MORRISSEY

THE ALBUMS

By The Same Author

Timeless Flight: The Definitive Biography Of The Byrds
Neil Young: Here We Are In The Years
Roxy Music: Style With Substance
Van Morrison: A Portrait Of The Artist
The Kinks: The Sound And The Fury
Wham ! (Confidential) The Death Of A Supergroup
Starmakers & Svengalis: The History Of British Pop Management
The Football Managers
The Guinness Encyclopaedia Of Popular Music (co-ed.)
Morrissey & Marr: The Severed Alliance
The Smiths: The Visual Documentary
The Complete Guide To The Music Of The Smiths & Morrissey/Marr
The Complete Guide To The Music Of Neil Young
Crosby, Stills, Nash & Young: The Visual Documentary
The Complete Guide To The Music Of John Lennon
The Byrds: Timeless Flight Revisited – The Sequel
The Complete Guide To The Music Of The Kinks
Neil Young: Zero To Sixty: A Critical Biography
Van Morrison: No Surrender

Anthology Contributions

The Bowie Companion
The Encyclopedia Of Popular Music
The Mojo Collection
Oxford Originals: An Anthology Of Writing From Lady Margaret Hall, 1879–2001

JOHNNY ROGAN

MORRISSEY

THE ALBUMS

CALIDORE

© **Johnny Rogan 2006**

ISBN 0-95295-405-2
[New ISBN from January 2007 ISBN 978-0-95295-405-7]

Exclusive distributors:
Music Sales Ltd
14–15 Berners Street
London, W1T 3LJ

To the Music Trade only:
Music Sales Ltd
14–15 Berners Street
London, W1T 3LJ

A catalogue record for this book is available from the British Library.

Front cover photograph: Vini Reilly.
Typeset by Galleon Typesetting, Ipswich.
Published by Calidore.
Printed in the UK.

Critical Reaction to Rogan's best-selling *Morrissey & Marr: The Severed Alliance*:

"The most controversial book of the year . . . tells as much about the Smiths as anyone could reasonably want to know . . . Rogan has more than done his homework and treads a fine line between academic rigour and breathless fandom. A major achievement."
New Musical Express

"Hugely entertaining . . . It is a tribute to the enduring brilliance of their music that their story still holds fascination. It is also a tribute to Johnny Rogan, a writer of real integrity. Rogan records the end of the band sympathetically but without missing one spasm of hubris. A page-turner of the first degree . . ."
Sunday Telegraph

"Mr Rogan is blessed with a brilliant mind . . . The research is exhaustive to the point of obsession . . . Quite superb."
Manchester Evening News

"A hugely readable and fascinating book . . . Flawlessly informed . . . expertly laid out . . . Whatever there is, Rogan's got it nailed. A superb achievement.★★★★★"
Q★★★★★

"Number one book of the year. This biography demanded to be written. An irresistible and illuminating account of the most influential British band of the 80s, a byword for diligent reporting and informed criticism."
Vox

"Exhaustively researched and containing interesting and sensible readings of the songs."
Sunday Times

"A painstaking account . . . highly sympathetic."
The Observer

"An essential purchase . . . a painstaking and thorough investigation."
Irish Times

"Rogan is a rock biographer's biographer . . . The guy is literally a method writer."
What's On In London

"A wonderful love story . . . Rogan turns over lots of stones, digs deep, reads Morrissey's juvenilia and dares to question the man's motives, sources and opinions . . . A bloody marvellous book."
Melody Maker

"*The Severed Alliance* has become an integral part of Morrissey's psychic self-torment, and thus an event of epic import."
Billboard

"The best Rock Biography of 1992 . . . Morrissey will be shaken and disturbed by Johnny Rogan's brilliant account . . . Rogan's analysis has the suspense and character development of a classy detective yarn . . . Excellently written with a novelist's grasp of pace, *The Severed Alliance* is one of the classic rock books. "
Record Collector

"One of the best books about music ever written."
Q★★★★★

"A typically thorough and ridiculously entertaining tome of the every-home-should-have-one variety. Rogan truly excels."
Select

"Rogan is a tremendous rock biographer. He collects intimate gems of information that thrill fans with their authenticity and then lends additional life through the eloquence of his prose."
Glasgow Herald

"I would sooner lose the use of both legs than read it . . .
Personally, I hope Johnny Rogan ends his days very soon in an
M3 pile-up."
Morrissey (1992)

"I made a statement when the book was published. Now I hope,
more so, that Rogan dies in a hotel fire."
Morrissey (1993)

"If God exists, then Johnny 'The Rat' will be devoured by his
German Shepherd dogs."
Morrissey (1994)

"I believe Rogan's now working on Volume 2. I believe he's
ransacking my dustbin for clues to lesbianism."
Morrissey (1999)

"Though Morrissey has expressed the wish that Rogan dies –
Johnny Rogan can feel proud of himself. He has written what is
certain to be the definitive book of the Smiths and though he is
capable of flexing his critical muscles, a clear-eyed love for his
subject suffuses every line."
Sunday Telegraph

"There is a greater sense of veracity in this book than you'll read
in a thousand music press interviews . . . Every descriptive
sentence seems curiously relevant . . . Morrissey's absurd and
unwise anti-Rogan outburst is no more than a finger prod against
the author's mighty wall of undeniable fact."
City Life

NOTES TO THE READER

Morrissey: The Albums is a detailed study of the recordings of Morrissey from his work with the Smiths through to 2006's *Ringleader Of The Tormentors*. It includes a track by track analysis of every album recorded by the singer in the UK/US territories. Collectors please note that the work concentrates solely upon officially released albums and does not include promotional releases, items exclusively produced for DJs/radio stations, special issues, samplers, cassette releases, various artistes collections, interview discs, videos, DVDs, radio/television appearances, bootlegs or unreleased recordings. Singles, from both the Smiths and Morrissey, are listed separately and, although beyond the specific remit of this book, are covered in detail throughout the text.

Finally, there is a round-up of those few songs that were officially released on single but have yet to appear in album form. The Index at the rear of the book can be used to cross reference songs.

Within the main text albums are printed in italics, along with books, poems, radio and television programmes, plays and newspapers. Individual songs are in single inverted commas; interview quotes are in double inverted commas. Numerical units are written out up to nine and numbered thereafter, except in the use of musical time, money and specific usages such as 8-track recordings. Acronyms have full points omitted, but names of people do not. Group/band names are preceded by a lower case 'the'. End spellings of verbs are 'ize' in accordance with *The Oxford English Dictionary* rather than computer spell checkers, with the obvious exceptions of words such as advertise, analyse, comprise, demise, improvise, supervise, surprise, televise *et al*.

Other rulings are generally in accordance with those suggested in *The Oxford Writers' Dictionary*, an invaluable asset in producing a consistent style guide.

CONTENTS

ACKNOWLEDGEMENTS   xi
INTRODUCTION   1

SMITHS ALBUMS   13
The Hand That Rocks The Cradle   15
The Smiths   20
Hatful Of Hollow   34
Meat Is Murder   46
The Queen Is Dead   60
The World Won't Listen   72
Louder Than Bombs   85
Strangeways, Here We Come   90
Rank   105
Best . . .   115
Best . . . II   117
Singles   118
The Very Best Of The Smiths   120

MORRISSEY ALBUMS   123
Viva Hate   125
Bona Drag   145
Kill Uncle   163
Your Arsenal   178
Beethoven Was Deaf   190
Vauxhall And I   199
World Of Morrissey   216
Southpaw Grammar   221
Viva Hate (Extended Edition)   229
Maladjusted   234
Suedehead – The Best Of Morrissey   247
Rare Tracks   251
My Early Burglary Years   255

The CD Singles '88–91'   259
The CD Singles '91–95'   264
The Best Of!   268
You Are The Quarry   269
Live At Earls Court   284
Ringleader Of The Tormentors   293

SINGLES/VIDEOS/DVDS   305
Smiths Singles   307
Smiths Video/DVD   314
Morrissey Singles   315
Morrissey Videos/DVDs   324

INDEX   327

ACKNOWLEDGEMENTS

This book offers an examination of Morrissey's work from the Smiths through to his solo releases. Previously, I have documented his life up until the breakup of the Smiths in *Morrissey & Marr: The Severed Alliance*. In another volume *The Smiths: The Visual Documentary*, I studied the group's live performances in detail. Hopefully, this modest volume complements those earlier efforts and does some justice to the recordings. Morrissey has produced a substantial body of work which has proven endlessly fascinating, particularly for those of us who have followed his career since the early days of the Smiths.

In compiling and writing this book, I owe much to the input of ex-Smiths Johnny Marr, Andy Rourke, Mike Joyce and Craig Gannon. Some of their comments I have rescued from my dusty archives and aeons' old tapes, others are from more recent encounters with certain ex-members. Humble thanks to Morrissey for putting me straight about several matters at the High Court. Additional greetings to other interviewees past and present whose quotes are featured, including the late Robin Allman, Stephen Pomfret, Phil Fletcher, Quibilah Montsho, Simon Wolstencroft, Dale Hibbert, Joe Moss, Gary Farrell, Richard Boon, Geoff Travis, the late Scott Piering, Tony Wilson, Matthew Sztumph, Grant Showbiz, Fred Hood, Ivor Perry, Vini Reilly, Andrew Paresi, Mark Nevin, Jonny Bridgwood, plus producers John Porter and Stephen Street.

I would like to thank Vini Reilly for allowing me to use the front cover picture of Morrissey which was taken at his Cheshire home. More recently Sarah Bacon, Jackie Cuddihy and Dave 'The Rave' Hill were on hand to help in various ways. On the production front, thanks to designer Lisa Pettibone, Susan Currie at Music Sales, plus Ken Shiplee and reader Pam Balaam at Galleon.

There are scores of other people I have spoken to over the years whose memories and insights were greatly appreciated. For a full roll call readers should consult the lengthy acknowledgements sections of *Morrissey & Marr: The Severed Alliance* and *The Smiths: The Visual Documentary*. Looking back at Morrissey's career, there are a small number of journalists who have interviewed him on a number of occasions, notably Nick Kent, Len Brown, Andrew Harrison and Stuart

Maconie. Their interviews were frequently enlightening. Several others of note are mentioned in the main text – and I thank them too. Over the years, many people have written to me about Morrissey. Let's hope the dialogue continues.

Any friends and family of Morrissey, former business associates, confidantes, musicians, engineers, record company personnel, agents, employees, plus others with information or memories of their time with the singer please contact the author as soon as possible or via an intermediary at the publisher's e-mail address:

calidore_@hotmail.co.uk

Similarly, any reader or critic wishing to offer comments, corrections or updates should also contact this address.

JOHNNY ROGAN

INTRODUCTION

Apart from obvious questions about M3 pile-ups, hotel fires, devouring Alsatians and similar Morrissey death wishes, the most common enquiries I used to receive from interviewers and fans revolved around the singer's sexuality, ethnic views and recording history. Years ago, a now famous writer and Smiths fan told me that *The Severed Alliance* had significantly altered his perception of Morrissey, or at least the figure he felt he knew intimately through the songs and media interviews. This surprised me somewhat as I felt the gap between the person and the persona was often negligible. As Vini Reilly once suggested to me, probably with a tinge of romantic overstatement: "There's not a moment of untruth in Morrissey's life." Applying that quote to his songwriting gets to the heart of Morrissey's appeal. Listening to such compositions as 'Suffer Little Children', 'Please Please Please Let Me Get What I Want', 'Half A Person', 'The Headmaster Ritual', 'Meat Is Murder', 'I Am Hated For Loving', 'Sorrow Will Come In The End', 'At Last I Am Born' and countless more, it is difficult to escape the conclusion that you have a direct line to the singer's heart and soul. But there is an ironic quality to Morrissey's songwriting that can make any listener feel uncertain or ill at ease. His mordant wit, sarcasm and love of ambiguity are as powerful as his naked confessional writing. One of the more gratifying aspects of writing about Morrissey all those years ago was discovering that many of the myths, exaggerations and probable inventions turned out to be true representations of his life. He did have a terrible schooling; he was a bed-sit misanthrope agonizing over sexual identity issues; he did write letters incessantly and find salvation in specific records, singers and groups. And the self-deprecating gallows humour that he used as a defence against music press writers was also there in his adolescence, shielding him from the slings and arrows of the outside world. Another aspect of Morrissey's complex appeal was his tendency to employ arch understatement and theatrical overstatement on a range of matters. This later worked spectacularly well in his songwriting as layers of irony undercut so many of his pronouncements, even when he sounded at his most earnest. For a writer so immersed in parochial gloom, it was intriguing to learn of not one but several trips to the USA, a luxury that some of his contemporaries compared to a moon visit. Of course, nobody is an entirely consistent caricature of themselves and these seeming anomalies in Morrissey's 'image' were simply part of a more complex whole. It was no coincidence that he later moved to America since that too had been such an important chapter in his adolescent story.

Morrissey always wanted to be a star, although he seemed unwilling to work for the privilege in the traditional manner. What money he earned was spent attending gigs and buying records. His love of pop music went right back to his childhood, but it was first made public in June 1974 when the *New Musical Express* printed a letter from the 15-year-old praising Sparks. Soon, Morrissey was bombarding the music press with snappy opinions and sterling defences of his favourite acts. Chief among them was the New York Dolls, who had first entranced the boy when they appeared on *The Old Grey Whistle Test* in 1973. When he attended one of the Sex Pistols' shows in Manchester during the summer of 1976, Morrissey wore a Dolls' T-shirt and carried a copy of their first album under his arm. Over the next few months, he continued his one-man campaign to rescue their faltering reputation, usually at the expense of the Sex Pistols. "British Punk Rock is second to the New York equivalent," he railed in *Melody Maker*. "It does not possess the musical innovation. The New York Dolls, Patti Smith, the Ramones and Jobriath can withstand accusations of novelty value because, although a great deal of their act was based on image, they also had the musical professionalism and variation to suitably recompense for their image-conscious inclinations."

Although Morrissey would later be hailed as one of the great saviours of British pop music, he was infatuated with America during the mid-Seventies. It is chilling to consider how close he came to leaving England. On several occasions he visited relatives in New York, New Jersey and Colorado and his family had firm plans to emigrate. In the end Morrissey decided to stay in Manchester and by the summer of 1977 he was working as a clerical officer at the Inland Revenue. One afternoon, while visiting Virgin Records, he was approached by a fellow Dolls' enthusiast, Phil Fletcher. Remarkably, Fletcher recognized Morrissey from the Sex Pistols' Free Trade Hall gig and had already reached the correct conclusion that he was that odd youth whose letters frequently appeared in the music press. Morrissey was taken aback. "He found it hilarious that somebody would notice him," Fletcher recalls. "I think he felt he was a star because somebody recognized him."

Morrissey was even more intrigued to discover that there was a clique of Dolls' fans among Fletcher's social circle in Wythenshawe. "He was very different from us," says Fletcher. "We gatecrashed everything. I couldn't imagine him doing anything like that." Nevertheless, Morrissey visited this Wythenshawe gang and became more involved after learning that a couple of them – Billy Duffy and Stephen 'Pommy' Pomfret – were forming a band.

Duffy was already quite a character among his peers, having recently applied unsuccessfully for the position of lead guitarist in Glen Matlock's Pistols-offshoot, the Rich Kids. Morrissey became friendly with Duffy for a time, even entrusting him with some lyrics. Before long, both were frequenting Pomfret's house and working on a group project. Those in attendance still recall Morrissey's strained vocals as he competed against loud guitar riffs clearly inspired by the New York Dolls and Johnny Thunders' Heartbreakers. In one of his more inspired moments, Morrissey even came up with a playfully exotic name – Sulky Youth – and encouraged Pomfret to write a song of the same title. "They were supposed to be New York kids, looking a bit upset like the Voidoids," Fletcher remembers.

Pomfret thought Morrissey was a "romantic and interesting character" but also "contrary and intense". He was not alone. In an attempt to enhance the group's chances, they invited another local player to join: Robin Allman. "We were almost being taught by Robin Allman," Pomfret stresses. "He was the svengali character as far as musicians around our way were concerned. He was teaching Billy Duffy, who was learning fast, and he later did the same thing with Johnny Marr." Allman met them at the Milk Bar in Manchester's

Piccadilly, but was put off by Morrissey's shyness. "He said nothing all the way through this so-called meeting."

With no money or proper equipment, the musicians continued desultory rehearsals, but had no solid plan. Morrissey suggested they change their name to the Tee Shirts, which sounded dull in comparison to Sulky Youth, but was reluctantly accepted. At one point, Morrissey turned up in the company of Quibilah Montsho, a black 16-year-old lesbian whom he felt might fit in. "I wasn't sure what type of music I wanted to get involved with," she says, "but we talked briefly about forming a band together." Pomfret found Montsho even more nervous than Morrissey and she never appeared at his house again.

Before long, Duffy lost interest and moved on while Morrissey retreated to his bedroom. Then, in the spring of 1978, Duffy reappeared with news that he had taken up with Ed Banger's old band the Nosebleeds and wanted Morrissey to be the vocalist. It was a wonderful opportunity as the group soon secured a couple of key gigs. On 15 April, the Nosebleeds appeared at the bottom of a bill hosted by Rabid Records. A month later, they supported Howard Devoto's new group Magazine at the Ritz. For Morrissey, these two performances were the closest he would reach to stardom in the years before the Smiths. The Wythenshawe clique was out in force for both shows and the general opinion was favourable. "Billy was doing his rock star bit and Morrissey was trying to look like David Johansen," Rob Allman told me. "He had his hair all over his face."

Phil Fletcher was also struck by Morrissey's Dolls' perm and make-up. "That was the first time I heard him sing 'Teenage News' by Sylvain Sylvain. At that time he hadn't learned to sing and had a very high-pitched scream."

Pomfret, who was amazed that they were playing the show, was among the converts. "Like Phil, I just went along, but I enjoyed the gig. Billy was great. He played well. I didn't have the best vantage point for hearing Morrissey because I was sat up on an amp trying to push the drum kit back every time it was edging forward. Morrissey had presence, but not as much as Billy, who really looked the part." A few weeks later, there was even a small write-up in *New Musical Express* in which Morrissey was described as "a minor local legend" and "a Front Man with Charisma", albeit under the incorrect name 'Steve Morrison'.

By this point, Morrissey had written several songs with Duffy, including 'I Get Nervous', '(I Think) I'm Ready For The Electric Chair', 'The Living Juke-Box' and 'Peppermint Heaven'. The latter, for one, was performed live and during their set Morrissey would proffer peppermints to members of the audience. No one I spoke to could confirm whether tapes of these recordings still exist, although Billy Duffy may care to differ. "Billy was quite pleased with the lyrics," says Rob Allman. "A lot of them were quite formulaic, like an update of the New York Dolls." What is certain is that the Nosebleeds folded soon after the Magazine gig, leaving Morrissey in limbo once more. Fortunately, the ever resourceful Duffy re-emerged a few months later, this time offering Morrissey a record company audition in London on 22 October 1978 as part of a revamped Slaughter And The Dogs. Evidently four songs from the period still exist on tape and appear to be self-penned compositions.

The Slaughter recordings led nowhere and within a month Morrissey was bound for Arvada, Colorado. Discontented, he returned to Manchester early in 1979, briefly securing a job at Yanks record shop. Thereafter, he went back on the dole and drifted aimlessly, spending far too much time watching trashy films and dreaming of fame. Instead of actively attempting to form a new group, he was reduced to doodling comic imaginary names for his dream combo, such as Stevie & The Socialites, Stevie & The Stepladders and the Silly Sluts. Some time later, he spoke of a new project, Angels Are Genderless, but seems to have got no further than coining a brilliant name. He ended the Seventies alone in his bedroom on New Year's Eve reading Jane Austen's *Pride And Prejudice*. It was not a happy time.

For much of 1980, Morrissey continued to drift aimlessly, seemingly bereft of motivation. With no forum for his imagined pop godhead, he reluctantly changed tack and attempted to infiltrate the music press. *Record Mirror* published a handful of gig reports, but nothing more substantial. At the time, *RM* was the least hip and worst selling of the weekly music papers, as Morrissey no doubt knew. Another opening came his way when a letter to a local publisher, Babylon Books, brought an unexpectedly positive response from owner John Muir. Unfortunately, Babylon turned out to be simply one man and his printing press and all that was on offer was a chance to produce a short booklet on the New York Dolls. Any opportunity for Morrissey to display his writing skills was squandered. Published in 1981, *The New York Dolls* was merely a fan's scrapbook, 24 pages long and devoid of literary merit. As a testament to his enduring fascination with the group, it was woefully inadequate. Encouraged by Muir, Morrissey quickly produced another short piece celebrating his idol, James Dean. When the first edition eventually appeared, it did not even feature the author's name on the cover.

If rock journalism and writing were producing limited critical or commercial reward for Morrissey, then his pop star aspirations seemed faintly delusional. Since the DIY punk explosion of 1976–77, the market-place had become overcrowded and it was harder than ever to make an impact. Morrissey was no great socialite and never pushed himself on other musicians. He still couldn't play an instrument, had severely limited experience as a live performer and was unfamiliar with recording studios or music technology. Nearly four years had elapsed since that brief epoch when he appeared onstage with the Nosebleeds. A recurring theme of his epistolary expositions and conversational asides was of time passing slowly, amid the purgatory of inertia.

By 1982, Morrissey's fantasies of pop stardom were receding rapidly. He desperately needed a Billy Duffy figure to offer fresh hope, but had lost touch with the old Wythenshawe gang. Fletcher had been exiled after daring to write to the music press criticizing Morrissey's beloved Patti Smith; Duffy was now in London chasing fame; and Pomfret had been out of touch for many months. Fortunately, Morrissey had not been entirely forgotten. Before leaving Manchester, Duffy had advised Rob Allman to seek out the Stretford bard and form a new band. Allman was unimpressed but passed on the tip to a friend.

Johnny Maher (later Marr) was four years younger than Morrissey, but already had a more impressive CV. Precocious, ambitious, charming and full of nerve and verve, he was a junior member of the

Wythenshawe set that Morrissey had encountered years before. At
school, Maher had befriended Andy Rourke, with whom he shared a
love of Neil Young and the Rolling Stones, among others. During
1976–77, the pair had formed a group with Kevin Williams (later
Coronation Street star Kevin Kennedy) and drummer Bobby Durkin.
Dubbing themselves the Paris Valentinos, they played at a Jubilee
jamboree in Benchill as well as folk masses at the Sacred Heart
Church. Maher also appeared briefly with some older players in Sister
Ray. In early 1979, his guitar mentor Rob Allman offered him the
chance to play in White Dice, a new group featuring former Freshies'
keyboardist Paul Whittall. Maher immediately drafted ex-Valentinos
Rourke and Durkin to complete the line-up. Soon after, Allman
entered one of his songs in a 'talent spotting' competition advertised
in *NME* and sponsored by Jake Riviera's F-Beat Records. Amazingly, White Dice won the chance to audition in London at Nick
Lowe's home studio. Although they weren't signed, they returned
home with seven professional recordings. It was a great start, but the
group failed to realize its potential, partly due to excessive partying.

By 1981, Maher and Rourke had left Allman and reinvented
themselves as funk merchants the Freak Party, roping in drummer
Simon Wolstencroft. They recorded a tape titled 'Crak Therapy' at
Decibel Studios but never performed live or found a suitable singer.
"It fizzled out in early 1982," Rourke told me. "I sort of lost interest
and Johnny was hungry for success." Maher had already considered
teaming up with a visiting Londoner, Matt Johnson, but that moment
had since passed.

The previous three years had taught Maher two key lessons: the
importance of strong songwriting and the need for a charismatic lead
singer. When Allman suggested Morrissey's name, Maher felt he
might be worth checking out. He was aware that the singer had col-
laborated with Billy Duffy and vaguely recalled seeing him at a Patti
Smith show talking to some of the Wythenshawe lads. Allman knew
from experience that Morrissey was preternaturally shy and might be
intimidated by a direct approach from a stranger. He suggested a suitable mediator. "I told Johnny he should use 'Pommy' as a means of
getting to Morrissey." Maher wasted no time in following Allman's
advice.

Pomfret remembers being accosted outside a newsagent by the over-eager Maher. "Johnny said, 'Hi Pommy,' as though he knew me. I didn't know him at all. He said, 'You know a guy called Morrissey, don't you? Let's get something together.' Johnny's personality is so strong that you feel consumed by him as soon as you meet him."

The meeting of Morrissey and Maher has been heavily mythologized over the years with Pomfret usually omitted from the script. "We got on the 263 bus," Pomfret remembers, "and went around to Morrissey's. His sister came to the door and I asked if Steven was in. He took an age to come down the stairs." Introductions were made and Pomfret explained that Maher wanted them to form a band. "I expected him to say he wasn't interested, but he said, 'Oh yes! Oh yes!' He was as excited as Morrissey can get."

Later Morrissey would speak of this meeting in mystical terms. "It was an event I'd always been looking forward to and unconsciously been waiting for since childhood. Time was passing. I was 22 and Johnny was much younger, but it seemed I'd hung around for a very long time waiting for this magical, mystical event, which definitely occurred. I had a slight tremulous feeling a long time before then, that something very unusual was going to happen to me, and I interpreted it as fame of some magnitude." Of course, that "tremulous feeling" had virtually gone prior to Pomfret's knock on the door. "It was very strange for me," Morrissey admitted, "because I tried to do it for a very long time and during this period that he [Maher] came I decided that I would no longer try. Then everything happened. It was very weird." In his more melodramatic moments, Morrissey has sometimes wondered if his life might have ended had that meeting not taken place.

Fired with enthusiasm, the trio began rehearsing several songs, a cover of the Cookies' 'I Want A Boy For My Birthday' and three originals: 'The Hand That Rocks The Cradle', 'Suffer Little Children' and the still unreleased 'Don't Blow Your Own Horn'. Pommy quickly realized that he was not wanted and bowed out. Maher next decided to find a rhythm section and brought in Dale Hibbert, a bass player who also worked as an engineer at Decibel Studios. Former Freak Party drummer Simon Wolstencroft also agreed to assist them in recording a demo. A cassette tape produced by Morrissey and

Maher was used as a blueprint for the new players. "I took it home, played it and added a bass line to it," Hibbert recalls. "Johnny said, 'This is how I want it to go,' and showed me what he wanted. I often wondered why he never approached Andy Rourke. They were in the same band so it seemed odd that he would come to me and not go for Andy." With Hibbert offering cheap studio time, Morrissey and Maher decided to record two songs: 'The Hand That Rocks The Cradle' and 'Suffer Little Children'. "I don't know why they chose those," Hibbert reflects. "There seemed to be something special about 'Suffer Little Children' which at the time was called 'Over The Moors'. I was intrigued because Myra Hindley was of interest in the Manchester area. I did ask Steve why it was so special to him, but he didn't say . . . I didn't pursue it. 'The Hand That Rocks The Cradle' wasn't one of my favourites. It was a bit bluesy and country & western [!]. It was supposed to be an 8-track recording, but we used about 11 tracks. The guy at Decibel had said he was either going to charge me for eight or 16 tracks, so I made out we just did an 8-track. It didn't take long, a couple of hours. I played the bass. It was quite easy. All I had to do was press a button to cue me in and that was it. A girl came in and did vocals and that laugh on 'Suffer Little Children' and then she disappeared." Morrissey and Maher stayed on late into the night in order to complete the mixdown. "They mixed it, but I wasn't too happy with their mix. Basically they weren't used to being in a recording studio. The sound they were getting from the big speakers wasn't the same sound that'd come out of a radio or a cassette player. I just let Johnny mess about with the faders until he was happy with it. They then went home with their version and I carried on with the mixing."

As a result there are two different mixes of these tracks in existence. In the summer of 1994, following the publication of both *Morrissey & Marr: The Severed Alliance* and *The Smiths: The Visual Documentary*, I corresponded with Hibbert and then visited his house in Manchester to listen to the recordings which he kindly allowed me to tape. "Johnny was really excited after we did these," he reminisced. "Let's listen to it. This one sounds muggy. On the other version I've got, which is the one that they did the mix for, the bass is really high." Although not radically different from the later recording featured on *The Smiths*, the versions Hibbert played me sounded subtly different. On 'The Hand That Rocks The Cradle', Wolstencroft's drums are prominent in the mix and Morrissey's deep baritone is noticeable. There's also the lyrical aside, 'I didn't even ask his name'. Surprisingly, Marr tackles the backing vocals, as he used to do in the White Dice days. 'Suffer Little Children' is more revealing and features lots of echo and reverberation, sounding almost double-tracked as a result. The female laugh and voice are more pronounced, but the major difference is Marr's haunting piano accompaniment at the close of the track and the discovered sound of children enjoying their break in a nearby school playground. After this listening session, Hibbert offered another surprise, a good quality cassette recording of 'I Want A Boy For My Birthday' which, he insisted, was initially considered as the group's first single. It sounds great, with Maher's chiming guitar already in evidence and Morrissey singing the words without any affectation or knowing references to gender alteration, just as he had once done onstage with the Nosebleeds when covering the Shangri-Las 'Give Him A Great Big Kiss'.

Although the Decibel demo was promising, the line-up of the group, soon to be known as the Smiths, remained in flux. Wolstencroft concluded that they weren't funky enough for his tastes and privately dismissed Morrissey as "old school miserable Manchester". Hibbert elected to stay and even agreed to acquire a flat-top haircut and an American bowling shirt, which he assumed was part of the group uniform. Meanwhile, the search for a new drummer continued. Several candidates were tried out, including former Sister Ray percussionist Bill Angstee, who knew both Maher and Hibbert. Morrissey even asked one of his King's Road neighbours, Gary Farrell, who was then playing in a group with Ivor Perry, later of Easterhouse. Perry remembers visiting Farrell and listening to a cassette tape that Morrissey had loaned him, featuring a rough of the demo, plus some other odd material including snatches of film music and what sounded like dogs barking.*

---

* Whether these cassette tapes survive is uncertain, as is their precise contents. During the Eighties, journalist Nick Kent, writing in *The Face*, related an apocryphal account of Richard Boon supposedly receiving a tape of Morrissey singing a

None of these approaches or auditions came to anything. "Every night we'd have a different drummer," Hibbert remembers. Finally, they settled on Mike Joyce, a former punk drummer with the Hoax and Victim, who had the audacity to turn up and play after ingesting some magic mushrooms.

On 4 October 1982, the Smiths played live for the first time, supporting Blue Rondo A La Turk at the Ritz in Manchester. At this date, they were a five-piece, with Morrissey's friend James Maker performing as a 'go go dancer'.

Thereafter they rehearsed at Spirit Studios where Hibbert was now working but by the end of the year he was replaced in the line-up by Andy Rourke. "I was told at Spirit," he recalls. "All Johnny said was that we should go our separate ways . . . I was involved with Spirit and that was taking up a lot more of my time than the Smiths. I had no regrets whatsoever. I wasn't bitter because it wasn't as if they'd made it. It was just another band. As far as I was concerned, I was more interested in a career as an engineer and producer." Various theories have been put forward to explain Hibbert's dismissal, including Joyce's damning criticisms of his bass playing. "I can't see that

bedroom version of 'The Hand That Rocks The Cradle' backed with what was assumed to be a Bessie Smith song titled 'Wake Up Johnny'. This was prematurely dated as 'around 1980'. For the record, and in answer to a query in Simon Goddard's book, when I interviewed Boon a few years later, he offered no such recollection, nor was he directly quoted as such in *The Face* piece. I therefore chose not to include the tale nor the likely erroneous dating in *The Severed Alliance* or *The Visual Documentary* since other evidence suggested that 'The Hand That Rocks The Cradle' was probably written considerably later. The Smiths were exceptional in their determination to release every Morrissey/Marr composition, leaving no completed outtakes behind. The early composition 'Don't Blow Your Own Horn' has never appeared, although Steve Pomfret briefly had a vocal copy. "Morrissey sent me a tape of him singing a cappella on quite a few songs, including 'The Hand That Rocks The Cradle', 'Suffer Little Children' and 'Don't Blow Your Own Horn'. Later, in August 1982, Johnny said, 'I believe Steven sent you some tapes . . .' and I gave them to him. I really do regret that bitterly." Even more remarkable is the apparent absence of other informal recordings containing new material. Ace sessionographer Goddard, who went through Joyce's extensive tape collection, found only one completed Morrissey/Marr song, 'A Matter Of Opinion'. Recorded on a ghetto blaster in December 1982, just after Rourke's recruitment, it betrayed the influence of his musical hero, Neil Young, sounding uncannily like the Buffalo Springfield's 'Mr Soul'.

myself," Hibbert retorts. "Any bass player could have done that first album. I don't think it was down to technical ability." Studio commitments, image and attitude may have played a part, but the most likely explanation is that the rechristened Johnny Marr was back in regular contact with Andy Rourke, a close friend whom he had played with in bands since the age of 13. The new rhythm section took a while to settle and there was even a momentary blip in the spring of 1983 when drummer Simon Wolstencroft was reconsidered. Effectively, this would have been the Freak Party backing the elusive singer that they had never found. But that idea was soon dropped and the Rourke/Joyce rhythm section established itself as a formidable unit, personally and musically.

1983 proved the breakthrough year for the Smiths. It began with their first headlining show at Manchester's Manhattan, with Maker joining them for the second and final time before moving on to his own projects. "James was there in a dinner suit," Rourke recalls. "I was a bit embarrassed by it all. I think everyone was. But Morrissey wanted him in, so we said, 'OK.'" With Factory's Tony Wilson and New Hormones' Richard Boon in attendance there was keen anticipation of securing a record contract. By February the Smiths were playing the Haçienda, surrounded by flowers, and the following month they were preparing their début single, 'Hand In Glove', financed by their generous manager Joe Moss. It was released on Rough Trade Records, the independent label that, seemingly against the odds, later won the signatures of Morrissey & Marr. In the meantime, the Smiths made their London début, undertook their first tour, signed a publishing deal with Warner Brothers and recorded BBC sessions for both John Peel and David Jensen. As summer approached, they were ready to record their first album.

SMITHS ALBUMS

THE HAND THAT ROCKS THE CRADLE

THE TROY TATE DEMOS (UNRELEASED)

In considering the Smiths' albums history, some attention should be given to this artefact which, in a different universe, might have been their first album. During the summer of 1983, the group spent weeks at Elephant Studios in Wapping, London, preparing what they hoped would be a significant début. Former Teardrop Explodes' guitarist Troy Tate was appointed producer and evidently enjoyed a friendly relationship with the group, particularly Johnny Marr. Unfortunately the sessions were terminated amid fears that the product was not strong enough. Manager Joe Moss, who always preferred these recordings to the ones that finally emerged on *The Smiths*, felt that Troy's removal was partly a political decision. "At first Morrissey was over the moon about Troy Tate working with the Smiths, but then Troy became close to Johnny whom he had more in common with. That was it. It was that triangle. If you were close to Johnny or weren't Morrissey's friend, then you were out."

Despite the conspiracy theories, there is no doubt that the other Smiths, including Marr, had strong reservations about these recordings and the quality of their performance. "We just weren't happy with the way it sounded and put the mockers on it," Marr told me. "That was it. Morrissey was more unhappy with it than I was – but he was right."

Bassist Andy Rourke felt the same uneasiness. "There was a mad heat wave and we were stuck downstairs in this tatty studio. It was really hard work. Troy would make us do 30 takes of one song so whatever sparkle there was we'd lost after the fifth take. We all had blisters on our fingers. Basically, we weren't enjoying it, and that came out in the final recording. We sounded like we were going through the motions. It just sounded like a demo, not good enough for a début LP. We weren't happy with it and the record company wasn't happy with it. But Troy was a nice guy and it was a difficult decision to make."

"We didn't fall out with Troy," adds Marr. "We were just really sorry to hurt his feelings. It was a professional decision and he obviously took it badly. He'd got himself wrapped up in it, and understandably so."

When I started writing *The Severed Alliance* at the end of the Eighties, Tate was one of the few people who declined to talk to me. His tone on the phone was chilling in its finality, as if the subject matter was so painful that even mentioning it in passing was enough to provoke unspeakable memories. "Don't ever ring again," he concluded.

His reaction came as no surprise to Rourke. "Troy was devastated. I think it was his first go at producing. He really did take it badly, and we felt badly about it but obviously we had to look out for ourselves. We couldn't bring out a substandard first LP. It had to be good."

Even Mike Joyce, an inveterate punk, went along with the general consensus. "I thought it was a bit too tame for what we were doing at the time. That first LP was so important. Troy had a good go, but I don't think it was as precious sounding as it could have been . . . it sounded OK but we needed somebody to tidy things up."

That person was John Porter who was initially contacted by Rough Trade label owner Geoff Travis with a view to remixing Tate's tapes. After hearing the work on a cassette, Porter listened to the original masters and reported back to Travis. "The sound was rotten . . ." Porter later told me. "This was no reflection on Troy Tate. The Smiths just weren't a good recording band. They had done lots of gigs but it's always different in the studio." Rather than remixing Tate's work, Porter offered to re-cut the material from scratch. At this point Troy Tate was effectively written out of the Smiths' story – never to return.

Despite its shortcomings, *The Hand That Rocks The Cradle* demos provide a fascinating glimpse of a young group coming to terms with working in a studio setting. Tentative at times, there is nevertheless a rawness to the sound that is arguably more faithful to the spirit of the band than the later re-recorded version. The Troy Tate Smiths were unpolished and understated, a group offering promise rather than greatness, but it was those inchoate performances that some, most notably Joe Moss, felt should have been shared with the world in

1983. Since then, the tracks have been included on bootlegs in a variety of permutations, including alternate takes from the sessions. Collectors can consult such bootlegs as *The Cradle Snatchers*, *Reel Around The Fountain*, *The Hand That Rocks The Cradle*, *A Nice Bit Of Meat 3*, *The Troy Tate Demos* and *Wonderful Woman* to sample the tracks. The CD bootleg *Troy Hand Rocks The Cradle* rounds up most of the stuff in circulation, but an official release would still be welcome. Perhaps if Morrissey and Marr ever approve a box set for release, room might be found for the best of this material.

Five compositions from the Tate sessions did not appear on *The Smiths*: 'These Things Take Time', 'Handsome Devil', 'Accept Yourself', 'Jeane' and 'Wonderful Woman'. Only two of Tate's productions ever saw release in any form: 'Jeane' and 'Pretty Girls Make Graves'. These are discussed below, along with the unreleased single 'Reel Around The Fountain' and the Porter-produced 'Wonderful Woman'.

Reel Around The Fountain

As if to compound Troy Tate's ill fortune, he not only lost the chance to produce the first Smiths' album but was dramatically robbed of the glory of seeing his name attached to the A-side of their second single. Even after he had been relieved of the producer's role, his recording of 'Reel Around The Fountain' was still confirmed for release. The song had been performed on John Peel's BBC Radio 1 evening show and Rough Trade duly placed an advert in the music press announcing that 'Reel Around The Fountain' b/w 'Jeane' was 'out now'. All that changed overnight when, on 25 August 1983, the *Sun* newspaper ran a feature titled 'Child Sex Song Puts The Beeb In A Spin' alleging that there was concern over the sexual connotations of the song 'Handsome Devil'. The *Sun*'s garbled account was actually bowdlerized from two previous pieces in the music paper *Sounds*. Ironically, the original articles featured some highly complimentary comments about Morrissey's opaque and controversial lyrics which journalist Dave McCullough nevertheless assumed might have paedophiliac undertones. "The subject of child molesting creeps up more than a few times in Smiths songs. They are hilarious lyrics, more so because they suddenly touch on the personal." Morrissey distanced himself from such interpretations, pointing out that the subtle motifs under discussion were not what he had intended when composing these songs. Unfortunately, what should have been a fascinating debate about a pop lyric was sensationalized by the *Sun* which misconstrued the words, failed to mention Morrissey's authorial point of view and caused sufficient consternation at the BBC to ensure that 'Reel Around The Fountain' was omitted from a forthcoming *David Jensen Show*. That was enough to seal the fate of 'Reel Around The Fountain' as a single, leaving Troy Tate's version to languish in obscurity.

Wonderful Woman

The Troy Tate recording of 'Wonderful Woman' was never released and no version of the song ever appeared on album. However, John Porter's later production was featured on the B-side of the 12-inch version of 'This Charming Man'. Written early in the Smiths' career, possibly even before the recruitment of Andy Rourke, 'Wonderful Woman' can be heard on tapes from their show at Manchester's Manhattan on 6 January 1983 where it was tentatively titled 'What Do You See In Him?' Over the next few months, some of the lyrics were amended with lines like 'She will plague you and I will be glad' disappearing. "The wonderful woman is actually an incredibly vicious person," Morrissey later mused enigmatically.

Pretty Girls Make Graves

Morrissey's comment on voracious women was an intriguing aberration given his teenage interest in feminist sexual politics. Particularly endearing is the comic, *Carry On*-style portrayal of the narrator, who resembles a Charles Hawtrey figure caught in the embrace of an enveloping Hattie Jacques who demands it 'now' in rough fashion, causing her prey to plead 'I'm so delicate'. Musically, the most notable feature of this first rendition was the inclusion of Audrey Riley's lachrymose cello accompaniment which provides the song with a spectral ambience, missing from the later arrangement. Tate's original version remained in the vaults until it was unexpectedly exhumed for inclusion as the B-side to 1987's 'I Started Something I Couldn't Finish'. By that time, of course, the Smiths had broken up.

Jeane

Although this song failed to appear on any of the Smiths' official albums, it was included on the B-side of the group's first hit single, 'This Charming Man'. At one stage, it was advertised in the music press as the flip-side to the unreleased 'Reel Around The Fountain' and, as such, might therefore have been excluded from the final running order of *The Hand That Rocks The Cradle*. Despite its relative obscurity, it was covered successfully by both Billy Bragg and Sandie Shaw. 'Jeane' sounds like Morrissey writing a Mancunian kitchen sink drama about a fragmenting relationship. He would later return to this theme with greater assurance using lines borrowed from Shelagh Delaney's filmed play *A Taste Of Honey*. In an early article on the Smiths, Nick Kent surmised that 'Jeane' might have been inspired by Morrissey's friend Linder (Linda Mulvey), although there are no specific references to her in the composition and the theme does not fit what we know of their relationship. Source hunters might be better directed towards Jeane Sheppard, Morrissey's aunt on his mother's side, whose Christian name, complete with an 'e' may have provided the song's title. Additionally, it might be worth noting that the bastard child of Oscar Wilde's friend, and rumoured lover, Lillie Langtry, was also named Jeane.

Troy Tate Demo Tape: *The Hand That Rocks The Cradle; You've Got Everything Now; These Things Take Time; What Difference Does It Make?; Reel Around The Fountain; Hand In Glove; Handsome Devil; Wonderful Woman; I Don't Owe You Anything; Suffer Little Children; Miserable Lie; Accept Yourself; Pretty Girls Make Graves; Jeane.*

THE SMITHS

Released: February 1984

Rough Trade Records, Rough 61, February 1984. Reissued Rough CD 61,
October 1986. WEA 4509 91892-2, July 1987, November 1993, February 1995.
US issue: Sire 9-25065, April 1984

With Troy Tate out of the picture, the Smiths' tapes were handed over to John Porter who suggested that the work should be re-recorded, a view supported by Rough Trade's founder Geoff Travis. Morrissey and Marr supported this decision and a £20,000 budget was allocated to the project. Porter, who had previously worked with the group on a BBC session for the *David Jensen Show*, was offered a fee of £500. The bulk of the new recordings took place at Manchester's Pluto Studios over a troubled two-week period in October/November 1983, and the tapes were then overdubbed and mixed at London's Eden Studios. It was not a happy time and there were bad feelings among the group. Marr later admitted under oath in the High Court that he had threatened to quit, even at this early stage. Obviously, any hope of issuing the album in time for Christmas was abandoned, but this only served to increase expectations. Many critics and fans, already sated with several treasured singles, B-sides and radio sessions, were quietly predicting an instant classic to rank alongside the greatest début albums of all time. The realization that the Smiths had actually recorded the work *twice* surely suggested that it must have been done to perfection. "We had all the songs," Mike Joyce recalls. "It was the first and only time that happened. The rest of the time Johnny would obviously be writing but they'd be things he'd done on the road or at soundchecks. The first album was great because we had the material. Some of the best stuff was written on that first LP."

Finally released in February 1984, *The Smiths'* impact was severely qualified by the tinny sound and sometimes leaden performances. Johnny Marr was initially pleased with the record and evidently unaware of its deficiencies. "It wasn't until people started mentioning the production that I noticed. People have made a lot of the production, but we weren't as good as we could have been. The only way to have nailed us down at that period would have been to record a gig because we were really good live."

His sentiments were echoed by Porter who felt the group's inexperience cost them dearly. Although the songs were obviously strong and well-rehearsed, the Smiths seemed uncomfortable working in a studio. The problems did not end there. Morrissey's reluctance to re-record or overdub meant that the album retained a minimalist, bare bones feel, with some tracks sounding closer to demos than accomplished studio recordings. "We were just bashing them out and trying them again," Porter laments. "It was a race against time and I was constantly thinking, 'This is not good enough.' Even when it came out I still wished we'd had more money."

Music press reviews of the period were revealing. Already, there was a sense that the Smiths were special and many writers were almost willing them to produce something great. Although the comments were generally positive, nobody seemed quite ready to proclaim the arrival of a life-changing record. It seemed that the Smiths may have had the songs but not the sound or performance to alter the trajectory of rock history. The major weekly music papers had not yet started the tradition of grading albums, so it was difficult to estimate precisely the gap between genuine appreciation and hyperbole. *NME* reviewer Don Watson focused on Morrissey to the detriment of the other group members, arguing: "Consideration of the Smiths always ends up as attempted penetration of Morrissey's singular charms, primarily because the Smiths in plural are as average as their uncharismatic name suggests. Where Morrissey is a wielder of the archaic art of the word, his cohorts are merely competent workers in the grimy craft of pop. Musically, the Smiths are little more than mildly regressive. What saves them is Morrissey's rare grasp of the myriad distortions of the pastel worlds of nostalgia. Much of the intrigue behind the Smiths is not what they have to offer but the seductive manner in which Morrissey offers it – his beguiling invitation to forget art and dance in a notion of animated camp."

The following week, *Melody Maker*'s Allan Jones wrote, somewhat more effusively: "The Smiths themselves seem to owe nothing very much to anyone; they appear to exist without convenient

contemporary comparisons. For music as lean and urgent, as passionately articulate and eerily beautiful as the most haunting episodes on
this record, you have to refer back to the stark emotional lyricism of
the Velvet Underground's third album."

After digesting the reviews, Morrissey attempted to 'talk up' the
album in interviews, extravagantly referring to it as a landmark in the
history of pop music. "I'm really ready to be burned at the stake in
total defence of that record. It means so much to me that I could
never explain, however long you gave me. It becomes almost difficult and one is just simply swamped in emotion about the whole
thing. It's getting to the point where I almost can't even talk about it,
which many people will see as an absolute blessing. It just seems
absolutely perfect to me." Behind the passionate justification and
characteristic overstatement, he realized that the Smiths had not done
themselves full justice, even though initial sales returns rewarded
them with an impressive UK chart position of number 2.

Critical reservations aside, there was no denying that *The Smiths*
highlighted the arrival of a strong songwriting partnership, well
versed in rock tradition but armed with a keen knowledge of the
power of pop music. Morrissey's engagingly ambiguous lyrics subverted the entire package with lashings of camp knowing and subtle
irony. At other times, the sense of desperation and unrequited
longing in the words was almost palpable in its intensity. Morrissey's
vocal, still very flat and occasionally uncertain, could nevertheless
shift from a deadpan moan to a hyena howl or an excruciating falsetto
at a moment's notice. Equally importantly, the Smiths looked the
part. Marr could still play the teenage prodigy with a strong sense of
rock fashion. Morrissey, by contrast, used spectacles and flowers as
anti-rock star accoutrements to bolster his image as the bed-sit misanthrope blessed with unlikely fame. The public perception of Rourke
and Joyce as solid, dependable, unselfish players testified to a sense of
camaraderie that made the Smiths special. Even their artwork was
carefully conceived to reflect Morrissey's affinity with gay culture as
well as serving as an ongoing gallery of his favourite icons. And, to
top it all, the closing track on the album would belatedly provide the
Smiths with some tabloid controversy which, although unwanted at
the time, ultimately worked to their artistic advantage.

Reel Around The Fountain

Appropriately, the opening lines of the album offered a stately voiced reflection on corruption and lost innocence. The 'taking' of a child who is suddenly 'made old' inevitably attracted attention from those inclined to see paedophiliac themes in the early work of the Smiths, although in this composition any such interpretation rests solely on the use of the word 'child'. According to Morrissey, he was unaware of such hidden innuendoes and intended the composition to suggest "loss of innocence, that until one has a physical commitment with another person there's something childlike about the soul." Despite his stated intention, the composition itself contains a strong underlying erotic frisson in its evocation of innocence under threat. The sexuality is aggressive, with phrases like 'pin and mount me' (the latter a borrowing from Molly Haskell's *From Reverence To Rape* in which she discusses the film *The Collector*). That the subject is a willing, indeed seductive, partner makes the composition even more intriguing and the fact that it is sung by a professed celibate provides additional tension. Morrissey later took the composition into the public arena by transforming the song's lines into a plea for stardom, informing one journalist, "I want to be pinned on everybody's wall – or pinned against everybody's wall. Can you make me a sex symbol?"

In keeping with the ambiguous theme, it is interesting to note that Marr originally composed the song as a cross between the dark introspection of Joy Division and the upbeat optimism of Jimmy Jones' 'Handy Man'. Although the Smiths were reluctant to employ session musicians on their records, producer John Porter persuaded them to use pianist Paul Carrack to enliven the arrangement. Unfortunately, what should have been a classic opening to the album never quite managed to take full flight, in spite of its underlying quality. "We didn't do anything like justice to the song," Porter admitted to me. "It was never as successful as it should have been. I put Paul Carrack on piano to add a bit of colour because it was a little lifeless on record. We needed more time. I subsequently wanted to do the song again, but nobody was into that."

You've Got Everything Now

A classic example of Morrissey's acerbic wit, this song satirized his materialist-minded contemporaries. In interviews he spoke frequently of the horrors of working for a living, but his amusing quotes paled alongside the instant aphorisms featured in many of the songs on this album. Here, conflicting feelings of jealousy, aloofness, arrogance and self-abasement mingle to startling effect, reinforced by the straightforward, uncomplicated arrangement. Some fans took literally Morrissey's claim that he had never had a job, although while researching *The Severed Alliance* I discovered that he had worked as a hospital assistant (courtesy of his father), in a local record shop and as a clerk for the Inland Revenue. Of course, he hated all of these jobs and none lasted for long. The truth was that, between leaving school and forming the Smiths, he did spend the majority of his time un-employed and living at home.

Miserable Lie

Often used as the closing song in the Smiths' early live sets, this dated back to late 1982 when it was first recorded at Drone Studios just after the recruitment of Andy Rourke, who initially made his pres-ence felt with some funky bass lines. Gradually, this more frantic version evolved. Morrissey sounds like a demented punk imitating Tiny Tim as he stretches his vocal cords to reach an unholy falsetto while denouncing love and locality with a combination of self-pity, loathing and scathing wit. Manchester itself is singled out for criticism in the references to scratching a living on the dole in Whalley Range. The notion of sex as some form of cosmic joke is expressed with typical self-deprecation ('I look at yours, you laugh at mine') and the plea to put your 'tongue away'. Morrissey's recurring theme of lost romantic idealism fits in well with the remaining tracks, posing inevitable questions about autobiographical intent. The singer made no attempt to separate his experiences from those expressed in 'Miserable Lie', archly telling one interviewer: "I always thought my genitals were the result of some crude practical joke." He also spoke of his own experiences as a brief resident of Whalley Range where he supposedly shared digs with his friend Linda Mulvey (Linder). If this indeed occurred it was, to use Morrissey's words, "a miraculously short time".

Pretty Girls Make Graves

Morrissey's love of gender play provides a tragi-comic feel to many songs on this album. Here, the 'flower-like' youth thwarted by love in 'Miserable Lie' is under greater threat, this time of being ravaged. Typically, Morrissey subverts traditional male/female roles to present the woman as sexually voracious and her male prey as a helpless innocent. There is a moment of rash braggadocio as the singer fantasizes about being wild and free before sex once again intervenes amid admissions of inadequacy. The coy 'I'm not the man you think I am' (possibly inspired by the chorus of Paul Jones' 1967 hit 'I've Been A Bad, Bad Boy', a song that Morrissey nominated 13th in a list of 'Singles To Be Cremated With') is reinforced by the disclosure about nature playing a trick on the narrator, a possible paraphrase of the words uttered by a heart-stricken homosexual barber in the groundbreaking 1961 film *Victim*. The song is full of narrative gender games and there is also a hint of misogyny in the treatment, but the predominant tone is playful, with continually self-effacing references thrown in at every opportunity.

The Hand That Rocks The Cradle

One of the first songs written by Morrissey/Marr, this was played at their initial rehearsal with guitarist Steve Pomfret. Marr's compelling arrangement may sound familiar for it was borrowed from Patti Smith's 'Kimberly'. This was proven to me by Marr's former White Dice colleague Rob Allman who magically produced a set list from a pre-Smiths rehearsal featuring Morrissey, Marr and Pomfret. Under the title 'The Hand That Rocks The Cradle' can be read 'G C D (Kimberly)' in Marr's own hand. Given the songwriting duo's mutual affection for Patti Smith's *Horses* and the fact that Marr first encountered Morrissey briefly at one of her concerts, the borrowing seems apt. The intriguing lyrics are arguably Morrissey's most unusual to date and much more oblique than anything else he was writing during this period. Later, Morrissey admitted that the song was partly autobiographical coming "from a relationship I had that didn't involve romance". His lyrical approach is almost cinematic as he focuses on innocuous objects which are magically transformed into disturbing images. Entering the child's imagination, he adds an air of inexplicable mystery as we successively witness a piano playing in an empty room, wardrobes disguised as birds and the sudden horror movie image of a bloodied cleaver. The sense of danger is hardly alleviated by the narrator whose obsessive, determinedly self-sacrificial love seems disturbingly suffocating. A claustrophobic ambience is reinforced by conspiratorial asides in phrases like 'your mother she just never knew' which prompts the inevitable question, 'What was it precisely that she never knew?' The Al Jolson inspired coda 'climb upon my knee sonny boy, although you're only *three . . .*' serves as both a poignant expression of innocence and additional fuel to those who detect unconscious paedophiliac connotations in the composition.

This Charming Man

If you happen to own the Warner Brothers re-release of this album, then this bonus track is included. On all previous British CD and album releases it was not issued, although it appeared on American pressings. It still seems strange to hear the original album with an extra song stuck in the middle, but there is no denying the power of this, the group's first hit single. Originally, it reached number 25 in the UK charts, but when it was reissued by WEA in 1992, the song climbed to number 8, the highest position ever achieved by a Smiths' single.

The song was first attempted at London's Matrix Studios in what producer John Porter described to me as "a mad 10-day rush". A distinctive feature of the recording was the emphasis on the guitar sound. Marr was allowed to use Porter's collection of Telecasters and an array of guitar segments were stacked, including acoustic parts, all given a keener metallic edge by the use of a knife scraping the strings. "It was incredibly linear at first," says Porter. "The introduction was about 28 bars and rambled. The Smiths were never a verse/ chorus/middle-eight band. Because there were no choruses, it was difficult and I couldn't get the hang of it. Then we knocked a few bars off and it all came together." During the playback, there was a general feeling that the mix was below par. Rough Trade's Geoff Travis listened in silence, then suggested they redo the song at Manchester's Pluto Studios, using the Matrix version as a guide. "He was right to tell us," Porter concedes, "because although the first version was good, it was better for doing it again. It was good for them having just played it and done the whole thing three days before. It made the song more focused . . . I remember when we did 'This Charming Man' again, we did the drums last. I got them to work with a click track because, although Mike was a good drummer live, it's a very different thing in the studio and you're so conscious of what you're doing. So I took a Linn drum up to Manchester, pro-grammed the drums on the Linn drum, put that down on tape, did the whole song (vocals and everything), and then put the drums on last and rubbed the Linn drum out." Porter remembers that many groups of the period preferred not to admit using a Linn drum. Although the Smiths had only employed the Linn as a guide, it was still amusing to hear Marr telling the press a year later: "We would never use a Linn drum or a drum machine."

The recording quality of 'This Charming Man', at least in terms of clarity and exuberance, eclipses most of the tracks on *The Smiths*. Its upbeat rhythm, complete with Marr's chiming guitars and Rourke's ascending bass lines, offers a fresh dimension to the reissue. Certainly, the reputation of *The Smiths* would have been considerably higher if they had elected to add 'This Charming Man' to the original vinyl album, but the inclusion of two singles was presumably considered too much, especially in view of the number of new compositions already recorded.

For many listeners, particularly older fans, the song remains a fond favourite, not least because it introduced the Smiths to a television audience. It was first broadcast on *The Tube* on 4 November 1983 with Morrissey flailing around, his feet deep in flowers; Rourke looks pale and interesting, Joyce intense and Marr's visage is largely out of camera range. On 24 November, the group fulfilled Morrissey's adolescent dreams by appearing on *Top Of The Pops* in a classic per-formance which gave notice of their musical prowess as well as trans-forming the singer into an iconic cult idol. Buzzcocks manager Richard Boon, who attended the performance along with Factory Records' Tony Wilson, remembers, "Morrissey was driven almost glowing. It probably seemed tiny on television but it was a big existential moment . . ."

In a determined attempt at promotion, Rough Trade simultaneously issued a value-for-money 12-inch vinyl version in November which included both the London and Manchester recordings, backed with 'Accept Yourself' and 'Wonderful Woman'. One month later, the company rush released a dance-floor version remixed by DJ Francois Kevorkian at the Right Track in New York. Its availability as an import persuaded Rough Trade that it would be expedient to produce a limited edition 12-inch for promotional use in clubs, but the public response was such that the company sanctioned a full release, retailing at £1.49. Although Travis insists Morrissey and Marr supported this decision, they rapidly regretted sanctioning such a mix and the offending disc was quickly deleted. Some months later, Morrissey could be heard complaining: "I'm still very upset about that. It was totally against our principles, the whole thing."

Still Ill

One of the longest running songs in the Smiths' live set, this was Morrissey's paean to hypochondria and self-reliance. As Marr wittily noted: "You listen to a song like 'Still Ill' and the title alone sums up Morrissey." The championing of the outsider was a key feature of the singer's appeal and opened up a wide market for the Smiths. The allusive lyrics, with their cod philosophical speculations on whether the mind rules the body or vice versa, merely enhanced the mystery of Morrissey. His mantra about England owing him a living endeared him to the indignant unemployed while its sentiments offered a glimpse back at his time in the dole queue. In later years, tourists of Morrissey's Manchester would visit the iron bridge near his former home on King's Road, which is mentioned in the song as a place of fumbling romance. Source hunters have since located these lines as borrowings from pools winner Viv Nicholson's autobiography *Spend, Spend, Spend* in which she writes, "We walked for miles, right over the iron bridge . . . we were kissing . . . and getting really sore lips from biting one another."

Hand In Glove

This album version of 'Hand In Glove' was remixed by John Porter with a stronger emphasis on Joyce's drumming. "Johnny tried to push the point home about a Phil Spector Wall of Sound," Joyce remembers. "It sounded big and Morrissey's vocal was so desperate." The composition was first heard in January 1983, shortly after Morrissey and Marr had settled on their long-term line-up with Joyce and Rourke as permanent members. According to Marr, the music was composed at his parents' house one Sunday evening while he was messing around on a 'crappy' guitar. His girlfriend Angie Brown felt the melody was attractive enough to be recorded, prompting some drastic action. "I was panicking because I had nothing to record it on," Marr told journalist David Sheppard, "so we decided to drive to Morrissey's, because he had a tape recorder. I sat in the back of the car playing the riff over and over so I wouldn't forget it. On the way, as is her wont, Angie kept saying, 'Make it sound more like Iggy.' I was just hoping Morrissey would be in. Well, I knew he would be, he was always in. When we got there he was a bit taken aback, it hadn't been arranged and it was a Sunday night – unheard of! He let me in and I played the riff and he said, 'That's very good.'"

Within a week of Marr's visit, Morrissey had a complete set of lyrics. "I was in my room, alone with a cassette recorder with a guitar tune on it and I was surrounded by lots of words, and I just sat there for two hours and threw the whole thing together . . . It was to be our first record and it was so important to me that there was something searingly poetic in it, in a lyrical sense, and yet jubilant at the same time." Throughout the group's career Morrissey always lavished praise on the song and its chart failure encouraged him to persuade Sandie Shaw to right the wrongs of pop history by belatedly taking a cover version into the Top 30. Even then Morrissey was not entirely satisfied: "From a recording point of view it was a tremendous success. From a sales point of view, it wasn't. It reached number 27, but it should have done much more. I feel slightly angered because of that."

What Difference Does It Make?
According to Marr's guitar mentor and former colleague Robin Allman, the riff of this R&B foray was partly inspired by Jo Jo Gunne's 'Run Run Run', although recently Marr has chosen to distance himself from any conscious influences in writing the song.

Composed early in the Smiths' career, this was not issued as a single until as late as January 1984. A far more immediate offering than their début 'Hand In Glove', for which it was not even considered as competition, it eventually peaked at number 12 in the UK charts. Despite its success, Morrissey was never happy with the recording which was primarily championed by Marr. "We explored overdubbing guitars and there's probably about 14 or 15 on there," John Porter recalls. "I remember 'What Difference Does It Make?' being a breakthrough. I liked it because it had a bit of an R&B groove."

Lyrically, the song was not one of Morrissey's greatest, although the opening line 'All men have secrets . . .' was suitably arresting. "People seem to look for quite staunchly philosophical edges in what I write, and certainly they're there," Morrissey added. "But 'What Difference Does It Make?' just struck me as a very necessary term. I don't know. What difference does it make? I just wanted to have a very easy attitude and that's what the lyrics imply. People get so really neurotic about themselves – their lives, their hair, their teeth – but what difference can anything make really?" Although the song was one of the group's more commercial offerings and featured in live performances at the time, it was soon dropped, and Morrissey has never said a good word about it since.

The recording took place at a time when there was some ill feeling in the group, serious enough to prompt Marr to consider leaving. "Johnny was upset about a lot of things that day," Andy Rourke later said in the High Court. "My main concern was getting the session done." Apart from his distaste for the song, Morrissey ran into trouble over the single's cover artwork, which was meant to feature a still of Terence Stamp from the 1965 film *The Collector*. When Stamp declined a request for clearance of the photograph, early copies of the single were recalled and replaced by a shot of Morrissey in the same pose, clutching a glass of milk.

I Don't Owe You Anything

Mike Joyce described this as "a massively powerful track and one of the most powerful that Morrissey has ever done". It may be neither, but it always worked well in concert, most notably at Dingwalls, London, on 30 August 1983 when, as Joyce remembers, "I was nearly reduced to tears. It was so powerful." Partly intended as a vehicle for their songwriting ambitions, the composition was offered to Sandie Shaw, whom Morrissey seemed intent on luring out of semi-retirement at the time. As Marr confirms, when he and Morrissey first got together, one of their main aims was to establish a formidable songwriting team. This was achieved when Shaw later recorded 'Hand In Glove' and 'I Don't Owe You Anything' , backed by the Smiths *sans* Morrissey.

Suffer Little Children

This moving and controversial tribute to the victims of the Moors Murderers was one of the first lyrics that Marr saw when he visited Morrissey's house. He was so impressed by the composition that he rapidly provided a lustrous melody which gave the lyrics even greater poignancy. As mentioned earlier, a prototype version of the Smiths recorded the song as a demo in the summer of 1983, when it was still titled 'Over The Moors' on the tape box and featured the sounds of children playing, an eerie effect not included on the album version. Apart from Morrissey's moving vocal, the composition was most notable for its subtle use of detail and some daring touches, including the naming of the victims and the chilling laughter of Hindley, pro-vided by Morrissey's friend Annalisa Jablonska, both of which added to the macabre feel. An important source for some of the lyrics and imagery was Emlyn Williams' 1967 study of the Moors Murderers, *Beyond Belief*, which included the chapter titles 'Suffer Little Children' and 'Hindley Wakes'. There were also the words 'Wherever he has gone I have gone', which echoed Hindley's statement to the police, "Wherever Ian has gone, I have gone." Although 'Suffer Little Children' was among the most accomplished of Morrissey/Marr compositions, it was only played live on one occasion which suggests that the singer may have regarded the lyrics as too personal for regular public exposure.

Unfortunately, the song returned to haunt the Smiths many months after the album's release. In May 1984, it was included on the B-side of their fourth single, 'Heaven Knows I'm Miserable Now'. A relative of one of the victims heard the song on a pub jukebox and voiced his objections to the *Manchester Evening News*. This titbit later found its way into the *Sun*, alongside the quote: "Whoever wrote the song must be as sick as the killers." Joining the debate was Ann West, mother of the murdered Lesley Ann Downey whose 'pretty white beads' had provided the song with one of its more powerful images. West, the most vociferous campaigner and fiercest opponent of clemency for the murderers, was bitterly opposed to anyone cashing-in on the families' grief. During the height of punk she had successfully scuppered the release of a sensationalist single, 'Free Myra Hindley', credited to the Moors Murderers, whose line-up included Chrissie Hynde. Assuming 'Suffer Little Children' was of that ilk, she contacted Rough Trade and succeeded in reducing the Smiths' representative Scott Piering to tears. West was eventually convinced of Morrissey's sincerity and the two later met, seemingly united in their antipathy towards Myra Hindley and Ian Brady. In later interviews, Morrissey maintained his condemnation of the pair, even suggesting that Hindley should have been hung. Meanwhile, the media onslaught was ameliorated by a moving press release prepared by Piering which read: "The Smiths stand behind 100 per cent of the lyrics to all of their songs and 'Suffer Little Children' is no exception. The song was written out of a profound emotion by Morrissey, a Mancunian who feels that the particularly horrendous crime it describes must be borne by the conscience of Manchester and that it must never happen again. It was written out of deep respect for the victims and their kin and the Smiths felt it was an important enough song to put on their last single even though it had already been released on their LP. In a word, it is a memorial to the children and all like them, who have suffered such a fate. The Smiths are acknowledged as writing with sensitivity, depth and intelligence and the suggestion that they are cashing-in on a tragedy at the expense of causing grief to the relatives of its victims is absolutely untrue. Morrissey has had a lengthy conversation with the mother of Lesley Ann Downey, Mrs West, and she understands that the intentions of the song are completely honourable. Furthermore, he's willing to speak to any of the families involved so there will be no misunderstanding."

One more controversy dogging the single release was a photograph of the bouffant Viv Nicholson on the sleeve, which some mistakenly assumed was Myra Hindley. As Piering confirmed: "The photo was taken in 1961 and was first published in the *News Of The World* years before the tragic event occurred. The decision to put 'Suffer Little Children' on the B-side was made well after the choice of Ms Nicholson's photo had been made and although it is a chilling coincidence, there is no further connection." One final coincidence, which I first noted in *The Severed Alliance*, was that the person who informed on the Moors Murderers was Hindley's brother-in-law David *Smith*.

Having already suffered at the hands of the tabloid press over the lyrics to 'Reel Around The Fountain', Morrissey was predictably vitriolic about this latest furore. "It's not a reflection of me, it really reflects the absolute and barbaric attitudes of the daily press. I don't feel that I was in the dock; I feel they were really. In retrospect, they were just really saying how narrow-minded and blunderous they were. Some of the reports in newspapers in Portsmouth and Hartlepool – all the places that really count – some of the reports were so full of hate, it was like I was one of the Moors Murderers, that I'd gone out and murdered these children. It was incredible."

HATFUL OF HOLLOW

Released: November 1984

Rough Trade Records, Rough 76, November 1984. Reissued: Rough CD 76,
December 1985. WEA 4509-91893, July 1987, November 1993, February 1995.
US issue: Sire 9-45205-2 CD, November 1993

The release of *Hatful Of Hollow* was partly a result of fan pressure and
a reaction against some of the criticisms of the previous album. During
their first year of fame, the Smiths had appeared on several BBC radio
sessions, home-made tapes of which were exchanging hands among
their more avid supporters. Morrissey was impressed by the number
of letters he received begging for an official release. Speaking of the
BBC recordings, he said: "As far as we're concerned, those were
the sessions that got us excited in the first place, and apparently it was
how a lot of other people discovered us also. We decided to include
the extra tracks from our 12-inch singles for people who didn't have
all of those and to make it completely affordable." Selections from
the BBC sessions, complemented by several rare flip-sides, provided
an opportunity to hear the Smiths in their primitive glory.

The release was an audacious move. At such a crucial early stage in
their career, few groups would have sanctioned what amounted to an
archival recording. Most releases of this nature tended to be post-
humous. Even Beatles' fans had to wait 24 years after the group's
breakup before their BBC radio sessions were deemed fit for the
market-place. If the Smiths had been signed to a major label *Hatful Of
Hollow* might never have been released. The beauty of Rough Trade
was its willingness to take risks, coupled with a firm understanding of
the independent scene. Their decision to issue the work at mid-price,
complete with a striking gatefold sleeve, was inspired. At nearly an
hour in length and 16 songs to savour, the package was an irresistible
bargain for those still curious about the Smiths but not yet willing to
risk paying out for a full-price album. Far from damaging the Smiths'
career trajectory, this unexpected compilation kept them in the
public eye, even reaching number 7 in the UK album charts. Those
lucky enough to hear the group for the first time could hardly have

had a better or more economical introduction. Even Morrissey, who had previously championed *The Smiths*, evidently preferred *Hatful Of Hollow*. "The situation we were in at the time of the release of the first LP . . . there was really no going back. It had reached a point where we had to release that record. At the time we were behind it completely and that LP means a great deal to many people who weren't even aware of the Peel sessions . . . *Hatful Of Hollow* was there because I absolutely felt that the first LP was an inaccurate representation of our skills, which is embarrassing, but I think we can survive the embarrassment."

William, It Was Really Nothing

This slight, urban comic drama was one of Morrissey's most delicately understated songs, but it proved commercial enough to reach number 17 in the UK charts. The scenario was most likely borrowed from Keith Waterhouse's *Billy Liar*, in which William Fisher fights a losing battle to escape the shackles of provincial life by dreaming of a scriptwriting career in London. For Morrissey, the theme had an acutely autobiographical significance. Only a few years before, he was walking the streets of Manchester, dreaming of a pop star fame which seemed as illusory as Billy Liar's fantasies. In several songs of this period there are unflattering portrayals of women and here the singer berates William for fraternizing with a provincial fat girl who seems intent on trapping him into marriage. Discussing the song, Morrissey said, "It occurred to me that within popular music if there ever were any records that discussed marriage they were always from the female's standpoint – female singers singing to women. Whenever were there songs saying, 'Do not marry'? . . . I thought it was about time there was a male voice speaking directly to another male saying that marriage was a waste of time – that, in fact, it was absolutely nothing."

The second male mentioned by Morrissey was the narrator himself, who sounds like a bitter misogynist. Echoes of *Billy Liar* can be detected in the portrayal of the girl, who resembles Barbara – the plump, orange-eating girlfriend who is intent on taming the wayward anti-hero. Morrissey may also have been influenced by one of his favourite northern comediennes, Victoria Wood, whose comic song 'Fourteen Again' contains the line 'an engagement ring doesn't mean a thing to a mind consumed by brass [money]' which echoes the demands of William's ring-fixated girlfriend. Some critics also suspected that the song might have been inspired by the Associates' doomed singer Billy MacKenzie, whom Morrissey encountered during this period. This theory was largely based on the flippant Associates' 'answer song' 'Steven, You Were Really Something'. Morrissey never confirmed the rumour and was decidedly ambivalent about MacKenzie, telling *Melody Maker*, "Billy was very erratic, quite indescribable. We spent hours and hours searching for some common ground but ultimately I don't believe there was any."

Musically, 'William, It Was Really Nothing' was a conscious attempt to recreate the great singles of the Sixties by compressing the contents into less than two-and-a half minutes. As Marr explained at the time: "We try and be adventurous . . . if you dig into either of our collections you will find music of quality from every period of popular music. For instance, in the Sixties, records were actually worth something. People went out and bought a 7-inch piece of plastic and they treasured it . . . It's good to take a part of pop culture and bring the human spirit back into it . . . The whole idea of two people getting together with lots of common ground but with separate influences to bring out something we believe to be the best we've ever heard is something we feel has been missing since the Sixties. The Seventies was the decade of the solo artiste and the solo writer and that really doesn't appeal to me at all. I really get a buzz from the unpredictability of the way a Smiths song turns out . . . 'William' is quite a whimsical song. I don't think it's broken all the rules in pop music, but to start with a short verse and then follow it with three choruses is quite good . . . It wouldn't upset me if tomorrow Morrissey wrote a boy meets girl type song, but it's good to have songs that cater for no gender specifically. One of the reasons our records are timeless is because the lyrics are so good, and whatever gay overtones are there I endorse 100 per cent."

What Difference Does It Make?

This less measured version of the song, produced by Roger Pusey and broadcast on BBC Radio 1's *John Peel Show* in May 1983, was preferred by Morrissey. Its most distinctive characteristic was the prominent drum sound which, not surprisingly, appealed to Mike Joyce. "The Peel session was myself and Andy playing the way we wanted to and at the time that sounded very indie, very busy, attacking and aggressive. The one that came out on the first album was a bit more solid. It pinned down the beat a lot easier for people to understand on the dance-floor . . . The Peel version was the way I wanted it to be and the John Porter version was the way he wanted it to be. John Porter thought he was right that it should be a more solid laid down track as opposed to a jumbled-up sound of rhythm."

These Things Take Time

Neuroses, insecurity and a sprinkling of gallows humour characterized this ode to unrealizable love. There is even a nod to *The Sound Of Music* in the line 'The hills are alive . . .' Bathos is used to humorous effect as we are taken from the holy vision of a sacred *wunderkind* to the sordid site of a disused railway line within the space of two lines. Celibacy, and possibly a degree of impotence, are hinted at in the wry lyrics. Produced by Dale Griffin on 26 June 1983, this was broadcast on BBC Radio 1's *David Jensen Show*.

This Charming Man

When Rough Trade founder Geoff Travis heard this song, he immediately suggested that it should be released as the next Smiths' single in place of the controversial 'Reel Around The Fountain'. It is not too difficult to understand why. With its infectious melody and tart lyrics this was undoubtedly the group's most commercial offering to date. Producer John Porter was impressed by Travis' certainty. "He was good like that. He had good ears and a good knowledge of the market he was trying to sell to . . ." Although this radio recording for the *John Peel Show* lacked the dynamics of the more polished single version, it was still impressive. Lyrically, it was one of Morrissey's more oblique compositions. Its deliberately elliptical verses featured subtle homo-erotic undertones, although there was nothing sexually explicit enough to cause offence.

The reference to a 'jumped up pantry boy' was allegedly borrowed from the film *Sleuth* but what struck most listeners was Marr's chiming guitar work. "We all felt a particular energy about the song," Morrissey noted. "There was a strange urgency to have it released straightaway."

How Soon Is Now?

Sire Records' supremo Seymour Stein called this "the 'Stairway To Heaven' of the Eighties". Unquestionably one of the Smiths' most loved and enduring songs, its recording history was a veritable comedy of errors. John Porter produced this version on 1 August 1984 for broadcast on the *John Peel Show* eight days later. The atmosphere in the studio was highly charged with the group bathed in red light in order to enhance the eerie mood. Marr presented a brooding arrangement inspired by Elvis Presley's Sun sessions and a recent immersion in the rhythms of Bo Diddley. He described the song to me as "a perfect cross between a sweaty, swamp backing track and an intense wired shock every few bars". Morrissey's opening words partly echoed some lines from George Eliot's novel *Middlemarch* in which the author described Fred Vincy as the "inevitable heir to nothing in particular". John Porter at first assumed Morrissey was singing 'I am the sun and the air', but was soon corrected. The lyrics transform feelings of self-pity into a triumphant cry of defiance in favour of the shy, awkward, maladjusted and unloved. After the recording was completed, Porter was convinced of its massive hit potential, but met with a cool response from the normally enthusiastic Geoff Travis. As the weeks passed, Porter was mortified to discover that the track was not even deemed suitable for official release on a 7-inch B-side. Instead, an alternate take was tucked away as an extra track on the 12-inch version of 'William, It Was Really Nothing'.

"They just threw it away, wasted it," Porter told me. "Everybody knew the Smiths' fans already had it. The record company blew it." Three months after the release of *Hatful Of Hollow*, 'How Soon Is Now?' was belatedly issued as an A-side in the UK but, by then, its impact was severely lessened and it peaked at a lowly number 25. Geoff Travis still hoped that the song might break the Smiths in the USA but, despite considerable airplay on college radio, it failed to dent the charts. Marr's backing track remained a favourite of radio and television broadcasters in search of a theme tune and the song's lasting appeal was indicated by its reappearance as a sample on Soho's 1991 hit, 'Hippiechick'. Morrissey and Marr responded to the unauthorized sampling by successfully securing 25 per cent of the royalties from Soho's recording.

Handsome Devil

Originally recorded at Drone Studios in December 1982, complete with an uncharacteristic saxophone accompaniment from Andy Gill, the song was subsequently recorded live at Manchester's Haçienda on 4 February 1983 and used as the B-side to 'Hand In Glove'. This later, more accomplished version was taped at the BBC on 18 May 1983 and aired 13 days later on the Smiths' first radio session for John Peel. Its arch allusions and Victorian use of the word 'handsome' demonstrated Morrissey's determination to invest pop lyrics with a degree of mystery. "People aren't used to thinking in a very charming or handsome way. I think words like that can sweep away a lot of the grime because people are becoming so mentally depressed and introverted that they can't think of a positive language any more. The language that people use totally erodes the heart, but modern life doesn't give much opportunity for really inflated language. The art of conversation has definitely been destroyed."

The song's playful gender confusion caused some listeners to highlight its homo-erotic content, while the inclusion of the phrase 'mammary glands' prompted a counter-offensive heterosexual reading. For the tabloids and *Lolita* hunters it provided a strong case for a more provocative analysis, made plausible by the arch references to helping a boy get through his exams, possibly with the assistance of oral sex. Even the S&M brigade could find some excitement with the references to cracking whips. It seemed that the celibate singer was offering his audience a cornucopia of sexuality. Interestingly, Morrissey's response to such interpretations was, in my view, either naïve or disingenuous. Completely ignoring the composition's explicit sexuality, he directed listeners to the final two lines which he termed "the essence of the song". Reacting to tabloid speculation about his motivations, he felt it necessary to offer a disappointingly reductive reading of the song's meaning: "We must stress that 'Handsome

Devil' is aimed entirely towards adults and has nothing to do with children and certainly nothing to do with child molesting. It's an adult understanding of quite intimate matters." Not for the first or last time, his defensive overview remained largely unchallenged.

Hand In Glove

Originally cut at Manchester's Strawberry Studios and financed by their manager Joe Moss, who proffered £213, 'Hand In Glove' became the Smiths' first single and only sole production. Marr opens the song with a harmonica break, just as the Beatles had done with their début 'Love Me Do'. Morrissey's strained vocal eulogizes a love threatened by public disapproval and mockery. The words proved equally appealing to star-crossed lovers, budding adolescent romantics and yet to be declared homosexuals. Morrissey evidently altered the line 'Everything depends upon how near you sleep to me' from Buffy Saint-Marie's reading of Leonard Cohen's 'Bells'. Underpinning the lyric was Morrissey's perennial self-effacing irony, for in the final couplet of the song his great love is exposed as little more than an ephemeral fantasy as he closes with a forlorn line taken from Shelagh Delaney, 'I'll probably never see you again'.

Joe Moss was willing to self-finance an independent label release for the single, but a one-off record deal was eventually secured when Marr and Rourke buttonholed Geoff Travis at Rough Trade's office in London. Thrusting a cassette into his hands, Marr implored: "Listen to this, it's not just another tape." After taking the cassette home for the weekend Travis concluded, rather extravagantly, that it was potentially a 'great' record.

Released in May 1983, it failed to emulate the achievements of fellow Rough Trade acts Aztec Camera and Scritti Politti by entering the charts. This was not entirely surprising for the song lacked the immediacy and commercial clout of its superior successor, 'This Charming Man'. For Morrissey and Marr, however, it was an all-important début and they were unwilling to entertain any criticisms about its weaknesses or shortcomings as an all-time great single. In interviews of the period, Morrissey characteristically overstated its significance, even calling it "the most important song in the world". One year on, he was still complaining: "The only tragedy for the

Smiths has been that 'Hand In Glove' didn't gain the attention it deserved. I won't rest until that song is in the heart of everything . . . It should have been a massive hit. It was so urgent – to me, it was a complete cry in every direction. It really was a landmark. There is every grain of emotion that has to be injected into all the songs and it worked perfectly with 'Hand In Glove'. It was as if these four people *had* to play that song – it was so essential. Those words had to be sung." Rather than the emphatic ending featured on *The Smiths*, this prototype used a fade and sounded noticeably muddier.

Still Ill

Positively primitive compared to the version that graced their first album, this radio session recorded for the *John Peel Show* on 14 September 1983 revealed Marr in uncertain mood. Occasionally, it sounded like the song was still at the rehearsal stage. This was also one of the few occasions when Marr provided a harmonica introduction, echoing the opening of their début single, 'Hand In Glove'. Not surprisingly, the instrument was replaced when they entered the recording studio. Given all the fuss about 'Suffer Little Children' it was fortunate that nobody connected the words 'England is mine and it owes me a living' with Hindley's comments after being moved to Durham prison in 1977: "Society owes me a living." The likelihood of Morrissey being aware of this coincidence was remote at best.

Heaven Knows I'm Miserable Now

New Year's Day 1984 was not an auspicious date in Morrissey's calendar. The previous night he had fallen off the stage at New York's Danceteria and when he awoke the next morning he learned that drummer Mike Joyce was stricken with chicken pox and might have to be replaced by Blondie's Clem Burke for the duration of their East Coast tour. That suggestion was soon dismissed and the Smiths returned home. Before their departure, Morrissey penned the lyrics to a new song that summed up his feelings: 'Heaven Knows I'm Miserable Now'. During the early stages of researching *Morrissey & Marr: The Severed Alliance*, I was busy rifling through my collection of 1960s copies of *New Musical Express* when I stumbled across a trade advertisement for an obscure and failed single by Sandie Shaw titled 'Heaven Knows I'm Missing Him Now'. That same week I interviewed Scott Piering for the first time and casually placed the ad in front of his eyes. He reacted with beer-spilling astonishment. "Morrissey hides his sources well. He never once mentioned that song to us, even though we knew of his love for Sandie Shaw. No one's ever mentioned that title or that connection before – and he may not thank you for sharing it with the world." Released in May 1984, 'Heaven Knows I'm Miserable Now' became the group's most successful offering to date, peaking at number 10. It was also the song that, more than any other in the Smiths' canon, equated Morrissey with the word 'miserable'. Yet, the composition was far from his bleakest work and amid the litany of discontent there is at least an acceptance of temporary happiness – albeit when drunk. There is also another humorous reference to excessive sexual demands from a female, evidently enough to make even the debauched Roman emperor Caligula blush with embarrassment. Morrissey's vocal is impressively confident throughout while Marr sounds as though he has been locked in a room and forcibly fed a glut of Sixties' instrumental albums.

This Night Has Opened My Eyes
This was the one song on the compilation previously unavailable in any form. Lyrically, the composition was largely inspired by Shelagh Delaney's play *A Taste Of Honey*. The recording was done in the wake of the paedophile controversy, so producer Roger Pusey was wary of broadcasting anything too offensive. "He was told to vet the lyrics," claims Mike Joyce. Pusey was naturally curious about the subject matter of the opening two lines which hinted at infanticide. As Joyce recalls: "The first words were 'In the river the colour of lead, immerse the baby's head' and it was like, 'Stop! What was that you sang?' It was ridiculous. They wouldn't ban a song, just not play it." In fact, it was broadcast on 21 September 1983. After a spell in the Smiths' live set, the song was dropped in November 1984 but was unexpectedly revived for their final show at the Brixton Academy on 12 December 1986.

You've Got Everything Now

Although this BBC radio session for the *David Jensen Show* lacked the organ and piano accompaniment that was later used on *The Smiths*, it still sounded surprisingly accomplished. Morrissey's falsetto is strong and the arrangement is consistent with the alternate version. Thematically, the composition fits well on *Hatful Of Hollow*, echoing the anti-work sentiments of the preceding 'Heaven Knows I'm Miserable Now'. In interviews, Morrissey repeated such protests, arguing: "Jobs reduce people to absolute stupidity, they forget to think about themselves. There's something so positive about unemployment . . . You don't get trapped into materialism, you won't buy things you don't really want."

Accept Yourself

Produced by John Porter in August 1983 and subsequently featured on BBC Radio 1's *David Jensen Show*, this was the definitive version of the song. Originally intended for their début album, it was first recorded by Troy Tate but failed to make the final running order of *The Smiths*, although a later version produced by Porter at London's Matrix Studios did appear on the B-side of 'This Charming Man'. It proved to be a powerful affirmation of individuality. The interrogative lyrics were accompanied by an appropriately uneven rhythm. While other Morrissey songs raged against imagined detractors, here the mood was stoical and the sentiments empowering. Its positive admonitions ensured the song a key place in the closing segment of the Smiths' live set during the summer and autumn of 1983.

Girl Afraid

It still seems amazing that this song could have been relegated to a mere extra on the rear of the 12-inch version of 'Heaven Knows I'm Miserable Now'. Within the context of *Hatful Of Hollow*, it emerges as a wondrous highlight. Marr's alluring arrangement, originally conceived on piano, provides a perfect counterpoint to Morrissey's morality tale of modern relationships. While it is possible to detect underlying hints of misogyny in the portrayal of the materialistically minded female protagonist, the predominant theme is a pervasive, mutual insecurity that gnaws away at the partners and ultimately separates them. As an observational study of human relationships, it was one of Morrissey's best songs of the period. Less didactic in tone than 'William, It Was Really Nothing', the omniscient narrator's point of view is kept at bay sufficiently to allow the characters' doomed relationship to unravel naturally. As Morrissey concluded: "'Girl Afraid' simply implied that even within relationships there's no real certainty and nobody knows how anybody feels. People feel that just because they're having this cemented communion with another person that the two of you become whole, which is something I detested. I hate that . . . It's not true anyway. Ultimately, you're on your own, whatever happens in life . . . You die on your own."

Back To The Old House
Yet again, this BBC radio version of the song, later broadcast on the *John Peel Show*, proved superior to the studio recording which was relegated to the B-side of 'What Difference Does It Make?' and failed to feature on *The Smiths*. A welcome inclusion on *Hatful Of Hollow*, it again underlined the power of Morrissey/Marr as a songwriting team. In the lyrics, Morrissey indulges a bleak sense of loss for something that was evidently unrealized. Marr's plangent acoustic work beautifully enhances the mood of empty nostalgia for a relationship that is never described, revealed or requited.

Reel Around The Fountain
Another crucial addition to the compilation, this was the BBC radio version recorded for the *John Peel Show* on 18 May 1983 by Roger Pusey, along with 'What Difference Does It Make?', 'Miserable Lie' and 'Handsome Devil'. The entire session was broadcast on 31 May and prefaced by the venerable Peel telling his listeners: "They've been touted as the latest prophets of northern doom. I should disregard that. At least you can judge for yourself on tonight's programme."

The recordings, 'Reel Around The Fountain' in particular, were so popular that they would be repeated several times. According to Scott Piering, this radio version of 'Reel Around The Fountain' was seriously considered as a single, although the later studio recording with Troy Tate was subsequently chosen. In the event, the single never happened due to the aforementioned tabloid furore over the lyrics. This resulted in a later radio recording on 25 August being excluded from the *David Jensen Show*. The controversy ultimately worked to the group's advantage when they were offered another BBC John Peel session by the crusading producer John Walters. As Scott Piering recalled: "Smiths fever was on. It wasn't just smouldering, it was aflame."

Please Please Please Let Me Get What I Want

Previously featured on the B-side of 'William, It Was Really Nothing', this was an inspired addition to the album. According to producer John Porter, Marr wrote the music quickly in the same period that he completed the masterful 'How Soon Is Now?' At a mere 110 seconds, 'Please Please Please . . .' proved the shortest song in the Smiths' canon, but its brevity was no impediment to its quality. As Morrissey rightly noted: "Hiding it away on a B-side was sinful. I feel sad about it now although we did include it on *Hatful Of Hollow* by way of semi-repentance. When we first played it to Rough Trade, they kept asking, 'Where's the rest of the song?' But to me it's a very brief punch in the face. Lengthening the song would, to my mind, have simply been explaining the bloody obvious." His simple expression of hope in the face of constant adversity features the usual sliver of mild irony. Marr provides a plaintive endnote to Morrissey's pleading with an impressive mandolin solo. Overall, it was a beautiful conclusion to a much loved album.

MEAT IS MURDER

Released: February 1985

Rough Trade Records, Rough 81, February 1985. Rough CD 81 March 1985.
Reissued: WEA 4509-91895-2, November 1993, February 1995.
US issue: Sire 9-25269-1, April 1985. Sire 9-25269-2, CD, July 1987

Following the release of their début album and the compilation *Hatful Of Hollow*, the Smiths toured extensively and built a sizeable following on the college circuit. Their success in music press polls indicated that they were not merely top of the indie pile but close to making a substantial impact on the pop mainstream. An endearing devotion to the three-minute pop single, backed by a promising songwriting partnership, suggested that they might yet follow previous music press heroes such as the Jam by topping both the singles and albums charts. But it was not to be. For all their awareness of pop history, it seemed the Smiths could not fashion the classic number 1 single to define their time for ever. Thankfully, their albums fared better and this great work, their sole chart-topper, supplanted Bruce Springsteen's *Born In The USA* during the same week that the Smiths won the 'Best Group' award in the influential *NME*'s annual poll.

Recorded at Liverpool's Amazon Studios, *Meat Is Murder* was also their first self-produced album. "When we came to record that LP, we were quite angered," Morrissey recalled. "We were distraught about the way we had been treated by the music industry generally over the previous 12 months . . . We produced it ourselves and that was a very important decision to make. For the first time we were on our own and devoid of any other influence."

The Smiths' impressive ascent since their début album coincided with Morrissey's emergence as pop's most provocative and newsworthy orator. His love/hate relationship with the media saw him lionized in the music press, even while the tabloids called for his head. As he said, "When we began, I thought there was a need to find somebody who was honest to a fault. Nobody had been like that before, because all the popular figures had become like early Seventies rock stars. There was nobody out there putting their heart on the line. There was no one singing as though they would die if they didn't. I had to be boringly personal. I'm beyond embarrassment now." Although his sexuality and apparent celibacy still fascinated journalists and public alike there was, throughout this period, a discernible shift in emphasis from the personal to the political. Suddenly, Morrisseyspeak was less preoccupied with the monochrome ideals of a lost verdant England and more concerned about contemporary events. His much publicized comments on Margaret Thatcher, British royalty, the IRA, CND, the Brighton Bombing and animal rights heaped controversy on controversy. The proselytizing tone could be glimpsed in countless captioned quotes as he effortlessly adopted the role of pop's most audacious orator. Wildean witticisms and political asides reinforced the lyrical thrust of what was arguably the Smiths' finest album. The self-righteous words were both passionate and compassionate, a fusion that was seen less often in his later work.

Meat Is Murder is a thrilling, spine-tingling extravaganza with an agenda that both transcends and reflects its time. In Thatcherite Britain, political pop was in vogue and a substantial number of artistes, from the New Pop of Culture Club to the Newer Pop of Frankie Goes To Hollywood and Bronski Beat, were making forthright political statements, usually backed by a sexual agenda. In many ways Morrissey was leading the charge simply by expressing opinions, ideals and prejudices that he had held since troubled adolescence. If *Meat Is Murder* had been mere sloganeering then it would now be little more than a faintly anachronistic curio. That it is much more than that is evident from its musical menu, which is as varied as any listener could desire. The contents offer pop, folk, rockabilly, psychedelia, flashes of funk and even a sprinkling of heavy metal. This was a major step forward from the Smiths' dour début album with a far crisper production, more accomplished musicianship and noticeably improved vocals. The rhythm section received a greater opportunity to explore new ideas, with Rourke introducing funk patterns and Joyce enjoying the freedom to play the way he chose. Having completed his apprenticeship under John Porter, Marr also found his *métier* as an arranger/producer, now ably assisted by Stephen Street. The strength in unison from the players enabled

Morrissey to translate his personal neuroses and political pronouncements into a potent body of work. *Meat Is Murder* may not have won as many critics' polls as its successor, but it is arguably the group's most abrasive and satisfying work. At the time of its release, *Melody Maker* reviewer Ian Pye remarked, "The Smiths have been misguidedly elevated to the level of gods by their followers but their music is well beyond the trivial novelty we've come to know as pop."

In retrospect, this album still sounds like the Smiths at their peak, although it is probably unfair to highlight one work during such a fertile period. For this was a time when they had acquired that palpable touch of greatness, by which you knew that almost everything they recorded displayed distinction. The aesthetic appreciation lay not merely in the moment, but in the sure knowledge that history would reward and enshrine this release. Great pop is captured amid a sense of temporal dislocation – an intense absorption in the moment, reinforced by the feeling that the instant is of such significance that it will later be recalled with similar and possibly greater intensity in the future. The additional attraction of *Meat Is Murder* lay in knowing that the group still had so much to offer. After listening to this fine work, there still seemed every chance that bigger achievements lay ahead. That dynamic always creates a dramatic and pleasing sense of witnessing history in the present while contemplating the future, and that was the story of the Smiths in 1985.

The Headmaster Ritual

Opening with one of Marr's greatest and most enticing riffs, the first few seconds alone confirmed a fantastic leap in the group's playing abilities, in striking contrast to the inchoate style of their first album. Joyce's steady rhythm and Rourke's interweaving bass enhance the arrangement which is one of the Smiths' best. Marr paid particular attention to this song which he told me took him longer to complete than any other in the Smiths' canon. "I first played the riff to Morrissey when we were working on the demos for our first album with Troy Tate. I nailed the rest of it when I moved to Earls Court. That was around the time when we were being fabulous." A combination of mid-Sixties Beatles' guitar lines and Joni Mitchell-style open tuning transforms the composition into a work of great invention. As Marr recalled: "I wrote 'The Headmaster Ritual' on acoustic. It's an open-D tuning with a capo at the second fret. I fancied the idea of a strange Joni Mitchell tuning, and the actual progression is like what she would have done had she been an MC5 fan or a punk rocker. I knew pretty much what every guitar track would be before we started. There are two tracks of Martin D-28, and the main riff is two tracks of Rickenbacker. I wasn't thinking specifically of the Beatles' 'Day Tripper' – even though it sounds like it – but I did think of it as a George Harrison part. The Rickenbacker belonged to Phil Manzanera of Roxy Music; I'm told it was originally owned by Roger McGuinn. All the guitars are in open tuning, except for one of the chorus guitars, which is done on an Epiphone in Nashville tuning, capoed at the second fret."

Marr's arrangement simultaneously sounded fresh and familiar, a modern song with more than a sprinkling of rock classicism. Morrissey's accompanying lyrics have the venomous spit of a revenger's tragedy. The victim of his wrath is ostensibly his headmaster at St Mary's, Vincent 'Jet' Morgan. Within the song, however, Morrissey's railing contempt transcends the particular locale and serves as a bitter indictment against all custodial educational institutions. His opening two words alone ('belligerent ghouls') instantly attract attention. Most pop composers might have written 'fools' but the bizarre image of grave robbers overseeing adolescents who have yet to experience adult life is oddly apposite in Morrissey's vicious narrative. Similarly the word 'belligerent' is the type of vocabulary that a sexagenarian High Court judge might apply to a truculent pop star. Taken together, the words conjure a Dickensian ambience which again serves Morrissey well in describing the authoritarian ethos of his school. While his account is to some extent exaggerated, most notably in the reference to dinner plate-sized bruises, this is not Morrissey merely creating agitprop protest but a bitter remembrance, the tone of which was shared by other pupils of the period. His horror of finding himself in this quasi-Victorian scenario is reflected in adjectives of disgust including, inappropriately for a supposed lover of animals, the phrase 'spineless swine', and a rare Morrissey expletive 'bastard'. The rage is so powerful and explicit that it comes as doubly shocking to hear the singer reduced to the emotional level of an over-sensitive, whimpering child on his first day at school, nervously pleading that he wants to go home. Ghoulish wailing adds to the disconcerting experience. With a less impressive backing, Morrissey's message might have sounded trite and facile but Marr's driving arrangement invests the lyrics with a power and resonance that is truly beguiling. Long before Morrissey considered writing this composition, the Department of Education and Science inspected his old school and their report, which I read with fascination, told its own story. Unlike Morrissey, they were positive about some aspects of the school and praised the pastoral efforts of staff members, but they also provided a conclusion far more damaging in its objective tone than anything Morrissey could ever have written: "It is therefore surprising to note that there were 92 recorded instances of the use of corporal punishment during the first half term of the current year. Its use for some offences scarcely seemed warranted."

Rusholme Ruffians

The debt that this song owed to Pomus/Shuman's '(Marie's The Name) His Latest Flame' was obvious from a first hearing and Marr would later acknowledge the source in live performance. If the music hinted at hidden influences, then so did the lyrics. Morrissey borrowed freely from the pen of comedienne Victoria Wood, remoulding her song 'Fourteen Again' for his own satiric purposes. What emerges is a striking adaptation in which Wood's humorously affectionate reminiscences ('The last night of the fair / French kisses as the kiosks shut / Behind the generator. . .') are subverted into a threatening landscape where casual violence is perpetrated. Morrissey also sings 'the last night of the fair' and mentions the 'generator', but in his scenario a boy is brutally stabbed and the threat of romantic suicide is menacingly present. The mutilating 'fountain pen' image also appears in both songs, but once again Morrissey uses the metaphor for melodramatic rather than nostalgic effect. Finally, he paraphrases another Wood song, 'Funny How Things Turn Out', transforming 'my faith *in myself* is still devout' into 'my faith *in love* is still devout' as a lyrical finale. With Morrissey and Marr each adapting material from separate sources, both the lyrics and music share a common sense of playful experimentation. As Marr told me, the primary idea was to create a song that captured the raw excitement of youths visiting a Manchester fairground. The rockabilly guitar work gave the song a Fifties' ambience in keeping with the theme and engineer Stephen Street added some fairground noises borrowed from a BBC sound effects record. Morrissey also travelled back to his earliest memories in dramatizing the dazzling unpredictability of fairground life. "As a child, I was literally educated at fairgrounds. It was the big event. It was why everybody was alive. On threadbare Manchester council estates once a year fairs would come around. It was a period of tremendous violence, hate, distress, high romance and all the truly vital things of life. It was really the patch of ground where you learned about everything instantaneously whether you wanted to or not . . . In Rusholme, it was the only thing people had."

I Want The One I Can't Have
This song included a series of catchy and amusing epigrams set against a basic chord sequence that came together in the studio surprisingly quickly. As Mike Joyce recalls, "It was just done like a jam and Stephen Street said, 'That's great.' We went through it a few times and that was the record. Then Andy put the bass on." The opening line, cleverly rhyming 'mentality' with 'biology', recalls the body/ mind dichotomy first voiced on 'Still Ill', while the offer to find self-validation in a railway-station alley takes us back to the disused railway line of 'These Things Take Time'.

There's an element of almost aristocratic condescension in Morrissey's suggestion that a double bed and a 'stalwart lover' are what constitute riches for the poor. Then again, like the upper-class central character in *Up The Junction*, happily slumming near Battersea, the narrator's tone is respectful rather than derogatory. Speaking about the 'double bed' line to Biba Kopf in the *NME*, Morrissey revealed, "That came from a sense I had that, trite as it may sound, when people get married and are getting their flat − not even their house, note − the most important thing was getting the double bed. It was like the prized exhibit: the cooker, the fire, everything else came later."

'I Want The One I Can't Have' was cleverly positioned on the album, neatly interspersed between stronger material, yet contributing to the music's forward thrust. In concert, the song invariably featured early in the set. During a performance at New York's Beacon Theater, Marr unexpectedly included a few chords of what sounded very much like the chorus of Jimmy Justice's 'When My Little Girl Is Smiling'. 'I Want The One I Can't Have' survived the *Meat Is Murder* tour and remained in the group's live set until as late as October 1986. Morrissey later revived the song in 2002 as an unexpected opening number for his solo shows.

What She Said

Mike Joyce was given leave to let rip on this song and his forceful drumming ensures its place as one of the hardest rockers in the group's varied canon. "With *Meat Is Murder* I realized the power behind us. We were becoming harder, which fitted more into my field of playing. 'The Headmaster Ritual' and 'What She Said' and others were all in your face. It was a lot harder and Morrissey was writing some of his best stuff." As in 'Girl Afraid', Morrissey adopts the persona of a neurotic woman – jobless, loveless, depressed and morbid. Yet there are some wonderful touches of black humour, such as the solace offered by the prospect of a premature death through chain-smoking, an allusion borrowed from Elizabeth Smart's best-selling *By Grand Central Station I Sat Down And Wept* ("I have learned to smoke because I need something to hold on to"). Blue-stocking intellectualism is also placed under serious threat by the emergence of a tattooed boy from the docks of Birkenhead. Like the ruffians from Rusholme, this sees Morrissey subtly introducing more laddish characters into his songscape, anticipating their seeming ubiquity in his solo work.

That Joke Isn't Funny Anymore

This is a candidate for the best ever Smiths' song – a view held by both myself and Johnny Marr. The majestic waltz-time arrangement and sublime acoustic and electric guitar work culminate in a startling refrain in which Morrissey chants a lament of inexpressible woe. As a dramatic device, the song is faded then returns from the ether, like a ghostly vision. Lyrically, the chorus appears to have been inspired and partly adapted from some lines in the 1935 film *Alice Adams* ("I've watched this happen in other people's lives and now it's happened in ours"). While irony is a common device for Morrissey, this is one composition where he appears to have stripped the mask away to reveal his true, unadorned feelings. At least this was the impression he gave when discussing the song. "When I wrote the words for that, I was just so completely tired of all the same old journalistic questions and people trying this contest of wit, trying to drag me down and prove that I was a complete fake. I was tired of that because it just seemed that even the people within popular music, even the people within the music industry, didn't have that much faith in it as an art form. And they wanted to really get rid of all these people who are trying to make some sense out of the whole thing, and I found that really distressing." There is an incongruously light moment where the singer eulogizes a car's cold-leather seating, a favourite image which can be traced back to the passenger's seat of 'This Charming Man'. In an innuendo-addled interview with *Sounds*, Morrissey unexpectedly alluded to his fixation with cars, albeit with a wry wit. "I do find many things erotic. As a child in the Sixties, when the seats of cars were made of leather, to me there was something highly erotic about actually being in a car. I have always found cars highly erotic . . . there was just something about the old leather seats . . ." Such humour is fleeting at best in 'That Joke Isn't Funny Anymore'. Coming away from the song, however, the feeling conveyed is both that of a quiet desperation and a sense of celebration. As so often happens with the Smiths' work, the music is uplifting to the point where even despair becomes therapeutic.

How Soon Is Now?

When WEA reissued the Smiths' CD catalogue in November 1993, they followed the American version of the album, which meant a surprise additional track for British listeners. It's somewhat ironic that America, which, back in the days of the Beatles, often short-changed the public by dropping a couple of tracks from over-generous UK releases, should now be the home of the bonus track. Then again, 'How Soon Is Now?' was always the most famous Smiths' song in the USA as a result of Sire using an unauthorized video to promote the work on MTV. Speaking to *Guitar Player*, Marr provided a musicological critique: "[It] was in F# tuning. I wanted a very swampy sound, a modern bayou song. It's a straight E riff, followed by open G and F#m7. The chorus uses open B, A, and D shapes with the top two strings ringing out. The vibrato sound is incredible, and it took a long time. I put down the rhythm track on an Epiphone Casino through a Fender Twin Reverb *without* vibrato. Then we played the track back through four old Twins, two on each side. We had to keep all the amps vibrating in time to the track and each other, so we had to keep stopping and starting the track, recording it in 10-second bursts. This sounds incredibly egotistical, but I wanted an intro that was almost as potent as 'Layla' – when that song plays in a club or a pub everyone knows what it is instantly. 'How Soon Is Now?' is certainly one of the most identifiable songs I've done, and it's the track most people talk to me about. I wish I could remember exactly how we did the slide part – not writing it down is one of the banes of my life! We did it in three passes through a Harmonizer, set to some weird interval, like a sixth. There was a different harmonization for each pass. For the line in harmonics, I re-tuned the guitar so that I could play it all at the 12th fret with natural harmonics. It's doubled several times."

Despite considerable efforts to push 'How Soon Is Now?' beyond the boundaries of college radio, that all-important chart crossover remained elusive. Even Rough Trade founder Geoff Travis was mystified by its relatively poor sales Stateside. "I can't understand why 'How Soon Is Now?' wasn't a Top 10 single," he told me. "Though perhaps I'm being naïve . . . 'How Soon Is Now?' is a rock record, it's one of their few ones, it's a lot of people's favourite Smiths track. It's one of those that contains more traditional rock elements and is much more palatable. That's the one I thought was going to break them in America and that would have made all the difference."

Nowhere Fast
Outrageous humour is the predominant mood of this song not least because it conjures up an image of Morrissey recklessly dropping his trousers in front of the Queen. That he should promote that peculiarly American ritual of 'mooning' in connection with an English

institution such as the monarchy was surprising, even for Morrissey. His lyrical outbursts were nevertheless consistent with numerous media tirades in which he derided the Queen, castigated Princess Diana and denounced the entire royal establishment. "I despise royalty. It's fairy-tale nonsense. The very idea of their existence in these days when people are dying daily . . . it's immoral . . . What I dislike is that they don't really care. There's a lot of people in this country who are living under serious and dangerous conditions . . . Old people die every single day and we accept that fact . . . Certain members of the royal family are of considerably advanced years, but they don't seem to care about people of their own time."

The remainder of the song centred on the narrator's own spiritual malaise. The sad sound of the train that Morrissey alludes to in the lyrics is echoed in the chugging backing track which drives the song along in rockabilly fashion, with Marr showing his current interest in Sun-period Elvis. Reading the lyrics, it almost comes as a surprise to consider the number of images of sterility and artificiality beneath the jocular exterior. Of course, all such considerations are rendered subservient to the overwhelming thrust of the second verse in which Morrissey denounces the monarchy in the cheekiest way imaginable.

An alternate version of 'Nowhere Fast' recorded for the *John Peel Show* by John Porter was belatedly issued in 1987 as a B-side on the 12-inch version of 'Last Night I Dreamt That Somebody Loved Me'. A live 'Nowhere Fast' from their Oxford Apollo Show (18 March 1985) can also be found on the flip-side of the single 'That Joke Isn't Funny Anymore'.

Well I Wonder

First heard on the B-side of 'How Soon Is Now?', a month prior to the album's release, this was unusual inasmuch as it was never played live by the Smiths. Marr's delicate acoustic arrangement frames Morrissey's elliptical lyrics which testify to an obsessive fixation with an unnamed object of desire. It's the frustration prompted by a longing for something imagined rather than experienced that gives the song a distinctive edge, made concrete by Morrissey's desperate vocal. The theme is reminiscent of 'Back To The Old House' with the narrator not merely musing upon what has been lost but cataloguing the genuine terror of being forgotten. Again, some of the lyrics appear to be adapted from Morrissey's latest favourite, Elizabeth Smart. Stephen Street encouraged the use of their trusty BBC sound effects record to recreate the patter of falling rain.

Barbarism Begins At Home

An excellent album is often made great by the ingenuity of its sequencing and the placing of 'Barbarism Begins At Home' after the slight 'Well I Wonder' was an inspired move. Maudlin introspection amid quiet acoustics is immediately replaced by an unlikely feast of funk in which Rourke revives the spirit of the Freak Party, the ensemble that he, Marr and drummer Simon Wolstencroft played in a year before the formation of the Smiths. The musical importance of Rourke has frequently been undervalued in profiles of the Smiths, but here his major contribution is self-evident. As Mike Joyce enthuses, "The bass line was a killer . . . It was interesting how Andy got his head around it. When we'd stop he'd continue with a Stanley Clarke bass line. It's incredible how he could shift into that."

The influence of Nile Rodgers' Chic is also paramount in Rourke's playing, along with an affection for Grandmaster Flash. As Wolstencroft told me: "What we were doing in the Freak Party was way ahead of its time. It was all dance stuff with wah-wah guitars and funk-style drumming . . . We weren't playing smoochy soul songs but hard, attacking funk like A Certain Ratio."

In spite of his perennial aversion to dance music, Morrissey loses himself in this seven-minute funk excursion, yelping like a recalci-trant puppy as he explores the casual violence of child abuse. 'Barbarism Begins At Home' gives the lie to the notion that the Smiths were purely one-dimensional in their musical approach. At this point in their career they seemed capable of trying anything.

The history of this song in concert is also unusual. It was actually premièred at London's Electric Ballroom on 19 December 1983, a full 14 months before it appeared on album. The early version was most notable for its faster pace and additional lyrics, with Morrissey singing 'I've always been such a decent lad' and 'I am the man to keep you in place'. During the group's performance at the Royal Albert Hall, Dead Or Alive's Pete Burns duetted with Morrissey on the song. It later became a live *tour de force*, sometimes lasting in excess of 15 minutes. "The crowd went mad and we enjoyed playing it," Rourke recalls, "so we carried on and on till Johnny gave us the nod." In terms of musical influence, it remains Rourke's most significant contribution to the Smiths.

Meat Is Murder

The album's finale opens with the harrowing sounds of the slaughterhouse, which are used to maximum melodramatic effect. Stephen Street recalls how the song was developed in the studio: "I remember trying to work out how the hell we were going to get those machine noises on 'Meat Is Murder'. We had the good old BBC sound effects records for the cows and sheep, but I had to make up some mechanical buzz-saw noises and work out how to do it. I actually came up with the idea of the backwards piano line because Johnny had done some piano and some really menacing things and I was into the idea of turning the tape round. I've always been into backward reverbs . . ."

Morrissey's proselytizing in favour of animal rights is confrontational rather than sentimental. The animal cries remind the listener of his feral yelps on the preceding 'Barbarism Begins At Home'. It is as if he is now equating the punishment of children with the fate of helpless cattle or, as the singer eloquently notes, 'heifer whines could be human cries'. Morrissey goes even further with the album's artwork, which clearly connects the soldier in battle to the helpless heifer. "Violence towards animals is also linked to war. I think as long as human beings are so violent towards animals there will be war. It might sound absurd but, if you really think about the situation, it all makes sense. Where there's this absolute lack of sensitivity where life is concerned, there will always be war. And, of course, there will always be war as long as there are people willing to fight wars in armies."

The dramatic use of the word 'murder' rather than 'slaughter' effectively reduces meat eaters to the level of cannibals in Morrissey's world. He cleverly employs such sophistry to intensify the emotive response. The high-risk strategy of introducing farmyard sound effects produces a similar reaction to the equally dangerous and disturbing

'Hindley laugh' in 'Suffer Little Children'. As a piece of agitprop, 'Meat Is Murder' fulfils its function all too well. Savouring his triumph, Morrissey noted gleefully: "'Meat Is Murder' is obviously a title that shouldn't be there and is obviously a title that will cause great discomfort and has done. I know it has done – which, of course, can give maximum pleasure."

The rhetoric is enhanced by Marr's funereal arrangement while the vocal performance is surprisingly compelling throughout. Within the space of a few seconds Morrissey moves from mournful sympathy to righteous indignation, bludgeoning home his point that the carnivore is an unnatural connoisseur of 'sizzling blood', a consumer of the life-force. The success of his proselytizing can be measured in the number of fans who became vegetarians after hearing the track. Even Marr, Joyce and Rourke gave up meat, along with others in Morrissey's circle, including members of his family.

"They even converted me to being a vegetarian," recalls Matthew Sztumph, who managed the group for a spell. "Nobody was eating meat so unless I snuck off to McDonald's there was no way I was going to get *any* meat. Having spent that much time not eating meat, the next time I did I felt really uncomfortable . . . physically uncomfortable."

Not that everyone was convinced. Suppressing carnivorous instincts ultimately proved too much for Andy Rourke, who returned to his old ways. "We all became vegetarian. Morrissey already was, and Johnny was, virtually. Me and Mike gave up meat at that time. Obviously, we couldn't tour and be seen eating meat with an album called *Meat Is Murder*. I stuck with it for about two years and used to sneak out for a burger and stuff. At that time there wasn't the variety of food, unless you liked egg and chips . . ."

Mike Joyce, who nominates this song as his favourite on the album, always felt it worked wonderfully in concert. "It was a very powerful track to play live. The stage was bathed in red. At the time everyone had their reasons for liking different tracks. That was mine because it actually changed the way that I was as a person, and I'm still a vegetarian. It shows you how strong the material was lyrically. Anything that can change the way I eat must be pretty powerful."

Morrissey's views on animal rights prompted some lively debate in the music press. *NME*'s weekly rival *Melody Maker* took a more irreverent attitude towards the singer and their mailbag included some dissenting voices. One wrote "Will *MM* give us a break from Mr Righteous God Almighty Morrissey?", another adding that "*MM* could solve most of Morrissey's problems by arranging a confrontation with a full-grown lion, a Bengal tiger, an alligator, or some other carnivore to see if his platitudes can influence their diet!" Morrissey was willing to discuss his beliefs with any section of the media, including the glossy pop magazine *Smash Hits*. Interviewer Tom Hibbert grilled the singer about his militant views and made some sarcastic comments about his 'unhealthy pallor', cheekily suggesting, "A good McDonald's quarter pounder would put you back on your feet in no time."

"I sincerely doubt it," Morrissey retorted, after which the conversation trickled to a halt.

'Meat Is Murder' became something of a Smiths anthem, and not just for Morrissey. Marr later surprised the world by performing the song as a lead vocalist at a Royal Albert tribute concert for the late Linda McCartney in 1999.

THE QUEEN IS DEAD

Released: June 1986

Rough Trade Records, Rough CD 96, June 1986. WEA 4509-91896-2,
November 1993, February 1995. US issue: Sire 9-25426-1,
Sire 9-25426-2 CD, June 1986

The lead up to the release of *The Queen Is Dead* was a problematic
time for the Smiths. They had failed to expand their market sufficiently abroad and, apart from a brief US foray, betrayed a distinct
unwillingness to tour outside Britain. At home, their singles sales had
declined, with four successive releases failing to crack the Top 20.
Worse still, they were beset by financial wrangling, management
changes and a dispute with their record company which was threatening to fester into downright war. For Johnny Marr, the background tensions and recent setbacks merely underlined the need to
create a work of lasting worth. "We knew it had to be special. Our
trajectory had gone up from day one, but although we were enjoying
commercial success it had reached a plateau. I was thinking that if we
wanted to be in the same league as the Who or the Beatles or the
Rolling Stones, we had to do it now." Unfortunately further problems dogged the recording. Extended negotiations over the Smiths'
Rough Trade contract effectively blocked the release of *The Queen Is
Dead* for the best part of eight months. In the interim, they suffered
the pain of purgatory punctuated by the worrying decline of Andy
Rourke into heroin addiction. Following a tour of Ireland, he was
unceremoniously fired from the group and, almost immediately after,
arrested on a charge of unlawful possession of drugs. Then, in a
surprise volte-face, he was reinstated as a Smith. In the meantime,
new boy Craig Gannon had been recruited and was kept on as a
second guitarist. The sudden changes caused consternation among
some fans who felt increasingly that the group was compromising its
old ideals and looked in danger of losing direction. Others argued the
opposite case, pointing to the brilliance of *Meat Is Murder* and suggesting that the Smiths might equal or even surpass past achievements. In such a climate the new album had much to prove.

Fortunately, *The Queen Is Dead* turned out to be a masterful work which received excellent reviews. Former *New Musical Express* journalist turned *Melody Maker* reviewer Nick Kent concluded: "This is neither the time nor the place to indulge in trivial banter; suffice to say that the Smiths' peculiar career manoeuvres, which have caused their audience much exasperation of late, are rendered utterly obsolete by the splendour of *The Queen Is Dead*, the album which history will in due course denote as being the key work in forcing the group's philistine opposition to down chisels and embrace the concept of the Smiths as the one truly vital voice of the Eighties . . . There's so much that I could write about this record, about the Smiths and why I still fervently believe they stand head and shoulders above the rest . . . this group is the one crucial hope left in evoking a radical restructuring of what pop could – nay, should – essentially be moving towards. *The Queen Is Dead* will help bury the one-dimensional misery-guts attitude so beloved of the group's denigrators, while further displaying to all and sundry the simple fact that this is essentially music brimming with valorous intent. The Queen is dead. England in ruins, but here, in the marrow of this extraordinary music, something precious and innately honourable flourishes."

The effusive notices, backed by extensive touring, expanded the group's following. *The Queen Is Dead* was later celebrated in various 'all-time great' critics' polls, even though it failed to secure any awards at the time of its release. *Melody Maker* voted the album the sixth best of the year while the usually loyal but now dance-orientated *NME* reckoned it worthy of eighth place beneath: 1. *Rapture* (Anita Baker), 2. *Control* (Janet Jackson), 3. *Evol* (Sonic Youth), 4. *Word Up* (Cameo), 5. *Graceland* (Paul Simon), 6. *Bend Sinister* (Fall) and 7. *Raisin' Hell* (Run DMC). The startling disparity between the writers' preferences and their readers' tastes would not be revealed until the New Year's 'Readers' Poll' in which the Smiths triumphed. Thereafter the album's stature seemingly grew with each passing year.

The most pleasing feature of *The Queen Is Dead* was its extraordinary variety of tone. *Meat Is Murder* had already displayed the Smiths' ability to tackle a wide range of musical styles in an earnest fashion; *The Queen Is Dead* added a splash of comedy to the mix. Over 10 songs Morrissey provided music hall frivolity, light satire, acerbic social commentary, romantic idealism, misanthropy, world-weary resignation, maudlin despair, comedic quips and *Carry On*-style innuendo. If nothing else, the album exploded the myth of Morrissey as a miserable bastard. Now, even his most myopic critics were forced to acknowledge his pre-eminence as a humorist.

Although the Smiths proved capricious in nominating their greatest work, there was a strong consensus in favour of *The Queen Is Dead* well into the Nineties. In 1993, Mike Joyce told me: "It was the album I enjoyed doing the most. Johnny had really come into his own in knowing how he wanted the Smiths to sound. We'd really slotted into our roles at that point. We knew we'd a couple of good albums under our belt and 'up' was the way we were going. That album was sheer strength. The whole thing is the four of us going, 'Listen to this, please do!' It was so powerful. I think it's my favourite album."

Johnny Marr was of similar mind and told *Guitar Player*: "*The Queen Is Dead* is certainly the best LP we made, the most focused from start to finish. It was a dark period in my life but, creatively, it made for something really brilliant." Morrissey also lauded the work in a letter to Stephen Street, concluding: "I cannot think of one second of any track which does not delight me."

The Queen Is Dead

This great epic in the Smiths' canon was Morrissey's most sustained and successful satire on the state of Britain. The stirring Cicely Courtneidge war-time sing-along which opens the track immediately dislocates the time scheme, presenting an image of England which appears to veer between past and present. Despite the song's title, Morrissey's lyrics are playful rather than vicious. There is fantasy talk of hanging the Queen but, within the dramatic context of the song, Morrissey seeks no more than a brief conversation with Her Majesty after breaking into the palace. He is making a topical allusion here, for the disturbed Michael Fagin achieved precisely that ambition after scaling the palace walls and provoking uproar in the popular press. Morrissey's satire shifts constantly from the serious to the comic. The allusion to Charles' fantasy transvestism stems from the same self-conscious vulgarity as the trouser-dropping incident in

'Nowhere Fast'. As the song progresses, there is a distinct move away from thoughts of regicide to more serious social issues. Morrissey regards the state of the monarchy as only one reason among many for the spiritual decline of England. It is not merely royal decadence, but church materialism, the escapism of the pub and the horrors of pre-adolescent drug addiction that erode society. Characteristically, Morrissey fails to resolve the unfolding drama and even turns the spiteful humour on himself, allowing the Queen to mock his singing ability while he lampoons his terrible piano playing. Adding another dimension to the song's title, the narrator confides, tongue-in-cheek, that a study of historical facts has exposed him as the distant descendant of some old queen. It is surely no coincidence that 'The Queen Is Dead' was also a chapter title in Hubert Selby Jnr's notorious, homosexually charged book *Last Exit To Brooklyn*. Having mixed the serious and the frivolous, Morrissey ends the song on a self-reflective note proclaiming his loneliness once more.

Musically, the composition is unquestionably one of the group's most startling and ambitious works. Joyce's forceful tape-looped opening drum roll and Marr's searing MC5-influenced guitar interplay are breathtaking. As Andy Rourke remembers: "'The Queen Is Dead' was done like a jam in the studio. Johnny had this riff and it erupted into this massive wall of sound. It was quite spontaneous."

Marr admits that some happy accidents occurred while they were completing the song which added to its power and passion. "It was Morrissey's idea to include 'Take Me Back To Dear Old Blighty', and he said, 'I want this on the track.' But he wasn't to know that I was going to lead into the feedback and drum rolls. It was just a piece of magic. I got the drum riff going and Andy got the bass line, which was one of his best ever and one that bass players still haven't matched. I went in there with all the lads watching and did the take and they just went, 'Wow!' I came out and I was shaking. When I suggested doing it again, they just said, 'No way! No way!' What happened with the feedback was I was setting my guitar up for the track and I put it onto the stand. Where it hit the stand, it made that note of feedback – really loud. And while we were talking, it was like, 'Wow! That sounded good.' So I said, 'Right, record that!' . . . I just started moving the wah-wah and it was getting all these different intervals, and it definitely added a real tension. I loved Morrissey's singing and the words. But it was very MC5. Morrissey has a real love for that music as well. I remember him playing the Ramones as much as he played Sandie Shaw."

Stephen Street recalls a euphoric feeling upon completing the track. "It came out really great. It was steady and constant. At the beginning there was the harmonized voice. The drum track wasn't really happening so I said, 'Let's do a drum loop.' There was this new sampler there, and I suggested we sample the drum and told them, 'We can read that and just play the bass and snare on top.' Which is what we did and it came out great. Then Johnny went in and did this wild wah-wah and it was one take. As he was changing the pedal it kept changing tone. He played blindingly. It was fantastic. In fact, we recorded eight to nine minutes' worth. I had to edit it. There was more on the 24-track than there is on the mix but we decided that it was a little bit too long so we cut it down."

Frankly Mr Shankly

Industry gossip suggests that the target of this song was Rough Trade founder Geoff Travis. If so, it was camp spite *in extremis*. "I'm not really upset by it," Travis told me. "Camp spite? I think there's a lot of that there, but I don't take it too seriously." The common wisdom is that Morrissey was again partly inspired by the novel *Billy Liar*, and based the Shankly/Travis caricature on Billy Fisher's employer, the funeral director, Mr Shadrack. In the song, Morrissey relishes the elongated pronunciation of the title, emphasizing each syllable with a roll of his tongue. In the novel, Fisher amuses himself by stretching Shadrack's name until it becomes a nursery rhyme chant: "Shaddy-shaddy-shaddy-shaddy". The quip about Shankly writing 'bloody awful' poetry was evidently directed against Travis, who once tried to empathize with the singer by revealing that he composed verse. Certainly, as a BA student at Churchill College, Cambridge, Travis was better versed in the study of English poetry than his Mancunian counterpart. While researching Travis' adolescence and educational background for *The Severed Alliance*, I unearthed a school magazine which confirmed that he did indeed write poetry, specifically the tautologically titled "The riff repeats itself over and over again". Alas,

Travis never exploited that talent to become a lyricist for any of his Rough Trade signings.

An amusing satire on Morrissey's role in the pop industry, 'Frankly Mr Shankly' was widely applauded for its ephemeral charm. In keeping with the Sixties' *Billy Liar* theme, Marr provided an oompah arrangement partly inspired by Chris Andrews' brass-heavy 1965 hit 'Yesterday Man'. At one point during the recording session Marr remembers an attempt to persuade Linda McCartney to play piano on the track but, not surprisingly, the request was rejected. Despite its lightness of touch, 'Frankly Mr Shankly' proved the most troublesome recording on the album and, as the credits reveal, it was the sole track engineered by John Porter. The original version, which Stephen Street claims featured a trumpeter from the BBC Orchestra, suffered a mishap which delayed the track's completion. "It was the first time I'd used digital 24 multi-track. We did a great version of that, but one day we came in and there was a drop-out on the tape so we had to record the whole thing again from start to finish. It wasn't finished when we were mixing the album."

As Porter concludes: "Johnny was so sick of it that he asked me, 'Could you finish it off?' The album did him in."

I Know It's Over

Arguably the bleakest composition in the Morrissey songbook, this remorseless lamentation sounded even more disturbing and jarring after the frivolity of 'Frankly Mr Shankly'. Interestingly, Marr remembers that both songs were recorded on the same evening, along with the epic 'There Is A Light That Never Goes Out'. 'I Know It's Over' is the cracked mirror image of 'Accept Yourself'; loneliness brings no compensatory strength of independence but instead unmitigated despair. It is not merely a situation that is over, but one that never began in the first place. Morrissey even taunts himself, and inadvertently his listeners, with a sarcastic self-questioning soliloquy on the state of loneliness. A series of suicidal images reach a maudlin zenith during the refrain in which the narrator pictures himself buried alive and crying to his mother. It is a chilling, metaphorical evocation of a premature journey from the womb to the grave. Death itself becomes a simile for an empty bed, rather than vice versa, prompting Morrissey to draw a veil over proceedings with the weary riposte, 'Enough said'. The emphasis on maternal assistance echoes the opening 'The Queen Is Dead' in which attachment to the mother's apron strings is equated with a form of castration. Later, Morrissey would take the burial/Oedipal theme of 'I Know It's Over' further in 'Rubber Ring' with the plea 'smother me, mother'. Hearing Morrissey in the recording booth singing words which so perfectly fitted Marr's funereal melody almost floored the guitarist. "I'll never forget when he did it. It's one of the highlights of my life. It was that good, that strong. Every line he was hinting at where he was going to go. I kept thinking, 'Is he going to go there? Yes he is.' It was just brilliant."

Stephen Street was less effusive. "I always thought 'I Know It's Over' was slightly too long. It overstated itself, but it was a good track."

Never Had No One Ever

The funereal mood was retained for this, Morrissey's elegy to a devastated life. A restrained dirge-like accompaniment ends with barely audible sighs and sobs. In the song, life's desperation is said to have lasted exactly 20 years, seven months and 27 days. Applied to Morrissey, who was born on 22 May 1959, this would date his great awakening from depression as 18 January 1980. It would be fantastic to report that something extraordinary happened to him on that day but a detailed study of his epistolary diaries reveals that all he did was read *The Murderers' Who's Who* and complain about a sore foot. He didn't even go out that evening, but stayed in his room alone. The recording of 'Never Had No One Ever' went through several stages during which Morrissey playfully experimented with canine yowls and sardonic laughter. "We even had this old guy from the BBC playing trumpet," Joyce remembers, "but it didn't fit, so Morrissey started whistling instead." The result was a bleaker, mournful arrangement which was retained as the preferred take.

Cemetry Gates

Morrissey's literary credibility was not seriously affected by his failure to spell cemetery correctly. It was unintentionally ironic that the error should appear in his most famous song of literary one-upmanship and plagiarism. The ironies multiply when you consider that Morrissey himself indulges in some borrowings during the first verse which bears a striking resemblance to lines spoken in one of his favourite films, *The Man Who Came To Dinner*. "All those people, all those lives, where are they now? Here was a woman who once lived and loved, full of the same passions, fears, jealousies, hates. And what remains of it now? . . . I want to cry." Other highlights include the preposterous critical notion that Wilde is superior to Keats and Yeats combined, and Morrissey's mock archaic utterance 'ere long done do done did'. Morrissey's cemetery jaunt vaguely recalls the graveyard scene in *Billy Liar* in which the reluctant anti-hero confronts his girl-friend Barbara (the Witch) "at the cemetery gates". For fans, there is the added attraction of knowing that the theme alludes to the days when Morrissey visited Manchester's Southern Cemetery, now a regular haunt on Smiths' excursion trips. On occasions, Morrissey was accompanied by two musical friends of the period, Howard Devoto and Linda Mulvey (Linder). "It wasn't done in any morbid sense," Mulvey stresses. "At the time it seemed quite natural."

For Morrissey, the banality of death was something he had little direct experience of in his everyday life. Rather, it was a state con-sidered romantic and dangerous. Facing the gravestones he could appreciate his own mortality which, in turn, helped break his lazy streak and encouraged greater creative productivity. As he concluded: "I can stand in a graveyard for hours and hours, just inhaling the indi-viduals. When they lived, when they died, it's all inspiring."

Musically, Marr once more added a striking melody, based around a light acoustic lilt which emerged when he was trying to compose something with a Ray Davies' feel. As he told me: "When I sat down my idea was for it to be a Kinks song. For some reason it was speeded up. It's strange."

Bigmouth Strikes Again
An alluring acoustic flourish presages Morrissey's politely acerbic vocal on one of the best Smiths tracks of the period. Joyce's speaker-splitting drum roll towards the close of the song is a show-stopper, while Marr adds a relentless gambolling rhythm. In those

few seconds you understand what the guitarist meant when he described this as the group's 'Jumpin' Jack Flash'. Morrissey's mock martyrdom (comparing his feelings to those of Joan of Arc on a burning stake, complete with his once familiar hearing-aid stage prop) is amusingly topical, given his heretical comments in the tabloids. His vocal is made doubly alluring by the presence of a certain 'Ann Coates' (a pun on the Manchester district Ancoats) on backing harmonies. As Marr explained, this was actually Morrissey's own voice sped up through a harmonizer. The punning continued when Rough Trade publicist and occasional photographer Pat Bellis adopted the pseudonym Jo Novark ('Joan Of Arc').

With such a powerful record the group must have been confident of securing a sizeable hit single. Amazingly, it only reached number 26. A disappointed Morrissey noted: "I often wonder if we shouldn't explain ourselves more, especially as an astonishing number of people completely misunderstand the Smiths' humour. Take 'Bigmouth Strikes Again'. I would call it a parody if that sounded less like self-celebration, which it definitely wasn't. It was just a funny little song." Although Morrissey's reputation as pop's Mr Bigmouth was current at the time, it is worth pointing out that he was beaten to this title by both Bob Geldof and the Fall's Mark E. Smith in such 1986 polls as *New Musical Express'* 'Biggest Mouth' and *Melody Maker*'s 'Lip Of The Year'.

The Boy With The Thorn In His Side

This slight but endearing vignette, issued in a different mix as a single prior to 'Bigmouth Strikes Again', was another chart disappointment, peaking at number 23, despite Morrissey's reluctant sanction of a promotional video. According to Andy Rourke, the song was recorded on 16-track at Drone Studios before being remixed by Stephen Street. "I think they were meant to do a demo," Street reflects. "Sometimes Morrissey would say, 'That sounds brilliant, we can't do any better.' That's what happened. So they decided to release the demo." According to Morrissey, the 'thorn' in the song's title was a catch-all symbol for the music industry, sceptical journalists, apathetic disc jockeys and others who stood in the way of the Smiths' success. "I think we've reached the stage where we feel – if they don't believe us now, will they ever believe me? What more can a poor boy do?" The composition is additionally interesting for those fascinated by Morrissey's psychology and willing to accept an autobiographical interpretation. In the song, he appears to excuse his much publicized hatred by turning inward and diagnosing his condition as resulting from a suppressed desire for love. The switch from singular to plural in the second verse entwines the listener in the drama as the singer urgently seeks sympathy and empathy. For those who would dare suggest that Morrissey should 'get a life' (as Marr later did, incidentally), the song ends sardonically by positing the pertinent questions: *how*, *where* and *who with*?

Vicar In A Tutu

Morrissey's saucy tale of a transvestite clergyman proved his gentlest satire to date. Typically, the singer ends by directing the humour against himself in the closing line. Real life comparisons between Morrissey and his fabled vicar took a bizarre turn around this time when Ian Pye of the *New Musical Express* was invited to interview the singer at his Kensington home. Upon arrival, Pye reported that he discovered Morrissey dancing wildly around the room, clad in a ballerina's tutu. For one brief moment it seemed that he had become the vicar of his imagination.

Musically, Marr's Scotty Moore-influenced rockabilly rhythm and Rourke's throbbing bass riff give the song a spontaneous feel which fits Morrissey's whimsical lyric. Indeed, Mike Joyce told me that the backing track emerged out of the air one evening when they were limbering up for a session. "We were playing away in the studio and jamming. Morrissey would look in and just say, 'Carry on.' Around that evolved 'Vicar In A Tutu'. Johnny was playing a riff and I started playing the drums . . . If we'd had a name producer I don't think that would have come out. I don't think that would've been the structure of the song."

There Is A Light That Never Goes Out

This, Morrissey's great song of romantic adventure, encapsulated his emotional dilemma in a series of melodramatic musings. There is an incredible lust for life and intense need to escape the shackles of home and family, but no happy ending. Life affirmation soon moves to thoughts of romantic suicide as the narrator pictures a double-decker bus hurling himself and his partner into oblivion. The desire to freeze this relationship while it can still be idealized is undercut by the familiar revelation that the romantic dreams are simply fantasy. Consummation is inevitably unrealized as diffidence strangles the possibility of communication, sexual or otherwise. Much of the humour comes from the extravagant tone and gestures, culminating in the arch reference to something erotic emerging in a darkened underpass. This, in itself, recalls a penchant for sex and cars previously charted from 'This Charming Man' to 'That Joke Isn't Funny Anymore'. Even the light that never goes out reiterates the light in the eyes referred to in 'The Boy With The Thorn In His Side'. While the lyrics betray an almost mock romanticism in the earnest tradition of death disc exponents the Shangri-Las and Twinkle, these morbid sentiments are given a sweep of ardent grandeur by the tasteful employment of woodwind and orchestration. Credited to the Hated Salford Ensemble, the studio's Emulator was again called on to provide the effects. "It was pretty straightforward at first," says Stephen Street. "We were using keyboards a bit more. We had an Emulator sampler and we started putting on these string and flute lines. It would be a case of Johnny hanging around and we'd start orchestrating the song and building it up."

Some Girls Are Bigger Than Others
A quiet fade-in introduces Morrissey's satirical comment on the pneumatic wonders of female sexuality. As he memorably noted: "I'm realizing things about women that I never realized before . . . The fact that I've scuttled through 26 years of life without ever noticing that the contours of the body are different is an outrageous farce!" Such ribaldry testifies to Morrissey's increasingly irreverent humour and love of comedy. The arrival of Anthony and Cleopatra in the narrative owes nothing to Shakespeare but rather testifies to his oft-quoted love of *Carry On* films. Amanda Barrie, the titular star of *Carry On Cleo*, was also a regular on the Mancunian television drama series, *Coronation Street*.

Musically, the song came about quickly, in common with several other tracks on the album. "I'd drop off a cassette of some music at Morrissey's house," Marr recalls. "He lived about two miles away, and I'd ride round there on my Yamaha DT 175 and post them through his letterbox. 'Some Girls Are Bigger Than Others' was done that way. All the music came in one wave while I was watching television with the sound down." Although this humorous composition added a welcome lightness to the album's darker elements and fitted in well with 'Frankly Mr Shankly' and 'Vicar In A Tutu', the comedic flippancy ultimately appeared unworthy of such a beautiful melody and arrangement. Then again, Morrissey always liked to combine music and lyrics that sounded completely incongruous, often with spectacular success. For added effect, he closes the song with a refrain from Johnny Tillotson's 1962 hit 'Send Me The Pillow You Dream On', which sounds as though it has just drifted through the ether to provide a muted conclusion to an extraordinary album.

THE WORLD WON'T LISTEN

Released: February 1987

Rough Trade Records, Rough CD 101, February 1987. WEA 4509 91898-2,
November 1993, February 1995

This was *Hatful Of Hollow* revisited and another chance to hear some
of the Smiths' rarer material, albeit with something of an over-
reliance on the recent success of *The Queen Is Dead*. The work testified to Morrissey/Marr's continued love of the singles format and
indicated that a full appreciation of the Smiths required some knowledge of their engaging B-sides and occasional radio sessions. Whatever else, *The World Won't Listen* served its primary purpose by
providing casual purchasers with the opportunity to sample the
group's work at a more affordable price.

The album arrived at a time when the British music press appeared
to be increasingly divided on Smiths' matters. Having previously
fallen out and made up with *Sounds* over the alleged 'paedophile
lyrics' argument, the group found new enemies at *Melody Maker*.
During the autumn preceding this album's release, an article was
published in which Morrissey was taken to task for his supposedly
suspect opinions. The single 'Panic' was called "the most explicit
denunciation yet of black pop". Morrissey added fuel to the criticism
by making insensitive remarks about the state of black music, including the strange and unfounded contention that there was some kind
of pro-black conspiracy on *Top Of The Pops*. Not surprisingly, this
provoked a stinging attack, followed by a howl of protest from
the Smiths' camp. The furore prompted a spate of accusative and
defensive letters in the music press. Marr reacted strongly to the
allegations and, during a sympathetic interview with the rival *New
Musical Express*, came on all macho by threatening the *Melody Maker*
freelancer who wrote the piece. At this stage, the *NME* had clearly
emerged as the most consistent champions of Morrissey/Marr,
although they too would fall from favour in later years after questioning the motives of their favourite cover star.

Amid the heated arguments over Morrissey's views and the continued relevance of the Smiths, it was no surprise that Britain's two major music publications found themselves divided on the merits of this latest compilation. Manchester-based journalist Dave Haslam gave the work a glowing review in the *NME*, concluding: "In their finest moments, the Smiths make music that tugs on our memory and gives you great hope." There were no such compliments from *Melody Maker*'s Steve Sutherland, whose antipathy towards Morrissey appeared to be growing with each release. He saw the singer as a cynical opportunist, claiming, "From the Moors Murders scandal early in their career, to the statements supporting the Brighton bombers, to the brief flirtation with the sensual, to the recent reclusive bemused intellectual, it's apparent that Morrissey will stop at nothing to manufacture confrontations with the norm in order that the Smiths remain special . . . A career in outrage is a fine place to be but some jokes just aren't funny anymore."

Public opinion went with the *NME* camp, the music ultimately triumphed, and the compilation became the third album by the group to reach number 2 in the charts.

Panic
With its chorus of 'Hang the DJ', this proved one of the Smiths' more 'controversial' songs. Interestingly, there was no problem with radio airplay and no hysterical criticism from the popular press. Debate about hidden racist connotations in the song seemed restricted to the music weeklies. Marr attempted to defuse the situation by explaining the genesis of the song. According to his version, it had been written on the day that he and Morrissey heard a news bulletin about the Chernobyl disaster on Radio 1. They were taken aback when this was allegedly followed by Wham!'s sing-along 'I'm Your Man'. Morrissey felt sufficiently indignant about the insensitive radio programming to pen a protest song with the stinging refrain 'Hang the DJ'. Marr concluded from this that the song was purely a reaction against the superficial tastes of disc jockeys and pop radio programmers.

Of course, 'Panic' was more than the above. Marr was merely distracting attention from the key refrain 'burn down the disco' which took the debate outside the boundaries of Broadcasting House and directly on to the dance-floor. Disco had been attacked before, most notably during the Seventies when 'disco sucks' car stickers were popular in the USA. The music press of that period tended to support such vilification. It was different in the Eighties when a new breed of writers fell in love with dance music and eagerly championed black singers. While the readership of the music weeklies, as demonstrated in polls and letters pages, lionized the Smiths and barely expressed any interest in black culture, the writers' annual awards indicated the opposite trend. This provided a fascinating tension. Unsurprisingly, some interpreted Morrissey's anti-disco line as a direct attack on the club scene, and therefore black music in general. Yet, the song was clearly far more than a provocative one-liner. Its controversial chorus aside, the composition could be read as a barbed comment on urban unrest at a time when memories of inner-city rioting were still strong. Derek Jarman's video captured the spirit of the single to great effect. Its image of children chanting the murderous refrain like some dark nursery rhyme was strangely disturbing.

Musically, the distinctive riff that made 'Panic' so appealing owed much to the influence of T. Rex's 'Metal Guru'. Both Morrissey and Marr had been keen fans of Marc Bolan during their adolescence so the tribute was appropriate. Although the Smiths were undertaking an American tour when 'Panic' was released, it gave them an impressive number 11 hit in the UK – their third best chart placing.

Ask

Controversy of a different kind surrounded the hit single 'Ask'. In the wake of Craig Gannon's departure from the Smiths, he brought an action against Morrissey/Marr claiming *inter alia* that he deserved a co-writing credit for the composition. His argument centred on a chord sequence idea that he claimed he'd come up with during the sessions for 'Panic'. Gannon explains: "Me and Johnny were sat in the library playing acoustic guitars and they must have been miked up as we were probably putting down the acoustic tracks for 'Panic'. I just started playing the chord sequence in exactly the way it appears on the record. Johnny then joined in playing the same . . . I then forgot about the idea and left it at that." At a later session, Gannon was convinced that the original idea, which he felt was his own, had been developed and was now to be recorded. "Johnny must have played Morrissey this idea or given him the recording I already mentioned. I was completely surprised as we were now recording this for the next single." Gannon was nevertheless quick to point out Marr's own contribution to the song stressing: "[One] section of the chord structure that I didn't come up with for 'Ask' was the middle eight section with the chords E-minor, D and C. That was actually what Johnny came up with. All the way through the song there is an overdub with me and Johnny sat around a mike with acoustics, playing a riff that he came up with towards the end of the recording of the song. That is a great riff and a real hook but it was still just an overdub and I felt the song was nearly complete without it. Up until the release of 'Ask' I still thought I'd be given a writing credit."

Marr disagreed with Gannon and clearly felt that his contribution did not merit a co-writing credit. "When he did come up with his own parts, others said it was like something I'd played on the last single. It wasn't exactly his own style . . . Craig really threw it away. He really screwed it up for himself." Eventually, the parties reached an out of court settlement over the matter, but the original song credits remained.

Another person bothered by the release of 'Ask' was producer John Porter, who felt that Morrissey's desire to have the song remixed by Steve Lillywhite thwarted its impact. "It was another one that didn't come off," he notes with regret. "There's some fabulous stuff on the tape. There were a lot of guitars and only I knew how they fitted together. There were too many of them – stuff that shouldn't be there all the time. It was a jigsaw puzzle of guitars. There was this great breakdown in the middle of the song with the big wave splashing. It was the most theatrical effect, with seagull noises done by Johnny on the guitar. It was fantastic but, on record, you don't notice it. It's just gone. I was really pissed off because that was a spectacular track." The disputes aside, 'Ask' was a sprightly single which justly maintained the group's recent promising run of hits, peaking at number 14.

London
A tense, driving arrangement characterized this tale of escape from provincial strangulation. The theme owed much to *Billy Liar* and

could be regarded as a sequel to 'William, It Was Really Nothing'. The crucial difference is that in Morrissey's scenario the protagonist boards the train and leaves for London, unlike the anti-hero of Waterhouse's novel who abandons his dreams on the station platform. Feedback and relentless drumming echo the movement of the train as the song reaches its frantic close. An alternate version, produced by John Porter for the group's last John Peel session in December 1986, remains unreleased.

Bigmouth Strikes Again

Still familiar from its recent appearance on *The Queen Is Dead*, this unjustly minor hit sounded almost as strong as ever in its new context. Stephen Street had fond memories of the song and with good reason. "I remember that night," he says of the recording. "At that point I was putting in a lot of ideas. When you're the only person working with the band, you start to become, by nature of the work, co-producer. That night the session went really well and I asked Johnny and Morrissey whether they'd consider giving me a production point, just one per cent of the sessions that I'd do. They thought about it and said, 'Fine.' So that's how I stepped up from engineer to co-producer."

Shakespeare's Sister

Taking its title from the Virginia Woolf essay *A Room Of One's Own*, 'Shakespeare's Sister' was an unusually upbeat reflection on the enticing nature of suicide. Morrissey constructs a cliff-top drama, throws in a hint of maternal repression, then ends the proceedings on a note of bathos by speculating on his prejudice against acoustic guitars. Stressing the positive aspects of the composition, and seemingly ignoring its darker elements, he explained: "The song was really about shrugging off the shackles of depression and shedding the skins of one's parents and getting out and living and doing what one wants to do."

Despite its intriguing literary title, 'Shakespeare's Sister' received a scathing critical response and its relative chart failure at number 26 was seen by many as a serious setback for the group. "'Shakespeare's Sister' wasn't a very happy session for me," says Stephen Street. "I never felt we recorded a great version of that. It was a bit of a hotch-potch. I know Morrissey and Johnny felt strongly about the song but I didn't really see it as being up there with the best of them."

Morrissey rallied to the song's defence with characteristic over-statement, telling *Record Mirror*: "'Shakespeare's Sister' – regardless of what many people feel – was the song of my life. I put everything into that song and I wanted it more than anything to be a huge success and – as it happens – it wasn't."

Despite such complaints, Morrissey could not stop people questioning the unexpected and sudden decline in the group's popularity as singles specialists. Marr was more stoical about the chart placing, but admitted, "It was a disappointment for me. As a 7-inch single for the group at that point in time, it was quite inventive. There was something about that riff that I always wanted to do. I just flipped all the way whilst we were recording it. I really loved doing it. We didn't get much support from Rough Trade on that one. They didn't like it very much. As with 'Bigmouth Strikes Again' it was a valid 7-inch single to own but maybe not to play on the radio but that's all right by me."

Record plugger Scott Piering did not agree with Morrissey & Marr's contention that the single lacked support. "All they wanted was to have the radio playing their records, and they didn't want to give anything back. They wanted to put out lots of singles but some were ill-considered, in retrospect. 'Shakespeare's Sister' was very intense, but it wasn't a radio record. Of course, *nobody* could tell them what singles were about."

Rough Trade's founder Geoff Travis concurred with Piering. "There was a problem with Morrissey thinking he had a divine right to a higher chart position. We did as well as anyone in the world could have done with those records."

There Is A Light That Never Goes Out

This was the second track on the compilation from the recent *The Queen Is Dead*. It was intriguing to hear this in a different context from its original setting and it must have been a welcome bonus for purchasers who did not own the former album. The song's popular-ity seemed to vindicate Travis' conviction that it should have been issued as a single. Five years after the group had ceased to exist, this dream was realized but by then its impact had been severely diluted and a chart peak of number 25 seemed scant reward. Johnny Marr later guested on Neil Finn's in-concert cover version, which can be found on the latter's *Seven Worlds Collide*.

Shoplifters Of The World Unite

By this point, even Morrissey's song titles were getting him into trouble. One tabloid dragged the singer over hot coals for supposedly inciting an outbreak of mass shoplifting. It was a ludicrous proposition. Even if the lyrics were taken literally, the possibility of a pandemic union of pilferers would have stretched the credulity of even the most optimistic anarchist. Slightly more interesting than the distracting title were the final few lines of the song in which Morrissey provides what amounts to an impressive diagnosis of his world-weary neurosis. His attempt to escape from his shell and confront the 'real' world was evidently doomed from the outset due to an ingrained apathy and crippling listlessness which left him 'bored' before he even encountered everyday experiences. Morrissey seemed equally jaundiced when asked about the meaning of the song, responding: "Every time we slap anything on to vinyl, one way or another, I have to give this great biblical sermon about 'Shoplifters Of The World Unite' and how it's immediately connected with a Colombian cocaine ring, or something."

NME greeted the release with a discernible lack of enthusiasm: "This record might be the stuff of tragi-comedy, but the funereal tone with cumbersome guitars and world-weary singing kills any irony that may be hidden in the lyrics." Although 'Shoplifters Of The World Unite' sounded terribly uncommercial as a single, it climbed to number 12, a firm indicator of the group's popularity in 1987. It was dedicated to Ruth Polsky, the group's American booking agent, '48-hour' manager, and recent victim of a bizarre, fatal road accident in New York. Eight years later Morrissey would revive the song in concert.

The Boy With The Thorn In His Side

This was another chance to hear Morrissey stating the validity of his

78

tortured persona. Although this track justified its inclusion on the grounds of its single status, the appearance of a third track from the recent *The Queen Is Dead* seemed a little overwhelming in the context. In fact, this was an alternate take of the song, minus the synth orchestration with a sparser sound. The acoustic rhythm guitar also appears lower in the mix, confirming that this was the original version recorded at Drone Studios. Marr recalls that this was the first time he ever played a Stratocaster guitar on a record. "I got it because I wanted a twangy Hank Marvin sound . . ."

Critical support for the single was surprisingly lukewarm. As *NME* said: "Seems like Morrissey himself gives up the song half-way through when he stops the words and uses up the rest of the needle-time with yodelling. If it's too much to expect a revision of world music with every record, we could at least ask for something a little less enervating."

Performing the song on *Top Of The Pops* the Smiths looked cool enough, with Morrissey perplexing viewers by having the word 'BAD' stencilled on his neck. By this point, he had agreed to sanction the limited use of videos, albeit with reluctance. "It was record company pressure," he insisted in defence of this volte-face. "The fact that we didn't want to make videos has always irked Rough Trade. They want videos, *Smash Hits* covers and to be heard on daytime radio. These are the things they live for . . ."

Money Changes Everything
Originally, 'Money Changes Everything' only appeared on the cassette version of *The World Won't Listen* but was later added to the CD reissue. Given their litigious history during and after the Smiths, the title of this instrumental was prophetic and truthful. Marr may have considered the title sardonic but it is worth noting that early in the group's career Morrissey had claimed, "Money doesn't change anything." The instrumental was played only once in concert, but survived the Smiths' story. It was later covered by Bryan Ferry who added lyrics and a new title, 'The Right Stuff'. Marr's endorsement and involvement in the recording came as something of a surprise given his caustic condemnation of Ferry's appearance at Live Aid.

Asleep

With its stark piano accompaniment imported from the original
demo of 'Suffer Little Children', this song could have been subtitled
'A Lullaby For Would-Be Suicides'. Unlike Morrissey's other songs
of self-destruction, there are no deflating, humorous asides here; the
mood is uniformly bleak and the melancholy dangerously alluring. It
is alarming to consider that in the wake of the Smiths' demise, there
were a small number of reputed suicides. Even as early as 1986,
Morrissey told the *NME*'s Ian Pye of six suicides from people
"alarmingly dedicated to the Smiths". "Their friends and parents
wrote to me after they'd died," he noted matter-of-factly. "It's something that shouldn't really be as hard to speak about as it is because if
people are basically unhappy and people basically want to die then
they will." Not that Morrissey offered any great prospects for the
afterlife. His conviction that there must be a better world following
death is undermined by the final line in which the narrator merely
clings to the hope that something may be there. The eerie sound of
howling wind adds a macabre feel to the song, while the music box
version of 'Auld Lang Syne' chillingly tolls out the old world for an
uncertain future . . . *sans* everything.

Unloveable

One of Morrissey's bleakest songs of self-deprecating diffidence, this
gained greater emotional force by what sounds like a delayed echo on
the vocal. If Morrissey felt unloveable then those sentiments seemed
to be reflected in a number of misanthropic asides. "I hate most
people. And I don't want to. It's an awful way to be. But the human
race gives me no comfort." The song's joyless desolation, marked by
an overwhelming sense of inertia, was perhaps a factor in ensuring
that it was never performed live. Its only previous appearance on
record was on the 12-inch version of 'Bigmouth Strikes Again'.
Stephen Street confirms that 'Unloveable' was the only completed
track left over from *The Queen Is Dead* sessions. "There were no
outtakes – everything was used."

Half A Person

This tribute to an obsessive, comic devotion was arguably the Smiths' finest minor work. "We just locked ourselves away and did it," Marr told me. "In the time it took to play it, we wrote it." Regrettably, the group never performed the song live, although an unissued BBC John Peel recording exists, and Morrissey would later incorporate the composition into his solo repertoire. Part of its charm comes from the autobiographical associations – for we know that Morrissey visited London when he was 16 years old, a period when he was decidedly clumsy and shy. There is also the additional charm of a possible gender reversal when the protagonist enters the YWCA and attempts to secure a job as a back scrubber. Has Morrissey taken on a female persona here? While researching the Moors Murders, I noticed that Myra Hindley visited London in 1958 and booked herself into a YWCA, although presumably that is nothing more than a macabre coincidence. It seems more likely that this is simply another example of Morrissey's playful coyness. The deliberately hesitant pause-for-effect 'Y . . . WCA' suggests that the singer was about to utter the more likely 'Y.M.C.A.'. Imagine the eyebrow-raising spectacle of Morrissey playing the Village People card with its attendant gay connotations? There is a wonderful pathos in the admission that the singer's whole life can be summed up in this adolescent drama of shyness and solitude. There may also be a tip of the hat to late Fifties pop as the words 'The Story Of My Life' echo the title of Michael Holliday's 1958 chart-topper. Holliday's life had ended in suicide which made the words sound even more chillingly appropriate. Desperate source hunters might also consider the Velvet Underground's 'That's The Story Of My Life'.

Stretch Out And Wait

This song may be as close as Morrissey ever came to celebrating teenage lust. It is only on keener inspection that you realize that his tortuous philosophical debate advocating the sex act may well be an inhibiting device in itself. The comedy is completed with what sounds like some sighs and mock kisses in the coda. Source hunters should note that the lines about the world ending were adapted from a scene in the James Dean-starring movie *Rebel Without A Cause*. "I'm still embedded in a fascination for suicide and intensified depression," Morrissey explained in a moment of near self-parody. "I have to sing about what is ensnared in me." Although this song was previously issued on the 12-inch version of 'Shakespeare's Sister' and a live recording can be heard on the 12-inch single of 'That Joke Isn't Funny Anymore', the rendition on this collection is an alternate take. It is noticeable that the accompanying lyric sheet and that used on the later *Louder Than Bombs* lists the opening line as 'Off the high rise estates' rather than 'All the lies that you make up' which Morrissey sings.

That Joke Isn't Funny Anymore
Arguably the finest moment on *Meat Is Murder*, this composition was one of the Smiths' greatest achievements and the oldest song on this collection. The new lyric sheet reveals that Morrissey is singing a muted 'Why must you kick them when they fall down?' which gratified those of us who could not decipher the words which were missing from the transcript of the original album. Speaking of omissions, it should be noted that this is an edited version of the song, presumably cut down for radio play. It fades prematurely, missing out the memorable closing reprise. Released ludicrously late, it deserved a strong chart position but its overfamiliarity on the parent album ruined its chances. Those who purchased the 12-inch version of the single were rewarded with four extra live tracks recorded at the Oxford Apollo (18 March 1985): 'Shakespeare's Sister', 'Meat Is Murder', 'Nowhere Fast' and 'Stretch Out And Wait'.

Oscillate Wildly
This attractive tune, complete with its painful pun on 'Oscar Wilde', was the first instrumental released by the Smiths, originally appearing on the 12-inch B-side of 'How Soon Is Now?' Improbably, it featured Rourke playing the cello. Morrissey's absence evidently had no political repercussions, as he was eager to make clear to the *NME*'s Len Brown. "I suggested that 'Oscillate Wildly' should be an instrumental; up until that point Johnny had very little interest in non-vocal tracks . . . The very assumption that a Smiths instrumental left Morrissey upstairs in his bedroom stamping his feet and kicking the furniture was untrue. I totally approved but, obviously, I didn't physically contribute." Despite his professed non-involvement, the publishing credits reveal that he was given a half-share in the song.

You Just Haven't Earned It Yet, Baby

This served as a spiteful riposte towards those imagined foes that had held back Morrissey's career by doubting his worthiness. It was originally intended as a single but was cancelled in favour of 'Shoplifters Of The World Unite' although some white label copies did surface briefly. According to Rough Trade, a clerical error resulted in the wrong stamper being used on several batches. "Without apportioning blame, there was a mistake at the pressing plant," the record company insisted. "We only knew about it when a couple of shops rang us."

Morrissey was less than convinced by this explanation and suspected that the white label error may have been a Machiavellian promotions scam. His final words on the composition were curt. "Ultimately, we felt it just wasn't good enough, so it went on the compilation LP."

Stephen Street adds, "The one used on *The World Won't Listen* was recorded on 48-track with John Porter . . . There were a lot of overdubs and I think they went too far. Morrissey felt that they'd wiped out the feeling of the song." Tellingly, it was never played live. This was the only previously unreleased composition to appear on *The World Won't Listen*. Fortunately, Kirsty MacColl saw greater value in the song and covered it with considerable aplomb on her 1989 album *Kite*.

Rubber Ring

Andy Rourke's prominent bass line introduced Morrissey's plea not to be forgotten by those who once loved his music. It was a fitting conclusion to the original vinyl album and seen by many as a personal message to those followers already in danger of outgrowing adolescent angst and abandoning Morrissey in adulthood. Oddly, the CD's lyric sheet transcribes the opening line as 'A sad factor widely known', instead of 'a sad fact . . .' The song ends with the Oscar Wilde aphorism "Everybody's clever nowadays" which also serves as a passing nod to the 1979 Buzzcocks' single 'Everybody's Happy Nowadays'. One chilling feature of the recording was the inclusion of dialogue taken from a spoken-word recording given away with copies of the 1971 publication of Dr Konstantin Raudive's *Breakthrough: An*

Amazing Experiment In Electronic Communication With The Dead. The doctor's translator Nadia Fowler can be heard interpreting sonic messages from the dead, including the jarring, 'You are sleeping, you do not want to believe'. When 'Rubber Ring' was first heard on the flip-side of 'The Boy With The Thorn In His Side', the sleeping motif was used as a segue into Morrissey's suicide ode 'Asleep', a powerful piece of sequencing that regrettably was not repeated on this compilation, despite the presence of both songs in the listing. Both the Fowler quote and the lyrics of 'Asleep' echoed the famous lines from Shelley's *Adonais* ('He is not dead, he doth not sleep / He hath awakened from the dream of life') which Mick Jagger famously recited as a tribute to Brian Jones during the Rolling Stones' 1969 Hyde Park concert.

Golden Lights

With an uncredited Kirsty MacColl on backing vocals, Morrissey tackled Twinkle's endearing vignette on the romantic perils of pop star fame. The unlikely pop god mentioned in the song was Bachelors' vocalist Declan Cluskey, who was dating Twinkle at the time. The Smiths' attempts at covering other people's recordings were rare and seldom successful and their efforts here had an oddly muted feel which disappointed producer John Porter. "I didn't hear it until it came out and I thought, 'Oh, no!' . . . We recorded it with these beautiful mandolins and it sounded fantastic. It had a Mexican feel. The stuff on the tape is beautiful, but the remix sounds appalling to me . . ." Ignoring such niceties, Marr clearly felt the song had no place in the Smiths' canon. In his black book, it appears to have been surpassed only by their equally anodyne cover of Cilla Black's 'Work Is A Four Letter Word'. Neither Joyce nor Rourke were featured on the final recording. Porter concluded that the song's failure was largely the result of interpersonal politics. "I think Morrissey was down on me because of my friendship with Johnny and it was just about the last time I worked with him." In fact, Porter would attempt one last single with the group the following year but, despite his consistently productive and friendly relationship with Marr, that too would end on a silent but regrettably sour note.

LOUDER THAN BOMBS

Released: March 1987 (US)

Rough Trade Records, Rough 255, Rough 255CD, November 1988. US issue:
Sire 9-25569-1, Sire 9-25569-2 CD, March 1987. Reissued (UK)
WEA 4509-93833-2, November 1993, February 1995

The release of this compilation in America, one month after *The World Won't Listen*, prompted brisk import sales. Of the 24 compositions featured, 20 had previously appeared on past albums, while the remaining four were culled from recent 12-inch single releases. Two other B-sides, 'These Things Take Time' and 'Back To The Old House', were familiar to non-collectors in superior versions recorded for BBC radio. In short, there was nothing new here for hard-core fans in the UK, while casual purchasers were offered better value on the aforementioned *The World Won't Listen*. Originally, *Louder Than Bombs* had been designated solely for US consumption, but the continued availability of import copies in the home market at inflated prices eventually persuaded Rough Trade to sanction its UK release.

In retrospect, it is unfortunate that the album was not compiled a little later as it might then have featured the group's final two studio recordings, a cover of Cilla Black's 'Work Is A Four Letter Word' and the George Formby-influenced 'I Keep Mine Hidden'. As it stands, Marr was pleased with the double album compilation, feeling that it enabled listeners, particularly in America, to sample a more extensive range of the group's work. "Now I say you can't ignore our singles entity," he stresses. "You have to take *Louder Than Bombs*. You can't just listen to *The Queen Is Dead* if you want to know about this group. You have to know our singles philosophy." Marr is quite correct, of course, but not too many people in the UK were entranced by *Louder Than Bombs* back in 1987-88. While *The World Won't Listen* had reached number 2, its unexpected successor barely scraped into the Top 40. Morrissey was well aware of these chart statistics and sent a letter to the *NME* arguing the case against the record's re-promotion. "Whilst endorsing *Louder Than Bombs* as a US equivalent of *The World Won't Listen* in early 1987, I agree that this record has no place in the Smiths discography, and in fact destroyed the Smiths' excellent chart record by charting at number 38 . . . No living ex-Smith can feel happy at the re-re-re-release of *Louder Than Bombs*, and the friendlier Rough Trade fraternity back away shyly. If I had personally known that the wretched thing would practically receive its own chat show on Channel 4, I would, of course, have given it a better title. If the Smiths' history is to remain virtually unblemished then Rough Trade cannot and must not release another related item until at least one ex-member has been found at the balcony of his bungalow home, half-eaten by his own Chihuahua."

Below are the versions of the songs featured for the first time on an album release, excluding the aforementioned 'Golden Lights' which made a belated appearance on the 1993 reissue of *The World Won't Listen*.

Is It Really So Strange?

The compilation opens with one of Morrissey's more humorous compositions. Using the old 'trip down south' motif, the singer presents us with a hilarious travelogue in which he loses his bag in Newport Pagnell and, amid great confusion, unintentionally kills a horse and a nun. Characteristically violent imagery is used as an expression of commitment, with words such as 'kick', 'butt' and 'break my face' preceding a carefree romantic declaration of love. The tight arrangement enhances the black humour which contrasts markedly with that other runaway anthem 'London'. This was one of two songs from their final John Peel session (broadcast on 17 December 1986) that was granted a release, appearing initially as the B-side to 'Sheila Take A Bow'.

Sheila Take A Bow

Here, the Smiths went glam rock with a thumping oompah arrangement, sounding like a cross between the bombast of Gary Glitter and a Salvation Army Band. On closer inspection the melody is reminiscent of David Bowie's 'Kooks', although the tempo is faster. Morrissey's lyrics are a veritable clarion call for teenage rebellion. The song champions the sexual confusion of early Seventies' pop, as narrator and subject swap gender in successive verses. The line about throwing your homework into the fire was clearly adapted from 'Kooks', wherein Bowie informs his son Zowie, 'If the homework brings you down, then we'll throw it on the fire'. In common with the T. Rex-influenced 'Panic', 'Sheila Take A Bow' displayed Morrissey and Marr re-creating themselves as Seventies pop idols.

Although the song was originally produced by John Porter, Morrissey appeared to have doubts about its merits and decided to recruit Stephen Street. The song was re-cut, but nobody bothered to inform Porter who, it turned out, had played a snatch of guitar on the record. When he heard the new version on the radio, he was extremely upset. "The first thing I knew it was out and it sounded slightly different. When I saw the record it said, 'Produced by Stephen Street'. They had gone in with Stephen Street, done the track again, but sampled guitars off the original and put them on this new one without mentioning it to me, asking me, giving me credit, paying me, or anything. That was the last I ever had to do with the Smiths . . . In theory I could have stopped the record and done a whole number . . . That was the end of it. The original version of 'Sheila Take A Bow' was just as good as the one they put out. It was just Morrissey trying to prove a point – that they didn't need me."

Porter's replacement, Stephen Street, stresses that the unauthorized sample was an accident. "With 'Sheila Take A Bow' I never knew until I read *The Severed Alliance* that it was John Porter's playing. If I'd known that I'd never have agreed to sample it. We were running a bit short of time and there was a guitar line that Johnny had on the last session with John and he couldn't quite remember who it was that did it . . . I think it was a slide bit . . . At the time I didn't think much about it . . . I thought it was just a piece of work that Johnny had done and couldn't be bothered to re-create. It was a guitar line and sounded good, so why bother doing it again?" Despite the confusion, the single emerged as a strong, commercial offering reaching number 10 and equalling the group's best ever chart placing prior to their breakup.

Sweet And Tender Hooligan
This strident rocker included some engagingly sardonic lyrics from

Morrissey on the treatment of violent offenders by liberal juries. The sarcasm is so biting that you are almost left with the impression that the singer is siding with the psychotic 'hooligan' who ends the song reciting a funeral oration ('in the midst of life we are in death'). Along with 'Is It Really So Strange?' this John Porter production was taken from their final BBC John Peel session. Although it was never performed live by the Smiths, it was featured as the finale of Morrissey's first live solo outing at Wolverhampton's Civic Hall on 22 December 1988, where he was backed by his litigious friends, Gannon, Joyce and Rourke. Writer Ian Pattison later borrowed the title *Sweet And Tender Hooligan* for a best-selling gangster saga.

These Things Take Time
Omitted from the Smiths' first album, this was originally included as the third song on the 12-inch B-side of 'What Difference Does It Make?' An early song in the Smiths' canon, it was first performed live at Manchester's Manhattan on 6 January 1983. The song was subsequently recorded for BBC Radio 1's *David Jensen Show* on 26 June 1983 and included on *Hatful Of Hollow*. By the time they attempted this B-side four months later, the Smiths should have been a tighter recording unit, but the aforementioned BBC version arguably has the edge in terms of feel. That said, the single take was a formidable flip-side, while the theme combining celibacy and neurosis was typical of early period Morrissey.

Back To The Old House
The last track on side 3 of the vinyl *Louder Than Bombs*, this haunting song was not the BBC version familiar from *Hatful Of Hollow* but the original 7-inch B-side of 'What Difference Does It Make?' Less impressive than its radio counterpart, which was recorded a month before, it was nevertheless useful to have on CD for completists. Whether this justified purchasing *Louder Than Bombs* was another matter entirely.

Full track listing: *Is It Really So Strange?; Sheila Take A Bow; Shoplifters Of The World Unite; Sweet And Tender Hooligan; Half A Person; London; Panic; Girl Afraid; Shakespeare's Sister; William, It Was Really*

Nothing; You Just Haven't Earned It Yet, Baby; Heaven Knows I'm Miserable Now; Ask; Golden Lights; Oscillate Wildly; These Things Take Time; Rubber Ring; Back To The Old House; Hand In Glove; Stretch Out And Wait; Please Please Please Let Me Get What I Want; This Night Has Opened My Eyes; Unloveable; Asleep.

STRANGEWAYS, HERE WE COME

Released: September 1987

Rough Trade Records, Rough 106, Rough CD 106, September 1987.
WEA 4509-91899-2, November 1993, February 1995. US issue: Sire 9-25649-1,
Sire 9-25649-2 CD, September 1987

Following the success of *The Queen Is Dead*, the Smiths were at a career peak. No longer the private property of the indie circus, they were branching out into mainstream rock with an ever expanding audience. Dogmas already outdated were now discarded: the group sanctioned videos; announced they were signing to EMI and even intended to conquer the USA by playing stadiums. Some fans felt uncomfortable or betrayed by these changes, but others understood that it was an inevitable progression. An eventful 1986 closed with the departure of Gannon, the rehabilitation of Rourke and a car crash that came close to costing Marr his life. The Smiths had come a long way but they were a stable four-piece once more.

1987 seemed sure to be a year of consolidation for a group on the brink of achieving international success. Instead, their attempt at reconstruction became the act of falling apart. The demise of the group was a sad tale, full of disillusionment, poor communication and comic confusion. Sessions for the new album took place at the Wool Hall, near Bath and, for the most part, the atmosphere was convivial. "The first night in the studio they all got a bit drunk," Stephen Street recalls. "I can remember bashing away at a DX-7 synth keyboard and the drums and bass were playing at the same time. Johnny was really out of it. As he admitted during the US tour, he'd taken a little liking to brandy and was getting a bit out of order. I can remember him shouting, 'Here, Streety, you don't like this, do you? You want us to sound jingle-jangly, like the good old Smiths days.' You could tell there was tension there. It was definitely, 'You don't like it do you? We're going to do *this*!' There was no holding it together. It was like a dirge. You really felt Johnny was pent-up. At this point, he fell on his back and the keyboard went crashing to the ground. I was sitting there trying to keep cool and telling myself: 'It's going to be OK. It's the first night in the studio and they've got to release a bit of tension. When Morrissey gets in tomorrow, we'll start doing it.' But it was a bit strange."

Following Morrissey's arrival, the recordings proceeded relatively smoothly and, despite some niggling moments, the old camaraderie was still in evidence. "There was no *musical* tension," Street stresses. "Johnny and Morrissey were fine in that respect. *Strangeways* was a great session. We had a really happy time and it was party night most nights . . . Andy was fine . . . He seemed to be a little more sprightly. They were happy and having a great laugh. It wasn't bad at all."

"The sessions were positive," Mike Joyce reiterates. "We were all getting out of it with the ales. Things were getting quite crazy at times, but that was the beauty of the Smiths – the craziness. A lot of people didn't realize how barmy it got."

Beneath this easy-going surface, Marr nevertheless detected subtle changes in the old Smiths' dynamic. As he later told journalist John Harris: "I've got loads of photos and loads of video footage of us making the album. You can see us talking and having a laugh. But towards the end of the band, when we weren't doing the music, we weren't able to be comfortable with each other any more."

While drink flowed freely in the studio, Marr expressed a desire to try out new ideas and explode the crumbling myth of the Smiths as a jingle-jangle guitar group cosy with their reputation as indie kings. In one respect, this seemed a healthy attitude but also testified to the group's underlying problems. Marr was clearly restless and although there was enough interesting music on the new album to satisfy his current needs, he resembled a man in search of fresh challenges.

In the background, the Smiths' perennial business sagas continued to fester. Marr made a firm stand, retaining American manager Ken Friedman with whom Morrissey had become severely disenchanted. "You could tell that Morrissey didn't want him around," says Stephen Street, "but Johnny was insisting that Ken stayed. Johnny said, 'I'm not going to stand down,' because up until then he always had. I think Johnny felt a slight regret at what they'd done to people who'd tried to manage them. He felt a loyalty to Ken, which was understandable."

The decision revealed Marr's increasing independence and suggested that the songwriting partners' magical union was less strong
than in times past. Morrissey's jealousy hardly helped matters. He had
always resented outside influences on Marr, particularly if they
affected the duo's creative partnership or close personal friendship. "I
didn't like Johnny bringing strangers into the studio. He allowed
anybody in, he was very free with people which I didn't agree with. I
wished to preserve our intimacy . . . The fact that I rejected his friends
implied that I was boring and hated the human race."

To make matters more disconcerting, there were clearly differences over career objectives. Marr saw the need to seize the moment
and transform the group into world beaters with an extensive international tour. Clearly he was tired of the Smiths' penchant for under-
achievement. At other times, Morrissey might have agreed to take on
the world but in early 1987 he was wary of extending his empire and
insisted that he did not want the Smiths to become a 'mega group'.
He claimed he would rather just make the records and then go home.
Promotional interviews and world tours were supposedly anathema.
Nevertheless, there were definite plans for another US tour and,
according to court records, a budget had already been drawn up. The
extent to which Morrissey's negative sentiments in the press were a
reaction against Marr's upbeat approach remained an interesting
question.

There was no doubt that the entire concept of the Smiths was
now under serious review. Once, Morrissey and Marr had seemed
uncannily united in their musical opinions, but Johnny was evidently
growing weary of the old kitsch icons associated with his partner. As
he told Manchester DJ Dave Haslam: "Towards the end of the
Smiths, I realized that the records I was listening to with my friends
were more exciting than the records I was listening to with the
group. Sometimes it came down to Sly Stone versus Herman's
Hermits. And I knew which side I was on." Always hip to
Manchester's musical undercurrents, Marr fully understood that
dance music was on the rise and sooner or later he would be forced
into a musical cul-de-sac under the reductive Smiths' banner. He
told his fellow players as much, suggesting that they were all in
danger of allying themselves to a musical dinosaur. "We're going to

end up like the Beach Boys in the blue and white striped shirts," he warned. Marr sensed that rival competitors would eclipse the Smiths if they failed to change . . . but in what way they should change remained uncertain.

Those close to the Smiths insist that the breaking point came later during an uneasy session in Streatham, south London, just days before Morrissey's 28th birthday. As usual, B-sides had to be completed for forthcoming singles releases. Marr suggested that they all deserved a rest after the arduous album sessions, but Morrissey was anxious to complete these commitments forthwith. Under duress, Marr attended the sessions, but he was clearly feeling suffocated by Morrissey's intensity. Probably the last straw was coming to terms with the unedifying material he was forced to work on. 'Work Is A Four Letter Word' and 'I Keep Mine Hidden' revealed Morrissey at his most whimsical, precisely at a time when Marr was uncharacteristically critical of his partner's superficial pop forays.

After completing the sessions, an obviously disillusioned Marr called a group meeting at Geales fish restaurant in Kensington and informed Rourke and Joyce that he was intending to leave the Smiths. They could hardly believe what they heard or face the truth. It wasn't as if Marr could articulate precisely why he wanted to end the Smiths. He offered only vague reasons: part musical, but also personal. As Rourke admits: "Johnny made it plain that he'd had enough. It had sort of taken over his life, and he wanted out basically. The demands of Morrissey he couldn't really handle any more. Like pandering to his whims. He got sick of all that after a while."

Marr was a little more circumspect, adding, "The pressure was far too much. I wasn't fed up with the guys, it wasn't that at all. I just felt all of us were in an unhealthy situation and unless we made some moves towards thinking about our future direction, we'd become an anachronism."

For the moment, Marr's direction lay abroad. He flew to Los Angeles, leaving the other Smiths to ponder his next move. At this stage, nobody was entirely sure that Marr would go through with his threats to quit. It was commonly believed that after a period of rest and re-evaluation, he would return to the fold. Morrissey clearly felt this to be the case, but he seems to have seriously misread the depth of his partner's disenchantment. Before long, the group found themselves overtaken by events. The music press had been noticeably tardy in discovering the current crisis in Smithdom, but it was inevitable that rumours would eventually be translated into headlines. Typically, the *NME* was first with the gossip about a rift and ran a major news story under the arresting title 'Smiths To Split'. Morrissey denied the rumours, while Rourke and Joyce kept a determinedly low profile. Marr, seemingly convinced that Morrissey had planted the story by some devious means, reacted by confirming that he had indeed left. At least he saved face by announcing the split himself. In one sense the *NME* rumours had given him the perfect excuse to conclude matters with a clean break and a minimum of psychological games. Any further prevarication or rationalization was now unnecessary: the cold fact was that Marr would not be returning.

Initially, Morrissey and the others insisted that they were carrying on and undertook a rehearsal with Ivor Perry of Easterhouse. "Morrissey was trying to keep the Smiths going," Perry remembers. "I told him he was daft. I didn't want to be Johnny Marr, Mark II. I didn't even play like him. It would have been embarrassing trying to live up to somebody. I thought it was a bit weird because the other Smiths were there and Morrissey didn't have enough guts to break clear."

Although a weekend session was booked, the audition foundered within 24 hours. "Me and Mike felt uncomfortable," Andy Rourke recalls. "It was the first time we'd played with a new guitarist in about five years." Nevertheless, the group managed to complete rough versions of a couple of songs, including an early version of 'Bengali In Platforms', using Perry's Clash–style arrangement.

"Obviously there was a large amount of stress going on in the band at the time," says Street. "I can remember sitting there with Mike and he said, 'I keep looking up and thinking Johnny is going to come through the door any minute and it'll be all right.' That summed up the feeling of the session." Joyce, in fact, summed it up more suc-cinctly in another comment to me: "The beauty of the Smiths had gone."

By mid-August Morrissey concluded that it was time to move on. He contacted producer Stephen Street and confirmed that he was going solo. The Smiths' demise prompted a flood of elegiac letters to the music press, although a significant number of fans accepted the announcement, feeling that it would be wrong for the others to continue without Marr.

One month later *Strangeways, Here We Come* was released. The title referred to the Victorian jail in Manchester, already controversial for its overcrowding. As Morrissey said at the time: "The way things are going I wouldn't be surprised if I'm in prison 12 months from now . . . Life is so odd that I'm sure I could manage it without too much difficulty."

The new album may not have been the group's best record, but in the circumstances it was guaranteed a eulogistic welcome. *NME* ran its review two weeks before the official release date and allowed Len Brown a full page to trumpet its importance. Brown's final words summed up the impact that the Smiths had made on the music press over the previous five years: "I don't think there's any point in comparing the Smiths with their pop contemporaries; a couple of dodgy singles aside they remained above and beyond the rest . . . I passionately hoped this was not to be their last breath, but nevertheless, in case you haven't guessed by now, *Strangeways, Here We Come* is a masterpiece that surpasses even *The Queen Is Dead* in terms of poetic pop and emotional power."

Three weeks after the album's release, a posthumous televised tribute was broadcast on ITV's *The South Bank Show*. Although nobody from the Smiths' camp was available to provide a suitable requiem, a snippet of Morrissey's earlier interview was salvaged as a suitable coda. Ever the controversialist, he proclaimed nothing less than the death of pop itself, with the Smiths cast as pall bearers. "The whole spectrum of popular music is that it is slowly being laid to rest in every conceivable way. I think it is more or less the end of the story. Ultimately, popular music will end. That must be obvious to almost anybody. I think the ashes are already about us if we could but notice them."

Strangeways, Here We Come is an album that continues to divide Morrissey's fan base. Even the Smiths themselves displayed ambivalence towards the work. "That was the swansong, and it sounds like it," Joyce told me. "The Smiths had become very serious at the time, although we were getting along well. We could really manipulate what we wanted to do musically. With *The Queen Is Dead* we were riding on the crest of a wave and with *Strangeways* it was very much sitting down and creating a *good* album, and thinking of them as album tracks . . . It was more of a studio album."

Marr also sounded ambivalent when discussing the record. "We were completely in sync about which way we should go for each record. But we started to lose that near the end of the last LP." While both Marr and Joyce felt *The Queen Is Dead* was their best work when I interviewed them in the Nineties, Morrissey always showed a greater affection for *Strangeways, Here We Come* and, judging from later interviews, the other Smiths may also have shifted allegiance in the same direction. Perhaps in another decade several of them might re-evaluate *Meat Is Murder* or even *The Smiths*.

Critically, *Strangeways, Here We Come* has yet to receive the endorsement provided by its creators as a glimpse at any music press poll of 'all-time greatest albums' confirms. A year after its release, an otherwise fulsome tribute in *Sounds* concluded: "Had *Strangeways, Here We Come* been released by a living band, it would have been roundly crucified as a tepid rehash of past glories. Instead, its many flaws were immersed in a moist-eyed funereal gloss. It's a sad valediction, appropriate in that it sounds like a band falling apart, with even the few excellent moments desperately bleak in a way the Smiths never were."

Although harsh, this overview correctly hinted at a key theme that went far beyond 'bleakness'. Lyrically, the work seemed dominated by songs about death, almost as if Morrissey was expecting the worst. He had sung of death in the past of course, but never as frequently as this. There was a discernible attempt to extend the Smiths' musical ideas on certain tracks, albeit occasionally at the cost of their melodic grace. Ironically, what the album displayed most clearly was a group in the midst of an uneasy, but interesting musical transition. Maybe the next album would have broken the magical spell irrevocably or perhaps produced a classic. That, like many other questions, would now never be answered.

A Rush And A Push And The Land Is Ours

Morrissey's uneasy relationship with love and death was seldom dealt with more obliquely than in this composition. The narrator announces himself as the spirit of 'Troubled Joe', a character hung a year-and-a-half before. The scene then shifts to what appears to be a humorous discussion between an adolescent and his father about the youth's listlessness, followed by morbid speculations on the trials of love. Marr's arrangement sounds different from any other Smiths record, as if he were intent on breaking free from the shackles of guitar-based indiedom. As Rourke points out: "'A Rush And A Push And The Land Is Ours' stands out because it didn't have any guitars on it at all. I thought that was a first."

The source of Morrissey's song title has produced some fanciful theories from internet enthusiasts, but the first and most convincing comments appeared in a note from David Tseng in issue 12 of the fanzine *Smiths Indeed*: "Paging through an Oscar Wilde biography by Hesketh Pearson, I came across a familiar maxim: '. . . a rush, a charge from north, south, east and west upon the English garrison, and the land is ours.'"

I Started Something I Couldn't Finish

Marr's bombastic rhythm, buoyed by a synthetic saxophone, provided a powerful opening to Morrissey's latest romantic saga. The comic, understated eroticism is destined never to reveal itself despite the singer's sexy attempt at a canine growl. Judging from the lyrics, it's not merely the narrator but the subject of his urges who seems unsure about how to react to a gesture which is deemed 'absolutely vile'. The vocabulary and the reference to '18 months hard labour' hint at the relationship between Oscar Wilde and Lord Alfred Douglas, although the link is tenuous. If the lyrics suggested uncertainty, then they were mirrored by some rare moments of tension in the studio. "It was when we recorded 'I Started Something I Couldn't Finish' that it happened," Stephen Street told me. "Johnny and I had been working on a guitar line all afternoon and got something that we felt had a strong glam rock feel like T. Rex. Morrissey came over to listen to it and said, 'I don't like it.' Johnny wasn't in the room, so I had to go back over to him in the cottage. I said to him, 'Morrissey doesn't like it.' So Johnny said, 'Well, let Morrissey fuckin' think of something.' I thought, 'Hold on a minute! This is the first time!' Normally, Johnny would have said, 'OK, I'll have a chat with him and sort it out.' Johnny was fed-up being relied upon to come up with something all the time and no one actually telling him what they wanted. Morrissey would just say 'yes' or 'no'. He couldn't say, 'I'd like to do *this*,' because he doesn't have a musical background. He knows what he likes – that's the main thing with Morrissey."

Although this track was not originally scheduled as a single, it was issued as such and reached a disappointing number 23, despite an amusing promotional video featuring a dozen Morrissey clones on bicycles following the singer around various Manchester streets. The 12-inch version of the single included an extended 'Some Girls Are Bigger Than Others' recorded at London's Brixton Academy on 12 December 1986.

Death Of A Disco Dancer
This was once compared to the work of Pink Floyd, but a more accurate musical antecedent would be late period Beatles. Marr cites 'I'm So Tired' and 'Cry Baby Cry' from the double album *The Beatles* as the most likely inspiration. Immersing himself in Sixties post-psychedelia, the guitarist concluded the track with a free-form freak-out in which even the untutored Morrissey was allowed to tinker on the piano. Some critics found the song turgid, but producer Stephen Street was not among them. "I still stand by it being a good track," he insists. "I know it was not liked by many people because it's not as catchy as the other tracks. We deliberately left it quite stark and didn't put on overdubs . . . You always need a track that's going to be the backbone of the album and, for me, that was the one." Lyrically, the song offers a gloomy perspective on the prospects of peace and love, casting a premature shadow over the next major youth movement. Acid house and E-culture were not far away, but Morrissey, while forlornly looking back to the past, also predicted the future. The suggestion that death in discos 'happens a lot around here' took on a chillingly prophetic ring several years later when the

Manchester club scene was blighted by drug-related slayings and the Haçienda was forced to close its doors.

Girlfriend In A Coma

After a troubled ghost and a dead disco dancer, we next encounter a coma victim. Despite the theme, the mood is jaunty and the song already familiar, having climbed to number 13 during the summer. The narrator's indecision about whether to see the girl is expressed in polite hospital clichés which neatly evoke the emotional confusion amid the drama. There is further comedy in the classic embarrassing utterance as the singer casually remarks about the times he could have 'murdered' her. Morrissey's lightness of touch has seldom been better. Musically, part of the song repeats Marr's favourite G C D chord sequence, taking us back to the origins of the Smiths when he first played the Patti Smith 'Kimberly'–influenced 'The Hand That Rocks The Cradle'. Source seekers for Morrissey's theme and lyrics are advised to proceed with caution. At the end of the Eighties, I was fortunate enough to unearth documentation confirming beyond doubt the exact date of Morrissey's first trip to New York after completing his O-level examinations in 1977. This was accompanied by detailed information about his stay there, written in his own hand. In order to learn more about what was happening during this important sojourn, and provide some background colour, I consulted various US newspapers. One feature that drew my attention was that of Karen Quinlan, a coma victim who had been unconscious for over a year and was taken to a nursing home to die in peace. Morrissey never admitted that he was even remotely aware of this news story which, as far as I know, was not even reported in the UK, but I included it in *The Severed Alliance* without additional comment or doubtful hypothesis. Theoretically, it could have been a subconscious influence in the composing of 'Girlfriend In A Coma' many years later but it was most likely an example of serendipity. Either way, it was the kind of small detail that I assumed would amuse or intrigue Smiths aficionados in thrall of life's coincidences, but nothing more. Alas, such subtleties are not always appreciated or understood and one later writer on Morrissey, who did not have any access to the information about the date or circumstances of the US visit, naïvely stated categorically that the song was about Karen Quinlan! Bearing in mind this cautionary tale, it can be confidently added that best-selling author Douglas Coupland later appropriated Morrissey's title for his novel *Girlfriend In A Coma*.

Stop Me If You Think You've Heard This One Before

Morrissey's increasing affection for lengthy song titles exceeded all previous attempts with this dissection of the fag ends of a relationship. The wry lyrics again touch on love and death. Indeed, this is the fourth song out of five on the album to mention death, this time with an allusion to the final '10 seconds of life' and even thoughts of a mass murder. Marr literally takes a knife to his guitar strings to provide one of the best and most dramatic openings heard on a Smiths song. He also achieves his ambition of making the group sound fresh and innovative even while they are performing a familiar reprise. Morrissey challenges his listeners in a similar way through the deliberately provocative title which virtually invites critics to consider whether he has lapsed into self-parody. This track would have made an excellent single and was intended as such before radio programmers voiced concern over the 'mass murder' line. Ostensibly, it was an innocuous enough phrase but, unfortunately, coincided with the recent massacre in Hungerford, during which the deranged Michael Ryan had shot 17 people dead and injured 14 more. The BBC concluded that the climate was far too sensitive to broadcast the song, so the single was cancelled. Looking back, the decision was understandable, but regrettable. Marr's dramatic closing break would have provided the perfect coda to the Smiths' career. "I can remember Johnny doing the lead guitar break at the end of it," Stephen Street attests. "I kept saying to him, 'Play it badly, Johnny, it's too good!' He kept playing these fiddly bits and it was more like the Buzzcocks – a two-fingered job. It was a very simple lead line of the last verse."

Last Night I Dreamt That Somebody Loved Me

The eerie opening section of this song, which Marr had originally intended to use elsewhere, was adapted from a BBC sound effects record. "It was basically a different song that Johnny had for the intro," confirms Stephen Street. What sounds like a trip through Dante's Hell or a journalist's nightmarish encounter with the brutality of the miners' strike serves as a dramatic introduction to Morrissey's woeful lament. Once again, the theme concerns the absolute hopelessness of finding love. Morrissey uses the phrase 'another false alarm', possibly inspired by Joni Mitchell's 'Amelia', although the link is tenuous at best. In the final two lines, Morrissey reiterates the sentiments of 'Stop Me If You Think You've Heard This One Before', fully aware that he is sounding like a worn-out record but insistent that the story must go on. His lovelorn persona may be predictable but the aching vocal is still moving, perhaps more so due to Marr's expressive 'Orchestrazia Ardwick' arrangement on the studio's Emulator. "I loved the song and when we did it I knew it was beautiful," recalls Stephen Street. "I just wish there was more vocal on it because Morrissey came in, sang, and it was quickly finished." Fans wishing to hear the song played live had to wait until the end of the century when Morrissey belatedly added it to his set list.

Unhappy Birthday
Marr's enticing acoustic arrangement provided a pleasing complement to Morrissey's politely sung but spiteful lyrics. Although the rhythm is upbeat, Marr detected signs of a melancholy lilt buried beneath. "There's an air of foreboding that's definitely there in that track 'Unhappy Birthday'," he told me. "Only Morrissey could do that to my music and only I could give him that music to sing . . ." Again, images of death dominate the narrative. Having previously alluded to the killing of a horse in 'Is It Really So Strange?' pop's premier animal rights lover this time threatens to kill a dog. The song concludes with the narrator shooting himself in a fit of romantic bitterness.

For Mike Joyce, this never sounded like a song they would play live. "'Unhappy Birthday' is a wild record, but it's very much a studio track. We'd all got together as a little family and became so close that we could toy with the idea of writing tracks in a certain way. The breakdowns you wouldn't do in a live situation. In 'Unhappy Birthday' there's small interludes where Morrissey sings over guitar chords and I'm just filling them out on the kit. You don't think of them being a live track. You don't do them live. Those breaks were created for a studio environment. They weren't created at a soundcheck. This was definitely studio time."

Paint A Vulgar Picture

With its Wildean title and bitter indictment of record company exploitation it was unsurprising that many interpreted this as an attack on Rough Trade. In particular the references to reissues and re-packaging took on an eyebrow-raising significance when applied to the recent compilations *The World Won't Listen* and *Louder Than Bombs*. Add to that the repeated use of one of Geoff Travis' phrases, "You just haven't earned it yet, baby", and the battle lines seemed clearly drawn. Morrissey denied the connection but it is difficult to believe that he was unaware of the connotations. Of course, he had no good cause for castigating his record company's marketing, for he had sanctioned the compilations and was therefore equally respon-sible for foisting them on the public. There has also been some fruit-less speculation on the identity of the dead star apotheosized in the song, with Morrissey's idol and cover star Billy Fury being an all too obvious candidate. The lyrics, however, give the lie to such a view. Fury's death did not unleash a record company feast of exploitative releases and he had nothing to do with radio A-lists, world tours or MTV, as mentioned in the song. The words are far more appropriate to modern-day stars and Morrissey may well have been musing on the after-effects of his own death while composing the lyrics.

The twin theme of the song is actually the relationship between star and fan. Morrissey captures the ambivalence of the obsessive star worshipper whose crowning moment was actually touching his object of devotion at a soundcheck and suffering not brutal rejection but a complete lack of acknowledgement and empathy. Ironically, death not only brings cheer to the rapacious record company but also enshrines the star's immortality for the sad fan. "'Paint A Vulgar Picture' was another song that we'd probably never have played live," Joyce told me, although Morrissey defied that prediction by introducing the song into his solo set during 1997.

Death At One's Elbow

The title was borrowed from the Orton diaries and, judging from the lyrics, so was the theme. Joe Orton was killed by his homosexual companion Kenneth Halliwell with a hammer, but Morrissey prefers a hatchet. In his scenario, it is the assailant who seems likely to die in a suicide pact, complete with the refrain of the Searchers' 'Goodbye My Love' in the background. Marr's harmonica work, recalling 'Hand In Glove' and the BBC version of 'Still Ill', is reinforced by a rockabilly arrangement, a combination that provides an incongruously sprightly feel to the singer's mournful musing. This was the seventh death-related song on the album, which was excessive even by Morrissey's morbid standards. "The music on side 2 of *Strangeways, Here We Come* is a little weak," says Stephen Street. "For me the low points of the album were 'Paint A Vulgar Picture' and 'Death At One's Elbow'. The former was a bit over the line, not so much sour grapes but not a great song. 'Death At One's Elbow' was this album's 'Vicar In A Tutu'. The album slipped half-way through side 2 and the songs weren't as strong as they were on *The Queen Is Dead*." Surprisingly, Morrissey chose 'Death At One's Elbow' for inclusion on his first solo performance at Wolverhampton's Civic Hall in December 1988. Presumably, the rationale was that, in common with the other Smiths' songs performed there, it had never been played live with Johnny Marr.

I Won't Share You

This poignant if understated conclusion to the album fades out with the forlorn singer reminding himself that this is his time. Marr's auto harp adds feeling to the arrangement. Inevitably, the title provoked speculation about the identity of the narrator's object of proprietorial affection, not least among some of the Smiths. "I always got the impression that was obviously about Johnny," Andy Rourke suggests. "Who he wouldn't share him with, I don't know! . . . Whenever anyone got close to Johnny they had to leave. I think maybe all that got to Johnny and he had enough." Certainly, Marr was increasingly frustrated by the never-ending business hassles and worn down by his partner's intensity. "I think Morrissey was almost infatuated with Johnny," Rourke says of the hero-worshipping singer. At one time, Marr remembers "counting his blessings" at having found such a close friend and musical ally, but after five years of plotting and scheming the Smiths' career, the adventure was no longer enjoyable. As Marr later admitted: "We had completely inflated senses of our own importance. Ultimately, I was giving every single second of my life to somebody else . . . he was my only friend really, my only close friend. And I'm not sure it was such a good thing for him either . . . we saw too much of each other. We worked together for five years, every single day of our lives, and that was getting boring as well as depressing." Morrissey never confirmed whether the lyrics were fictional or autobiographical, though he later admitted that Marr was the subject of at least one song following the Smiths' split.

RANK

Released: September 1988

Rough Trade Records, Rough 126, Rough CD 126, September 1988.
WEA 4509-91900, November 1993, February 1995. US issue: Sire 9-25786-1,
Sire 9-25786-2, September 1988

One year after the release of the Smiths' final studio album, this post-humous live set was issued and rapidly climbed to number 2 in the charts. The group could have chosen almost any phase of their career and conjured a live set of interest but, not unexpectedly, they selected a date from their last tour. This was a time when they were at their rocking best, with a full five-piece line-up hardened by an arduous American adventure. However, it was also a troublesome period in which live gigs took on a more menacing aspect. Cumulative success had brought larger audiences, whose constituency not only included indie fans and college students, but a sizeable number of hard rock fans. Although the group's followers were well used to packed halls and sandwiched bodies, they were less enamoured of this macho and often brutal element. Spitting, jostling, punching and near rioting were now more representative of Smiths' concerts than gladioli, National Health spectacles or loving embraces.

Even before the arrival of Craig Gannon, the 1986 shows were provoking critical comments in the music press. One disgruntled customer from Newcastle upon Tyne expressed his disillusionment with a stinging missive: "After 45 minutes onstage the band walked off in the middle of 'Hand In Glove' and refused to come back due to some dickheads down the front gobbing on them. Sounds fair enough? Don't you bloody believe it. The Smiths' attitude all night sucked – the fact that they were charging £6 (or £6.30 on the door) to get into the Mayfair was a disgrace to begin with, but their whole outlook seemed to be geared towards getting off as quickly as possible. Not only that, but they now look like the new Rolling Stones and sound like Led Zeppelin. Johnny is actively pushing his rock star image as far as he can – it was bloody horrendous to see him pandering to the 'Johnny clones' in the audience and 'rock, rock, rockin' his axe'. If I want to see the Rolling Stones I'll go and pay £20 to see the Stones, not £6 to see a second-rate impersonation."

In America, the tradition of Morrissey-worshipping stage invasions was already in full swing. Obviously, the American visit had a significant effect on the Smiths' 'rockist tendencies' and the five-piece faced a riotous reception during their final UK tour. "When we came back from America with all the histrionics, we then did the north of England, and you're giving off the same kind of vibe," Mike Joyce explains. "We came back and we were like, 'Rock 'n' Roll!' America was a pretty big tour and we were screwed up by the end of it. Then we had a bit of time off, and it was – 'Yeah, let's go!'"

The strong rock elements in the Smiths' performances were immediately translated into critical cliché, with Rolling Stones comparisons mentioned in various reviews. *Record Mirror*'s Dave Sexton was clearly intrigued by this apparent metamorphosis: "The more I see, the more I'm convinced of two things. The first is that the Smiths are probably the best band in Britain. The second is that they are, slowly but surely, turning into the Rolling Stones. This is not as daft as it may sound – think not of the Rolling Stones of today, the flabby, flatulent, dried out and dried up Stones. Think rather of old film of them – very old film – and you'll see what I mean. It is the unlikely brooding sexuality and skittish posturing of the Morrissey/ Jagger figure and the now unashamed 'axe-hero' stance of Johnny Marr – the new Keith Richards."

The British tour was beset by dramatic events, and a series of worrying injuries. In Newport, Morrissey was dragged from the stage, struck his head on the floor, and was forced to retire hurt. When sound engineer Grant Showbiz announced the news of the singer's departure to the angry audience, he was struck by a flying bottle, then taken to hospital to be treated for cuts and concussion. Police arrived on the scene to prevent further ugly outbreaks and afterwards several complaining letters to the music press castigated Morrissey for not being a trouper and coming back on. Nor was this gig an isolated incident. In Preston, one week later, the Smiths played the shortest set in their history, when the evening came to a dramatic close after just one song. Morrissey suffered another injury, this time from a flying missile which was later identified as a drumstick. The fact that the opening song was 'The Queen Is Dead' encouraged the *Sun* to spout the implausible notion that the group were the recipients of violence from a bunch of pro-royalists.

It was between these two riotous gigs that *Rank* was recorded at the National Ballroom, Kilburn, on 23 October. It was an eventful evening for all concerned, not least the support group, Soil. Their drummer Gary Farrell, a former pupil of Morrissey's hated school St Mary's, had once turned down the chance to join the Smiths. Now, four years on, he was playing with them on the same bill. The newly scarred Grant Showbiz could also look back fondly at the live recording, for it brought him a much deserved 1 per cent royalty which turned out to be an unexpected financial windfall.

The Smiths played 21 songs that night, 14 of which were extracted for inclusion on *Rank*. There must have been some temptation to include the entire concert on a double set, but Rough Trade restricted themselves to a single album comprising 56 minutes of music. Few customers would deny that they had got a bargain. Completists were left to track down the original bootleg concert tape which featured the additional 'I Want The One I Can't Have', 'There Is A Light That Never Goes Out', 'Shakespeare's Sister', 'Frankly Mr Shankly', 'Never Had No One Ever', 'Meat Is Murder' and 'How Soon Is Now?' There was even some small consolation for those Mancunians unable to make the trip to London for the big show. That same evening, Morrissey was featured on Tony Wilson's regional arts programme, *The Other Side Of Midnight*, reviewing Norman Tebbitt's autobiography. His scabrous comments were not available to southern audiences.

The Kilburn gig could not have come at a more eventful time. One week later, the unfortunate Craig Gannon was ousted from the group in the most casual way imaginable. He discovered his fate not from any of the Smiths, but through Gary Rostock, the drummer in Easterhouse. The news had already been passed on through Geoff Travis and Ivor Perry, who was stunned by the announcement. "To be told your own mate has been kicked out of the Smiths, and he doesn't even know. That was shocking. It was pretty callous."

Gannon had mixed feelings about his dismissal. "I received no notification from the Smiths or anyone connected with them," he later told me. "When I first heard the news that I wasn't with them any more I did feel a big relief and glad in a way that it was all over, although I don't think I would have left them at that point. I felt relieved not to be with them but, at the same time, disappointed that it never did work out because I still had enormous respect for their music . . . They were all great musicians."

Two weeks later, Marr was hospitalized after a near fatal car crash. "I'd been out with Mike Joyce and his girlfriend. He didn't live too far away, so I dropped him off. Then I got to literally 150 yards from my house. There's some lights stopping you from getting to the road, and the road forks off one way. There was a cassette in the machine and it had gone round to the other side and, just as I was at the lights, the other side of the tape had started up, so I put my foot down and thought, 'Right, I'll take a two-minute diversion around the block.' But I just put my foot right down and drove at this bend in the pouring rain at full speed as fast as the car would go. It went completely out of control and ended up bouncing off a couple of walls and into the middle of the road. I jumped out and saw that the car was completely crushed. I just couldn't believe I was still there." Marr literally ran home, falling over several times along the way. He was put to bed, but the following day awoke with shooting pains in his arms, fingers and neck.

Joyce later saw the car wreckage and was shocked. "It was like a concertina up to the windscreen. One corner of the car had completely disappeared. I'm surprised the engine hadn't come through the front and removed his legs. Johnny was very lucky to keep his legs really." This almost James Dean-like conclusion to the Smiths' saga turned out to be part of the closing act. Marr went to hospital the following day where he was fitted with a neck brace and splints.

A show shortly afterwards for the Anti-Apartheid organization was necessarily rescheduled for December at the Brixton Academy. That turned out to be the last ever gig played by the Smiths on British soil. After just over four years of performance the dream was over. *Rank* served as a belated and much treasured memento of a turbulent period that nobody realized was actually the denouement of the Smiths' career. The album's release was greeted with due reverence, most notably in the *NME*, whose critic James Brown awarded the work a maximum 10 points: "Live LPs rarely work. *Rank* does. It captures the Smiths during their most creative period, playing their music with speed, passion and ferocity – three qualities the band possessed that were so often overlooked. For those of you seeking a re-formation *Rank* will only make matters worse. It is a live recording of rare raw talent . . . I think the journalists have stopped throwing things now, Morrissey."

The Queen Is Dead

The Philadelphia Orchestra's version of Prokofiev's 'March Of The Capulets' from *Romeo And Juliet* provides the perfect dramatic opening to this live album. The classical refrain brings an enormous sense of expectancy, complemented by the swirling lights which announce the imminent arrival of the group onstage. Then, suddenly, they are there. A raucous "Hello" precedes some powerhouse drumming before Marr emerges with what is undoubtedly the *tour de force* of the entire set. The song is taken at a furious pace as Marr wah-wahs into the stratosphere backed by some sterling work by Gannon and Rourke. Morrissey is left almost breathless at times as he tries to keep up with the players. For tricky word endings he substitutes guttural noises and almost sings in tongues during the word 'castration'. For the Smiths to open a show with an epochal track like this displayed an extraordinary confidence and gave notice that they were intent on rocking out, perhaps like never before.

Panic

A long drum solo precedes this powerful composition which, in 1986, had restored the Smiths to the UK Top 20 after a two-year absence. In concert they were unable to compensate for the loss of the children's choir in the final verse and during this performance Morrissey sounds in urgent need of vocal accompaniment. Instrumentally, there are no cracks to paper over. The addition of Gannon gives Marr the necessary space to fatten the sound and he closes proceedings with another wah-wah flourish. At some shows Morrissey dramatized the song by wielding a noose and wearing a T-shirt featuring the face and name of BBC disc jockey Steve Wright under the heading 'Hang The DJ'.

Vicar In A Tutu

Not surprisingly, this live set featured a high proportion of songs from the still recent *The Queen Is Dead*. This faster paced version of 'Vicar In A Tutu' offers some amusing vocal dexterity from Morrissey while the group sound like they are enjoying the comic romp. Although rough and ready in parts, it serves the same function as the original album version in lightening the intense mood.

Ask

"This is our new single," says Morrissey, before growling, "Ask." The performance is tight and sounds impressively like the recorded version. Marr and Gannon combine their guitar work which meshes well. Morrissey appears to make a special effort in enunciating the hard northern 'a' sound for emphatic effect. The song still surprises with its casual sting in the tail line about 'the Bomb' achieving what love cannot by bringing the protagonists together. Although the legal problems with Gannon were already under way at this point, no attempt was made to remove this song from the set. He was philo- sophical about the dispute. "When I found that I wasn't given a writing credit, it didn't really bother me, but I thought it was pretty bad that no one even acknowledged that it was my idea in the first place. The thing I hate is that in the past I've been accused of trying to put my name to a song as if I was trying to grab what I could get when that was not the case at all. In any other situation where it would have been up to me to choose to make a song out of such a basic song idea, I probably wouldn't have expanded on that idea, although I do think the song ended up really good."

Rusholme Ruffians

Morrissey and Marr mischievously acknowledged this song's debt to Pomus & Shuman's '(Marie's The Name) His Latest Flame' by incor- porating its first verse as an amusing introduction. It is worth noting that the inspiration for 'Rusholme Ruffians' emerged after Marr had been listening to his parents' copy of the classic Elvis Presley record- ing. "I loved 'His Latest Flame'," Marr admits. "But from being a kid I noticed how many other songs had that chord change. When Morrissey sang it, it sounded really brilliant." The segue into

'Rusholme Ruffians' was expertly done, with Marr suddenly shifting gear and speeding up the song, much to the audience's appreciation.

The Boy With The Thorn In His Side

Another impressive guitar introduction reveals Marr and Gannon working well together. Morrissey's vocal is very confident, complete with a growl or two and the customary falsetto. Given the song's bitter subtext, the lightness of touch is surprising but successfully creates a more complicated response from the listener than might otherwise be the case. Ultimately, it is the confused feelings of the boy rather than the metaphorical thorn that attracts our sympathy.

What She Said

A Morrissey belch launches the group into a fierce driving version of this relatively minor song from *Meat Is Murder*. The tempo is slightly slower than the studio version, but the hard-rocking intensity of the original is retained. The real surprise comes with the additional outro from 'Rubber Ring' which works extremely well, proving that the Smiths could string a short medley together and still sound unique.

Is It Really So Strange?

A polite introduction is followed by another belch as Morrissey canters through this tale of his zany journey around England. It's intriguing to hear the way he pronounces Newport Pagnell and rolls the 'r' sounds around his tongue as if he's practising for a French oral exam. Obviously a live favourite, particularly given its obscure geographical references, the song was belatedly brought back into Morrissey's solo repertoire in 1999.

Cemetry Gates

At first blush this was far less impressive live than might have been expected. The charm of the album version is missing despite Morrissey's attempts to invest some verve into the song by pointedly growling the words 'dizzy whore'. Marr's little false ending is a pleasant touch, but the delicacy of the original melody is somewhat lost in translation. Ultimately, this composition became something of a self-fulfilling prophecy, turning many Morrissey fans into overimaginative source hunters. While his previous debts to Shelagh Delaney, Victoria Wood and Elizabeth Smart were self-evident, some interpretations of his later 'borrowings' were less convincing, often consisting of nothing more than a couple of words or a strained paraphrase from another book. Although such similarities were amusing, intriguing and certainly worth noting, the tendency to transform conjecture or coincidence into stated fact without offering at least some qualification, all too often proved irresistible. Marr later confessed to the magazine *Guitar* that the composition began as a playful experiment. "When we signed to Rough Trade we were being hailed as 'The Great New Songwriters' and I was on the train coming back thinking, 'Right, if you're so great – first thing in the morning, sit down and write 'A Great Song'. I started with 'Cemetry Gates' Bm to G change in open G . . . Sonically, we got it right . . ."

London

In contrast to the fragile 'Cemetry Gates', 'London' works extremely well as the group are given freedom to rock out. What emerges is an unexpected highlight with Morrissey dragging out the syllables to add some new drama to the proceedings. Joyce flails away mercilessly for the obligatory emphatic ending. "*Rank* gives you the depth and thickness of sound that we had," he says. "That wall of sound was very much the Ramones' style. Obviously, the tempos shoot up in live performance, but I've no qualms about that at all." After Gannon's departure from the group, Marr incorporated the song into another medley of sorts with 'Miserable Lie', which was heard at their final UK concert at the Royal Albert Hall on 12 December 1986.

I Know It's Over

When Morrissey sings about death by rivers and razors you can't help wondering whether he has been reading Dorothy Parker's *Résumé*. What's missing is any sign of her wry humour as a grim, despairingly claustrophobic mood overwhelms him like the funeral soil he describes. This version builds up to an impressive climax, lasting in excess of seven minutes. It serves as the morbid centrepiece of the live album.

The Draize Train

The studio version of this Marr-composed instrumental was previously premièred as a B-side on the 12-inch version of 'Panic'. Its unusual title was evidently inspired by animal research scientist John Draize. In concert, it worked well and served as an opportunity to focus attention on the players. The decision to feature the instrumental on *Rank* was fortuitous for Marr, who thereby received a larger share of the album's publishing income than his partner. This was the track that Geoff Travis and others felt should have been issued as a single with some suitable Morrissey lyrics. Despite various solicitations, however, the singer was unimpressed and declined to pen a single word, insisting that it was the weakest track Marr had ever produced. As Marr admits, "That was his feeling, yes, and there was strong pressure on him from Rough Trade. It could have been really good but it became a matter of principle with him. He felt the way he did. It didn't click with him. Simple as that, really."

The evening after this performance, the group stayed in London for a show at the Brixton Academy which, uniquely, included a second drummer – the Impossible Dreamers' Fred Hood. In a parody of the Glitter Band's two-drum line-up, Hood joined the group for 'The Draize Train' and stayed on for a powerful rendition of 'How Soon Is Now?' As he told me: "It was like scoring a goal at Wembley."

Still Ill

This was the oldest song in the live set and the only representative from the group's début album. It's immediately evident how much Morrissey's voice has changed over the years. As if aware of this, he plays with the lines, looking back with comic affection at his younger self. This time when he ponders the 'body ruling the mind' conundrum, he screams 'I dunno' *loudly*, as if tired of all the cod philosophical questions.

Bigmouth Strikes Again

This, the final encore, offers a less arresting finale than we might have expected. Marr, for once, seems incapable of reproducing the studio guitar sound to spectacular effect. Even Gannon's presence does not compensate and Marr could really do with a third guitarist here. Fortunately, Morrissey plays up the song's drama to maximum effect with an endearing range of gargles, grunts and vocal pyrotechnics. The tapes continue to roll after the Smiths have left the stage and it is a welcome closing touch to hear the frustrated handclaps and nostalgic echo of Shirley Bassey's 'You'll Never Walk Alone'. Those final moments, along with the dramatic Prokofiev opening, take the listener back to the concerts of 1986 almost as poignantly as the songs contained herein.

BEST . . .

Released: August 1992

WEA 4509-90327-2, August 1992. US issue: Sire 94542-2, September 1992

The first retrospective offered by WEA following their acquisition of the Smiths' catalogue was something of an anti-climax, although its sales performance exceeded expectations. Released at a time when Morrissey's younger audience was ready to investigate the Smiths' back catalogue, it had its place, but the decision to stagger the 'Best Of' concept over two albums seemed nothing less than cheap and exploitative. What could have been a great album sounded little more than a superior sampler. This was reflected in several music press reviews. "Serving no evident purpose save making money, with music and fans as secondary considerations," concluded Q, while NME overstated WEA's reissue policy, describing the work as "Just another brick in what is becoming a veritable Hadrian's Wall of Smiths' exploitation."

Although none of the Smiths were keen on the later compilations, the existence of a chart-topping album underlined their importance which surely provided compensatory pride. Best . . . also paved the way for the complete reissue of the Smiths catalogue on CD in 1993. Mike Joyce welcomed this at the time, telling me: "It has to be done. If it comes across to lads who are now 17 or 18, it's cool. It means that it resurfaces. I don't want to get left by the wayside and be seen as just a cult band. I want people to listen with fresh ears. For too many of these kids now, it's just Morrissey and they don't know the Smiths because they couldn't see them play live. So, in a way, I think it's good. A lot of stuff around at the moment is so sterile. There's very little out there for people who want to say something. The lyrical content of the Smiths is too important to be forgotten or to be heard only by people who were around at the time."

Full track listing: *This Charming Man; William, It Was Really Nothing; What Difference Does It Make?; Stop Me If You Think You've Heard This*

One Before; Girlfriend In A Coma; Half A Person; Rubber Ring; How Soon Is Now?; Hand In Glove; Shoplifters Of The World Unite; Sheila Take A Bow; Some Girls Are Bigger Than Others; Panic; Please Please Please Let Me Get What I Want.

BEST . . . II

Released: November 1992

WEA 4509-903406/2, November 1992. Sire 9-45097-2, December 1992

Even the Smiths' faithful following gave this compilation the cold shoulder and it barely dented the album charts, peaking at number 29. Essentially a mopping up exercise after the first 'Best Of', its target audience appeared to be those hard-core collectors who might buy any old product in a new sleeve. This was reflected in such limited editions as the 'wooden box' set, which featured both volumes, and various other artefacts. The unseemly haste with which this was issued was probably due to the record company attempting to recoup its investment at the earliest opportunity. At the time, it caused many fans concern about what might be foisted on the public next. Fortunately, WEA's marketing zeal cooled and the next compilation would prove a more dignified and welcome collection. It should be stressed that neither Morrissey nor Marr were actively overseeing these compilations, having agreed to allow Warner Brothers complete control over marketing such product. In an interview with David Browne, Morrissey observed: "It's peculiar not to be involved in the artwork at all or in the discussion of the track listings. When the catalogue was bought by a major label, it was a bit like leaving a child at school on the first day and saying goodbye. But life goes on, and I've got other things to do."

Full track listing: *The Boy With The Thorn In His Side; The Headmaster Ritual; Heaven Knows I'm Miserable Now; Ask; Oscillate Wildly; Nowhere Fast; Still Ill; Bigmouth Strikes Again; That Joke Isn't Funny Anymore; Shakespeare's Sister; Girl Afraid; Reel Around The Fountain; Last Night I Dreamt That Somebody Loved Me; There Is A Light That Never Goes Out.*

SINGLES

Released: February 1995

WEA 4509-99090-2, February 1995. US issue: Sire 9-45932-2, May 1995

Although offering nothing previously unavailable on album, this compilation of singles was a welcome addition to the Smiths' catalogue. It immediately made the previous 'Best Ofs' not merely redundant but unnecessary. For older fans this was a chance to luxuriate in the recording history of the Smiths as a singles entity, a process that was not without some regrets. During their lifetime, the group had never fashioned a zeitgeist-grabbing number 1 single to equal their Liverpool rivals Frankie Goes To Hollywood who achieved the feat on three consecutive occasions. Morrissey often spoke of conspiracies and lack of daytime radio play, but lesser groups than the Smiths had broken through with a chart-topping single on numerous occasions with little or no promotion. Indeed, the Smiths benefited from regular appearances on the hugely chart influential *Top Of The Pops* and still found problems getting anywhere near the number 1 position. The unpalatable truth was that, although the Smiths recorded excellent quality singles, they never seemed likely to rival the Beatles or Stones as Morrissey and Marr had intended. Instead, partly thanks to their strong student following, it was the albums format that provided them with consistent commercial successes. Their potential crossover appeal from indie to mainstream was never realized by a single song that had number 1 indelibly written in its grooves, not even the famous 'How Soon Is Now?' Nevertheless, their run of singles was impressive and, most importantly, was always executed with an emphasis on fine quality B-sides and bonus tracks. This compilation makes its own case for the Smiths as singles specialists but it should be noted as a caveat that the versions of 'Hand In Glove' and 'The Boy With The Thorn In His Side' included here were not the same mixes originally issued on single. A television campaign featuring clips of cover star Diana Dors from the 1956 movie *Yield To The Night* enhanced the album's performance in the market-place with a chart peak of number 5.

Full track listing: *Hand In Glove; This Charming Man; What Difference Does It Make?; Heaven Knows I'm Miserable Now; William, It Was Really Nothing; How Soon Is Now?; Shakespeare's Sister; That Joke Isn't Funny Anymore; The Boy With The Thorn In His Side; Bigmouth Strikes Again; Panic; Ask; Shoplifters Of The World Unite; Sheila Take A Bow; Girlfriend In A Coma; I Started Something I Couldn't Finish; Last Night I Dreamt That Somebody Loved Me; There Is A Light That Never Goes Out.*

THE VERY BEST OF THE SMITHS

Released: June 2001

WEA 88948-2, June 2001

Six years after *Singles*, this 'best of' attempted to pull all the famous Smiths songs into a single package for the digital age. With the original 'Best Ofs' largely forgotten, this compilation was a good introduction for younger listeners belatedly catching up with the legacy of the Smiths, but largely irrelevant to anyone else. Elitism aside, the work probably served its purpose for casual listeners eager to sample the essence of the Smiths without wishing to purchase their complete catalogue. Marr, who chose to sell his work to WEA after acquiring the rights from Rough Trade and accepted the terms and conditions of that transaction, making a small fortune in the process, still had the audacity to complain on his website: "The band were not asked for approval on this record and consequently it is a disgrace. It has the worst cover I've ever seen [Charles Hawtrey] and has been re-mastered poorly. I believe Morrissey is less than pleased about the album, but I can only speak for myself when I say it should be ignored by fans." Warners retorted that the mastering overseen by Bill Inglot was "brilliant", adding "He's done a terrific job." That argument aside, Marr's objections still seem unconvincing. Why should Warners ask the *band* for approval when the Smiths were contractually Morrissey & Marr? And if Morrissey & Marr felt so precious about the quality of compilations, why did they not exercise greater control over the exploitation of such rights, as the Beatles had done from a far more disadvantageous position?

Full track listing: *Panic; The Boy With The Thorn In His Side; Heaven Knows I'm Miserable Now; Ask; Bigmouth Strikes Again; How Soon Is Now?; This Charming Man; What Difference Does It Make?; William, It Was Really Nothing; Some Girls Are Bigger Than Others; Girlfriend In A Coma; Hand In Glove; There Is A Light That Never Goes Out; Please Please Please Let Me Get What I Want; That Joke Isn't Funny Anymore;*

I Know It's Over; Sheila Take A Bow; I Started Something I Couldn't Finish; Still Ill; Shakespeare's Sister; Shoplifters Of The World Unite; Last Night I Dreamt That Somebody Loved Me; Stop Me If You Think You've Heard This One Before.

MORRISSEY ALBUMS

VIVA HATE

Released: March 1988

HMV CSD 3787, CDCSD 3787, March 1988. US issue: Sire 9-25699-2,
Sire 9-25699-4 CD, March 1988

The most extraordinary aspect of *Viva Hate* was the speed with which
it was completed and released. After the dramatic breakup of the
Smiths, one might have expected Morrissey to fall into a despondent
gloom resulting in stasis. Instead he responded to the challenge of a
new solo career with an alertness and confidence which was most
surprising. After writing to Stephen Street during August 1987 and
announcing his intentions to complete a new album, the two spent
the early winter at the Wool Hall near Bath working with apparent
ease on new material. Street brought in Durutti Column guitarist
Vini Reilly, whom he had previously worked with and, despite some
aesthetic disagreements in the studio, there was much to recommend
the partnership. Reilly was also a Mancunian of Irish stock and his
world-view would have appealed to Morrissey. A creature of mood,
Reilly could relate to Morrissey's forthright attitude without pandering to his whims. The guitarist's frailty, exacerbated by an eating dis-
order that precluded touring, meant that Morrissey was dealing with
someone whose problems outweighed his own. Both were essentially
outsiders, working in a music business that enabled them to transform
their neuroses into an art form. Their work was all the more striking
because of its painful roots. Reilly's non-rock pedigree ensured that
he could work with Morrissey without being overwhelmed by the
Smiths' myth. Inevitably, there would be comparisons with Marr,
but Reilly was such a strikingly different guitarist that these proved
irrelevant.

The drummer chosen by Street was the uproarious Andrew Paresi,
an experienced session player who had recently worked with, among
others, Bucks Fizz. Ever cautious, Street ensured that the new recruit
was given a subtle image makeover. "Stephen was worried that
Morrissey might pick up on something which he didn't need to

know about and he asked me not to mention anything about Bucks Fizz," Paresi recalls. "In addition I was asked to genetically alter my appearance in such a way that the bright, dazzling Eighties gear I was wearing turned into jeans, DMs [Doc Marten boots] and a short haircut. So I was subtly altered."

The burden of composing the songs was taken up by Street, whose cassette tape of melodies would launch Morrissey on the hazardous road to solo success. Street was not a known songsmith and Morrissey took a considerable risk working with somebody whose writing potential was untested. Not for the first time, Morrissey saw something in a partnership that others might have cautioned against. It was partly the security of familiarity. Morrissey had worked closely with Street during the Smiths years and clearly admired his work both as an engineer and a producer. Evidently Morrissey heard something in the demos that Street posted to him that sounded commercial yet interesting enough to be allied to his lyrics. Perhaps more importantly it seemed a relatively painless way to break the Marr spell.

Upon arriving at the Wool Hall in the autumn of 1987, Paresi was instantly struck by the group dynamics, which were in evidence during their first meal together. "What impressed me most was that when Vini and Morrissey sat down at the table there was clearly a connection. They were already talking about people they knew in Manchester, so immediately you could sense they were getting on and had a lot in common . . . There was a tremendous respect between Morrissey and Vini. Morrissey seemed to really appreciate Vini's work and there was a reverse relationship there too . . . Certainly, I got the impression that Morrissey was fascinated by and also quite protective of Vini. Morrissey is routinely fascinated by personalities and people that are not of the ordinary nature of things, of which Vini is definitely not. So there was a connection there. But there were a lot of problems too. Vini felt very strongly that he should be writing the material and this was a bit difficult given that Morrissey had written the songs around Stephen's chord shapes . . . Morrissey had clearly written shapes and ideas around those songs and felt confident enough to go into the studio and record them. Then Vini comes in. If you know Durutti Column's music you appreciate that Vini is not some session guitarist that you yank off the street and say, 'Hey, come and put some hip chops around this.' You get the *total* effect which is a fantastically beautiful work. Playing guitar on some of these songs was to him composing for them really. It may be hard to swallow in some respects but I think that's how *he* saw it . . . But that's not really how it is, is it? I felt Vini was effectively the hired guitar hand who was contributing his very special and unique style to the record."

One feature of the album that proved surprising, particularly when considering the speed with which it was recorded, was the existence of several outtakes. Unlike the Smiths, who seldom left anything on the cutting-room floor, Morrissey had several songs which did not even register as B-sides or bonus tracks. Early in the sessions, there was an attempt at 'Please Help The Cause Against Loneliness' to which Sandie Shaw later added backing vocals. "It was intended for *Viva Hate*," Andrew Paresi points out. "But we just got nowhere. We were hammering around that for three or four takes and it didn't seem to work." Morrissey felt uncertain about the song and it was eventually handed over to Shaw who recorded a passable version.

When I visited Stephen Street at his home in 1993, he unveiled more rarities, including a tape box whose contents featured 'Life-guard On Duty', 'Safe, Warm Lancashire Home', 'Treat Me Like A Human Being' and 'Untitled'. There were also several DATs of outtakes from the sessions. Included on these were works in progress, including the amusingly titled 'I Know Very Well How I Got My Note Wrong', a track that was included as a free CD single (credited to Vincent Gerard and Steven Patrick) on the first 500 copies of the Durutti Column's *Vini Reilly*. "That was me and Morrissey trying to do this very intense song. I was playing it like someone performing in a bar or a restaurant, like a Spanish guitar player. I thought it was very effective and worked really well. It was the one outtake I liked and enjoyed."

While fans were still mourning the Smiths and pondering the likelihood of a reunion, Morrissey was preparing for an eventful New Year. "We finished the album literally a week before Christmas," Stephen Street remembers. "Afterwards I felt absolutely drained. People were amazed how quickly it came together. It takes a while to wait for release schedules so the earliest they could issue a single was

February, with 'Suedehead', and the album appeared the following month."

The general critical reaction to *Viva Hate* was warm surprise. It followed on so quickly from the Smiths that the reverential attitude towards Morrissey had yet to cool. Even *Melody Maker* gave the record a positive review. Critic David Stubbs concluded: "It's tempting to say that we don't need Morrissey any more, that his ghostly grey presence in the relentlessly gaudy pop terrain has faded as it has persisted. But Morrissey is needed, not as an ombudsman, or a figure of the Eighties but as a horrified figure against the Eighties, who has turned his back on the march of pop time as the last keeper of the sanctuary of self-pity, apartness, exile . . . And *Viva Hate*, a further act of simple faithlessness, is, its lapses withal, another great album by our last star, our last idiot."

The album was not an outright classic and occasionally seemed uncertain in places but there was an exuberance of discovery that was at times irresistible. Several songs stood as likely candidates for a future Morrissey all-time greatest hits collection and, most importantly, the work proved beyond doubt that the singer could survive and thrive without Johnny Marr. Musically, it sounded contemporary, complete with drum machines and smart effects. But lyrically it was almost a concept album based on the Seventies. Of course, Morrissey had always been obsessed with his own past, but usually the landscape he created in song was strangely out of sync, its northern imagery redolent of the Sixties, while also conjuring monochrome, celluloid visions of the Forties or Fifties. Sometimes it seemed an imaginary world of Morrissey's creation, naturalistic in part, but made up of scattered fragments from favourite books and films. *Viva Hate* was like witnessing the switch from black and white television to bad colour, then flashing through a decade highlighted by decidedly unglamorous memories. From the axed child star at the start of the decade in 'Little Man, What Now?', through to the condescendingly treated Bengali with his platform shoes and the ordinary boys and girls with their supermarket clothes, this was no era to feel nostalgic about. 'Break Up The Family' also recalled his early teens; 'Angel, Angel Down We Go Together' took its title from a 1970 movie and 'Suedehead' referred to Richard Allen's cult novels of the same period. Tellingly, the album closed with a vicious denunciation of the most prominent political figure to emerge from the tail-end of that decade. It may not have been a concept album in Morrissey's head but the sheer weight of Seventies' imagery in theme or title told its own story.

As a solo début, *Viva Hate* was far better than most of us anticipated but that in itself provided expectations which Morrissey could not necessarily meet immediately. Looking back at the work two years later, he told Nick Kent: "I feel it was more of an event than an achievement. I think the audience was simply relieved that I was still going on with living . . . I've always been fiercely self-critical and – it wasn't perfect. And it wasn't better than *Strangeways, Here We Come*. There's at least six tracks on it that I'd now willingly bury in the nearest patch of soil. And place a large stone on top." Later still, Morrissey identified these weaker songs, while admitting, "*Viva Hate* is an uncomfortable record . . . I wanted to make a record straightaway, but I was still in a state of shock, still upset and very angry. That's why I called the album *Viva Hate*. I find the second side weak but I like the first side: 'Alsatian Cousin' and 'Bengali In Platforms'. I think 'Everyday Is Like Sunday' is one of the high points of my career."

Morrissey's overview sounds largely convincing. As it turned out, Street's greatest forte was in the area that the Smiths most prized – the ability to write a strong single. Both 'Suedehead' and 'Everyday Is Like Sunday' were class records that brought Morrissey his greatest success to date and their chart placings would be unequalled until as late as 2004. It seems odd to consider that Morrissey was a hot tip to register a number 1 single at the time of *Viva Hate*'s release. In retrospect, the early Street era represented his commercial peak as far as *Top Of The Pops* was concerned. He may have recorded better material but he never looked quite such a happening singles artiste after this exciting early run. But *Viva Hate* wasn't just about singles success. The album also reached number 1, equalling the achievement of the great *Meat Is Murder* and suggesting that Morrissey was poised for a formidable albums career at will.

Alsatian Cousin

Morrissey opens his solo album with a sound more in keeping with an ambient-tinged hard rock band on the rampage. Vini Reilly's distorted guitar and Andrew Paresi's booming drums take us as far away from the familiar Smiths' sound as possible. The lyrics betray a prurient, almost voyeuristic, character as the narrator seeks eroticism in quizzing his subject about whether or not sex has taken place in an open tent. Knowing that such questions are likely to be interpreted by certain fans as some kind of autobiographical admission merely adds to the song's appeal.

Having previously heard harsh testimony from Vini Reilly, who felt the song was largely his own, it was instructive for me to listen to the original demo at Stephen Street's house and witness his account of the composition's genesis. "I played it to the guys and they fell about laughing because it was as basic as you've just heard it – just a drum machine with a bass line. I said, 'I want to leave it open so you can just go mad over the top of it.' It happened that Morrissey was doing his high, wavering stuff, those high yelps, so I gave Vini a free hand. He did a great job. The beginning I really liked. Andrew's drums worked very well and Vini added to the chords that I'd originally written. He added some harmonies to it. It was nice and solid. But there was a chordal structure to it and I can play you it. It's true that on the verse patterns where all the wild guitar sessions were going on I said, 'Look, it's a bass line groove here, I want you to wig out on guitar.' The chordal bit where Morrissey sings had always been there and it's there on my demo. Look, I'll play it for you! It's basically the same chords I had on my demo. Vini did add extra harmonies to the chords. He added a *lot* to it, but that was the whole point. That's the reason why I got him in because some tracks needed that."

Vini Reilly adds some memories of his own: "Stephen Street had a cyclical, repetitious bass line and a drum machine. *That* was the demo – just a bass riff. It didn't really change. He decided that we should jam because there was no structure to it." Reilly feels his wild guitar work provided the song's essence. "I know Morrissey thinks it's vaguely interesting. That was very satisfying because I freaked out on it and it was radical. I got a really distorted guitar sound with the help of Stephen Street, who's a first-class engineer. Praise where it's due – he's a brilliant engineer. The guitar sound I wanted he was able to get for me with over-the-top distortion. That one I really enjoyed . . . From day one I insisted I be paid a session fee that wouldn't take into account any contribution I made, musically or otherwise. As far as I'm concerned I did write 'Alsatian Cousin' but an agreement was made in order that I could do that. And that was fine."

"It was less of a structured song," Paresi adds, "and one of the earliest recordings in the session. It might have been a bass line and a couple of chords when Stephen gave it to Morrissey. At that stage the Vini/Stephen axis hadn't come off the rails so Vini was happy to play along with some things and maybe Stephen was giving me more space . . . I wasn't sure of the album order then, but it struck me as a very strong opening track just because it was so meaty and funny. There were some great lines in it. Looking back now I'd have played it slightly differently but that's just drummer stuff really. Overall I was very pleased with it."

Little Man, What Now?
One of the album's stronger songs, this was also recorded and completed early in the sessions. "I loved the track," says Stephen Street. "It was one of the songs I had demoed with Morrissey before we went into the studio, so I really knew what I was doing. The flamenco rhythm reminded me of David Bowie's 'Andy Warhol' from *Hunky Dory*." Morrissey again showed his penchant for borrowing song titles. 'Alsatian Cousin' had come from Alan Bennett's play *Forty Years On*, while this track shared its name with a 1932 book by German writer Hans Fallada (*Kleiner Mann, Was Nun?*). The song details Morrissey's perennial interest in minor celebrities and documents a period when he spent an inordinate amount of time in front of a television set. He takes us back to Friday nights in 1969 to witness the early career of a minor celebrity who was dropped and ended up appearing on an afternoon panel show during the Seventies, where even his fellow contestants failed to identify him. Fanzine enthusiasts later claimed that the child star was Jack Wilde and the obscure television programme *Looks Familiar*, although Morrissey has confirmed neither of these propositions in print. However, he did insist that the character was "a real person but I don't want to name names".

Everyday Is Like Sunday

With a nuclear theme that recalled Poet Laureate Sir John Betjeman's *Slough*, this was one of the highlights of the album and a deserved UK Top 10 hit. Morrissey's commentary on the English holiday resort was one of his most pointed satires. As he wittily observed, "The idea of a resort in Britain doesn't seem natural." His dissection of the unnamed coastal town, with its greasy tea, cheap souvenirs and grey weather, prompts fantasies of Armageddon, which are all the more amusing when you consider his aversion to nuclear weapons. Back in the mid-Eighties, he spoke often about his support for CND, saying: "Above all, the world should be nuclear free. So much is at stake that if we don't get rid of nuclear weapons we're all in an immense amount of danger." Here, such danger is life's only blessing. Indeed, by the end of the song the fantasy appears to have been realized as a strange dust descends upon the disgruntled holiday-goer.

According to Stephen Street, the melody line was one of the oldest pieces of music used on the album, having been vaguely inspired by an Echo & The Bunnymen bass line that he had heard a couple of years before. "Morrissey's vocal took it somewhere else entirely. I hadn't heard the lyric before we went into the studio. But we recorded it in exactly the same format as the demo. We might have changed the key to suit his voice. With Morrissey, two or three takes and you've got a vocal take. I know John Porter felt he didn't have it in that time, but with Morrissey I felt, 'Catch him quick,' because those early performances were superb."

Andrew Paresi remembers the genesis of the recording. "'Everyday Is Like Sunday' was in the second set of recordings we did. There was nothing on that track apart from Stephen Street, who was playing bass at the same time. Vini was playing a guitar line and I was just humming along. I had the click track in my head . . . The speed of the track was pulsating in a New Order kind of way, but it was quite groovy. It had a bit of a groove going. Sometimes in a studio when you've very little to play with, particularly if there's no vocal to get off on or it's just a cowbell or a tambourine, it's useful to place a tune over the top that you might have practised or played along with. I was listening to Stephen's bass line but because I had nothing else to go on, I was hearing Steely Dan's 'Deacon Blues' in my mind and I was using the drumming from that as a kind of groove guide. What I was trying to do was play a very straightforward rhythm that had a rocking groove to it so that it didn't sound too indie England but it also didn't sound too funky. It had a nice lolloping groove about it and, in order to help me through the changes, that was the tune I slung over the top while I was playing along. But it was purely a guiding influence. When I went to hear it afterwards, it suddenly had a string section on it."

The classical flourish gave the song its haunting lilt – but was it a genuine string section? Vini Reilly claims otherwise. "'Everyday Is Like Sunday' had loads of guitars and I put hook lines in and played all the string parts on the keyboard. The Musicians' Union wouldn't have allowed the video or record to be played if it had been credited to a keyboard player because I had effectively replaced a string section so it would have been a very bad idea to credit me with having done that."

Bengali In Platforms

This controversial song actually dated back to the final days of the Smiths, minus Johnny Marr. "When Johnny left I wanted to con-tinue with the name," Morrissey later told *Record Mirror*. Although the guitarist would probably have thwarted Morrissey's wish through legal channels, the notion of simply carrying on seemed like a happy delusion. As a result, the remaining Smiths sought a replacement, sounding out several possible candidates, most notably Craig Gannon and Roddy Frame. In the end, Morrissey settled on an old friend, Ivor Perry, the guitarist in fellow Mancunian band Easterhouse.

In August 1987, the group got together at the Power Plant in London with a view to recording B-side material for likely inclusion on a posthumous Smiths single. According to Perry, two tracks were completed, an untitled instrumental and a prototype version of 'Bengali In Platforms'. "They were putting down this slightly chopped-up reggae rock on 'Bengali In Platforms'," Stephen Street recalls. "It was a totally different song. The only similarity with the version on *Viva Hate* was the title. Morrissey often carries around titles. I think the lyrics were different too with the words 'misguided Bengali'. We were in the studio and I thought, 'We might as well try and see if it works,' although I didn't have much faith in Ivor Perry and Morrissey becoming a songwriting team . . ." The idea of continuing the Smiths soon foundered and Perry was informed that his services were no longer required.

By the time of the *Viva Hate* sessions, Morrissey was ready to revive what many regard as the most controversial or offensive of his lyrics. "It's not being deliberately provocative," Morrissey later insisted, although it seems inconceivable that he was unaware of the song's underlying ambiguities. The tone throughout is politely mocking, with Morrissey commenting patronizingly on his subject's displeasing sartorial style. As if that's not enough, the singer takes on a role akin to a disdainful immigration officer, advising, 'It's hard enough when you belong here' (thereby implicitly suggesting that Bengalis *do not* belong here). 'Break the news to him gently,' Morrissey confides, as if the poor Bengali is such a fragile, pathetic creature that he might fall apart at any moment. It was small wonder that the lyrics caused people to question Morrissey's point of view, even before *Viva Hate* was issued.

After hearing a pre-release copy, *Sounds* journalist Shaun Phillips politely questioned the singer about a likely negative reaction. Morrissey was defensive, but confident. "There are so many that are obsessed with racism that one can't mention the word Bengali; it instantly becomes a racist song, even if you're saying, 'Bengali, marry me.' But I still can't see any silent racism there . . . If *you* went to Yugoslavia tomorrow, you'd probably feel that you don't belong there." This was sophistry on Morrissey's part, for the song is not about a foreigner's feelings of alienation, but the imposition of that point of view by an omniscient narrator purposely telling him to shelve his western plans. It was even more explicit in the original version's teasing 'misguided Bengali'. Some fans, seemingly immune to satire, have defended Morrissey on the grounds that he is simply advising Bengalis of the difficulties of adjusting to western ways, but such a naïve reading fails to take into account the song's unsubtle nuances. There is so much condescension, even in the description of the platform shoes, a laughably stereotypical and outdated image, although accurate enough if the scene were set in the Seventies. Indeed, the song achieves some redemption as a satire of the type of 'polite racism' prevalent during that decade when a television show like *Love Thy Neighbour* was seen as hilarious mainstream entertainment and the term 'multi-culturalism' was unknown outside sociology classes. Unfortunately, Morrissey evidently never saw 'Bengali In Platforms' as satire and even implied that the narrative was a present-day drama rather than some flashback to the Seventies. But perhaps it is best to ignore his interview comments which tend to reinforce his detractors' worst accusations.

Speaking to *NME*'s Stuart Maconie, for instance, Morrissey painted himself as a victim of political correctness. "You mustn't do it. You can't mention 'Asian' or 'Bengali' regardless of what follows lyrically, regardless of what you're trying to say about the situation." While this objection might have applied to the tabloids and certain liberal sections of the music press, it was by no means universal. Many critics have applauded Morrissey for tackling difficult subject matter – it's one of his most loved traits – but it was no coincidence that so many otherwise supportive voices saw 'Bengali In Platforms' as clumsy or supercilious.

Even Vini Reilly felt it came out wrong. "I'm not quite sure what Morrissey was getting at with 'Bengali In Platforms'. Whatever he was trying to say, I don't think that was the best way of saying it." The only mystery is that Morrissey never realized or admitted to the song's cruel, playful undertone. Perhaps the later 'racist' debate over the song is misconceived. Irony and ambiguity have always been part of Morrissey's songwriting apparatus, usually when writing about his own neuroses and psychology, but also when tackling wider issues. Although he professes a singular point of view in interviews, the songs sometimes tell a different story. He can embrace and identify with the afflicted and the outsider, but also poke fun at their failings, seemingly with the same relish as their other tormentors. Here the tone says as much as the lyrics and even the Indian sounding violin adds a slight air of ridicule to the proceedings.

Angel, Angel Down We Go Together

This time the string section *is* in force for what sounds like Morrissey's plea to a potential suicide. The Angel persona is so close to Morrissey's world-view that he might almost be addressing himself in a mirror. "I'd demoed that with Morrissey at home," recalls Stephen Street, "so I knew the lyric . . . I wanted to do it with a proper string section, which I did." Street's main inspiration in writing the original melody was Kate Bush's evocative 'Cloudbusting' from *Hounds Of Love*. Both songs share a driving, pulsating string arrangement. The orchestration suits Morrissey's voice, adding a poignant edge to the lyrics.

Judging by Morrissey's private correspondence around this time, this was the song that excited him the most. He subsequently admitted: "'Angel, Angel Down We Go Together' was written with Johnny Marr in mind . . . I saw him in the industry being used and being manipulated and I felt I was in a similar situation." As ever with Morrissey, the lyrics exaggerated real events in their fantasies of a worst possible scenario. Far from being downtrodden, Marr was fancy free and in good spirits during this period. Morrissey's 'I will be here' plea fuels false dreams of a Smiths' reunion, a fantasy most of those around him felt was an accurate representation of his feelings about the group. The song ends with the eyebrow-raising 'I love you more than life' which, given Morrissey's admissions about the song's subject, requires no further comment.

Late Night, Maudlin Street

This seven-and-a-half minute sentimental opus contained some of Morrissey's most self-pitying lyrics, alleviated by several of his most humorous. He sets the scene in 1972, amid a backdrop of power cuts and house moves, while waging an inner battle against ugliness, pill-taking, family death and fantasy love. Paradoxically, it seems that the singer's greatest act of nostalgia is reserved for a place in which he never experienced a single happy hour. The arrangement plays up the pathos to a staggering degree, but Morrissey cannot resist moments of self-effacing comedy. The phrase 'Goodbye house, goodbye stairs' sounds like Morrissey has been listening to Neil's comic version of 'Hole In My Shoe' in which he sings 'hello shoes'. The bathos reaches an apogee with the amusing riposte, 'Me – without clothes?' followed by the image of an entire nation turning away and gagging at the prospect. This revulsion was itself a reiteration of similarly self-loathing lines in the Smiths' 'Miserable Lie', not to mention an old interview where Morrissey wryly referred to his genitals as the sad product of a cosmic joke.

According to Stephen Street, the music was written during their residency at the Wool Hall studios. Morrissey had specifically requested a "long rambling structure" in the tradition of jazz-period Joni Mitchell, so Street took 1975's *The Hissing Of Summer Lawns* as an inspirational source. Vini Reilly's contribution cannot be over-estimated. "The one I really liked was 'Late Night, Maudlin Street', simply because when we did it most of the chords were mine and my particular style of playing, even though the structure of the song was Stephen Street's. As soon as Morrissey put guide vocals down, which actually was 'late at night', I was able to find an emotional kick from what he was saying. It rang true and touched me deeply."

The producer, while crediting Reilly's excellent work, contests his point about the chord sequence. "I did give Vini a lot of room, but I can play you the demo and you can tell straight away that it's 'Late Night, Maudlin Street'. I needed Vini to put in one of those ambient guitar lines . . . The chords were the same. The one chord he changed was the first chord which he made a G Major 7th instead of a G Major. The rest of the chords were exactly the same as the demo, but in a different key. Obviously, there's more than one way to play a chord – he might not have played them the way I would, but the main chords are there on the demo."

As Andrew Paresi remembers, "Stephen had taken the bass drum from a Prince song and he just had this looping guitar line running around it. It was a very straightforward bass line which he played and Morrissey had put a vocal over the whole thing. So there wasn't an awful lot there when I came in. But at least there was a guide vocal and it was that which I got a tremendous amount of inspiration from. I definitely reacted to what he was doing and what he was saying and I know Vini did too because he was playing guitar along with me at one stage. That was one of the few tracks where I could hear Morrissey singing. It made me think that if there was sufficient confidence around for Morrissey to put the vocals down first, then maybe I could go in and play some drums, or even have us all playing at the same time. Instead of having to play along to guitar sequencers or drum loops, just to actually have Morrissey's voice in the cans while I was playing was absolutely fantastic. But that didn't happen on *Viva Hate* very often. We certainly didn't play live. Stephen and Morrissey had been listening to a weird selection of songs. Amongst them was a track from *The Hissing Of Summer Lawns* with some interesting drumming from John Guerin. They'd been listening to that and they wanted some kind of jazzy, free drumming. They wanted to be freed from indie pop bland drumming on this one section at the end. So, they ran it past me a few times and then I went downstairs and did some bits and pieces. What we did was pin the first half of the second take to the second half of the first take. For me 'Late Night, Maudlin Street' was fantastic. It's very rare to get a chance on a number 1 album to play something that is completely off the wall or for the drummer to be given full rein where you can play exactly what you want. So I just let go and I was very pleased with the results. It's wonderful because it was a bit of pomp rock jazzy drumming in amongst an indie hit album, and I was very happy with that. I would like to think that what I played on that represents the pinnacle of my drumming career!"

Suedehead

Richard Allen's violent teen cult novel *Suedehead* added another Seventies reference point here, albeit in title only. The lyrics, sarcastic and vindictive in equal measure, display Morrissey's usual mixture of false humility (he's sorry) followed by sneering contempt (he's sickened). Missing from the lyric sheet was the teasing final line 'It was a good lay' which pricked ears among his following and provided more copy for the celibate exposé hunters. Musically, the track was one of the most commercial Morrissey has ever recorded and resulted in his highest UK singles chart placing of the century when it reached number 5. For Stephen Street the song represented a breakthrough in their songwriting relationship. "It was the first song we recorded for the album. I knew then it sounded really good and could work. But it wasn't until we got in a studio and cut a tune proper with Andrew and Vini, and Morrissey sang 'Suedehead', that I thought, 'Wow, this is great. It's going to work really well.'"

Reilly stresses that Street deserves full credit for the composition. "'Suedehead' was more musically Stephen Street than any of the other things. Yet that was the only thing people started to credit me with. In fact, the guitar break on 'Suedehead' is Stephen Street's tune. I play, but it's Stephen Street's tune: the lead guitar, the chorus, the structure, the whole thing is Stephen Street. If he achieved one thing he did write a good single with Morrissey. It was a good choice and began very dramatically, very up and quite hard."

That hardness was largely down to the combination of Street's strong bass line and Paresi's powerful drumming. "The bass leaps out and it's a wonderful counterpoint to Morrissey's singing," says Paresi. "I also remember giving 'Suedehead' some wellie. One of the things I did throughout the whole of *Viva Hate* was to make sure that the drums were, where necessary, *loud*. By that I mean that I hit the drums incredibly hard because that way they had much more presence. It takes a lot of energy to do that. You're quite wasted after the second or third take. But the flip-side is that the drums, even when they're low down in the mix, have great power and energy which, if you're just playing along, they don't have. You have to crank the volume up and put compressors over lots of things to get them to come to life. So I realized that the tracks that would stand out best were the ones where I really hit them very hard but very accurately as well. 'Suedehead' was one of those. It was a forward sounding drum take and I was powering away on the kit. I was extremely satisfied with the drum track. I also felt the other elements worked well. It's an unimpeachably excellent pop single."

Break Up The Family

This was apparently recorded towards the end of the album when producer Stephen Street was ill with stress. In common with several other songs here, it documents a past that is far from idyllic, but strangely inescapable. As Morrissey explained: "The song 'Break Up The Family' is strongly linked with 'Suedehead' and 'Late Night, Maudlin Street', that whole period in 1972, when I was 12, 13. [It's] about a string of friends I had who were very intense people. At that age, when your friends talk about the slim separation between life and death . . . well, if you utilized that period in a very intense way, that feeling never leaves you." Morrissey sounds trapped by the paradox of knowing that today is better while obsessing over a dead past.

The subdued, simple arrangement complements the poignant lyrics. "I really like that song," Street notes. "I think it's a really nice vocal and lyric. Great drumming from Andrew Paresi and some fine touches from Vini. Exactly the same format as I had on the demo, really. Again, I hadn't heard the lyric before we got into the studio. Morrissey just said to me, 'Can we record that one?' We did the backing track, then he sang and it sounded great. It was the same trick I'd done on 'A Rush And A Push And The Land Is Ours'. I trapped his vocal into an intimate reverb so that you get the 'aaah' effect."

Paresi takes up Street's point about the percussion. "'Break Up The Family' was putting the emphasis back ever so slightly on the drumming. By that I mean we were in the territory of a groove and it does have a groove to it. I was keen just to keep it very simple but absolutely rock solid with the click track. The only thing I played in each of the choruses was a little snare drum roll to bring us out each time. I was pleased with how that worked out."

Hairdresser On Fire
At this point, the UK version of the album began to flag somewhat but American purchasers were fortunate to have the surprise addition of this song, previously unveiled as the B-side of the single 'Suedehead'. One of Morrissey's most attractive and witty songs, its inclusion on the US album was an absolute delight. Bathos was always one of Morrissey's favourite lyrical devices, and it was seldom better executed than in this light satire. Who else but Morrissey would write a song of affectionate vengeance against a Sloane Square hairdresser who failed to fit him into his appointments book? There's the expected tale of an accident at the salon, but the fiery hairdresser emerges as a hero and is even lauded as a psychic healer. The backing, including a mock dramatic orchestral opening, simulated xylophone chimes played on a Yamaha DX-7, and some spectacular Vini Reilly guitar work, adds to the exuberant air. Morrissey tops it off with an engaging vocal, including perhaps the most memorable growl in pop since Roy Orbison's 'Oh Pretty Woman'. Among the rehearsal tapes and outtakes of *Viva Hate* is an out of tune, imperfectly worded reading of the song by Vini Reilly. "I really like that version of me

singing 'Hairdresser On Fire'," he says. "It's quite funny because my voice is unbelievably bad and I was trying to sing like Morrissey . . . We did have fun and it was brilliant."

Why this song was fobbed off as a B-side remains a mystery. "I think it was just the luck of the draw," Paresi suggests. "There was a time when it was considered as a possible album inclusion but it lost out to something else. Funnily enough, it is on the American version. From a drumming point of view 'Hairdresser On Fire' was one where I was able to react to what Morrissey was singing about. I remember the vocal in my head while I was doing it. And it was great because I could play these implausible, ridiculously complicated drum patterns flying all over the place in reaction to what he was singing in the chorus. I was very pleased and thought it came out really well. I was hitting the drums really hard but I was deliberately breaking up the choruses with these drum fills. There was just something in the song which I wanted to be completely predictable like you'd expect from the drummer. But then you suddenly get to the 'hairdresser on fire' and it was there that I lifted it up by playing the snare and hi-hat open. There was a little tag at the end of each chorus and then there'd be this little two-bar break and I thought I'd just chuck a fill in there and see what happens, something completely mad. I think there were two takes. We took the first take, then we used a bit of the second take for the outro. It was completely mad drumming but it seemed to be quite an effective counterpoint to what was going on."

The Ordinary Boys
The theme of this song was not dissimilar to 'William, It Was Really Nothing' and 'London' in its portrayal of an outsider and non-conformist attempting to escape the stifling ordinariness of small-town life. Yet there is a curious ambiguity in Morrissey's description of the vacuous boys and heartless supermarket girls who achieve happiness in spite of themselves. As he admitted: "They don't need to use their imaginations all that much, they act upon impulse – and that's very enviable. Theirs is a naturalness which I think is a great art form, which I can't even aspire to. I don't feel natural even when I am fast asleep."

With its percussive opening and waltz-time arrangement, the song started well but lacked punch. "It's not one of my favourites," says Stephen Street. "It was OK. I'd demoed that one with him so I knew exactly what it was. I'd heard the lyric before. It went down basically as we'd demoed it. I always thought 'Margaret On A Guillotine' and 'The Ordinary Boys' were the weakest tracks on the album."

Andrew Paresi was characteristically more exuberant in describing a song which, surprisingly, he saw as anything but ordinary. "'The Ordinary Boys' was one of my favourite tracks because rather like 'Break Up The Family' I just heard the need to do very little but to have a picture of some kind and paint a picture with the drums. I had this 'rock ride' which is an awful cymbal because it has such a wide sound. It just doesn't work on lots of songs but on this one it had a way of making the track sound very grey and misty and rather miserable. I kept it at the same dynamic so it would just be firing the odd ride cymbal once around the chorus. I wanted to keep this consistency, this monotony, like some steam hammer in a factory going the same way as in *Saturday Night And Sunday Morning*. I had a sense that the track demanded that but I had no idea lyrically what it was going to be like. As it turned out my instinct was right and 'The Ordinary Boys' was another story of isolation and avoiding being swept away by the mediocrity of everyone around you."

The song later inspired the naming of chart toppers the Ordinary Boys whose singer Samuel Preston subsequently attempted to extend his fame by entering Channel 4's *Celebrity Big Brother* house in 2006, alongside Morrissey's former friend Pete Burns, who gained more notoriety following a spurious suggestion that he was wearing a coat made from the skin of an endangered species of gorilla.

I Don't Mind If You Forget Me

Morrissey later complained that *Viva Hate* was severely weakened by several of the closing tracks and this may be one he had in mind. The lyrics are Morrissey by numbers: the old story of the maladjusted hero taking pyrrhic revenge on the person who once had the audacity to reject him. The Motown-influenced arrangement is pleasant and the melody catchy but never strong enough for consideration as a single. Only Vini Reilly's wasp-buzzing guitar breaks stand out as particularly funny or inventive, while the drumming is so-so. "I was very keen to keep the energy up on that," Paresi adds. "So I was doing a lot of flying around the kit and the hi-hat was going on quite intensely. Then we decided to put some synth drums over the outro which was almost electro." Even the normally effusive Street could not muster much enthusiasm for the track. "I don't think we ever captured that right on the album to be honest, but it's a good scathing lyric . . . I did that guitar. I wanted it straight and quite simple so I knew I couldn't ask Vini to do it; he'd throw an incredible wobbler. It's not one of the stronger songs. I feel that if 'The Ordinary Boys', 'I Don't Mind If You Forget Me' and 'Margaret On A Guillotine' had been taken off and we'd put on the tracks we recorded three months later ['Disappointed', 'Will Never Marry' and 'Sister I'm A Poet'] then it would have been a really strong album."

Dial A Cliché

In keeping with the underlying theme of life in the early Seventies, Morrissey looks back at a dysfunctional adolescence when a fey image was still frowned upon. It's the old 'square peg in a round hole' story which, as Morrissey knows, is something of a cliché. Hardly a candidate for *Morrissey's Greatest Hits*, it leads the album towards an uneventful close. "It was a very peculiar time for me making that record so suddenly," Morrissey admitted. "I wanted to try something different. Because of the particular status I have, where people concentrate on every comma, I reached a stage where I wanted to be entirely spontaneous, without writing the words down and memorizing them. Rather, just step into the vocal booth and sing."

Stephen Street enjoyed the song, which was his attempt to write in a Beatles' style. Vini Reilly was less impressed and felt frustrated by his minimal creative role. "I put lots of hook lines in, played French horn on a sampler on 'Dial A Cliché' and played fast and wild guitar on some tracks but, apart from that, there wasn't really anything satisfying for me. It was all too rigid, all too predictable."

Andrew Paresi agreed with Reilly's negative assessment of the song. " 'Dial A Cliché' just seemed like a very wimpy ending. I thought it might be a B-side when I first heard it with the vocal. When I saw it in the album placement I thought, 'This is a shame.' "

Margaret On A Guillotine

Here, Stephen Street's simple melody was mischievously subverted by Morrissey into a vitriolic attack on the British Prime Minister. The lyrics pleading for the PM's death made even 'Meat Is Murder' sound subtle and sensitive by comparison. The agitprop concludes with a macabre comic touch as a plangent flamenco-style guitar solo by Vini Reilly is suddenly interrupted by the thud of decapitation, followed by a deadly silence. This was a track that was often talked about but seldom loved. Speaking to *Melody Maker*'s astute critic Simon Reynolds, Morrissey admitted: "The song is silly, it's also very heavy and very brave. And I sit back and smile. Surely you can see that the very serious elements in it puts the kind of straightforward demonstration, 'Maggie Maggie Maggie – Out Out Out' protest song in its place and makes it seem trite and a little cosy?"

It's interesting to note that 'Margaret On A Guillotine' was originally considered as the title to *The Queen Is Dead*. However, you need only listen to both songs to hear how much fresher, inventive, forceful and accomplished the Smiths sounded when tackling political issues. It must have been a shock for Stephen Street when Morrissey presented his lyrics for this seemingly innocuous melody. "I was taken aback," the producer admits. "Then again, it wasn't the first time I was taken aback. I felt it was a little bit strong. But it was his domain. You don't mess with his lyrics. I remember thinking it wasn't quite what I expected! He chuckled. He's got a dry sense of humour. I went, 'Phew! Well, what can I say?' He'd just come upstairs from doing his vocals . . . All of that guitar is me apart from the acoustic at the end. I know people think Vini did all the guitar on that, but he didn't. I put down the rhythm guitar, Morrissey sang, Vini put on his little bit of Spanish guitar at the end which was beautiful and we put the guillotine chop from the BBC sound effects record. I think, in fact, it's a door being closed. It worked. It's not one of my favourites. I'm not going to defend it and say it's a brilliant piece of work, but it's an OK track."

BONA DRAG

Released: October 1990

HMV CLP 3788, CDCSD 3788, October 1990. US issue: Sire 9-26221-2,
November 1990

Bona Drag revealed Morrissey at another crossroads in his career.
Having completed *Viva Hate* in surprisingly quick time, nobody
could have anticipated the torturous delays and indecisions that
followed. At first all seemed well and anticipation was high for a new
album and possible tour. Despite impending legal problems, Morrissey
was keen to work with his former colleagues, Rourke, Joyce and
Gannon. On 22 December 1988, the Smiths' line-up *sans* Marr were
reunited onstage for a one-off performance at Wolverhampton Civic
Hall. It was a chaotic affair which ended in pandemonium. Morrissey
had suggested offering free entry to any followers who arrived
wearing a Smiths T-shirt. In the event, over 17,000 fans converged
on the city and the fraction that successfully gained admission
witnessed Morrissey besieged by well-wishers during an all too brief
seven-song set. *NME*'s Terry Staunton was at the scene to provide an
effusive commentary: "Forget Jacko, forget Bros, tonight the air is
swamped with screams that started life in the groin. The man of a
thousand wet dreams, a man who has fostered more clones than any
British singer ever is actually in the same room as us! This is not
sarcasm on the part of the writer, we are witnessing a bona fide
musical event." His colleague Danny Kelly added, "Everywhere lies
the evidence of the stir Morrissey's return has caused – twisted metal
sculptures that were recently police crush barriers, and the trampled
detritus of the campers. Constabulary and security race from potential
security breach to potential security breach. The Alamo comes to
Wolverhampton . . ." If nothing else, the gig was proof positive that
Morrissey could look forward to an invigorating tour whenever he
chose.

With three other Smiths back in camp, a full reunion seemed a
distinct possibility, but it never came about. Marr was clearly not

interested, while Gannon, Rourke and Joyce were in the strange position of performing with a singer whom they were also chasing to the High Court. What appeared to be the start of Morrissey's solo career as a live performer became little more than an exercise in stasis.

The litigation dragged on. Gannon eventually reached an out-of-court settlement of £44,000, Rourke dropped his case in return for frozen funds of £80,000, but Joyce continued the fight, never realizing that it would not reach the High Court until 1996. His claim was for 25 per cent of the Smiths' earnings, bar songwriting, rather than the 10 per cent he had been receiving. At the beginning of the Nineties, Joyce told me: "As far as I was concerned, if 10 per cent was put forward to me [originally] I probably would have accepted that, or said *maybe* I will accept that, but the fact is it never was. People who know me know that I'm not stupid enough to accept a certain percentage and then, when we split up, say I want some more. I wasn't trying to reap some benefit from the fact that the band had split up – it was more the fact that, as far as I was concerned, I was always on 25 per cent. When we split up I found out that I was on 10 per cent and I was pretty upset about it."

Outside of the Smiths, Morrissey faced further flack from his producer Stephen Street who was sufficiently concerned about their business affairs to seek an injunction, which briefly delayed the release of 'Interesting Drug'. "I didn't want to hold the single back," he told *NME* at the time, "but I still haven't received a production contract for *Viva Hate* even, and I have to protect my rights. I have to put pressure on Morrissey to speed up the paperwork – he just disappears and shuts himself away and, because he has no manager, nothing gets done. I'm very disappointed . . . it's made me look like a money-grabbing bastard whereas, really, I'm just protecting myself legally." Looking back, Street now adds, "The single wasn't delayed that much. People get the impression that because of my actions it had gone back by weeks." By the time Street's injunction was lifted, his friendship with Morrissey had been irrevocably damaged and their working relationship would not survive the year.

Unsurprisingly, Morrissey sought new producers, teaming up with Clive Langer and Alan Winstanley for 'Ouija Board, Ouija Board', which garnered the worst reviews of his career up until this point and

barely climbed into the Top 20. At least there was now the promise
of a new album, tentatively titled *Bona Drag*. By the end of 1989,
Morrissey had several tracks ready, including the still unreleased
'Striptease With A Difference'. While studio work continued, he
agreed to be interviewed by Nick Kent and spoke haughtily about his
place in pop, even stepping outside the first person as he announced:
"I find the notion of Morrissey as a continuing singing artiste in
the Nineties suddenly very, very interesting. Very challenging and
exciting. Having hit 30 and got over that particular barrier, I feel
better about my standpoint in the scheme of British pop music. And
though I dread the Nineties, I believe my position in this coming
decade is perhaps one of the most challenging and interesting things
that's ever happened in British pop music."

Hubris awaited Morrissey within weeks of this interview. The
recording sessions ended abruptly with less than half an album completed and eventually news filtered through that the project had been
cancelled. Most of the completed tracks were issued as singles and the
title *Bona Drag* was retained for this compilation album which was
issued as a stopgap between releases. Morrissey was unusually cautious about its reception, warning, "People will view it suspiciously
in England but not in the rest of the world where all those funny little
singles were never released. It was initially for the rest of the world
but EMI were determined to release it here."

Contrary to Morrissey's fears, it was a welcome release, allowing
fans and casual purchasers to savour a solo equivalent of *Hatful Of
Hollow* that once again showed how much fine work there was to be
found on the flip-sides of his 12-inch singles. *Bona Drag* still sounds
fresh. Listening to the songs it is difficult to believe that the original
lost studio album was so quickly abandoned. There is no crisis of
confidence here. Indeed, every track has merit and some of his most
underrated and strongest material can be found nestled among the
familiar hits. Of course, this is a composite, so what we are hearing
are nine Stephen Street productions with five from Langer &
Winstanley. Nevertheless, it proved a surprisingly complementary
collection of songs that performed the psychological trick of distracting attention from the current state of Morrissey's career. He had not
toured for four years, the Smiths were dead, his singles no longer

commanded a Top 10 place but, listening to this record, it was difficult to resist the conviction that further great work lay ahead. Producer Clive Langer felt it served its purpose perfectly. "We didn't have a whole album that was finished. I don't think we had the songs at that point. But we had *some* great songs. So *Bona Drag* was put together and I thought it was a really good compilation and a really entertaining album. It was quite a clever idea in the end. I didn't feel any problem sharing an album with Stephen Street songs."

Piccadilly Palare

Dogs howl as Morrissey plunges deep into Madness territory, with clanking piano and some brief dialogue from Suggs. Despite the prominent Langer/Winstanley influence it was pleasing to see Morrissey moving away from self-reflection to create new characters in song. Adventurous and humorous, the song reached a modest number 18 in the UK charts. "It's not a particularly strong song," Morrissey conceded during an interview with Len Brown. "It's not overwhelming, the subject is even slightly dated. 'Piccadilly Palare', which will receive blanket horrendous reviews, is a song about male prostitution. But I'm not running around in the street saying, 'Look at me singing about male prostitution. Isn't that incredibly unique?' I don't want plaudits for examining a new subject, but I will say that even coming across a pop record with a reasonably unique situation is in itself interesting."

As described in Neil Bartlett's book *Who Was That Man? A Present For Oscar Wilde*, 'palare' or 'polari' was a type of slang used by nineteenth-century male prostitutes. Later, this street vernacular was taken up by homosexuals as a secret language to disguise sexual predilections which, up until 1967, could result in imprisonment. Phrases such as 'sharpie homie' for policeman, 'eek' for face, 'bona' for good and reversed lettering like 'riah' for hair could be thrown freely into general conversation without fear of detection from hostile heterosexual eavesdroppers. As Morrissey elaborated to Nick Kent: "'Palare' is gypsy slang that was adopted by the theatre and in the Seventies I heard it being used by male prostitutes. They had their own code words for sizing people up and talking among themselves. The song is about male prostitution in Piccadilly . . . In the north, among people I knew, there was something oddly romantic about the whole thing. It spelt freedom. Catching a coach and spending a day in Piccadilly was extraordinary."

Morrissey's use of such slang also displayed his appreciation of *Round The Horne*, the 1960s BBC Light Programme radio comedy which introduced the outrageous and incomprehensibly camp duo Julian and Sandy, whose hilarious use of 'polari' entranced a nation of innocent Sunday afternoon listeners. Inevitably, 'Piccadilly Palare' encouraged a spate of articles translating Morrissey's 'palare' for music press and fanzine readers.

Morrissey's translation of polari into song was enjoyable, but not everybody was pleased. It came at a time when his asexual stance in the media was being questioned in the gay press, most persuasively by cultural commentator Richard Smith, a long-standing Morrissey fan who felt betrayed by his hero's evident refusal to confirm the precise nature of his sexuality: "So why all this talk? If he's just mucking about, I really don't like it one bit. If the man is merely 'posing as a sodomite' then he is doing us a disservice. I don't want a straight man to rip off our culture and profit from it through cultivating a com-mercially 'naughty' image. To steal the things that are ours and throw them out into straight society, like pearls before swine, is divorcing these things from their meanings and is cultural imperialism of the very worst kind . . . If you're not gay, then get your hands off our history. You can't steal the words from our lips just so you can embellish your songs with (pardon the pun) a bit of rough . . . Outside his never-never world where homophobia doesn't exist . . . adolescent lesbians and gays are, just as I once did, buying his records by the truckload and feeling far more miserable than he could feasibly fake as they think they're the only ones in the world due to the dearth of positive and out role models." Smith later partly retracted this attack and, in less polemic mode, acknowledged Morrissey's 'ambi-sexuality' as a liberalizing force and, presumably, a more acceptable set of 'pearls' to throw at us heterosexual 'swine' among his audience. Interestingly, in an earlier more primitive take of 'Piccadilly Palare', Morrissey undercuts the jaunty tone with a verse in which he describes the runaway boy in his 'cold water' room agonizing over the morality of his West End escapades: 'Am I really doing wrong?'

Interesting Drug

This was another social commentary from Morrissey, condemning government youth schemes and championing the escapism of recreational drugs. " 'Interesting Drug' is about any drug, legal or illegal," he pointed out. "We have to face the very simple fact that drugs can help people in many ways. Even with acid house parties and constant police invasions, it almost seems to me that whenever people in working-class situations try to enjoy themselves or escape from what is forced upon them, they are stopped. It's almost as if this current government want people to be sheepish and depressed and not seen, and whenever they attempt to break out of that bubble, they are hit on the head."

Morrissey cannot have failed to notice that his home city had become England's unofficial capital of acid house. The scene owed much to the Smiths' old rivals New Order whose journey from guitar-based miserabilism through New York disco to Ibiza-inspired rave would later culminate in the chart-topping football anthem, 'World In Motion' (more interesting for its original title 'E For England'). At the centre of the new E-culture were the Stone Roses and Happy Mondays, whose stories dominated the pages of the music press in similar fashion to the Smiths. Unfortunately, a combination of pharmaceutical excess and Mancunian *laissez-faire* bloody-mindedness would blight their progress and productivity, ensuring that there was never a legacy to rival that of the more prolific Smiths.

Engagingly light in texture, 'Interesting Drug', with Kirsty MacColl on backing vocals, was commercial enough to provide Morrissey's fourth consecutive solo UK Top 10 hit. The original lyric sheet claims that there are bad people 'on the rise' while Morrissey appears at times to sing the more accusative 'on the right'. In the video version, the word 'right' is emphatically scratched on a blackboard as if to emphasize the correct interpretation.

After the song's release, Morrissey surprised many fans and commentators by openly admitting that he had experimented with Ecstasy. "I've taken it a couple of times. The first time I took it was the most astonishing moment of my life. Because – and I don't want to sound truly pathetic – I looked in the mirror and saw somebody very, very attractive. Now, of course, this was the delusion of the drug, and it wears off. But it was astonishing for that hour, or for however long it was, to look into the mirror and really, really like what came back at me. Now even though I had that wonderful experience, and it was a solitary experience – there was nobody else present – I'm not actually interested in drugs of any kind. I'm not prudish, I don't mind if other people take them, but it's not for me."

November Spawned A Monster

This powerful single was something of a return to form for Morrissey following the unfair criticism he received over 'Ouija Board, Ouija Board'. In common with 'Interesting Drug' and 'Piccadilly Palare' the lyrics were mildly controversial with Morrissey tackling the plight of the disabled. As ever with Morrissey, the tone and sentiments are riddled with ambiguity. What seems a genuine display of sympathy is consistently subverted by the very power of the language. The most extraordinary aspect of the composition is its point of view. In attempting to strip away the offensive condescension shown towards the invalid, Morrissey does not merely empathize but appears to act out the self-revulsion of his subject and adopts a disconcertingly mocking tone as narrator. There is an element of cruelty as well as sympathy as early as the first line in which he advises the invalid to 'dream hard', because that is the closest '*you'll*' get to finding love. Later, there is sexual black comedy in the line about kissing the invalid on the mouth or '*anywhere*'. The loaded vocabulary with its deliberately provocative use of words like 'monster' and 'twisted' produces a strange mixture of revulsion, sympathy and black comedy. Like Joe Orton in the play *A Day In The Death Of Joe Egg*, Morrissey uses casual cruelty and macabre humour to disturb and enlighten his audience. Mary Margaret O'Hara's theatrical, gurgling outpouring is at once horrific, humane and comic – in keeping with Morrissey's ambiguous approach. The backing adds to the drama with some effective touches such as that strange harmonica break in the middle of O'Hara's babbling. Morrissey chooses to end the song on a note of pathetic fulfilment with the girl defiantly promising to purchase her own clothes. The genuinely moving and sympathetic tone of Morrissey's voice in the final line further complicates our response.

By adopting the ambivalent persona of tormentor and saviour, Morrissey forces the listener to confront their own prejudices head on.

As with so many songs in the Morrissey canon, from 'Suffer Little Children' onwards, 'November Spawned A Monster' presents the type of slippery ambiguities that the songwriter appears to relish. In pop terms, this is a dangerous but courageous tactic, easily open to misinterpretation. There will always be people who insist 'November Spawned A Monster' is a sick or offensive song, and it's no use telling them that their critical faculties are not sophisticated enough. They have a point. In such circumstances what Morrissey says in interviews about his intentions are only of passing consequence. In the end, it is the song that matters and, for some, the use of the word 'monster', the Hindley laugh in 'Suffer Little Children', references to a child in 'Reel Around The Fountain', the condescension in 'Bengali In Platforms' *et al* are proof enough that Morrissey's love of outrage outweighs whatever noble intentions he may claim. Others, this writer included, revel in his ambiguous point of view and are delighted by the 'controversial' darker undertones of 'Suffer Little Children', 'Handsome Devil', 'November Spawned A Monster' and beyond.

The importance of Mary Margaret O' Hara in helping Morrissey to realize the comic horror implicit in the composition proved crucial. Far more than Annalisa Jablonska in 'Suffer Little Children', O'Hara brought a spooky melodrama to the proceedings. "She's the oddest, most eccentric person I've ever met," Morrissey told Len Brown. "I went into the vocal booth and said, 'Just simply give birth,' which she most expertly did, while I stood behind with a mop and a bucket." An earlier take of the song featured more prominent feral growls from the opening of the song onwards.

O'Hara herself was evidently bemused and uncertain about her contribution. "It was strange because he just happened to ring up the record company the same week I came to England to tour for the first time. I knew the Smiths because a friend of mine loved them absolutely, so I said I'd do it knowing they wouldn't believe it. We went down to the studio and he was really nice – making tea and stuff – and he just told me to do whatever I wanted. It was kind of scary because I didn't really know what he wanted and I wasn't familiar with the song ['He Knows I'd Love To See Him'] because I didn't have a tape player for the cassette they'd sent me. But I took several takes and did something and then they said there's another song ['November Spawned A Monster'] which they played a couple of times over the monitors, and Morrissey told me he liked stuff like 'Year In Song' [from *Miss America*], so then I felt happier about going in and getting looser. I did it once and the production guys said, 'Fine,' and that was it. I don't know what Morrissey thought."

Will Never Marry

Brett Anderson once said of this song: "It's moving, human and passionate, but strangely not in an explicitly lyrical sense. There is an overwhelming feeling of loss but with desolation. I always thought it was a touching reply to a piece of fan mail." Anderson's final sentence is insightful. However, the song's tone and vocabulary are more reminiscent of a nineteenth-century epistolary novel. The polite opening line sounds like the measured response of a Victorian lady declining a marriage proposal. Morrissey's paean to solitary life is voiced with regret rather than celebration. His acceptance of the unremitting inevitability of loneliness leaves no room for the usual disarming humour or ambiguity. The sound of children playing, courtesy of a BBC sound effects record, adds a poignant edge to Morrissey's confessional.

Originally, the song appeared in longer form on the 12-inch version of 'Everyday Is Like Sunday'. "We got a lot of praise for the B-sides of that 12-inch," Stephen Street recalls. "We put three brand new tracks on it – 'Sister I'm A Poet', 'Disappointed' and 'Will Never Marry'. I think they're better than a lot of tracks on *Viva Hate*, so I felt it was really working well and Morrissey was getting the message. Those three tracks were written between Christmas 1987 and March 1988. They were all strong and helped make 'Everyday Is Like Sunday' a really good record."

" 'Will Never Marry' was much lighter in terms of drumming," adds Andrew Paresi. "I was fiddling around a lot on the hi-hat for that one. As it built I was opening the hi-hat in a funny kind of way. It worked really well but it didn't have the full-on drum parts that the other songs had demanded. So, I was really getting into the musical minutiae of the recording. I was focusing on that and I was very pleased with what I did to the point where I felt confident to say to Morrissey: 'What do you think about touring with this?'"

Such A Little Thing Makes Such A Big Difference
Given that this was the B-side of 'Interesting Drug' it is tempting to interpret the title as a coded reference to a tablet of Ecstasy. However, there are no further drug connotations in the song which offers a different type of urban commentary. Morrissey's narrator sounds like a well-meaning social worker advising a bicycle-chain-wielding delinquent on the virtues of politeness and being 'nice'. Of course, in Morrissey's world-view the notion of 'nice' is seldom, if ever, positive. In the song 'Disappointed' the word was enough to provoke him into a rant about how his life had been ruined by people who were nice. At first, he pokes fun at the heartless hooligan but even when mocking those whose brains remain between their legs, there is a grudging admiration for this triumph of instinct over intellect. By the end of the song a role reversal is effected and the plea to be left alone because '*I* was only singing' firmly identifies the criminal outsider with the singer.

In composing the music, Stephen Street was told by Morrissey, "I want you to write something that sounds like Sparks." What emerged was a keyboard-dominated piece, broken into sections, which Street attempted to piece together during an intense afternoon session in the studio. As he recalls: "There were quite a number of other songs that we tried to record that just didn't work out and I didn't think I was actually getting over to the people what I wanted. But we managed to get quite a few at that session, including 'Such A Little Thing Makes Such A Big Difference'."

The Last Of The Famous International Playboys
Morrissey's abiding affection for criminal glamour reached its apogee with this confused tale of a lad entranced by the Krays. Morrissey attempted to dissociate himself from the character in the song telling the *NME*: "I'm interested in the sense of celebrity, even on the level of murder, and the fame attached to grizzly crimes. I often wonder

why people who commit such crimes are treated like celebrities. It doesn't do the crime rate much good does it? It's interesting also the way notorious people can be quite glamorous. I don't have admiration for the Kray Twins at all but I am fascinated and almost amused that they've been confused with minor celebrities. In theory they were, but they murdered." When asked the identity of the unnamed international playboys in the title, however, he added a wry autobiographical touch by suggesting that they were Devoto, Bolan, Bowie and himself. One of the more amusing aspects of this song was that it actually prompted a reply from the still imprisoned Reggie Kray. The murderer turned music critic decreed, "I liked the tune but I thought the lyrics in their entirety were lacking a little." Kray was spot on about the melody which proved commercial enough to elevate the song to number 6 in the UK.

Morrissey seemed equally impressed: "'The Last Of The Famous International Playboys' is the first record that I feel hysterical about. And I'm very pleased to feel that way."

For Stephen Street, the song was "very straightforward, a great pop single." It also signalled a change of line-up with the departure of Vini Reilly in favour of Craig Gannon, and the return of Rourke and Joyce as rhythm section. "Suddenly the idea was to use Craig Gannon," Street remembers, "which I found quite strange because I was aware that he was going through a court procedure at the time. I thought, 'Fine,' because I'd worked with him before on 'Half A Person' and had no problem."

Ouija Board, Ouija Board

This single caused the first serious critical backlash of Morrissey's solo career, which was compounded when it failed to emulate the Top 10 success of its predecessors. Yet, it was an amusing song in the grand tradition of the death disc genre, complete with a wry punchline. As usual, Morrissey cannot resist turning the wit upon himself as he relates the perils of afterlife communication. From beyond the grave, his reluctant old friend dismisses his advances with the surly riposte, 'Steven – Push Off!' "I try and instil a degree of humour in the record," Morrissey told Mat Snow. "I know it isn't terribly apparent but I find it amusing. The song is primarily me, once again for the

8,000th time, losing faith in the human race and almost turning to the other side of life for communion and friendship."

Morrissey's dark comedy was ably captured in the memorable video of the song which featured *Carry On* star Joan Sims. But none of this could stem the ridicule from certain sections of the music press. Producer Clive Langer was nonplussed by the seemingly universal negative reaction. "We didn't understand why everyone hated it so much. We loved it. It was very light-hearted, but I really liked the sound. I thought of it like an Eno record or something soundwise. Actually, recording it was really difficult. After about two days, the session collapsed – there was just a really nervous atmosphere in the studio – and I was wandering around the garden with Morrissey and we both realized it wasn't working. So it was like, 'All right, we've had a go,' and then we wandered back to the studio where Alan [Winstanley] was mixing the B-side and it sounded great."

Co-writer Stephen Street was surprised to learn that the song was scheduled as the follow-up to 'Interesting Drug'. "I went to see Morrissey and he said, 'I want to do this track.' It was 'Ouija Board . . .' which I wrote in my attempt to do an Eno-type keyboard track. I saw it as an album track but I never saw it as a single."

Understandably, Morrissey made no great claims on behalf of the song, but was stoical about the criticism, telling Len Brown: "While I admit that 'Ouija Board, Ouija Board' wasn't 'Chirpy Chirpy Cheep Cheep', I do think the backlash has been slightly overdone . . . But I don't mind that 'Ouija Board, Ouija Board' never received an Ivor Novello award. I never believed that sitting on top of the pop arena was a nice place to be."

Several interviewers questioned Morrissey on his interest in spiritualism which, at the time, seemed genuine. During his late teens he had written to several people about everything from ghosts to flying saucers, even vividly describing the presence of a troubled spirit at his home at 384 King's Road, Stretford, on Friday 18 April 1979. When he confided these experiences to his mother, she admitted that she had also felt this chilling 'presence' and, after further research, they concluded that it was probably the spirit of a 50-year-old woman who had died on the premises. Oddly, when later speaking about his supernatural experiences to the magazine *Q*,

Morrissey told a suspiciously similar story, relocating the place and time. "I had an experience in 1984. I lived in a rented flat for a while and there was definitely a presence, and a friend of mine who is a medium came to the flat and I didn't tell her that I'd had vibrations. When she came in she immediately went into a semi-trance, walked around every corner of the flat and stood outside the bathroom door and said, 'It's here.' It's coincidental that each time I'd stepped outside the bathroom, even though I'd always kept the heating on high, I'd felt a great chill. I found out that somebody had died in the flat – the usual story."

His ghostly anecdotes continued when he visited New York in November 1991. Speaking on WDRE FM, he said: "Yes I do believe in the afterlife. I have a very open mind and I have tried a few things . . . If you stare into a mirror at midnight in a completely darkened room with a candle below your face, your face supposedly changes into a face of somebody who has died and who wants to reach you or somebody who has died and doesn't particularly want to reach you . . . It's extremely frightening because most people's faces do change automatically and it's not just a matter of darker shades of a moustache."

In England, Morrissey found himself back in the tabloids following a hysterical snippet suggesting that his single might promote occult dabbling or devil worship. He retorted with the memorable quip: "The only contact I ever made with the dead was when I spoke to a journalist from the *Sun*." Judging from more recent comments, Morrissey has become increasingly sceptical in middle age and now claims that he does not believe in any afterlife. "You're born, you live, you die and that's the end."

Hairdresser On Fire
Although this appeared previously as a B-side and featured on the American edition of *Viva Hate*, many people first heard the song on *Bona Drag*. A superlative production, it opens like a film theme as Morrissey takes us to the centre of the action in London's Sloane Square. According to Andrew Paresi, the story of Morrissey visiting the magical hairdresser was partly autobiographical. "I think it did stem from a real incident . . . You can imagine all kinds of interesting

hair-styling ideas being discussed over Morrissey's head as he sits mumbling, 'Well, actually, no, I just want to keep my quiff.'" Probably the finest B-side of Morrissey's career, the song revealed some excellent interplay between Reilly's sinewy guitar work and Paresi's powerful drumming. Morrissey later revived the song, famously performing an irreverent version at his 45th birthday celebration in Manchester where he changed the words to 'psychologically *shave* me', '*stoned* around Sloane Square' and 'too busy to *kiss me*'.

Everyday Is Like Sunday

It seems strange to hear this famous song so late on the album. Perhaps its placing was indicative of Morrissey's ambiguous feelings about featuring so recent an album track on successive releases. No doubt its UK Top 10 success ensured its inclusion here. "When 'Everyday Is Like Sunday' came out it received tons of airplay and hit the charts in a really strong position," Stephen Street remembers. "I think Morrissey then realized, 'This is working.'"

Andrew Paresi was equally impressed when he heard the orchestrated version played on the radio. "Everything was deep in reverb and it was a brilliant single. The moment I heard the chorus I just knew 'that's gonna be a big hit single'. It felt like a classic, which is a wonderful feeling if you've never played on a classic single before. That suddenly does hit you in quite a big way. You think, 'My God, that's me on that hit single.' So it was great." Clearly, by siphoning the best moments from *Viva Hate* the compilers ensured that an album of even greater quality was created.

He Knows I'd Love To See Him

The fact that Morrissey hadn't seen Johnny Marr since the Smiths' split was enough to convince the world that this was a thinly disguised letter to the guitarist. Maybe it was. Then again, it could have been directed towards his old friend Johnny Daly or others from his secret past. With vocal assistance from Mary Margaret O'Hara, Morrissey reflects on a seemingly forbidden friendship that is either repressed or can only proceed in subtle degrees of closeness – as much as 'is allowed'. O'Hara's presence ensures that Morrissey is able to blend his singing perfectly, sounding both passionate and resigned, even within the space of a single line. Midway through the song Morrissey switches attention to a recent drama in his life when he was interviewed by the police after wishing death on the Prime Minister in 'Margaret On A Guillotine'. Assuming Morrissey's account was not invented, the visit seemed a severe over-reaction. "Yes, ridiculous grounds," he agreed. "But they don't need grounds, they've got a funny little hat and a truncheon. They recorded a conversation for an hour and searched the house for a guillotine. Curiously, they found one. They thought I was public enemy number 72. And at the end of the grilling they actually asked me to sign various things for ailing nieces, which I thought was a bit perverted." After listening to the constabulary's caustic comments on his bedroom radicalism and lazy behaviour, the narrator turns the tables by languidly agreeing with every thing they say. The tone of world-weary resignation in the phrasing of 'I know I do' sums up his subversive stance with a wonderful flourish of irony.

Yes, I Am Blind

Co-written with Andy Rourke, this was a lyrically morbid diagnosis of Morrissey's neurosis in which anything positive must always remain unseen. At one point, Morrissey takes his case to the celestial court, invoking a Marlovian atheism that recalls Tamburlaine's cry for God to come down from the heavens. Literary analogies abound. If not Marlowe's *Tamburlaine The Great*, then there is the telling comparison with Milton's *Samson Agonistes* – the blind, fallen hero demanding one last favour from the Saviour. There's also a touch of *King Lear* in the declamatory title, especially when you consider Morrissey's pun on that same title on the succeeding *Kill Uncle*. The anti-Christian sentiments in the last verse are undeveloped, just at the point when they are getting interesting. Oddly, Morrissey uses the lamb – a symbol of Christianity – as the object of slaughter by Christians rather than Romans. He would take up this theme in more light-hearted vein later in his career with 'I Have Forgiven Jesus'.

Musically, 'Yes, I Am Blind' shows signs of the Smiths' influence in its attractive acoustic guitar flourishes. Rourke consciously fashioned a bridge connecting Morrissey with his past, but alas their working relationship failed to last. Only one song of theirs remained on the cutting-room floor. "There was an orchestral arrangement which he liked but he couldn't really get a grasp on," Rourke remembers. "That was the only one he didn't really use. I sort of wrote songs to order. He'd phone up and say: 'I want this sort of song or that sort of song.' I'd write them with that in mind."

Lucky Lisp

The title puns on Cliff Richard's 1963 hit 'Lucky Lips' with Morrissey placing himself in the role of the super-fan, fully indulging his hero worship with some light ironic touches. So whom, if anyone, might Morrissey have been thinking of? Again, the name Johnny Marr comes to mind, especially when you consider how he occasionally pronounced his 'r' and 'w' sounds. Or could it be Marc Bolan whose 'Larry The Lamb' vocal inflexions were initially deemed uncommercial but later became a distinctive pop parlance? Whatever the source, Morrissey's tonsorial and lyrical touches transform the composition. It's full of clever internal rhymes and ascending lines that create a sense of euphoria. During one verbal aside, Morrissey even rhymes 'fool' with 'fool' and makes it sound original and funny. In common with the preceding 'Yes, I Am Blind' there is a sprinkling of religious imagery, with the saints themselves shining their beatific approval upon this fortunate son. Stephen Street's clean, sharp production is given greater scope by the percussion, particularly the DX-7 xylophone effect which sounds like peeling bells of celebration as Morrissey proclaims his fan worship.

Suedehead

Arguably, the most commercially successful song of Morrissey's solo career is tucked away almost unnoticed as the penultimate track on the album. With its distinctive combination of guitar and keyboards, this showed the Street/Morrissey relationship to best effect in the pop market-place. It sounded sparkling and new, but also strangely familiar, largely due to the fluid bass line which Street admits was strongly influenced by the work of Andy Rourke. The lyrics contain lashings of irony with Morrissey offering humble entreaties in a polite voice that is nevertheless full of vituperation and contempt. For those who bought *Viva Hate* this was probably one single too many and Morrissey was no doubt aware of this. Its inclusion draws attention to those other tracks from the period that failed to win a place on the compilation: 'I Know Very Well How I Got My Name', 'Oh Well, I'll Never Learn', 'Sister I'm A Poet', 'Michael's Bones', 'East West', 'Girl Least Likely To', 'Get Off The Stage' and 'At Amber'.

Unusually, the musicians involved in 'Suedehead' had the pleasant experience of collectively hearing the song become a hit. Having returned to the Wool Hall to record additional B-side material for 'Everyday Is Like Sunday' in February 1988, their ears were glued to the radio in anticipation of a massive chart smash. "There was a feeling that this is going to go," Paresi remembers. "The album hadn't been released but 'Suedehead' was getting played on Radio 1. John Peel was also playing it, along with one of the B-sides. It was being played three to four weeks before release on rotation. So it was great just to hear that and think, 'Wow.' A wonderful experience. This was the first time I'd ever heard my drumming coming through radio speakers on average every two-and-a-half hours. Everyone was playing that song and it was a great pop single. It was the archetypal Morrissey pop record. It had everything – the inbuilt fizzy excitement and that wonderfully laconic voice over the top. It was a brilliant piece of work and construction. So from a radio producer's point of view it was the perfect song. It had the risk element in it but it also had the beauty and that wonderful pop dimension."

Disappointed
This had to be the closing track, given its marvellously humorous ending. As Morrissey announces his retirement the assembled crew cheer, then jeer when he adds that he's again changed his mind. The 'Goodnight and thank you' not only concludes the album on an appropriate note, but serves as a farewell to Vini Reilly whose simmering guitar work, alongside Paresi's powerful drumming, makes this track one of the most memorable of Morrissey's minor works. Despite the quality of the song, producer Stephen Street had few fond memories of the recording. "The tension with Vini had got even worse. That session was unbearable . . . but I still loved 'Disappointed', especially the line, 'This is the last song I will ever

sing'. You can hear Andrew Paresi, Vini, engineer Steve Williams and me doing the 'aahs' in the background."

Although Street remembers the session as a fractious affair, Paresi was blissfully unaware of any tensions, partly because of his excitement over this recording. "Oh joy of joys," he exclaims. "My memory of that session is that even Vini didn't seem to protest too much about playing. But he and Stephen may think differently. Stephen had sent me a copy of 'Disappointed' and I went away and thought about how to play it because it was a very powerful groove. I knew that if I played it right then the song would benefit. So I worked out something where I could have the hi-hat coming all the way through, like disco, and then have this glammy tom-tom pattern going on. That way, the whole thing could trundle its way through the mix like a steam engine. This also meant we wouldn't have to do an overdub which would have been boring. So I was really happy that I'd come up with this pattern . . . I'd written a bit of drumming and I'd got it on to this track and it was *de facto* a definition of disappointed. Everyone loved it. I can say that with confidence."

KILL UNCLE

Released: March 1991

HMV CSD 3789, CDCSD 3789, March 1991. US issue: Sire 9-26514-2,
March 1991

Kill Uncle was a puzzling record. Sparse and superficial, it had none of the momentum of *Viva Hate* nor the breadth of *Bona Drag*. At just over 33 minutes, it was insubstantial to the point of insult. So what happened? The history of *Kill Uncle* is a complex story with no easy answers. By the time of its completion the singer was tired of the long studio sessions and seemingly uncertain about the work's merits. A few months before the album's release I phoned Morrissey at his Cheshire home and he seemed disconcertingly weary of everything, with a Greta Garbo-like attitude to fame, albeit with a customary tinge of gallows humour. "I feel pretty fatigued to be honest," he told me. "I'd rather just, as much as I can, stay in a cupboard at the end of the foot of the stairs." At the time, he had no official band, no plans to tour and seemingly no zest for life. More than anything, this might explain the jaundiced quality of *Kill Uncle*, an album bereft of passion, drama or any deeply held conviction or emotion. Upon its release, Morrissey could barely muster any enthusiasm for its content. "It's a very simple album, a pop record that can be easily appreciated. That's its only purpose. It was high time I made a straightforward record . . . This album won't threaten anybody, nobody will be traumatized by it but, having said that, this record is unapologetically me."

Despite its brevity *Kill Uncle* was far from a rushed affair and had been in gestation for an age. The abandoned *Bona Drag* sessions arguably contained superior songs which, had they been allied to the poppier songs herein, might have produced a minor classic. Instead Morrissey seemed intent on pursuing a lighter pop direction, minus the melodrama and confessional intrigue that most people considered his forte. "The fact is we were in this very English pop territory," argues drummer Andrew Paresi. "These were great pop records he was making and in theory this was a great trajectory to be on at the

163

time. I thought things like 'Ouija Board, Ouija Board', 'November Spawned A Monster' and 'Piccadilly Palare' were great songs. We had people like Suggs and Mary Margaret O'Hara coming in. It was just a fantastic mixture. To me it had all the right hallmarks of a great album."

A surprise feature of the later recordings was Morrissey's decision to abandon Langer and Winstanley as co-writers in favour of Mark Nevin, a light pop specialist most famous for composing Fairground Attraction's catchy chart-topper 'Perfect'. "Mark's a very creditable songwriter," Paresi notes, "a songwriter to the bone. So Morrissey felt confidence in him and that explains why Mark went on to do some stuff on *Your Arsenal*. He could have done a lot more. With Clive, Alan and Mark, it was a really good team."

Nevertheless, Nevin was perplexed by Morrissey's working methods which largely consisted of requesting tapes through the post with little or no feedback. "I never really knew what he liked about me and I didn't know what he wanted me to do . . . He wouldn't send me the lyrics or tell me what they were about. He wouldn't even tell me the titles."

Nevin was understandably tentative about his contributions which were often preliminary sketches or song fragments which he expected to flesh out after consultation with Morrissey. There was no consultation. Instead, Morrissey listened to the tapes over time and suddenly announced, "I've finished the album!"

With this material in hand, they entered the studio but the songs obviously required considerable attention. "We'd record a track," Nevin remembers, "then Morrissey would come in, hear the song for the first time and sing the guide vocal. Clive Langer embellished what we did. But all the time, I was thinking, 'How can this work? This can't work.' It was amazing how it worked at all."

Langer and Winstanley spent considerable time attempting to improve the songs, but there were clearly moments of uncertainty. By Morrissey standards, a large amount of material, including fragments, backing tracks and even completed songs, languished on the cutting-room floor. Earlier, there had been a fleeting attempt at a Stephen Street tune, 'Jodie's Still Alive', which nobody revived. Presumably the recent dispute with Street discouraged Morrissey from seeing it through to release. There was the powerful 'Oh Phoney' with its passing reference to Hitler, the shelved 'Striptease With A Difference' and the comic macabre 'Kill Uncle', inspired by the mid-Sixties film *Let's Kill Uncle*. None of these were in contention when the final order of tracks was selected.

Apart from Nevin, there was no shortage of songwriters ready to assist and Morrissey had already received a constant supply of backing tracks for consideration. Paresi remembers: "At the tail end of the *Bona Drag* sessions we had Andy Rourke supplying songs, Kevin Armstrong offering material and me putting my stuff in. It quickly became clear that Clive Langer's songwriting was attracting Morrissey's attention. I think we had an album's worth of songs and they were good. Clive was a real music machine at that point. He would constantly be giving him stuff and the tracks that Clive thought were good were often the ones Morrissey would reject. He actually tried to bridge the gap between 'Ouija Board, Ouija Board' and 'November Spawned A Monster' with as many songs as possible to keep Morrissey inspired. Everyone was putting stuff in the pot. And this was the object of all of us, even when we weren't in the studio. So there was lots to choose from."

Given this wealth of material, it seems doubly amazing that *Kill Uncle* was so short. The selection now looks embarrassingly lightweight, as if they were struggling to find enough songs to fill the album which was not the case. While some tracks impressed, others were as dull as dish water with sparse melodies and trite lyrics. Looking back, Nevin is phlegmatic about his contribution. "It was nobody's baby that record. Obviously I started to realize that in the Smiths, Morrissey had his role and Johnny Marr had his role which was musically to lead the band . . . I loved the Smiths as much as anybody else. As a fan, I'd have preferred Morrissey to have got back with Johnny than make a record with me because that would have been brilliant. I didn't do what I wholeheartedly felt I should have because I was trying to double guess what Morrissey might want . . . Without Marr there, Morrissey needed someone to do that. Previously, Stephen Street did that but he'd been with them for years and knew how it worked. When we did that record Clive was the nearest person to that but I think he really wanted to be writing the songs as well as producing. So it wasn't his baby any more. I think a record has to have a parent, somebody to say, 'This is *my* record, this is *my* baby.'"

Incredibly, just as the album was being signed off, Morrissey had a rush of blood to the head. Nevin remembers that when they returned to London, Morrissey spent Thursday nights visiting the Camden Workers' Social Club watching some younger musicians playing rock 'n' roll. Suddenly, he seemed re-energized. "We hadn't stopped doing *Kill Uncle*," Nevin stresses. "We were mixing it and a lot of things were being done in the studio. One day Clive rang me up and said, 'Can you write a rockabilly album? We want to go straight into the studio and carry on.' So we started this rockabilly thing. I sent Morrissey some tracks and guitarist Boz Boorer came in with Jonny Bridgwood on bass and Woodie Taylor on drums. The first songs we did were 'Pregnant For The Last Time', 'Born To Hang' – which wasn't released – plus 'The Loop'. We did a few tracks but then Morrissey just decided not to do it."

Given the brevity of *Kill Uncle* it was regrettable that the new tracks could not have been developed and added to the work during post-production. "The amount of studio time was probably getting silly," Nevin suggests. "Maybe Morrissey thought, 'What's the point?'" By this stage, the new album was overdue and Morrissey was no doubt acutely aware of the problems he had faced the previous year when the original *Bona Drag* had been scuppered. Another volte-face would probably have proven a nightmare. More importantly, having found some new musicians who looked the part, Morrissey was keen to get back on the road at the earliest opportunity.

Whatever reservations had been felt about the new album were evidently forgotten after hearing the final playback. Langer and Winstanley professed satisfaction with the work and Nevin admits he felt the same. "I loved it at the time. It's difficult to be objective about it now."

Surprisingly, initial reviews in the music press suggested that *Kill Uncle* was a winner. *Select* magazine proffered an impressive four out of five rating while the *NME* reckoned it was worth an exceptionally generous 8 out of 10. Reviewer David Quantick concluded: "*Kill Uncle* is a collection of songs that are both very good and like nothing much else in pop. They range every which way across styles and themes and they still sound like only Morrissey could have sung them. *Kill Uncle* bodes immensely well for the future, not least because this is the first Moz album where half the songs are about someone other than himself."

The accolades proved short-lived and the chart statistics gave a truer reflection of the album's worth. Despite all the anticipation, it entered at a disappointing number 8, only to plummet the following week. Worse still, *Melody Maker*'s Steve Sutherland savaged the work in one of the most damning album reviews ever published. The paper's readership were left in no doubt that he considered Morrissey a sorry, spent force. "*Kill Uncle* is Morrissey comfortably slippered, feet on the pouffe, tea and scones, and a welcome guest in the home of the so-bad-it's-good Sally Army. *Kill Uncle* is Morrissey revelling in mediocrity . . . *Kill Uncle* is such a tragic, turgid, pathetic record one can only assume it's an act of spite . . . I guess it's a miracle that *Kill Uncle* exists at all, considering its overriding impulse appears to be that the world doesn't deserve it. But if Morrissey thinks he has framed himself in a halo of righteousness by putting out an album that makes a virtue of not mattering any more and, furthermore, if he reckons we give a shit that he's making a meal of not mattering, he's got another think coming. So Morrissey doesn't matter any more. OK. RIP."

Morrissey was not about to lay down and die. A world tour was immediately booked to promote *Kill Uncle*, signalling the end of a strange period of indecision. Appearances in the UK, USA and Japan gained him fresh column inches and also distracted attention from the more negative aspects of the album by allowing critics to focus on his charisma as a performer. Some of his former collaborators, most notably Stephen Street and Mark Nevin, were appalled by these shows and the band's rough treatment of their material. Others concluded that Morrissey was disguising the weaker moments of *Kill Uncle* by transforming its lightness into a barrage of sound. For some, the album now served as a touching memento celebrating his return to the stage and first tour in five years.

Unfortunately, when the tour ended some niggling questions returned and Sutherland's scabrous views gained currency. Was

Morrissey effectively a jaded creative force now reduced to parodying his finer moments in the Smiths? Was *Kill Uncle* the nadir of his career? Such questions dogged the album down the years and there were no positive critical reappraisals. Finally, in 2004, *Q* commissioned a special edition featuring the Smiths and Morrissey which boasted 'every album reviewed'. Tellingly, perhaps, the person chosen to celebrate *Kill Uncle* was David Quantick, the same journalist who had provided that pleasing review in *NME* back in 1991. Looking back, Clive Langer feels the album was something of a lost opportunity. "I suppose I thought we were going to continue from where 'November Spawned A Monster' had gone and that maybe I would be more involved, but I had a good time with Mark and everybody. I just accepted it. Morrissey didn't choose the kind of music that I would necessarily choose but it was my job to make the most of what I'd been given and that's what I felt we did, and it was really enjoyable. But it was really an album out of time . . . I'm always disappointed when things don't go well that I've worked on. I was disappointed because it felt like a personal record . . . but it was a very unfashionable album."

Our Frank

Appropriately, the album's opening track was in correct chronological sequence with the recording sessions. "The first song we did was 'Our Frank'," Mark Nevin confirms. "I remember me and Mark Bedford, who played bass, were wetting ourselves because we were very nervous. Morrissey is unnerving: he's so quiet and looks so amazing and cool with his quiff and glasses. He stands there and looks just like Morrissey – and that's amusing. When he came into the vocal booth, he started to sing and they put an Elvis-like echo on his voice. We got to the chorus and he's singing about being sick over somebody's 'frankly vulgar red pullover'. Mark and me were wetting ourselves and trying to keep it together with tears running down our faces. First day nerves. It was a release of tension as much as the effect of the lyrics."

Morrissey's plea for some frivolous conversation is set against a raga-like violin backing which leads into a piano break reminiscent of both Madness and Roxy Music. Nevin's original demo was very

stark so the producers added some vocal effects courtesy of an Eventide Harmonizer. "It was quite folky when we started," noted Clive
Langer. "We booted it up a bit and the intro is actually the same as
the outro . . . For that main chorus I was thinking early Roxy with
the ding-ding-ding piano chords and stuff . . . The end vocal effect is
just a preset in the Eventide Harmonizer."

The lyrical tone was similar to the equally scathing and sarcastic
'Frankly Mr Shankly'. Midway through, Morrissey demands a smoke,
an odd request given his aversion to tobacco. "I despise cigarettes,"
he once told an interviewer, although several ex-Smiths recall him
saying, "Give me a ciggy," after consuming too much alcohol during
the 1986 tour. On the later *Kill Uncle* tour, the 'cigarette' line
prompted fans to litter the stage with 'ciggies'.

Despite being issued as a single prior to the album's release, 'Our
Frank' only climbed to number 26, evidence enough of Morrissey's
sudden commercial decline. During an interview between Johnny
Marr and *NME*'s Danny Kelly, the song was spitefully referred to as
'Alf Wank'. Although the lyrics are ostensibly superficial and inconsequential, the repeated plea to cease thinking so deeply about
matters probably summed up Morrissey's feelings at the time and may
well explain his approach to the entire album.

Asian Rut

Classically trained violinist Nawazish Ali Khan added further raga
touches to this track which complemented the theme of racial unrest.
Morrissey's melodrama focuses on the righteous vengeance of an
Asian boy who is felled in an uneven fight against white oppressors.
Unlike 'Bengali In Platforms' the lyrics do not invite controversy,
although Morrissey still suffered criticism in some quarters simply for
tackling the racial theme. There is a sense of detachment in the
reporting of the slaying and even the narrator, who is merely passing
through the area, admits that what he hears is second-hand ('as far as I
can tell'). As a result, the Asian is poorly characterized, a mere sketch
on a police officer's report. His sole significant trait is that he has only
one friend in the world for whom he is ready to lay down his life.

Morrissey's decision to transform the melody into a 'death song'
was no doubt inspired by the bleak-sounding arrangement. "The

track I sent him for it was called 'Idiot's Funeral'," Nevin recalls. "Normally, I never titled a song but for some reason I did with that. It had this funereal quality. If you just listened to the music you'd say it sounded like an idiot's funeral."

Roger Beaujolais, then a member of the Chevalier Brothers, played vibraphone on the track but failed to receive a namecheck in the credits. "There was something about Morrissey not wanting to have that name on it because he thought it was stupid. I think he said, 'We'll have him, but not the name.' He wouldn't have Steve Nieve's name in the credits either. So he became Steve Heart. When Morrissey did the vocal on 'Asian Rut', it was fantastic and I thought it was an amazing song. I really loved it."

Co-producer Alan Winstanley was also impressed. "I liked the harmonium on it. It was just lying in one of the bedrooms in the house, so we got it down, and it was a bit out of tune so we had to varispeed the tape, but it sounded perfect."

"It was just a case of colouring the track in," added Clive Langer. "The tune was pretty doomy anyway, and Mark had most of the parts, so it was just a case of creating a really dramatic backdrop for the lyrics, which are like a poem really. A lot of the songs were like poems . . . While we were making the album, I kept thinking about Lou Reed's *Transformer* . . . Lou Reed just kept telling the stories and the music's very simple. Hopefully we achieved something along those lines. The use of the violins and the double bass sort of gave it a Victorian air."

Sing Your Life
Morrissey's love of simple pop was crystallized in this track. The minimal chord sequence and delicate, fragile arrangement enhanced his DIY guide to pop stardom. The subject of his confidence boosting lyrics, if indeed it was a particular person, remains unstated although it sounds suspiciously like he is addressing his younger self. 'Sing Your Life' is evidence enough of the gap between the flat-voiced Morrissey of 1982–83 and the measured assurance on display here. Issued as a single, the song reached a paltry number 33, ending Morrissey's run of Top 30 hits. Its slight air was clearly of concern to the producers, who brought in keyboard player Steve Heart to add texture to the arrangement. As Clive Langer told journalist Tom

Doyle: "It was always a very simple sort of chord sequence, and Morrissey came up with these words and it was our job to try and make a great pop record out of it. We mixed it once and then decided it wasn't really happening, so we got Steve to do a string arrangement on it which we wanted to sound like an old Adam Faith record, and that's really when the track came alive. We gave Morrissey's voice that early Sixties' vocal sound with the short delay. I think the song just gets better and better as it goes along, which is good because it's so frighteningly lightweight."

Recorded towards the end of the sessions at a time when Morrissey was showing an interest in rockabilly, the song included Suggs as guest vocalist. The Madness frontman was probably not alone in wondering whether the lyrics might have been written about him. " 'Sing Your Life' was a lovely song. It was one of those songs where you think, 'Was that written about me?', as you often do being as egotistical as we are in this industry . . . The sentiment of it was that anyone can sing as long as you're singing with your own voice and you sing about things you understand which is very important to me as an artiste in my own career. I just remember we did a vaguely yobbish chorus possibly with a drink or two, a crowd sequence, and I think it turned out very well."

Mute Witness
Co-written by Clive Langer, this tune owed much to the influence of Roxy Music. Indeed, the opening sounds uncannily like 'Virginia Plain'. "Clive refers to himself as 'Clanger' because of his piano playing," Mark Nevin reveals. "He put that piano on everything, which I wasn't too keen on. I preferred guitars."

According to Langer: "We'd been talking about Sparks a lot and I sent Morrissey a demo of this track I'd written which had that feel on the piano. Since I was in a pop/rock Seventies band [Deaf School] who used to emulate Roxy Music a lot of the time, it kind of comes naturally to me, so that's why it ended up like it is. It worried me whether it fitted into the album or not, simply because it was a song I'd co-written." Alan Winstanley felt the music was reminiscent of Mott The Hoople and recalls a wild synthesizer part that originally appeared throughout the song, but was later cut and pasted on the end.

Lyrically, Morrissey presents a comedy of the afflicted, just as he had done in parts of 'November Spawned A Monster'. Although the tone is less serious on 'Mute Witness', the narrator's mockery is relentless as he describes the confusion caused by the mute, adding that it would have been easier if she'd never appeared as a police witness. The benign condescension reaches a peak in words that might more accurately be applied to a performing animal ('see her move in time so nicely') and the final dismissively polite 'my dear' as the unfortunate mute is bundled into a taxi. Although it was refreshing to hear Morrissey moving away from self-analysis into social observation, his cruel wit had limited comedic appeal. This was not so much a commentary on people's attitudes towards the disabled as an excuse for Morrissey, the playful narrator, to have some fun conjuring a 'hilarious' drama about an overexcited mute witness. It spoke volumes about his dark sense of humour that he should consider the subject matter amusing.

As elsewhere on the album, Morrissey's singing was impressive and Langer, like John Porter and Stephen Street before him, noted a tendency to insert vocals in unexpected places. "Morrissey's backing vocal in the instrumental was quite amazing. In fact, he didn't put it in the instrumental, he put it in the chorus, but then we moved it. He's got a great pop sense which people don't realize. I think for a long time he was singing within a certain range and [then] opened up a little . . . We were surprised when we first worked with him how precise he was and how sure he was of exactly how he was trying to sound . . . His first take could be the best, but we always did three or four of them. Even the guide vocals were good sometimes."

King Leer

This appallingly bad pun was made worse by the lyrics, which were probably the worst of Morrissey's career, thus far. The wordplay was cringeworthy at times with Morrissey acting out the role of a pathetic suitor whose final achievement is merely to bore a selfish girl. There is a touch of sexual innuendo in the attempt to lay beside her but, predictably in Morrissey's fictional universe, nothing physical happens. If the lyrics lacked inspiration, then the melody and arrangement were little better. "It's funny isn't it?" Nevin remarks. "I don't know! There was that line about the boyfriend with one knee! It's like elevator music, isn't it? Da da da . . . What I found frustrating was that afterwards I felt, 'Now, I know how he works,' and I would have done things differently in the first place. I was sending him what I thought was a sketch of an idea and he would take it as the finished song. I thought he'd come back and say, 'I like it but we need a middle bit,' or something. Often the songs didn't have a middle because I wanted to see where the first bit went before thinking about the middle. But he thought it was a finished track. There was no communication. The songs could have been more complete if I'd known the way he worked."

Drummer Andrew Paresi was also perplexed by the song's inclusion on the album. " 'King Leer' to me was the weakest song. I didn't quite get it. I found that one the most difficult. I didn't quite see what the point of it was. And once again, what I am playing? The brushes! I'm convinced that it's me playing brushes which is the kiss of death for these songs. I've just got to stay away from them. Not that there's any connection to be made there!" Langer and Winstanley were left with the unenviable task of transforming the basic track into something listenable. After replacing the guitars with piano, Langer heard what sounded like a 'tea-room dancing song' in his head, but the results proved ultimately uninspiring.

Found Found Found

According to Langer this tune was "knocked out in about five minutes" at a time when they were thinking about likely B-sides. Although an obvious attempt to add some musical weight and sonic variety to the album, it partly succeeded in distracting attention from the predominantly lighter material. Mark Nevin plays a Hofner Violin bass, just like Paul McCartney, while Langer provides the heavy guitar work, backed by programmed drums. The lyrics are both portentous and platitudinous and sound as rushed as the music. There's even a possible borrowing from Noël Coward's 'If Love Were All' ('I do believe the more you give your love . . .'). Discussing the lyric, Morrissey said: "It's more of a reflection upon what happens in your life when you don't find somebody. Because I think we all secretly must believe that it may take a hundred years but we will eventually find someone with whom we're fantastically compatible. At the core of the song is not really finding that person, but wondering what will happen if I don't." One long-standing myth about the lyric is that it was specifically written for R.E.M.'s Michael Stipe. This piece of conjecture, usually stated as fact in media profiles of Morrissey, can be traced back to an interview in *Select*. After commenting on 'Found Found Found', Morrissey was casually asked *in the very next question* about his recent friendship with the R.E.M. vocalist. Neither he nor the journalist made any direct comparisons between Stipe and the song but the placing of the quotes encouraged others in search of good copy to connect the two. Morrissey's actual words were, "I don't think I mention sexuality in the song at all. But even in the limited capacity of finding a real friend and realizing that it actually does take a lifetime to find one, I'm always slightly exalted by coming across someone with whom one has an instant rapport, an instant harmony . . ."

Driving Your Girlfriend Home

Probably the most attractive pop melody on the entire album, this gossamer production, complete with prominent bass and an attractive backing vocal from Morrissey's friend Linder, showed how strong the work might have been with a keener sense of discrimination. Indeed, the song might have been even more powerful if she had sung the girlfriend's part alone. As it stands, it was probably too fragile to release as a single. "When we'd first finished the album, for months after – this was my favourite," Langer remarked to Tom Doyle. "I love the pathos in this track . . . it feels like a musical journey from the beginning to the end, really satisfying . . . We got up to our old tricks a bit on this one, a few backwards bits and stuff."

Paresi was equally impressed. "It was beautiful. I loved Mark's work on that, particularly the chord structures which were gorgeous. A beautiful song."

In common with the narrator of 'King Leer', Morrissey plays the role of father confessor, listening without comment as the girl lists the inadequacies of her boyfriend. As driver, he appears a mere functionary and is treated like a cipher, unable to comment upon or contradict the girl's point of view. Like the protagonist in the Smiths' epic 'There Is A Light That Never Goes Out', Morrissey is driving and seemingly thinking of making some kind of romantic gesture, which never happens. Perhaps it is the 'strange' fear of the former song that grips him once more but, as in 'King Leer', the drive ends in a gesture of bathos with a shake of the hands rather than a kiss on the lips.

The Harsh Truth Of The Camera Eye

One of the longer songs on the album, this rather dull composition required special effects to provide even a modicum of interest. "The ending of it musically, for me, is almost jazz with sound effects," Langer fancifully noted. "Instead of a trumpet, it's got the click of a camera . . ."

Nevin agrees: "It was Clive's idea. While we were in the studio he went to a fashion show. He saw and heard all these people taking photographs and thought, 'That's great,' so he put it on the track. We were doing that song for ages. A lot of the time we were walking around in the garden while Clive and Alan were in the studio."

It was Alan Winstanley who elected to sample the sound of a skateboarder playing under a bridge which can be heard criss-crossing between the speakers. "We recorded this track with a long ending, and when Steve Heart came in to do the keyboards, the piano and sound effects, he just kept going on to the end. The album needed a bit of playing, a bit of something loose." The sampled sounds were intended to add some much-needed life to the track but failed to disguise the composition's shortcomings.

At times Morrissey seems about to make some comment on the nature of celebrity and the voyeurism of the camera in the macabre tradition of the disturbing film *Peeping Tom*, but nothing that interesting emerges. Indeed, the cover artwork says more than the song, featuring Morrissey heavily made-up with a towering quiff and lavishly applied eye-shadow. On reflection, the song's sole saving grace is the psychologically revealing last verse wherein Morrissey appears to sum up a narcissistic insecurity by saying he would prefer to be blindly loved than coldly judged, a subtle echo of Oscar Wilde's arrogant aphorism: "I have never adored anyone but myself."

(I'm) The End Of The Family Line

Morrissey's self-mythologizing reached new heights in this slight but vaguely interesting speculation on his decaying dynasty. Unfortunately, like several other tracks on the album, the composition was fragmentary and undeveloped. "It was pretty similar to 'Driving Your Girlfriend Home'," Langer told journalist Tom Doyle. "We added some sound effects because we wanted the atmosphere of a family watching television or listening to the radio which is in the middle. Mind you, maybe if you're not used to it, it doesn't sound like that at all." For Nevin, the song was one of his favourites on the album – "I liked it, there was something really haunting about that song."

Paresi agreed. "'(I'm) The End Of The Family Line' is my favourite song on the album. I don't know if I had the advantage of hearing the lyrics while I was playing, but it absolutely speaks 100 per cent Morrissey . . . I was very pleased with my playing on it because there was some dynamics that I played around. There was something incredibly sad about it and that was the bit that got me excited. This, to me, was the perfect crystallization of Morrissey."

Unconsciously perhaps, the reprise of the fade-out recalls the same trick employed on 'That Joke Isn't Funny Anymore', itself an echo of Elvis Presley's 'Suspicious Minds' and other tracks. Those who take Morrissey's lyrics literally may be disappointed to learn that he is not the last of the Morrissey family line. In fact it was this song that prompted me to commission Pete Frame to draw a family tree revealing the still flourishing Morrissey clan. The Morrissey surname lives on in the sons of his uncle Thomas Morrissey – Peter, Kevin and Thomas – and in their male offspring, Rhett, Lee, Perry and Rheece.

There's A Place In Hell For Me And My Friends

The funereal piano and familiarly maudlin tone close the UK album on a suitably anti-climactic note as Morrissey speculates on the redeeming aspects of damnation. Having ended his mortal life on the previous track, he pictures himself among his friends in hell. The arrangement is deliberately minimalist and features Mark Nevin playing piano into a cassette recorder. "It was taken from my original demo. I had a wonky old piano at my house in Camden at the time.

When they tried to redo the piano it didn't sound as atmospheric so they kept the original."

The lyrics owed much to Morrissey's schooling at St Wilfred's where he made his first confession, communion and confirmation. "As a child I went to this Catholic school and they gave us the idea of Heaven and living for ever and ever and ever. It used to petrify me. Can you imagine living this life without end?" In the song, Morrissey offers a benign view of damnation in which pain is mysteriously absent. His theology was more fire and brimstone during promotional interviews, in which he insisted: "Some of us have to end up in Hell and I'm ready to suffer the flames. Anyway, there won't be enough room for all of us in Heaven."

Tony The Pony

Released on the CD single of 'Our Frank' this was inexplicably added as a bonus track to the American issue of *Kill Uncle*. "I've no idea whatsoever why it was on the US version," Mark Nevin says. "I really liked 'Tony The Pony', it was one of my favourites and I was really shocked when it wasn't on the UK album." Despite Nevin's recommendation it sounds decidedly out of place here, a B-side oddly relocated for Stateside purchasers.

Recorded at the start of the sessions, the song lacked the familiar Langer/Winstanley trademark. Morrissey's throwaway lyrics about an over-protective big brother are uninspiring and the arrangement sounds closer in feel to the abandoned rockabilly experiment that occurred just as the album was being completed. "Well, I think it's a sweet song," Paresi adds. "Mark had his little solo which was routed around three chords at the end. I remember Morrissey saying, 'I don't need to hear any more of this!' as if to say, 'This is sweet enough now, fade out.'"

YOUR ARSENAL

Released: July 1992

HMV CDSD 3790, CDCSD 3790, July 1992. US issue: Sire 9-26994-2, July 1992

Morrissey took to the road for a world tour after *Kill Uncle* with a band of rockabilly-loving musicians comprising guitarists Boz Boorer and Alain Whyte, bass guitarist Gary Day and drummer Spencer Cobrin. Meanwhile, Mark Nevin, who had declined to join them, tracked down former David Bowie sideman Mick Ronson who agreed to produce Morrissey's next album. During the tour, Morrissey was joined onstage by Bowie for a cover of T. Rex's 'Cosmic Dancer'. It all augured well for the recordings which turned out better than anyone could reasonably have expected. In almost every respect, *Your Arsenal* was the complete opposite of its predecessor. Instead of low-key arrangements and light, reflective tunes, Morrissey seemed hell-bent on reclaiming the oompah glam rock sound of his teenage years. Mark Nevin found himself out of favour at the precise moment when he finally understood how best to present his songs to Morrissey. Alas, he was allowed only two contributions to the album, the remainder being passed over to guitarist Alain Whyte. What emerged was a genuine group sound, the obvious legacy of months spent on the road. It did not escape the public's attention that Morrissey had at last found a band which he could promote as a gang. Clearly, this was what had been lacking in his musical life since the demise of the Smiths.

"Before *Your Arsenal* I felt very lonely," Morrissey confessed. "I didn't have any regular band and the last album I'd recorded, *Kill Uncle*, frustrated me. I needed to rebuild a gang spirit, to be back permanently with the same people . . . I love being surrounded, even if I dread human relationships . . ." Significantly, *Your Arsenal* did not include a lyric sheet, a sure sign that Morrissey wanted to shift attention away from his authorial pronouncements and encourage a more direct appreciation of the music. As a further indicator of confidence, neither of the last two singles, 'My Love Life' and 'Pregnant For The

Last Time', were deemed necessary to pad out the album. Here was a work which demanded all new material. At a time when Morrissey's career was in the descendent, this must have proven the ultimate confidence booster. "I wanted it to have a less isolated sound," Morrissey said at the time. "I wanted it to sound less lonely than previous records, and it is. It's possibly the noisiest record I've ever been involved with."

The reviews were almost universally enthusiastic. *NME*'s Andrew Collins, who had recently become a Doubting Thomas, found himself won over by the album's sparkly effervescence. "When Morrissey was King Of The World – not so long ago – the very notion of downfall, of imperfection, of embarrassment, of vicious, cold-hearted betrayal was unthinkable. The years 1983 to 1987 were industrial light and magic . . . The Smiths were the greatest bet of the 1980s; it shouldn't even need stating. It does need stating. For since their premature demise, Moz has gone about making the Smiths' memory look and feel like shit. He might be a big Morrissey fan (the biggest), but he cares little for the Smiths these days. Do we not have ears? Is that not the sound of one man clapping himself on the dire likes of 'Ouija Board, Ouija Board', 'Our Frank' and 'You're The One For Me, Fatty'? . . . The fourth solo album, so misleadingly fanfared into the market-place with Morrissey's worst two singles ever (the contrary bastard), is, if not a revelation, certainly less than a war crime. And that's incredible enough. It ought to have been his tombstone, instead it is a milestone. Of sorts . . . How we laughed when Morrissey recruited those YTS rockabillies as his band, started hanging out with Mensi, issued some Carry On Fatwah on Johnny Rogan the author of a book about his old band, and angled for reflected glory off Mick Ronson . . . *Your Arsenal* could've been a contender for fifth Smiths album. It's only good, but it's not shite, and if you still hate it when Morrissey becomes successful, tune in. The Queen's not dead."

Writing in Q, John Aizlewood was even more enthusiastic and awarded the album a maximum five stars: "There comes a point in many major artistes' careers where they have to make an album of some significance or the game is well and truly up. Morrissey is exactly at that point. The solo career had reached a stage where the song titles were more interesting than the songs themselves, and many a revisionist knife was sufficiently sharpened to suggest that the Smiths have had little lasting influence – unless James and Raymonde really count – and that, bar a few cracking singles, they weren't actually that great. *Your Arsenal* is his musical salvation. *Your Arsenal* is his best solo work yet and easily stands comparison with the best of the Smiths."

Arguably the ultimate accolade was provided by *Select*, which commissioned 17 'top pop celebrities', ranging from Brett Anderson and Mark E. Smith, to myself, Linder, Billy Bragg and Tanya Donelly to evaluate the new album. Titled 'The Feast Of Steven', the six-page feature was evidence enough of Morrissey's enduring appeal.

Critical approbation was reflected in sales and a UK chart placing of number 4, which proved a significant improvement on *Kill Uncle*. More importantly, *Your Arsenal* gave Morrissey his first proper taste of success in the US charts, peaking at number 21 in *Billboard*. With a touring band and a best-selling album, Morrissey sounded more confident than at any time since the breakup of the Smiths. There was a strong sense that, against the odds, he had been vindicated in choosing to work with musicians whose pedigree and potential had previously been ridiculed by most observers. Characteristically, Morrissey could not resist slipping into heretical hyperbole when discussing their contribution. "They are central to everything I do and they are, though you won't believe me – well, you might in five years – they are the best musicians I've had the joy of working with . . . I do hope people will not constantly want to write about the Smiths and the 'good old days'; the days when we got bad reviews and we didn't play very well sometimes. These musicians are better – and the harmony of the set-up . . . well, let's just say it's all very precious to me." With such an upbeat message, backed by an aesthetically impressive and highly commercial album, there seemed every likelihood that Morrissey was ready to establish himself as a worldwide phenomenon.

You're Gonna Need Someone On Your Side
The opening riff of the album neatly fuses Eddie Cochran's 'Something Else' with 'The Batman Theme' to create an arresting backdrop

in marked contrast to the insipid sound of *Kill Uncle*. For the first time in ages, Morrissey actually sounds as if he's part of a group again. Lyrically, the song stresses the need for friends, a theme that would be developed more fully on his next studio work. One of only two Mark Nevin songs on the album, this was clearly superior to most of the material on *Kill Uncle*. Nevin agrees, adding, "When I did 'You're Gonna Need Someone On Your Side' and 'I Know It's Gonna Happen Someday' I knew how to do it so they're more realized . . . I think that Clive Langer was maybe a bit too clean for Morrissey. When Mick Ronson did the album there was something more immediate about it. It was in your face."

Several critics singled out the song for praise, including Q's John Aizlewood who suggested, "'You're Gonna Need Someone On Your Side' promises a new improved Morrissey. At once it resembles the grumbling murmur of Richard Thompson's 'Read It In Books', the rush of the Smiths' 'The Queen Is Dead' and some old swamp-rockabilly tune even the Polecats never heard. Later in the same song, Morrissey tells a joke: 'And here I am,' he declaims, as if there were any debate as to whom the 'someone' you need is. 'Well, you don't have to look so pleased,' he moans, right out of Frankie Howerd."

Glamorous Glue

Mick Ronson's influence was strikingly evident here allowing Morrissey to indulge himself in a veritable cornucopia of glam rock. Half of the fun lay in spotting the influences which took in David Bowie, the Sweet's 'Blockbuster' and Gary Glitter's 'Rock And Roll (Parts 1 and 2)'. Lyrically, the composition reiterated Oscar Wilde's famous dictum: "We really have everything in common with America nowadays. Except, of course, language."

Morrissey's love/hate relationship with the USA and his regrets about England's lost glories were manifest throughout the song. The much quoted line 'London is dead' and the suggestion that the English language has been hijacked by Los Angeles sum up Morrissey's feelings of disillusionment. In a syndicated interview with Lorraine Ali, he explained, "What I mean by this is all television and radio broadcasters now speak with American accents . . . Everything that happens in America is constantly reported on the English news while in America England is never referred to and British politics are completely meaningless. The country could explode and disappear into outer space and America would not mention that on the daily news. That's a big failing in American culture. It's entirely self-obsessed. If America finally realized that other countries actually exist, this country would be a nicer place. British broadcasting is obsessed with LA, which is really upsetting and sad." Elaborating on this theme elsewhere, he qualified his assertion that London was culturally dead. "Well I don't think it's totally true that London is dead but that line concerns the language that we use and London no longer has an influence on language. In England now, people are very influenced by Los Angeles. London has no strength so, in that respect, London has died, but in other respects it is a very voluble place with a great deal to do and see."

Morrissey's ambivalence towards America went back to his teenage years when he visited New York and Colorado and never seemed entirely happy, even though he was quick to lambast Britain. In 1992, his sarcasm spoke volumes and he was quick to take a shot at an old adversary. "It's not that I dislike America – I think America is fine on the other side of the Atlantic. It works quite well and is interesting. If Margaret Thatcher was a strong person, which she isn't, she would not allow this Americanization to happen. But because she is such a weak Prime Minister, it happens, and any influence American business wishes to have on England, it has. They've completely taken over Newcastle."

We'll Let You Know

Warming to his theme, Morrissey adopts the persona of an English football hooligan as a dubious embodiment of enduring patriotism. Evidently, he was able to identify with his troubled protagonist. "I understand the level of patriotism, the level of frustration and the level of jubilance. I understand the overall character. I understand their aggression and I understand why it must be released . . . When I see reports on the television about hooliganism in Sweden and Denmark or somewhere, I'm actually amused. Is that a horrible thing to say? As long as people don't die, I am amused." The singer makes no attempt to disguise the predatory nature of his subjects. But there is typical Morrissey ambiguity in the plea that the songs which the moronic football fans chant do not mean a thing. Is he also defending the controversial nature of his own lyrics against literalist critics?

Musically, the acoustic arrangement works well, culminating in the sounds of chanting football fans, followed by a loud whistle and a final chilling declaration from the protagonist that these are the last genuinely British people of their time.

Interestingly, the song ends with the sounds of battle, albeit complicated by a woodwind accompaniment more in keeping with a re-creation of the American Civil War. Guitarist Alain Whyte recalls how Morrissey influenced the song's structure. "Morrissey writes the lyrics after I've given him the tune. Sometimes he'll make some changes . . . That happened in 'We'll Let You Know'. I remember when I wrote it, Morrissey said, 'I want this part to go around 10 times,' and I was saying, 'But 10 times?' He said: 'Just do it.' He's really clever and knows what sounds good."

The National Front Disco

The nationalist theme continued on this ominously titled and unjustly controversial lyric. Inevitably, the song attracted racist accusations in certain sections of the press and particular attention was paid to the inflammatory line 'England for the English', even though this was spoken by the protagonist rather than Morrissey. In adopting the persona of Davy, Morrissey paints a vivid picture of an ordinary, suburban boy 'lost' to the lure of the NF. References to the love of a country that does not exist pinpoints the follies of right-wing nationalism rather than promoting its philosophies. Although there are poignant moments in the song, most notably when the mother laments the departure of her indoctrinated son, the catchy chorus presents a more upbeat, comic mood. The notion of a 'national front disco' may sound absurd and ridiculous but those words were actually used to open the sixth chapter of Bill Buford's examination of football violence *Among The Thugs*.

As for Morrissey's own views on nationalism, they were anything but straightforward. He firmly denied any racist intent in writing the song, telling *Select*'s Andrew Harrison: "The reason why 'The

National Front Disco' was pounced upon was really because it was actually a very good song. And if a song is utter crap, no one would have cared. I was stopped by many journalists who obviously raised the topic in an accusatory way, and I would say to them, 'Please, now, list the lines in the song which you feel are racist and dangerous and hateful.' And they couldn't. Nobody ever could, and that irked me . . . On 'Asian Rut' or 'Bengali In Platforms' or 'The National Front Disco' one can plainly hear that there is no hate at all. But you soon realize that they are just out for you, and that it doesn't matter what you say or do . . . I think that if the National Front were to hate anyone, it would be me. I would be top of the list." Yet, Morrissey was strongly against the broadcasting ban imposed on the extreme right. "If the BNP were afforded television time or unbiased space in newspapers, it would seem less of a threat and it would ease the situation. They are gagged so much that they take revenge in the most frightening way by hurting and killing people. But part of that is simply their anger at being ignored in what is supposed to be a democratic society." To complicate matters further, Morrissey displayed the rigidity of a Little Englander with an anti-Euro rant. "I don't want to be European. I want England to remain an island. I think part of the greatness of the past has been the fact that England has been an island. I don't want the tunnel. I don't want sterling to disappear. But that doesn't mean that I'm some great twit who lives in a hut and eats straw. I'm actually quite modern in some respects."

As ever, Morrissey's unwillingness to follow a predictable party line stoked the fires of suspicion among his detractors but, unlike the politely condescending 'Bengali In Platforms', there was nothing here to warrant condemnation. What the composition demonstrated most forcibly was the songwriter's continued fascination with the disenchanted outsider whose world-view, however questionable or hopeless, was marked by a pyrrhic defiance.

Certain People I Know
More than anything else on the album, this song testified to both Morrissey's and guitarist Boz Boorer's enduring appreciation of Marc Bolan with a hook line that recalled 'Ride A White Swan'. A limited edition version of the track was later issued featuring a pastiche sleeve

with Morrissey in Bolan pose pictured underneath the word 'Moz' instead of 'T. Rex'. As the third single issued from the album, its chart placing was always likely to be low and a UK peak of number 35 proved worse than even 'Sing Your Life'.

Morrissey's porcine grunts towards the close of the song are highly amusing, while the mannered delivery disguises his authorial intent. Once again, there is a distinct ambivalence in his appreciation of pro-letariat pleasures. He adores those buccaneering spirits that face danger and laugh their heads off, but professes to hate others who break their own necks, a distinction which seems at best contradic-tory. The extreme, visceral imagery recalls the nail-swallowing antics of the rough boy in the Smiths' 'I Want The One I Can't Have'.

We Hate It When Our Friends Become Successful

Issued as a single three months before the album's release, this light effort returned Morrissey to the UK Top 20 after an absence of 17 months. Not that it was greeted with enthusiasm by the music press. *NME*'s Andrew Collins, who would later review the parent album favourably, saw this as a new low in Morrissey's career. "Start your sobbing, this is by far and away the ex-Smith's worst single. Playing alongside it, 'Ouija Board, Ouija Board' sounds choppy and inspired. Sure, the ambiguous title allows 30 seconds of salacious conjecture, but that double-bluff 'Ha ha ha ha ha ha' non-chorus scores a direct miss, and the sound of five men bashing around in the darkness in search of a tune merely drains you of the will to live. And the live B-side of 'Suedehead' was played by monkeys who clearly hated *Viva Hate*. Use the money you save by not purchasing this record, do yourself a fucking favour and invest in *Morrissey & Marr: The Severed Alliance* by Johnny Rogan . . . Moz is history, and we'd all do well to learn it."

What saved the song from accusations of banality were the sarcas-tic, spiteful lyrics. Oscar Wilde once said that "friends sympathize with one's troubles, but not with a friend's success" and Morrissey takes this aphorism to cruel extremes by exploring the feline destruc-tion of so-called friends as good sport. "The song is my vision of the Manchester situation – which is quite strong. In that city there is an intense feeling of jealousy and I don't like it . . . People in Manchester seem to be accepting of anything except success. They are very supportive if you fail, but when you succeed and they can't, they instantly begin to destroy you."

In some respects, this song was a bitter extension of the playful putdown previously voiced against old friends in 'Girl Least Likely To'. The lyrics leave you wondering whether Morrissey might have been equally cynical and back-stabbing if pop star fame had proven elusive. Given his later references to 'northern leeches' on 'You Know I Couldn't Last', an affirmative answer seems most likely.

You're The One For Me, Fatty

Having previously championed the physically and mentally handicapped, the deformed and the culturally alienated, it was fun to see Morrissey subverting the love song tradition by cooing to the overweight. As ever with Morrissey, ambiguity is present and the gaps between celebration, sympathy and mockery tend to be wafer thin. It may be worth noting that as an adolescent Steven had little time for fatties and was wont to blame them for over-eating. With its catchy, Buddy Holly hiccupping 'hey hey' chorus and novel lyric, the song provided Morrissey with another UK Top 20 hit. As before, his whimsical work tended to leave certain critics cold. *NME*'s Barbara Ellen lamented, "Oh dear. Steven Patrick, please release us, let us go . . . Forget 'Fatty's' tune, once again it is well within the reach of any second rate bar band with too many Jam albums. And Morrissey, though more purposeful than on recent efforts, still comes across like the quintessential one-trick pony, helpless without its trainer, but still lured by the roar of the crowd and the smell of the greasepaint to hobble into the arena and humiliate itself time and time again." Fans were left to play the parlour guessing game of identifying the 'fatty' of the title, resulting in such humorous and improbable nominations as Oscar Wilde, Kirsty MacColl, Victoria Wood's husband Geoffrey Durham, the recently plumper Johnny Marr and even Morrissey himself, whose girth had visibly expanded during this period.

Seasick, Yet Still Docked

For older Morrissey fans, this was probably the album's crowning glory. Starting with the ominous ticking of a clock, it catalogues in poignant detail the plight of a frozen soul whose life journey has never properly begun. It's both impressive and disconcerting to observe the ease with which the 33-year-old singer draws on experiences more appropriate to a tortured adolescent, but such is the nature of Morrissey's appeal. The neuroses documented herein uncannily recall the subject matter of any number of Smiths songs. Morrissey sings of the despair of never being able to find love, then switches to earnest self-deprecation, self-pity, dreamy wish-fulfilment, excessive sleeping and finally romantic narcissism.

Any listener familiar with 'Unloveable', 'Half A Person', 'Asleep' or 'There Is A Light That Never Goes Out' will know this terrain well. And in case the reference points need further clarification, Morrissey tells us 'I've got no charm', echoing the title of the Smiths' first hit 'This Charming Man'.

Musically, the Smiths' influence is even more pronounced with a sad, waltz-time melody that is almost a pastiche of 'That Joke Isn't Funny Anymore'. The homage was no coincidence. Alain Whyte, in conversation with Rob Nebeker, admitted that the composition was a conscious attempt to recreate the Smiths' sound. " 'Seasick, Yet Still Docked' and 'We'll Let You Know' are very Smiths-like, but that's the way it came out. What can I say? I wrote the tune and Morrissey put the lyrics down. The same principle as with Johnny Marr . . . I studied a lot of the Smiths' stuff, so I've got a feel for that . . . you get an idea of the kind of music Morrissey likes and what would suit him. That's probably why *Your Arsenal* was quite successful. We did exactly what we wanted to do, and it was what the fans wanted. The sad songs on there are really sad."

I Know It's Gonna Happen Someday
The second Mark Nevin composition on the album was originally written as part of the rock 'n' roll experiment at the end of *Kill Uncle*. Although it was hardly rockabilly, the melody captured the period feel that Morrissey was seeking and his vocal here is reminiscent of a Fifties balladeer. This was the closest he ever came to re-creating the sound and ambience of those pre-Beatles singles he so loved. Even the twirling of the radio dial that opens the song sets the mood

dramatically, recalling a similar trick used by Dexys Midnight Runners at the start of *Searching For The Young Soul Rebels*. Nevin's attractive lilt successfully conjures images of Johnnie Ray and other lost icons while Morrissey's melodramatic singing style and optimistic lyrics contrast markedly with the negation and despair of the preceding 'Seasick, Yet Still Docked'.

Given Mick Ronson's involvement, it was a remarkable coincidence that the closing riff recalled one of the classic Bowie songs. "The 'Rock 'n' Roll Suicide' riff was an absolute accident," Morrissey insisted. "David Bowie mentioned to Mick that he thought the end of the song was from 'Rock 'n' Roll Suicide' and it's true. Now when I listen to it I can hear it but, at the time, it was completely uninstigated." Morrissey received what seemed the ultimate accolade when David Bowie recorded a cover version of the song on his album *Black Tie, White Noise*. At last, Morrissey's teenage hero was eating from his hand.

Mark Nevin first learned about Bowie's decision when visiting Morrissey in Hollywood. "Morrissey said, almost as if he'd forgotten it, 'Oh, I've got some good news for you, David Bowie's recording 'I Know It's Gonna Happen Someday'.' At first I thought it was a wind-up but, bit by bit, it emerged as the truth. My publishers managed to get me a copy of the tape. I felt I couldn't truly believe it until I bought a copy. On a Monday morning I went to the shop and I was horrified because they'd left my name off the credits. It just said, 'Morrissey'. I was mortified. My publishers made them correct it for the second run but a lot of people who'd heard me say I wrote it must have thought, 'Sure you did!'"

While Nevin's account suggests that Morrissey was preternaturally cool about Bowie's involvement, this was not manifested during promotional interviews. According to Morrissey, "David's version of 'I Know It's Gonna Happen Someday' made me wail tears of pure happiness, actually. David is an extraordinarily nice man. He's very gentle and he has a tremendous ability to put people at ease. David and I don't talk about life as major rock stars. We like to talk about books and flowers a lot." Alas, this display of fan worship would not last.

Tomorrow

The final track reiterates the personal rather than the political themes on the album. Its title may have been borrowed from Sandie Shaw's 1966 Top 10 hit but, if so, the mental landscape is decidedly different. As so often happens in Morrissey songs, sex, affection and emotion are expressed furtively. A request to be embraced is cautiously qualified by reassuring words. The narrator promises not to tell anybody, as if there is something taboo about even the slightest physical contact. Images of physical and emotional pain, clandestine sexuality, psychosomatic illness and frustration flash by. For those doubters preparing to sharpen their quills in anticipation of a killing, Morrissey disingenuously quips that he never said he wanted to achieve fame in the first place. In common with the other songs on the album, the production and arrangement are impressive, with guitars prominent. But there is a surprise at the end with a disembodied piano coda that recreates the same eerie effect previously heard on the Smiths' 'Asleep'.

BEETHOVEN WAS DEAF

Released: May 1993

HMV CSD 3791, CDCSD 3791, May 1993

Following *Your Arsenal*, Morrissey could afford to feel optimistic about his drawing power as a live performer and this was confirmed when he sold out the Hollywood Bowl in record time. Back in England, however, all was far from well. Branching out from his usual fan base, the singer had agreed to appear on the same bill as Madness for two evenings at London's Finsbury Park. It was to prove a costly error. The 'Madstock' affair ended in disarray and controversy when Morrissey displayed a Union Jack flag onstage. The Nutty Boys' hard-core followers took exception and pelted the singer with a variety of missiles. After a relatively short set, he left the stage and declined to fulfil his engagement the following evening.

The following week *NME* reopened the old racist debate prompting a barrage of letters, defending and condemning the singer. Morrissey refused to address his detractors and it was only later during a US visit that he spoke more openly about the affair. "My relationship with England has been slandered and ridiculed because, in England, you're not allowed to be patriotic in any way. It's construed as racism. I don't know why; that doesn't happen in any other country in the world. In England if you display the Union Jack, it's considered racist and extremist. I do that and it becomes very, very difficult. I'm really the last in a long trail of unshakably English pop artistes, from the Who, the Jam, the Kinks, whoever you care to throw in there, groups who were just unswayably English."

Throughout this period, Morrissey's concerts were as frenzied as ever, with passionate fans clambering onstage at every opportunity. The singer's commercial upswing persuaded him to sanction this live album, which came as something of a surprise. The Smiths had never issued a live recording during their lifetime, but after three solo albums and a compilation, Morrissey and EMI felt that the time was right. Although the live work contained three songs previously unavailable on album, it was in most respects a predictable tour memento. The opportunity to feature his cover of Suede's 'My Insatiable One' from an earlier taped concert was not taken. Unsurprisingly, there were no Smiths tracks available, nothing from *Kill Uncle* and only one track from *Viva Hate* – his big hit 'Suedehead'. Nine out of 10 songs from *Your Arsenal* reappeared, a regrettably high ratio in the circumstances. In short it was an accurate illustration of his current live show, a pleasant enough souvenir for new fans, but little more. At least with 16 live selections Morrissey came close to capturing a complete concert, although three songs escaped: 'Tomorrow', 'Alsatian Cousin' and 'The Last Of The Famous International Playboys'. To confuse matters, there was a bit of jiggery-pokery in the ordering and selection of tracks. According to the accompanying notes, the album was taped at the Zenith in Paris on 22 December 1992. However at least two tracks, 'The National Front Disco' and 'He Knows I'd Love To See Him', were culled from the London Astoria show two days before. The provenance of 'You're The One For Me, Fatty', 'Certain People I Know', 'We'll Let You Know', 'You're Gonna Need Someone On Your Side' and 'Glamorous Glue' was also in doubt. Such minor inconsistencies aside, the album was a faithful representation of Morrissey's live shows of the period with a decent remix by Bob Clearmountain.

The reviews were an accurate reflection of Morrissey's confused standing at the time. In the increasingly disenchanted *NME*, John Harris – usually a fair-minded critic – felt obliged to end his review with a set of marks for both the album and Morrissey's character: "It's all changed now, of course. He's soiled our view of him as an eloquent crusader for ethical decency by dancing with the flag-waving devils, now stamping their hooves all across Europe. And he's become one of those regimented pop stars by running into needless media–phobic seclusion, appearing far more willing to satisfy his burgeoning American fan base than to reward his British admirers . . . All of which, in the light of what this album represents, is something of an irrelevance. There is a nightmarish spectre lurking in the grooves of *Beethoven Was Deaf*: it's of a once-great man who's decided to turn up to parties dressed up as a jingoistic thug and talk to men in suits about marketing ploys. (7) for the music, (2) for the lamentable stench."

At the other extreme there was former *NME* writer Tony Parsons, then in the midst of defending Morrissey in *Vox* as a national treasure. Unfortunately, his partisanship seemed to have robbed him of his usual critical faculties. In an outbreak of Morrissey worship, he proclaimed *Beethoven Was Deaf* as "possibly the best live record since the Rolling Stones' *Get Yer Ya-Yas Out*". It was left to the broadsheets to provide a more sober analysis. The *Independent* probably summed it up best with the withering conclusion: "Apart from a few extra shards of guitar from Alain Whyte and Boz Boorer, there's little to distinguish these versions from the originals."

You're The One For Me, Fatty
The running order was resequenced so that this bouncy tune opened proceedings rather than 'We Hate It When Our Friends Become Successful'. The audience was very familiar with Morrissey's ode to Fatty, which had been released as a single the previous July. In concert, the musicians were given a free hand to play in a more raucous fashion although, given the simplicity of the song, the sonic differences were not profound. Morrissey seems poised to have fun with the 'a-hey' vocals but avoids any attempt at inventive scat singing in favour of a more restrained approach.

Certain People I Know
Another former single followed, maintaining the commercial opening to the album. The group again appeared reasonably confident, fusing Bolan-style riffs with a distinct rockabilly edge. Boz Boorer's fascination with Bolan was something he shared with Morrissey. Although this version was faithful to the original, the playing sounded beefier, the backing vocals more flirtatious and Morrissey provided a subtle lyric change, telling us that '*life*'s absurd'. Midway through there were some audible screams from the audience before Morrissey offered those familiar grunts, albeit in less comic fashion than the album version. The slightly cod ending was appealing and the guitar work economical ensuring that the song barely exceeded the three-minute mark. During a show in Texas, Morrissey used this rather urbane composition to express his displeasure at the

over-zealous security, sneering the line 'I'd hate to be like certain people . . .'

The National Front Disco

In concert, it was rather disconcerting to hear the extent to which the chorus 'England for the English' seemed to serve as a clarion call. Morrissey had already expressed his opinions on racial disharmony in an interview with Q prior to the album's release. In view of his Paris performance, it was interesting to hear his comments on Anglo-French relations. "I don't really think black and white people will ever get on or like each other . . . The French will never like the English. The English will never like the French. That tunnel will collapse." Speaking in France, Morrissey defended the composition even though few serious commentators ever regarded the work as contentious. "The people who listen to the whole song, to the way it is sung, the tone of my voice, will know that I'm not a racist, that I don't glorify xenophobia. Very simply, if one considers a song as history, the line 'England for the English' is between inverted commas: it is a quotation. 'The National Front Disco' evokes the sadness of having lost a boy who has joined the National Front. Those who say, ''The National Front Disco' – what a racist song!' don't listen to it. Melancholy runs through the song which expresses deep sadness, a deep feeling of loss . . . It is a fact that people join the National Front, that there are racist people. The song talks about the regret and sadness of someone joining the movement."

Morrissey's exuberant live reading had a slightly harder edge cul-minating in a dramatic conclusion during which the group flew across the stage like exploding rockets colliding in a frenzy of rever-berating guitars. Amid the cacophony of clawed strings and feedback squeals, there is a snatch of Jimi Hendrix's 'Purple Haze' for the guitar purists. During the fade-out Morrissey mischievously announces: "We might release this as a single. Do you think it would be a hit?"

November Spawned A Monster

Here, the audience are teased by the opening of 'Ouija Board, Ouija Board' before Morrissey abruptly segues into 'November Spawned A Monster'. He provides a suitably dramatic reading of the song, with the group adding a solid, tight backing. At the time, Morrissey was still thrilled by the composition, which he evidently regarded as among his finest works. "It was a pinnacle. In its invasion of the mind of a 'poor twisted child, so ugly', trapped and unlovable in its wheelchair, it expresses me most accurately . . . It's a record I have striven to make." Live, the most revealing aspect of the song occurred when Morrissey almost burst into laughter while singing 'Oh, no, no', a clear enough indication of the comic revulsion in his sardonic lyrics. The crowd's enthusiasm and curiosity were evident as the song approached the section where Mary Margaret O'Hara appears on the studio version. She is replaced by handclaps, a clarinet interlude from Boorer and finally some fierce drumming. Regrettably, Morrissey made no attempt to take on the O'Hara role by 'giving birth' onstage even though his bizarre vocal yelps might have transformed this live reading. At least the audience appreciated the composition's importance and there was a great roar of approval at the end followed by the chant "Morrissey, Morrissey" with a discernibly French pronunciation.

Seasick, Yet Still Docked

After the crowd-pleasing, upbeat openers, Morrissey attempted one of his more mournful compositions. In some ways it was a surprisingly brave attempt to feature such a personal song live, especially if we are to believe guitarist Alain Whyte who recalls, "Morrissey said to me one day about 'Seasick, Yet Still Docked': 'I've got to be in the right mood to listen to it because it makes me feel really sad.' It's just one of those songs. We wrote the tune just with an acoustic and electric guitar and Morrissey asked me to lengthen it . . . Everyone's contribution made it an amazing tune." Although some of the song's studio subtleties such as the ticking clock and delicate brush and cymbal work were missing, this is largely an identikit version, with a suitably stately vocal reading. Displaying extraordinary precision, the band end the song at the five-minute mark, with a time difference of less than two seconds in comparison to the studio original.

The Loop

Something of a rarity, this non-album composition was previously available on the 12-inch version of 'Sing Your Life'. The song's title was not mentioned in the lyrics as the 'loop' is probably a reference to the way the track was recorded during the *Kill Uncle* sessions. Alan Winstanley confirms that they "sampled all these old rockabilly beats off the original records and then just looped them over one another." Unlike the pleasingly authentic original single version, this live cut sounded more rock than rockabilly, with a full drum kit and greater instrumental body in deference to contemporary audiences' expectations.

Sister I'm A Poet
Another non-album track, this first appeared in different form on the 12-inch version of 'Everyday Is Like Sunday' and also featured in the video *Hulmerist*. Morrissey's decision to include the song during his famous performance at Wolverhampton in December 1988 ensured that it became a live favourite over the years. The Paris version is not the best rendition, but you still come away wondering what Morrissey is referring to in those oblique lyrics in which the word 'poet' is conspicuous by its absence. As an arch comment on the nature of evil, the composition fitted well alongside Morrissey's other ruminations on criminality. Its inclusion on this live album partly compensated for its surprising failure to appear on *Bona Drag*. At the end of the song, Morrissey announces his linguistic deficiencies, a likely leftover from his time at St Mary's Secondary Modern. "I still cannot speak French. I am very lazy."

Jack The Ripper
The trilogy of non-album songs was completed with this unusual number, previously premièred in studio form on the flip-side of 'Certain People I Know'. Oddly enough, it was also the third consecutive song on the live album whose subject is not named in the lyrics. At one point this version was considered as a possible single, but the idea was soon vetoed. However, a DJ-only promotional release was issued. Speaking at the time, Boz Boorer explained: "It's a bit different in concert from the way it is on the record, as we do it a little bit slower, and Morrissey doesn't sing the last part. We didn't have enough time to do it in the studio properly as we were going

away to America, and we only had two days. That's why it's different onstage." In fact, this live version is remarkably similar to the studio original, although Morrissey's vocals are clearer in the mix and the overall mood is more subdued. In common with several compositions in the Morrissey canon, from 'Suffer Little Children' through to 'The Last Of The Famous International Playboys', this testified to his fascination with celebrity murderers. On reflection, Morrissey was fortunate to escape further controversy. When Screaming Lord Sutch performed his song of the same title during the Eighties, his concerts were boycotted by feminist protesters.

Such A Little Thing Makes Such A Big Difference
Morrissey's vocal wavered here, but the effect was not unpleasing. Indeed, the performance worked reasonably well in Paris although the absence of Stephen Street's memorable harpsichord–like keyboards was noticeable. The band attempted to compensate with some power chords and drum thrashing, thereby offering a beefier backing than the more sophisticated and attractive original. Although Morrissey did not introduce any new material at the show, he concentrated on reviving a number of songs previously issued as B–sides. Slight rather than significant, this song served as a welcome prelude to 'I Know It's Gonna Happen Someday'.

I Know It's Gonna Happen Someday
There is no time for a break as 'Such A Little Thing Makes Such A Big Difference' segues seamlessly into this big ballad. A Mark Nevin song, as opposed to one by Whyte or Boorer, this provided the band with a keener challenge in reproducing the original. While some of the drama was missing, along with the sampling and effects from the studio original, the band valiantly attempted to disguise their technical shortcomings with guitar pyrotechnics. Morrissey provided a sustained vocal performance to accompany the engagingly chaotic backing. At this stage, however, the concert required more upbeat material to sustain the early excitement.

We'll Let You Know
Another studiously faithful attempt at reproducing a track from *Your*

Arsenal, this revealed Morrissey in fine voice, complete with an impressive falsetto midway through. At the end there is a greater stress on the suggestion that the protagonists are the last truly British people you *wouldn't* want to know, which emphasizes the ambivalence at the song's centre. Apart from that, there is little to choose between this enervating rendition and its studio counterpart. By this point in the album there is a sense of overfamiliarity with the recent material, understandable given that Morrissey was promoting a new CD, but ultimately an impediment to long-term listening enjoyment.

Suedehead

Morrissey's first single, an obvious crowd favourite, was greeted by loud cheers. When the group first played this song live it was very ragged, but over the years they improved their interpretation. It came as no surprise to learn that the song's co-composer had no love for the concert version. Stephen Street: "I just think the band he formed after working with me were terrible. They killed songs like 'Suedehead' live. But there you go, that was his choice." Here, the rhythm section sounds noticeably weaker and the upfront drumming and pounding bass work that powered the studio track is occasionally rendered lacklustre. Morrissey enjoys some playful vocal gulping and sounds as though he is throwing in a few different lyrics, although they may be merely guttural growls. The coda, with the reference to a 'good lay', is sung loud and clear without ambiguity. Loud applause follows.

He Knows I'd Love To See Him

This song, slotted in from the London Astoria gig two days before, abruptly changed the mood of the set. Morrissey inexplicably omits the opening line of the composition and places a slightly different emphasis in his pronunciation of the word 'arse'. Although the original version, co-written by Kevin Armstrong, long predated the arrival of the band, they tackled the song with forceful aplomb and it worked far better in concert than might have been anticipated. Even the absence of Mary Margaret O'Hara's eerie backing vocal was less noticeable than expected.

You're Gonna Need Someone On Your Side

The opening song from *Your Arsenal*, complete with the familiar tribute to 'The Batman Theme', was a welcome encore. It was interesting that both of Mark Nevin's final contributions were featured in the show. Had he not declined Morrissey's invitation to join the band in concert, he might have enjoyed many more co-writing collaborations. Neatly placed on the album, this upbeat rocker allowed the group the perfect opportunity to show their credentials, which they do with considerable confidence.

Glamorous Glue

The *Your Arsenal* show continued with this glam stomper which emerged as the most bombastic track on the album. The group improvise slightly and finally go wild as the song reaches a powerful conclusion, amid a burst of interweaving guitars and feedback. Ever appreciative, the French audience even applaud Whyte's guitar riffs. By this point, the album is heading towards the one-hour mark, a creditable length for a single CD during this period.

We Hate It When Our Friends Become Successful

This was a pure sing-along in which the French audience followed every nuance of Morrissey's vocal. More passionate and energetic than the lighter single version, and taken at a faster pace, it provided an exciting and pleasant ending to the album. Ironically, this actually opened the show in Paris, but you'd never guess that listening to the emphatic close. Tagged on to the end is a brief, "Thank you, I love you, goodbye" – and the show is over.

VAUXHALL AND I

Released: March 1994

Parlophone PCSD 148, CDPCSD 148, March 1994.
US issue: Sire 9-45451-2, March 1994

After the success of *Your Arsenal* and an impressive concert invasion of America, Morrissey's career was at an all-time high. Nevertheless, this was a time to ponder friendships past and present. In the fallout of *The Severed Alliance*, Andy Rourke was threatening to return as an embittered litigant and follow Mike Joyce who was still planning to take Morrissey to the High Court. Meanwhile, Rough Trade ceased trading and the entire Smiths catalogue reverted to Morrissey and Marr, only to be sold on immediately to Warner Brothers. News gradually reached the press that Morrissey and Marr were not only back in contact but had resolved their former differences. Inevitably, there was speculation about a Smiths reunion or at least a fresh collaboration between the group's two songwriters. Rourke held little hope of the rhythm section being invited to participate. "If we all did agree to get back together, it'd probably be a bad move," he told me at the time. "It could be a real letdown. We've all changed. We've all moved on. Musically, we couldn't really sound like that any more. Maybe we could, you never know until you've tried it. But in the press it would always look like a money-making idea. Like that's the whole reason we'd re-form – to do a massive tour, a reunion album, make a lot of money and split up again."

With the substantial profit Morrissey had made from selling his back catalogue and the current standing of his career internationally, he certainly did not need the money. Moreover, his negative comments on Rourke and Joyce in the music press suggested that he now saw them as part of his past. If old friends were at a premium then some of the newer ones had already abruptly departed. In the space of a few short months video director Tim Broad, business manager Nigel Thomas and producer Mick Ronson all passed away. At a time when Morrissey should have been celebrating, he was surrounded by news of death.

These sudden losses obviously affected Morrissey and profoundly influenced his songwriting. Gone were the trite lyrics that had blighted *Kill Uncle* and even parts of *Your Arsenal*. Instead, he produced some of the finest writing of his career. *Vauxhall And I* was undoubtedly his most subdued record to date, but arguably his finest as a soloist. Producer Steve Lillywhite brilliantly extracted the melancholia at the heart of the compositions using an array of subtle effects, both simple and complicated. There was also a change of personnel with bass player Jonny Bridgwood and drummer Woodie Taylor, who had previously played on the single 'Pregnant For The Last Time', replacing Gary Day and Spencer Cobrin, respectively.

The sessions for *Vauxhall And I* commenced at Hook End Manor on 1 June 1993 and continued until 31 August. Bridgwood and Taylor assumed that the recordings would faithfully follow what they heard on the demo tapes, but they were in for a surprise. Even early in the sessions, it was evident that this album was something special. "I was aware of this end of reign atmosphere while recording," Morrissey remembers. "I was even quite happy about it. The album wasn't as fiery or passionate as its predecessors; it seemed a bit resigned, which quite pleased me."

Bridgwood also realized that the work was taking a fresh direction as each new song was completed. "I remember being really excited that I was part of this thing. We had no idea that the album would evolve as it did. Suddenly we were there and started doing things and it just took on its own life and its own personality."

Originally scheduled for release in November 1993, *Vauxhall And I* was delayed by several months, but proved well worth the wait. It was rightly hailed as a major work and emulated *Viva Hate* by climbing to number 1 in the UK charts. A respectable number 18 in America was achieved without the benefit of a promotional tour. Andrew Collins, who had lampooned Morrissey's recent singles, showed no hesitation in proffering a five-star review in *Q*. "The lyrical tone of *Vauxhall And I* is, while predictably melodramatic and self-pitying, more resigned and even peaceful . . . Thank heavens he's come round to making exceptional, unique music again. What was his old band called?" A similar note was struck in *Select*: "The record fascinates because Moz himself is still fascinating – only now he's not hiding behind a remnant of the Seventies or a smart line. *Vauxhall* is better than *Your Arsenal*, so it's his best record since *The Queen Is Dead* – and if he keeps making records like this you won't want the Smiths back."

Even the exiled *NME* bore no grudges and responded with an impressive 8 out of 10 rating. Reviewer Stuart Bailie offered a number of insightful points, noting how the album begins with "an assertion of life's mad, high-frothing possibilities", after which "we witness the bombing of children, a skull gets hammered in, a sailor dies, there's a bizarre swimming fatality, a sprinkling of skin cancer plus innumerable brickbats and back-stabbings". Bailie also offered a series of passing 'Moz meditations' including some speculation about the album's title: "Vauxhall is the London manor of Smiths' biographer Johnny Rogan. Coincidence or not?" I would say 'coincidence'. Although it was true that I lived just off Vauxhall Bridge Road before and during that time, the street in question was on the other side of the river in the Westminster/Pimlico area, a completely contrasting locale. However, my girlfriend Teresa Walsh lived adjacent to Vauxhall and naturally I spent a lot of time with her there. In another quirky coincidence, one of the musicians in her band was currently working on *Vauxhall And I*. Morrissey never fully explained the significance of the album title beyond the oblique suggestion that it was a "reference to someone who was born and braised in Vauxhall". Bailie concluded his review with a series of rhetorical questions: "Shall we forgive him? Will he forgive us? Isn't he the oddest, richest, most royally messed-up fish in the pond? The debate continues."

In addition to the abundance of riches on the album, there were a handful of outtakes, some of them incomplete. 'Black-Eyed Susan', which was recorded at the start of the sessions, was held over for use as a B-side. 'Interlude', a collaboration with Siouxsie Sioux, suffered innumerable delays before appearing as a single in July 1994. The string section that appeared on 'Interlude' also played on 'Stay As You Are', for which Morrissey failed to complete a vocal. The same fate befell 'Honey You Know Where To Find Me', a title that Morrissey assigned to an Alain Whyte tune and later revived for a melody by Boz Boorer. Finally, there was the pre-Beatles, early Sixties-styled 'Sharp Bend, Fast Car, Goodbye', another example of Morrissey tackling the 'death disc' song tradition with his usual mixture of morbidity and comedy.

Perhaps the most flattering comments on the album were offered by Morrissey himself. He frankly admitted that he would *never* top this album – and history may well have proven him right. For one moment, at least, the work even prompted him to consider lowering the curtain of retirement. "I'm starting to see the time when I'll feel like I've expressed all the things I want to say."

Now My Heart Is Full

Distorted guitars open the album in ominous fashion as Morrissey announces that trouble is brewing and everyone in his house will require a spell on a psychiatrist's couch. What emerges is both a serious and celebratory acknowledgement of the onset of happiness, an emotion which Morrissey fails to express in words. He frequently tells us he simply 'can't explain'. Not for the first time, he finds solace in a gang mentality, this time namedropping the deviant characters in Graham Greene's *Brighton Rock*, a novel that was adapted for film, with Richard Attenborough playing the part of the psychopath Pinkie. The scenario is another seedy seaside town, but more glamorous and dangerous than the decaying place dramatized in 'Everyday Is Like Sunday'. Morrissey identifies with the heady rush experienced by Pinkie's gang while also acknowledging that it ends up nowhere. Then there is the character of Pinkie himself: damaged, devious and amoral, with a particular loathing for the sex act. His Catholic upbringing leaves him resigned to damnation, just like the character in Morrissey's 'There's A Place In Hell For Me And My Friends'.

'Now My Heart Is Full' is simultaneously chilling and liberating. Its sense of joyous release is complicated by the knowledge that Morrissey is still locked in his own private mythology with its fictional anti-heroes and apotheosized actors, in this case the doomed suicide Patric Doonan, whose film-starring roles included *The Blue Lamp* and *Cockleshell Heroes*. As Morrissey later admitted, he even attempted to contact the occupants of Doonan's Chelsea home, almost as though it were a shrine. While the song ushers in a sense of newly discovered freedom, it leaves the listener wondering whether any escape is ultimately possible. Discussing the composition in *Select*, Morrissey was more optimistic. "I think I was certainly really tired of the past. 'Now My Heart Is Full' has a sense of jubilant exhaustion with looking over one's shoulder all the time and draining one's reference points . . . I have perhaps overtapped my sources and now all that is over, basically. I have a vast record and video and tape collection, but I look at it now in a different light. It's no longer something I feel I need to be embroiled in night and day. I have realized that the past is actually over, and it is a great relief to me . . . I feel free to do absolutely nothing at all, and it is exhilarating."

In common with the majority of songs on *Vauxhall And I*, 'Now My Heart Is Full' was originally an instrumental demo, written in advance of the album. According to Jonny Bridgwood: " 'Now My Heart Is Full' was one of the more finished demos for that album. We did a version before Steve Lillywhite arrived that was a little slower but it lacked a bit. Then we got an arrangement that we later played live and that was transferred on to the studio desk – so I had a bass part. But Steve kept coming back to the demo. Some of the guitar effects were kept and some bits added. There was a drum machine on it originally that was replaced by Woodie's drums. I worked on it for a couple of days trying to duplicate the bass line. We came in one day and Steve had a think about it and he decided that he preferred the overall feel of the original demo with Boz's bass line. So I wasn't on it. I'm on everything bar 'Now My Heart Is Full'. I remember it being mentioned as a single, but not as the first one. It was always perceived as the third single and never was."

Spring-Heeled Jim

Source hunting for themes and titles has always been part of the puzzle in analysing and appreciating Morrissey's lyrics. During the Smiths' era, a grounding in Shelagh Delaney, Elizabeth Smart and Victoria Wood ensured a rich harvest of borrowed quotes, but since the beginning of his solo career the fount of Morrissey's inspiration has been either more original or simply less obvious. This has not stopped fans from tracking down and documenting key sources, no matter how unlikely or improbable. The long defunct fanzine

Morri'Zine reckoned this song was based on Spring-Heeled Jack, a mythical, devilish creature who inhabited London in the 1830s. Like Jack the Ripper he terrorized women, albeit in more feral fashion with his claws. His speciality was spitting dragon-like flames into their eyes. While all this was fascinating, it appeared to have little or nothing to do with the actual song which was another of Morrissey's ambivalent tales of hero-worship. Here, the hedonistic, womanizing wide boy is portrayed as a creature of instinct, an anti-intellectual who has no need or desire to be 'knowing' and whose *carpe diem* recklessness is an end in itself. But by the close of the song, the chill of passing time leaves him feeling toothless and old. The samples from Karel Reisz's 1959 documentary *We Are The Lambeth Boys* provide an indispensable accompaniment, resurrecting the voices of untamed youth while also instilling the realization that such verve and energy will be eroded in the same way as the laddish exploits of spring-heeled Jim.

"'Spring-Heeled Jim' was the first thing we did with Steve Lillywhite," says Jonny Bridgwood, "and the second track in the can after 'Billy Budd'. We had a meeting with Steve before we went into the studio. He said, 'I'm not one of those producers that works on things all day. If it's not working we'll leave it and move on to something else.' The bizarre thing was that we then spent the entire day on it! It's got the staccato bass and literally I was doing that all day. That evening my entire arm ached. I was thinking, 'Why does my arm feel like this?' It was like I'd been gripping something for a whole day. When you're working on a track and something about it isn't quite right, you lose perspective. You don't know how many times you've been playing it. You just think – 'Apart from a couple of breaks here, it's been about six hours,' and you've got no idea if you're doing it well or terribly. You feel, 'Take 50? That was good enough, I thought!' We were thinking, 'Is it going to be like this every day?' But that was the only track we did like that."

Billy Budd

After the recording sessions had been booked, news came through that producer Steve Lillywhite would not be arriving at the same time as the band due to a prior commitment. "I think it was five days he wasn't there," Bridgwood says. "So we did 'Billy Budd' without him and we kept it. Chris Dickie engineered and Danton Supple assisted. We did a couple of tracks, actually. We didn't think we were going to keep any of them, but we kept 'Billy Budd'. We did the basic backing track live and, as with the other tracks, it evolved. We played it because it was 'vibey' and we wanted to rock 'n' roll. You can hear the live track underneath the overdubs. That's the bed of the thing. It's quite wild in parts and builds up. I like where it takes off. It was very much a live song and we used to start off with it in concert a fair bit at one point."

The song's title was presumably borrowed from Herman Melville's famous short story of incorruptible innocence faced with inexplicable evil. Regrettably, Morrissey's lyrics display none of the moral complexity of Melville's *Billy Budd*. Perhaps the singer took his inspiration from the movie version, which starred his old idol Terence Stamp. There is another cinematic reference at the end of the track with the words 'Don't leave us in the dark' sampled from the Artful Dodger's closing plea to Fagin in David Lean's 1947 film, *Oliver Twist*. As Morrissey noted: "Charles Dickens was very exciting to me because he was a terribly gloomy character, terribly embittered, and quite depressed . . . I love the grim, dim descriptions of the East End, all those murky, winding passages, full of desperate characters – like our friend Fagin."

Another possible subtext to the song was the elusive Johnny Marr. When Morrissey sang that it was 12 years since 'I took up with you', it was difficult to forget that a dozen years had now passed since the formation of the Smiths. The fact that these lines were followed by what sounded like a light pastiche of Marr's pyrotechnic work on 'The Queen Is Dead' merely added to the song's mystery. Passing consideration might also be given to the title of Melville's 1888 collection of poems, *John Marr And Other Sailors: With Some Sea Pieces*.

Hold On To Your Friends

Friendship has been a constant theme in Morrissey's writing and although this composition seemingly emphasizes the need to retain close relations, it was hardly consistent with his general viewpoint. As a teenager, he was quick to dismiss everyday friendships as ephemeral and easily replaceable. More often, he indulged a fantasy relationship with unattainable stars or even inanimate objects like vinyl singles. In 1985, surrounded by a symposium of fanzine editors, he said: "In a very fundamental way, everybody needs friends and a lot of people don't have them. And a lot of people who buy records believe that the artistes who make the records are their friends. They believe that they know these people, and they believe that they're actually involved in these people's lives and it's a comfort." A decade later, during an interview with William Shaw, he admitted: "Some friendships aren't necessarily meant to last forever. It's not because I suddenly wake up and despise them, it's just for the common good that it's best to move on." He was even more dismissive in another feature insisting "most of the people I come into contact with are quite disposable anyway."

Vauxhall And I uses these themes of vulnerability and persecution to subtle effect. It is difficult to believe that Morrissey is not singing about himself when he refers to fighting those who would gallantly fall defending his name. Similarly, the advice to be rash and squander cash sounds like a dialogue between self and soul. There is also criticism of a certain fair-weather friend who only calls the singer when depressed and ignores him in happier times. Who can he be referring to? According to Morrissey: "It was written about somebody I know in relation to their treatment towards me. I'm simply waiting for people to do something damaging and they inevitably do . . . I often wonder, if I was a penniless pauper, would a lot of people that I know want to know me? Maybe they would, but it's more than likely they wouldn't because when I was a penniless pauper, nobody wanted to know me." The motto appears to be that with enemies so prolific, it is pointless to squander time turning on friends.

Musically, the song is most noticeable for its rhythmic use of language and guitar accompaniment. As Bridgwood testifies, "'Hold On To Your Friends' was a huge production. Song-wise it's fairly straightforward, maybe that's why Steve wanted to make it more epic. Steve gets inspired and has these ideas. He's a very creative producer. We did the backing track to it, and then he had Alain do a guitar part. It was essentially how we later played it live but he had

Alain record each string separately. He had to break down the guitar part note by note and then spend hour upon hour working on it. I can't even remember why Lillywhite did that to be honest with you. He literally spent long into the night doing the track. It was exhaustive."

The More You Ignore Me, The Closer I Get

As a single, this was something of a return to form, both lyrically and melodically, and gave Morrissey his first UK Top 10 hit since 'Interesting Drug' five years before. His presentation of love as a psychological chess game, complete with connotations of vengeance if unrequited, contains some impressive lines with analogies to high court judges and even some appropriately fiscal imagery. When Morrissey exclaims 'It's war' and sings of stalking somebody like a 'bad debt', the persona sounds closer to the tenacious Mike Joyce than to himself. The new image of Morrissey as an over-confident suitor also seems out of character and he was quick to qualify such a portrayal. "But as the song ends I don't necessarily succeed. Though I am quite determined, which is new to me. I feel a lot more comfortable the older I get, which is a song title in itself."

Steve Lillywhite's upfront production greatly enhanced the song while the solid riff ensured decent radio play. Originally attempted early in the sessions, it was retrieved and worked on till Morrissey was satisfied. "We seemed to be cracking on," says Bridgwood. "We listened back and it wasn't bad really. So we did a live arrangement of 'The More You Ignore Me . . .' and built it up from the drums. I was happy enough it did well. It's quite catchy and gets in your head. A good pop record. I liked it. I was pleased to come up with the bass line. I remember we were working on it and I was thinking, 'There's a particular part in here I want to play,' and then it just clicked. When we came to the outro I did a completely different descending part. It's essentially the same chords but it starts and descends whereas the rest of the song ascends. All the descending guitar parts were put on afterwards which may or may not have been because I'd done the bass line. I don't really know. But personally I was very pleased with it. It was very straightforward, studio-wise."

Why Don't You Find Out For Yourself

This mini-thesis on the plight of the beleaguered pop star was far more impressive than Morrissey's previous bitter examination on the Smiths' 'Paint A Vulgar Picture'. Here, he rails against money-grubbers, manipulators, skin-peelers, back-stabbers and those that dare to write disparagingly about his career. The repeated song title is a petulant riposte seemingly directed towards both friends and enemies, fans and critics. Biographers and journalists are advised not to rake up his past errors on the grounds that he is already well aware of them. His impatience and annoyance are expressed in chiding, capitalized words on the lyric sheet: 'You Just Sit There'. By the end, his exasperation is replaced by a stoical acceptance and painful shrug of the shoulders in the closing words, 'that's just the way it goes'.

"At first 'Why Don't You Find Out For Yourself' was a straight-ahead rock song," Bridgwood reveals. "It was really rocky. That was one of the tunes we played at Nomis along with 'Now My Heart Is Full', 'The More You Ignore Me, The Closer I Get' and, I think, 'Billy Budd'. If not the latter, then certainly the first three. The first recording was all right, but nothing special. It sounded a bit throw-away but the song was obviously very good so it was recorded, including the vocal. Everything. Although it was not finished, the track had gone down. Then there was a wholesale rethink because it was very rocky. Maybe it sounded a bit too much like the material on *Your Arsenal*. As it stood it didn't have a place on the album that was evolving. I think Morrissey said, 'Let's try it another way.' So what we did was keep the vocal and completely replace the track which was kind of bizarre because it had a pumping bass and loads of electric guitars. And that was completely stripped down. An acoustic guitar and double bass made it much lighter. It was almost like a remix in one sense whereby you keep the original vocal and replace every-thing else. We decided to go completely in the opposite direction. As it was 'full-on electric' the obvious opposite was stripped-down all acoustic which is why it just had the long, bowed bass lines. There wasn't much happening. I recall there were brushes put on the track rather than full-on drumming."

Morrissey's singing has seldom, if ever, been better, while the acoustic guitar, high in the mix, testifies to the care with which Steve Lillywhite produced the track. In the background, there's an eerie, keening vocal and some whispered words that seep through. As Bridgwood recounts, "If you listen to it closely, following the opening part you can hear the words 'some men here' in the distance. Here's how it happened. At Hook End, there's a huge mixing desk that I always likened to the bridge on the Starship Enterprise – there's the screen and everything. Boz was doing some percussion on the table worktop and there was a tray on it with a teapot and cups that were all rattling. Steve said, 'I like that – let's sample it,' and he recorded a bit of it along with the track and leaked it. So on the song you can hear the faint echo of 'some men here' and that goes on throughout the track. Later, Boz was working out a part, just messing about with one of his guitars, a semi-acoustic that wasn't plugged in. Steve took a mike and ended up recording a hollow-bodied guitar acoustically. And that's on there as well. There were loads of little things like that. Steve was really enthusiastic – he'd say, 'Let's do that!' and then stick it on. Everything evolved, and suddenly something different emerged that was much more exciting and in keeping with the overall flavour. We spent so long on that album. We probably did only half of the tracks as they were originally conceived. This was not necessarily going to be the follow-up to any previous album. Suddenly it was quite different and apart . . . which is why I think a lot of people like *Vauxhall And I* who may not necessarily like other Morrissey albums."

I Am Hated For Loving

A simple melody and delicate arrangement frames this less than convincing plea of persecution aimed against anonymous callers and poison pen pushers. The echo on Morrissey's voice adds a poignant element to an otherwise average composition. Although the songs begin to overstate the central theme here, the sheer air of defiance that Morrissey oozes proves compelling. Moreover, his insistence that he does not 'belong' places him in the same space as the subject of 'Bengali In Platforms', a move which complicates and defuses any simplistic accusations of racism.

Musically, the song was far more radical in demo form and

underwent significant changes. "It was a bit like 'Why Don't You Find Out For Yourself'," Bridgwood told me, "in the sense that we never attempted it this way. The song wasn't on the original tape that we had a copy of, but there was a demo which I heard which we didn't work on. It was vaguely Clash-like and Alain's a huge Clash fan. Morrissey and Steve obviously decided to try something unlike the demo, possibly so that it enhanced everything else that was developing on the album. It became a complete production number. We hadn't worked up an arrangement or played it live as such. I think the rhythm guitar part was put down first and Woodie was playing drums in the control room. He did lots of contrasting takes and you'll notice how the drums build during the track and get louder. We had him doing it different ways with brushes and different takes were used for different parts of the song. After we did the drums, Steve produced his Hofner violin Beatle-bass and said, 'Why don't you try this on this track? Let's do a bit of a McCartney thing.' He obviously had something in mind. It actually worked really well because I naturally play that kind of way. I wrote the part on Steve's bass but, when it came to recording, parts of it would be out of tune, so we decided not to use it. I'd borrowed a semi-acoustic Hofner bass from Dave Brolan of the Shanakies which I used on that track. It was the closest to the Beatle-bass sound. So that was me doing my McCartney thing. Then everything else was put on. It was a fairly simple track. When I heard it, I thought it was back to front musically and vocally. Morrissey was singing a verse as a chorus and a chorus as a verse. There are parts I play where I doubt I would have done if I'd known he was going to sing there. And yet it works. Now when I listen back to it I can't imagine it being any different."

Lifeguard Sleeping, Girl Drowning
There's a sprinkling of the old Morrissey misogyny in this tale of an attention-seeking woman who tries somebody's patience once too often. A string quartet is present alongside an impressive clarinet arrangement from Boz Boorer. Morrissey's whispered, sensual vocal is both extremely seductive and menacing.

"It was Steve Lillywhite's idea to do something completely different vocally in a very un-Morrissey way," says Bridgwood. "We did an arrangement, played it live, got the drums and built it up from there. Having recorded the album pretty much instrumentally, we cleared out for a few days while Morrissey did his vocals because he wanted to get on without any distractions. Some string people came down for 'Interlude' which was done at the sessions, so any strings on there are real."

The result was one of the more unusual compositions in the Morrissey canon. "It's a song inspired by real facts," Morrissey claims, "but what's the use of talking about it since the girl in question sank a long time ago. Yes, I can be cruel with women, as with men." Within the context of the song it's difficult not to feel sympathy for the drowned girl who is finally dismissed as 'nobody's nothing'. Thematically, the composition recalls both Stevie Smith's *Not Waving But Drowning* and Patti Smith's 'Redondo Beach', but with a far more vindictive edge. Morrissey may also have been inspired by his own composition 'Lifeguard On Duty', recorded during the *Viva Hate* sessions, although the lyrics here are different.

Used To Be A Sweet Boy

At a crucial stage in the album, Morrissey addresses the very root of his childhood neuroses. Here, for the first time on record, he expresses his uneasy and unresolved relationship with his father. The song followed comments from the singer about the breakup of his parents' marriage when he was 17. "Realizing that your parents aren't compatible, I think, gives you a premature sense of wisdom that life isn't easy and it isn't simple to be happy. Happiness is something you're very lucky to find. So I grew up with a serious attitude, but my parents weren't the basis of my neuroses."

Morrissey's father was puzzled by the song's sentiments at the time of its release, but was intrigued when I suggested to him that the plea 'I'm not to blame' was more likely to be the parents speaking rather than the son. Many years later, Morrissey confirmed that this was the interpretation he intended. "In the song, it is the parents who speak and decline all responsibilities. To me though, parents must assume responsibility: they bring children up, not the other way round."

Musically the understated backing, highlighted by piano and

compressed harmonies, made this autobiographical confession the most evocative and moving composition on the album. "It was done fairly late in the sessions," says Bridgwood. "By that time we were really into our stride and had a good working relationship so it was really easy. It was very much an Alain Whyte track. There was the guitar and I think he added the piano afterwards. It was not done live, but evolved in a very studio way. We never had an arrangement as such, although it was fairly close to the demo. The song was just as it was. I sat back in the control room while Alain was playing. The track was going round and round while he was doing some stuff and I just wrote the bass part in my head. It was fairly simple anyway, it just follows a progression. Steve said, 'Right, do the bass,' and within 15 minutes I was done. We laughed about it at the time. From having just heard the track played through the speakers I got up and played it. And that was that. It was probably the quickest track on the whole album. The easiest track I did — the easiest day's work I've ever done."

The Lazy Sunbathers
The setting for this odd composition prompted one writer to reach the dubious conclusion that it was inspired by events in World War II. A more likely explanation is that Morrissey is projecting forward into a dystopian future. Significantly, he sets the scene a few days after the outbreak of *a* world war (with no capitals). I always interpreted the lyrics as a satire of Hollywood and Costa Rica values, with sun worshippers portrayed as immune even to the news of a probable nuclear war. The sound effects suggest splashing waves or acid rain in the background. In this sense, the theme is not dissimilar to that evoked in 'Everyday Is Like Sunday', except that the weather is hotter and the fantasy of the bomb dropping suddenly becomes even more real.

"It was one of the songs we did very early in the sessions," Bridgwood reveals. "We were working it out live and Woodie was wondering what was happening because we weren't getting into a groove as a band. So Steve Lillywhite set up a mike and Morrissey sang it. He stood in the booth and we could hear him through the headphones and, after he sang, it just fell into place and went down fairly easily. During the time I played with him, over three albums, that was the only track that ever happened that way in the studio. Elsewhere, we'd always do the instrumental track first. There were a lot of things added to that song. Two double basses were used and the whole album is awash with guitar effects. Alain had a really active pick-up on his Gibson Les Paul and he used to do backing vocals through his guitar."

Speedway

There's a school of thought that says Morrissey pre-empted Eminem during the opening of this track by using a chain-saw for dramatic effect. "It's not a chain-saw," Jonny Bridgwood insists. "It's engineer Danton Supple with a drill. I am positive about that. He told me afterwards." If the sound effects were confusing, then the lyrics seemed even more puzzling. Morrissey playfully keeps his critics guessing by suggesting that the rumours that kept him grounded were not entirely unfounded. The *NME* interpreted this as an admission that there might be some truth in the racist allegations, but it was more likely a wind-up, with Morrissey proving as oblique as ever. This was borne out in an interview with *Q* where he was quizzed about whether the unspecified 'rumours' were indeed true.

"Yes, partly," he responded, "but if you're going to bring up the issue of racism, it simply gives too much credence to the bitty, scattered rumours that abound. But I'm well aware that rumours are more important than truth. I've been called many names in my time, not all of them ill-fitting. Rather than defend myself I simply feel beyond it all."

Within the song, the tease continues to the very end when Morrissey unexpectedly introduces another character into the story. Having portrayed himself throughout as the victim, then admitted that there might be something in those unexplained 'twisted lies', he finally tells us about an unnamed person, guilty by association, whom he is protecting. It's fascinating to witness Morrissey transforming a song of victimization into a conspiracy theory, complete with an unresolved ending.

In certain respects, the composition sounds distinctly Smiths-like. The allusion to being swallowed by the earth recalls the enveloping soil described in 'I Know It's Over', while the speedway itself is an image familiar from 'Rusholme Ruffians'. Indeed, the speedway becomes a recurring motif that echoes through the respective child-hoods of both Morrissey and Marr. "I spent a lot of time at the fair in Wythenshawe Park and I worked at a speedway in a place down in Cheshire," Marr once told me.

His nostalgic memories were not entirely shared by Morrissey who encountered violence beneath the ersatz glamour. "I remember being at a fair in Stretford Road: it was very early, about 5pm, and I was just standing by the speedway. And somebody just came over to me and head-butted me. He was much older than me, and much bigger. I was dazed for at least five minutes. What I find remarkable is the way you just accepted it. That was just the kind of thing that happened. I don't think that it was even that I looked dif-ferent in those days. There never needed to be a reason."

'Speedway' provided a suitably epic ending to the album, building to a climax during which drummer Woodie Taylor appeared to be inhabited by the ghost of John Bonham. The recording was a saga in itself. " 'Speedway' went from being a straight-ahead band effort to a big production," Bridgwood recalls. "We recorded that track in a different key in a slightly different version. Then we did 'Interlude' and towards the end of the sessions we tried 'Speedway' again. We were working towards getting a backing track for it in a new key. Morrissey sang it in E originally, then it went up to F-sharp which was more his range. During recording, we changed the arrangement, particularly the intro. We did the track as it is and the first half of it was ready to be used on the album. While we were doing it, Steve Lillywhite said: 'I've got this idea!' There's this big dining-room at Hook End Manor. It has a wooden floor and wooden panels all the way up the walls and across the ceiling. He decided that the drum for the second half of the track should be recorded there. Although the dining-room wasn't that far away from the desk, we had to set up mikes and everything, so we needed cables about 500 metres long. There was a wait of several hours while these cables were brought in from London. We just went off for a walk, played pool and amused ourselves until these cables arrived. There was this huge break and I think we finished the rest of the track the next day with Woodie doing the drums. I don't know why exactly but they did the cymbals in the laundry-room! It was incredible. We'd recently done 'Used To Be A Sweet Boy' really quickly but this was the opposite. The epic end with the rim shot on the drums is not an effect. The sound of the drums is literally the sound of that dining-room. It was a big finish."

WORLD OF MORRISSEY

Released: February 1995

Parlophone PCSD 163, CDPCSD 163, February 1995. US issue: Sire 9-45879-2

The second UK compilation of Morrissey's solo career proved a relative disappointment for those who had hoped he might at last round up all his B-sides on CD. Rather than emulating *Hatful Of Hollow*, *The World Won't Listen* or even *Bona Drag*, the patchy *World Of Morrissey* seemed closer to an unimaginative record company marketing exercise. The only mystery is why Morrissey allowed his work to be issued in such a lazy and haphazard fashion. Perhaps, he no longer held any contractual control over reissues.

As a compilation, this was a rag-bag of recent singles, fleshed out with three tracks from *Beethoven Was Deaf* and four from the recent *Vauxhall And I*. As if to sum up the wayward nature of the exercise, the compilers even included 'The Last Of The Famous International Playboys', conveniently forgetting that it had already featured on the previous compilation, *Bona Drag*.

Not surprisingly, *World Of Morrissey* left some reviewers baffled. *NME*'s Keith Cameron concluded: "*World Of Morrissey* isn't so much a vulgar picture as an extremely bizarrely conceived collage. One presumes motivated solely by the need to have some 'new' product in the racks for the UK tour, this generation's most exhaustively compiled living artiste has decided to release a new old album that appears to entertain no rhyme or reason whatsoever."

The album title was obviously borrowed from the famous *World Of* . . . series of Decca compilations that were available during Morrissey's teenage years. Generally, these were quick-fire bargain compilations put together without too much thought, care or attention. If this was intended as an ironic parody of those, then it succeeded. At least EMI followed Decca's route by issuing the album with a mid-price tag. Presumably, it was hoped that the compilation might attract casual listeners to investigate Morrissey's better work.

All the tracks included have been previously discussed, except the following:

Whatever Happens, I Love You

The album begins impressively with the highlight of the entire set. Criminally placed as the third track on the single 'Boxers', this gem was one of the more adventurous and musically interesting moments in recent Morrissey history. Lyrically an extension of the obsessive love described on 'Speedway', it echoed that song's sonic assault. The musicians are given full rein to use their imaginations and Boz Boorer manages to take the tune into some strange places with his expressive saxophone work, which interlocks bizarrely with Whyte's wild lead guitar, abetted by sound effects and a strong rhythm section. At times it seems like some throwback to the experimental sounds of mid-period Yardbirds complete with a raga rock tinge. Morrissey provides a passionate and beguiling vocal for added effect and Woodie Taylor's drumming is strong. As Jonny Bridgwood concludes: "'Whatever Happens I Love You' was quite a powerful song but it got a bit lost as a B-side. If there had been more songs completed at the time, it would certainly have been on an album. But the 'Boxers' session didn't evolve like *Vauxhall And I*, even though the same people were in the studio."

Have-A-Go Merchant

In common with its A-side 'Boxers', this revealed Morrissey's current penchant for singing about rough boys, complete with a line of pub cockney patter. The lyric also deals with the intricacies of a father/daughter relationship set against backing vocals that sound as though they have been adapted from a sea shanty. Not the greatest Morrissey song, but a reasonable B-side which was typical of the band sound he had developed on recent releases. The song's title revealed Morrissey's affection for dated London slang, although some wily commentators maintain that it may have been a coded slight directed towards 10,000 Maniacs' Natalie Merchant who sang a cover version of 'Everyday Is Like Sunday' on the B-side of their single 'Candy Everybody Wants'.

The Loop

Recently released in live form on *Beethoven Was Deaf*, this was the original studio version that appeared on the 12-inch single and CD of 'Sing Your Life'. An out of character experiment from the 'rockabilly' sessions attempted towards the end of *Kill Uncle*, it remains an interesting curio. At the start it sounds like some Western theme performed by an early Sixties instrumental group. Morrissey's lyrics, which may well be addressed to Johnny Marr, are an open invitation to pick up the telephone when he is ready. Although the credits on 'The Loop' state that Jonny Bridgwood played bass, this was not the case. "I did 'Born To Hang' and 'Pregnant For The Last Time' but I wasn't on 'The Loop'," Bridgwood points out. "It was Bedders on that. People often assume it's me. But if you look at the record, it also says 'Alain Whyte – harmonica'. He actually played harmonica on 'Pregnant For The Last Time' but at the mixing stage they decided not to use it. Obviously there's no harmonica on 'The Loop' but he gets a credit for it on the back of 'Sing Your Life'. So it's right credits – wrong song, wrong sleeve."

Boxers

The current single at the time of the compilation's release, this was Morrissey's paean to pugilists past with a snatch of commentary from, I think, Reg Gutteridge, among others. Unfortunately, Morrissey fails to create a musical equivalent of *Raging Bull* and his tale of the defeated boxer lacks any drama. Both the wife and nephew described in the song appear like pasteboard figures and Morrissey fails to enter the boxer's mind to realize the poignancy expressed in his vocal. The song was originally conceived as the lead track for an EP but devolved into a three-track single with the fourth song 'Sunny' issued separately. Eminently uncommercial, 'Boxers' flopped, reaching only number 23 in the UK charts.

Nowadays, the song is remembered less for its tune than its promotion, which featured Morrissey brandishing a knuckleduster while attempting to look menacing. He was even photographed in a gymnasium, posing with boxers, including the super middleweight champion John 'Cornelius' Carr. In the accompanying 'Boxers' tour, Morrissey took the image further by displaying cuts and bruises, courtesy of the make-up department. Inevitably, his new hobby attracted media interest, sometimes to his chagrin. "I released a single called 'Boxers' and everyone assumes I'm some authority and I'm not," he told *Q*'s Stuart Maconie. "I'm not an expert on the manly art or the sweet science as it's called. I just enjoy the violent aspect of it. I think it's quite glamorous." Elaborating on that point, he told *Select*: "For me it's the sense of glamour that's attractive, the romance, but mainly it's the aggression that interests me. It has me instantly leaving my seat and heading for the ropes to join in."

Moonriver (Extended)
In 1961, Danny Williams topped the charts with this Henry Mancini/ Johnny Mercer classic. Familiar to anyone who has seen the film *Breakfast At Tiffany's*, the song had long been a standard and seemed an odd choice for Morrissey. Frequently, he sounds out of his depth and although his Mancunian vowels are disguised, the mannered style required of such an evergreen merely emphasizes his vocal limitations. Released as a B-side, this did not feature the same line-up that recorded *Vauxhall And I*. With rumours of a tour, the old rhythm section of Gary Day and Spencer Cobrin returned, although the former did not appear on the track. "Boz played bass," Bridgwood remembers. "Gary had problems with the song. Afterwards, Boz told me that Morrissey was saying, 'What happened?' and he told him, 'Well, half the band's different now!'"

The 'extended' version of 'Moonriver' that appears here originally featured as an extra track on the 'Hold On To Your Friends' single and lasts for nine-and-a-half minutes. It is most noticeable for the different sound effects and a spooky ending during which Morrissey sings the refrain while a girl can be heard crying her eyes out.

My Love Life
Something of a lost single from the Morrissey canon, this only reached number 29 despite the fact that it had never appeared on album. It was a reasonable, if unadventurous, single from the pen of Mark Nevin. Morrissey's lyrics are as slight as the arrangement, serving as a doomed address to somebody who is already in love. Even the additional harmonies from Chrissie Hynde sound oddly

understated, although this was presumably intended. Why this was chosen as a single still seems odd, particularly when you consider that Nevin had previously shown a strong pop sensibility with the anthemic Fairground Attraction chart-topper 'Perfect'. As drummer Andrew Paresi recalls: "The last thing I did with Morrissey was 'My Love Life' even though it was credited to his rockabilly group. It was done at Clive and Alan's West Side Studio. You could tell that things were coming to an end."

Full track listing: *Whatever Happens, I Love You; Billy Budd; Jack The Ripper (Live); Have-A-Go Merchant; The Loop; Sister I'm A Poet (Live); You're The One For Me, Fatty (Live); Boxers; Moonriver (Extended); My Love Life; Certain People I Know; The Last Of The Famous International Playboys; We'll Let You Know; Spring-Heeled Jim.*

SOUTHPAW GRAMMAR

Released: August 1995

RCA Victor 299531, 29953-2 CD, September 1995.
US issue: Reprise 9-45939-2, August 1995

In December 1994, the band relocated to the south of France to commence work on a new album, retaining Steve Lillywhite as producer. Evidently nobody was too sure how the project might develop. As Jonny Bridgwood remembers: "We were thinking, 'What shall we do?' So we started some demos, literally bare bones – acoustic guitars, bass and drums – for an album that we generally perceived (whether Morrissey did is another matter) as a follow-up to *Vauxhall And I*, principally because it was the same personnel. Some of the songs we demoed in France were just scrapped completely. I never heard them again. They were more in keeping with *Vauxhall And I* than *Southpaw Grammar* . . . We then flew home for Christmas and then we went back . . . We started working on things like 'The Teachers Are Afraid Of The Pupils', 'Dagenham Dave', 'The Boy Racer', 'Reader Meet Author', 'Best Friend On The Payroll' . . . pretty well most of the album. After that Steve Lillywhite decided it was pointless because Morrissey wasn't there to approve the tracks."

When Morrissey heard the results he was unimpressed. During February, Spencer Cobrin returned to replace Woodie Taylor, and the group set out on the 'In Person' tour which coincided with the release of 'Boxers' and *World Of Morrissey*. The following month, they were back in the studio at Hook End Manor. Fresh from playing live, they swiftly completed a work which was radically different from its predecessor. "We'd just come off the road so it made sense to do the album," Bridgwood says. "We were prepared by then, so there weren't any great surprises. It happened quickly and became quite a rocky album. It wasn't as creative as *Vauxhall And I*. That's why I always say *Vauxhall And I* is more something completely separate. If you didn't know the chronology and just listened to the albums you'd naturally assume that *Southpaw Grammar* was the follow-up to *Your Arsenal*."

It was never going to be easy following up an album as strong as the great *Vauxhall And I*, as Morrissey himself no doubt realized. Evidently, his instinct was to try something different while retaining most of his former backing musicians. Rather than the glam stomp of *Your Arsenal* or the introspection of *Vauxhall And I,* this was a heavy, tough-rocking record dominated by the band. "I didn't want to give birth to *Vauxhall And I Part 2*," Morrissey explained, "so I asked the producer Steve Lillywhite to work with me again, explaining that I wanted to record a hard and solid album without a slow song. I wanted to reinvent myself."

Part of the reinvention involved a change of UK label with Morrissey choosing RCA Victor, the former home of Elvis Presley, Lou Reed and David Bowie. By this point Morrissey was beginning to resemble an elder statesman at the grand old age of 36. Britpop was in the ascendant and a legion of groups, spearheaded by Oasis and Blur, were achieving mainstream success and record sales beyond anything achieved by the Smiths. Although most of these acts acknowledged the importance of the Smiths, the general attitude towards Morrissey was more ambivalent and soured soon after the release of *Southpaw Grammar*. The work sounded conspicuously out of place amid the pop-fixated albums of the time which, in theory, was no bad thing. Unfortunately, despite several strong tracks, the album tended to dip in the middle and lacked the songwriting consistency of *Vauxhall And I*. There was evidence to suggest that with greater discrimination and more time, Morrissey might have constructed a more substantial album, but with only eight songs on offer the work sounded oddly incomplete. It still works well as a band album and probably served Morrissey's purpose in 'capturing the moment' after some solid touring but, like *Kill Uncle*, its better moments were obscured amid the debate over songwriting consistency, length and number of songs featured.

Critical reaction was generally negative and worsened with passing time. *NME*'s David Quantick, the critic who had once championed *Kill Uncle*, awarded *Southpaw Grammar* a measly five points out of 10. This time around, the lighter songs left him cold and he could muster no enthusiasm for the epic tracks that bookended the album. "Morrissey's sacrificed light and shade, and wit and insight just to make two portentous musical non-statements. The other songs, tuneful though they are, comment about issues for which the word 'trivia' is too mighty, and substitute thumping around in an attic full of tin boxes for production and arrangement. In the end, there's no reason why anyone who already owns a record made by Morrissey – or, more particularly, the Smiths – should even want to hear this record, let alone buy it. Its maker should call himself 'The Morrissey Formerly Known As Artist'."

RCA Victor's parent company chose to issue *Southpaw Grammar* in August, a quiet month for record releases but a good time to maximize chart action. Alas, after entering at number 4, the album plummeted. In the US, it fared even worse, peaking at a lowly number 66. Critics seized upon these setbacks to pose the inevitable harsh questions about Morrissey's continuing role in the brave new world of Britpop. Could it be that his time as a great pop icon was at last over?

The Teachers Are Afraid Of The Pupils

A deceptively thrilling opening, this inspired 11-minute epic featured a sample of Dmitri Dmitrievich Shostakovich's *Symphony No. 5* set against the sound of sawed strings for added dramatic effect. Morrissey seldom changes his point of view on key issues but here we have him reversing the sentiments of 'The Headmaster Ritual' and empathizing with a downtrodden and cowed teacher. Tellingly it's the only track whose lyrics are featured on the inside of the CD insert, as if Morrissey wanted us to read these words above all others. Strong lines and double meanings abound, most notably the phrase 'we'll have you' which serves as a legal threat from the parents but also has connotations of violence in its colloquial usage. Similarly, the refrain 'to be finished would be a relief' expresses both the teacher's frustration and Morrissey's own ennui. However, what truly empowers the track is the full-on production and Boorer's foreboding effects which combine to make this a wonderful companion piece to 'The Headmaster Ritual'.

According to Bridgwood: "We started playing and working on 'The Teachers Are Afraid Of The Pupils' at soundchecks during the

'In Person' tour. Steve Lillywhite came to a couple of the shows and there were discussions then about the forthcoming sessions. So we had some clues . . . Obviously this was Boz's track and he built it on the strings sample. Essentially, it's just the same track twice really. It was only half that length originally and we built it up into an epic. There was all the bowed double bass to begin with. We recorded it in two parts – the first and the second half. It literally kicks in, then it becomes fully electric which is how we did it live on the later 'Outsiders' tour with Bowie. It was a huge number. I suppose Morrissey wanted to do something different. There was no point in making another *Vauxhall And I*."

Reader Meet Author

Seizing significance in the title some reviewers reckoned this was written about 'Johnny Rogan'. For the record, Morrissey never mentioned this when I met him in the High Court and when asked the same question by *RTE Guide*'s Alan Corr, he emphatically denied this lazy interpretation: "No! No! [very amused] Not at all. He should be so lucky . . . 'Reader Meet Author' is about a lot of middle-class journalists I know who think they have an understanding of the working classes and their fascinations, which they patently do not." Elaborating on this for Stuart Maconie, he added: "I've come across it many times. It's a fascinating phenomenon. Especially among music journalists who pretend to understand all aspects of life however degrading. It amuses me that these people are middle class and their preoccupation is meddling with the destitute and desperate as a hobby. Middle-class writers are fascinated by those who struggle. They find it righteous and amusing . . . I sing, 'The year 2000 won't change anyone here' and that's true. It won't change their lives. They won't be catapulted into space age culture and mobile fax machines. The poor remain poor. Someone has to work in Woolworth's."

As a comment on cultural tourism and the upsurge of laddism, the song was apposite, while the sprightly arrangement provided an ironic bite. Some of the acerbic lines displayed Morrissey's cold sarcasm at its best and there was even a subtle nod to 'Handsome Devil' (in which he'd told us there was more to life than books) in the suggestion 'books aren't Stanley knives'.

The Boy Racer

Immediately after commenting on the class divide and the current state of music journalism, Morrissey's urban observations turned to the new phenomenon of the terrorizing boy racer. Once more, Morrissey oozes sarcasm, picturing the boy at a urinal, then singing the title of Laurie London's 1957 hit, 'He's Got The Whole World In His Hands'. At other times, the gap between derision and admiration appears wafer thin.

The frantic musical accompaniment brings the song to a thundering climax in keeping with the album's overall mood. "I just remember lots of guitar, lots of Boz and Alain, it was very much a guitar album," Bridgwood concludes. "On his Gibson Les Paul, Alain's got a really active pick-up and you can particularly hear it on songs like 'The Boy Racer'. All those screams, all those backing vocals – that's coming through his guitar. It's incredible. I've never seen another guitar in the same model that you can do that with. He just discovered that he could do it through the pick-up and it was used a fair bit. Alain was incredibly creative with sounds and Steve Lillywhite would exploit that to produce those interesting effects. I remember 'The Boy Racer' principally for the James Bond-like progression in the middle. We'd changed the key and needed to get from one key to another so we put that bridge piece in. It sounded different."

The Operation

The idea of Morrissey sanctioning a drum solo straight out of the progressive rock school seemed inconceivable, but here it was. Spencer Cobrin is let loose for nearly two-and-a-half minutes before the singer and band intervene. Bridgwood was as mystified as everyone else about Morrissey's decision. "I have absolutely no idea why or what was in his head. He just wanted a big drum intro and we thought, 'Fine.' We repaired to the pub while Spencer spent hours doing loads of takes on the drums with the assistant engineer Tom Elmhirst. If you listen closely, you can hear lots of squeaking during the song. That was the sound of a vehicle doing a handbrake turn in the courtyard outside." The track includes another ferocious guitar interlude which takes this otherwise average composition close to seven minutes in length.

Given the title *Southpaw Grammar* it seems odd that the protagonist mentioned here fights with his right hand rather than his left, which is evidently used for caressing. Accusative and contemptuous, Morrissey plays the bitter admirer who rejects the object of his affection for undergoing a personality makeover. Ironically what draws his greatest ire are changes which most people would consider extremely positive ('you say clever things . . . pleasant things').

Dagenham Dave

The birthplace of Sandie Shaw was the subject of this light satire which, like 'The Boy Racer', focuses on the vacuity of young life in suburbia. The empty existence of the titular anti-hero sounds too easy a target for Morrissey's curmudgeonly wit and the lyrics are so tired that the narrator effectively gives up during the first verse: 'I could tell you more but you get the picture'. Although it was the only song on the album to be issued as a single, it climbed no higher than number 26, despite the presence of two new studio tracks, 'Nobody Loves Us' and 'You Must Please Remember'. Blandly catchy but insubstantial, 'Dagenham Dave' attracted one of the fiercest reviews of Morrissey's career. *NME*'s Tommy Udo sneered: "We know that any criticism of Morrissey will have a whole host of you pasty-faced sensitive little pantywaisters throwing fits of the vapours and putting green ink to yellow paper to bleat abuse at us, but what the hell . . . come and have a go if you think you're hard enough. The fact is that this simply isn't very good . . . Actually, it's pure shite. If any further proof was needed that Morrissey has become the embarrassing incontinent grandfather of Britpop, look no further than this tune-impaired three-minute drone. He must have difficulty keeping a straight face as he dashes off this piss-poor old crap, secure in the knowledge that enough hard-core sycophants will keep him in royalties for a while longer, their loyalty making them selectively deaf when they listen to their Morrissey-god's increasingly dire efforts. 'Dagenham Dave' really smacks of 'Will this do?' – just a generic Morrissey track that sounds like a weak album-filler – even the title is borrowed from the Stranglers."

Do Your Best And Don't Worry

With its solid, if workmanlike, instrumental backdrop and unremarkable lyrical content, this sounded somewhat half-baked, as if Morrissey
had achieved his aim of writing a good chorus, but neglected to fill in
the remainder of the song. Perhaps the title stood partly as a comment
on the artistic process during this time of 'low spirits'. Bridgwood
confirms the suspicion that the song was something of an afterthought. "It was done very quickly towards the end of the sessions. I
went home for a couple of days then went back on a Sunday and
when I got there it was like the *Marie Celeste*. Nobody was there. So I
thought, 'Oh, I'm not going to stay here by myself if everybody has
gone,' so I got in the car and went back home. I phoned the next day
and Steve said, 'I don't think you're needed any more.' I said, 'Right,
OK.' I called back in a couple of days and he said, 'No, we definitely
don't need you to come in and finish it.' Which is why 'Do Your
Best And Don't Worry' has Boz playing bass because I wasn't there
when it was recorded. It was a song that was just pulled out and I've
absolutely no idea why. Boz probably had a tune and they just did it
and knocked it out. I never even heard it till I got the album. I was on
every other track except that one. It was done just before they mixed
it."

Best Friend On The Payroll

Given Morrissey's penchant for autobiographical allusions, it was
tempting to interpret this as a message to his friend and former
employee, Jake. Lyrically, it pushes home the point that business and
friendship seldom mix well. Again, there is a sense of a potentially
strong song that ultimately does not emerge. It opens promisingly
with Morrissey's casually petulant observation about having to
placate his employee by turning down the music in his own house.
But the wit ends there and the musical accompaniment is at best
unremarkable, leaving Morrissey to carry the song through persis-
tence rather than genius.

Southpaw

This 10-minute epic finale begins with the sounds of guitar strings
being brutally clawed, after which the listener is treated to an

ambitious musical backdrop full of unnerving effects. Morrissey was amused by one writer's suggestion that he was the new king of progressive rock. "Oh, definitely. I'd love to continue where Van Der Graaf Generator left off. No, we just didn't know how to stop the tape. There's no great point . . . As musicians, they've improved enormously . . . We've become a group and it shows. It's not a matter of me saying, 'You get on with it while I go and ski somewhere.' We're just getting better. That simple; that complicated."

Along with 'The Operation' and 'Do Your Best And Don't Worry' this was the only song that the band had not worked on during their sojourn in the south of France. Lyrically, the composition reads like an exercise in self-therapy, confirming how key childhood experiences are destined to be re-enacted in later life, with particular emphasis on lost friendship and the intense relationship between mother and son. Using two lengthy tracks to bookend the album was a clever device, although the work would surely have benefited from an extra song or two. Nevertheless, it provided a powerful conclusion to an album that was both intriguing and frustrating.

The dramatic outro was recorded in a single take and the sudden cessation at the end was literally the tape running out. "Rather than fading it, we let it run," Bridgwood confirms. "The ending went on for about four minutes and I had to replace the bass for some reason. I remember standing in the control room and replacing it in the one take. Obviously I knew the part − it's the same thing, just going round and round. But when you're repeating a phrase over and over, you've got to focus. In that particular song, it had to be the same. I remember Danton Supple saying, 'You looked like you were hypnotized.' I was really concentrating − I thought, 'I don't want to do this over and over I just want to do it once and that will be the end.' And it was great and it was a relief when we got to the end of the track."

VIVA HATE [EXTENDED EDITION]
Released: April 1997
Parlophone 7243 8 56325 2 5, April 1997, February 2002

In April 1997, as part of EMI's 100th anniversary celebrations, *Viva Hate* was reissued in a new cover, minus musicians' credits and song lyrics, but with the surprise addition of eight early B-sides previously unavailable on album. With Morrissey's commercial currency at a worrying low, this was an opportunity to recall a time when he was universally acclaimed and number 1 in the album charts. Although he later admitted that *Viva Hate* was a flawed record, it remains a fascinating example of Morrissey attempting to come to terms with the demise of the Smiths by proving his worth with a work of considerable quality. The presence of two of his biggest solo hits – 'Suedehead' and 'Everyday Is Like Sunday' – ensured that the album would always feature among his best. Oddly, this new version did not include the classic 'Hairdresser On Fire', which featured on the US edition of *Viva Hate*, presumably because EMI had already included the song on the excellent *Bona Drag* compilation. The sparse credits, not an untypical occurrence on reissues, particularly annoyed Vini Reilly who already felt his contributions had been severely undervalued.

Below are the songs not previously discussed.

Let The Right One Slip In
With its ring-out-the-old, ring-in-the-new theme, this song sounded like a thinly veiled farewell to the Smiths ('let the wrong ones go') complete with a desire to end the mind games, tricks and schemes. In typical Morrissey fashion the word 'slip' adds a slight sexual connotation to his admonitions, while the festive 'oh ho's offer a cautious celebratory air. The track was previously not part of Morrissey's official UK discography having appeared as the final song on the US single 'Tomorrow', although it was, of course, available on import.

229

Pashernate Love

Originally to be found on the B-side of 1991's 'You're The One For Me, Fatty', this Mick Ronson production premièred the glam rock style of *Your Arsenal*. In keeping with the glam tradition, Morrissey follows Slade's annoying habit of misspelling song titles. There may also be something in the theory that the title was inspired by 'Mad Passionate Love', a 1958 UK Top 10 hit by *Carry On* actor Bernard Bresslaw. Bassist Gary Day receives a rare co-writing credit alongside bandmate Alain Whyte.

The lyrics play on the popular image of Morrissey as pop's great celibate as he sings about making love in any form, whether real or in a dream. Some of the imagery is amusing, including the frightening spectacle of someone's sister covered in boils and blisters and a grandmother roller-skating back from her grave, presumably in the hope of finding 'pashernate' love. At just over two minutes, this was Morrissey at his most economical.

At Amber

Morrissey had already displayed his antipathy towards seaside resorts on 'Everyday Is Like Sunday' and here we find the singer in the foyer of the Sands Hotel on the phone to an invalid friend. His litany of complaints lacks the acerbic, deadpan humour of 'Everyday Is Like Sunday', and there is nothing as dramatic as the call for a nuclear war. Indeed, the major faults of the patrons appear to be an over-indulgence in the simple pleasures from which he is detached. Originally attempted under the title 'The Bed Took Fire' and previously featured on the 12-inch single of 'Piccadilly Palare', this light-hearted lament is complemented by a sprightly arrangement, typical of Andy Rourke, which offsets Morrissey's comic empathy with the phone-bound invalid. Here, he partly follows the theme of 'November Spawned A Monster' which had been issued as a single six months before. Of course the treatment is less adventurous or serious. As he told Len Brown: "If you're a genuine artist you have a very powerful vision of most situations, whether or not they're painful, as in my case they most often are. I don't have to know people. It's a matter of understanding many extreme situations in life."

Disappointed
Recorded live in Holland, this was a perennial concert favourite and much loved encore. It's a wonderful example of Morrissey's playfulness and although this terribly rough live cut cannot hope to compete with the original studio version, it is still pleasing to hear again even in such chaotic fashion. Precious little attention has ever been given to the witty lyrics, except for the teasing finale in which the singer retires then changes his mind. However, earlier there is a neat dramatic device in the form of a devastating anonymous letter that causes the singer to voice the reason for his disappointment. Such nuances were not easily conveyed in concert. At this show, Morrissey was besieged by stage invaders throughout the song and at times sounds breathless while the dull thud of the microphone is captured in unwelcome audio-vérité. This composition was first available as the fourth track on the 1991 single 'Pregnant For The Last Time' where it appeared with unedited applause.

Girl Least Likely To
The final track on the CD single of 1990's 'November Spawned A Monster', this was co-written by Andy Rourke during his brief spell back in the Morrissey camp. It is regrettable that the pair did not do more work together as this pithy but catchy song was quite impressive. At times it recalls early period Smiths and, fittingly, the lyrics look back to a period when Morrissey wrote to fellow teenage aspirants in search of unlikely fame. The clever, sarcastic lyrics may sound bitchy, but it is important to remember that many of the sentiments applied to the teenage Morrissey of the late Seventies. Moreover, lines like 'one more song about the queen' and the complaint about turning a knife on everything bar your own life could easily apply to several songs in Morrissey's own canon. Drummer Andrew Paresi was mightily impressed by Rourke, both as a bassist and potential songwriter, and regretted that his reunion with Morrissey proved so brief. "'Girl Least Likely To' is one of my favourite Morrissey songs, at least that I've ever played on. I really went to town on that one. I felt an energy pulsating through me and I just couldn't get enough of it. And as it got to the end I started doing wackier and wackier fills. I started to shift the pattern from being very straight to a

slight shuffle. And then I was doing double bass drum stuff toward the fade-out. I really got off on that one. No disrespect to Mike Joyce, obviously, but that was a building block that we could maybe have moved on with."

I'd Love To

The final track on the 12-inch B-side of 1994's 'The More You Ignore Me, The Closer I Get', this tune, co-written by Boz Boorer, was one of Morrissey's most mournful and despairing songs. However, it did focus on the three great themes of literature: love, time and death. While protesting the sorrows of unrequited love he reflects on how time will wipe us all out and the melancholic tinge in his voice suggests that it is probably already too late for change. His familiar role as the diffident suitor is resurrected along with the usual furtiveness in admitting to love. The emphasis on a singular object of desire recalls 'Hand In Glove', albeit from a gloomier perspective. The band provide a suitably sombre arrangement with funereal organ effects and 'otherworldly' backing vocals.

Michael's Bones

First available as the last track on the 12-inch single of 'The Last Of The Famous International Playboys', this rivalled 'Suffer Little Children' in terms of morbidity, but lacked that song's sensitivity or musical complexity. The dirge-like arrangement is at least in keeping with the lyrics which tell the tale of a boy's death on a sports field, complete with a forensic examination of his body. Just as he had focused on Lesley Ann Downey's pretty white beads, Morrissey spares no adjectives in the macabre description of the victim's frozen hands and death-blue lips. Nor is there any respectful valediction but merely a flippant dismissal, not unlike that offered to the swimmer in the later 'Lifeguard Sleeping, Girl Drowning'. "Yes there's a cruel streak in it," Paresi agrees, "but it's got a tenderness when he sings it. It's almost like 'you're worthless' as he's stroking his head!"

There was considerable confusion about the lyrics as a result of mis-information from the *NME*'s Danny Kelly, who wrote, "'Michael's Bones' is a mournful lament to another of the Moors Murders' victims. The fact that the latter is seriously brilliant won't save it from the wrath of the knee-jerk brigade. Morrissey reckons he's fully aware of, and prepared for, the likely reaction to the record . . ." In fact, Morrissey was referring to the A-side and its 'glorification' of the Krays. Contrary to Kelly's assertion 'Michael's Bones' had nothing to do with the Moors Murders and none of the victims was even named Michael.

I've Changed My Plea To Guilty
What sounds like a tape recording of some Americans talking in a corridor is followed by a stark but stately piano introduction that sets the scene for Morrissey's latest confessional. Originally heard on the B-side of 'My Love Life' this song represented that uncertain stage between the end of *Kill Uncle* and the beginning of *Your Arsenal*. The opening lines about standing in the dock now sound prescient in view of the 1996 court case and the increasing number of songs in which courts, magistrates and the legal system are mentioned. Here, Morrissey employs some metaphorical plea bargaining in the hope of improving his love life while simultaneously realizing that freedom is a wasted reward. The Langer/Winstanley production is characteristically slight and poppy with a sparse piano accompaniment that puts greater emphasis on Morrissey's vocal. At one stage Morrissey rather fancifully described this as "the best song, in my mind, that I've ever recorded".

MALADJUSTED

Released: August 1997

Island ILPS 8059, CID 8059, August 1997. US issue: Mercury 314 536 036-1, 314 539 036-2 CD, August 1997

The mid-Nineties were a tricky period for Morrissey, who seemed embattled on all fronts. It was bad enough seeing him outflanked commercially by the practitioners of Britpop, but playing second fiddle to Bowie on an ill-advised tour was worse again. This was not a good time to be seen genuflecting before an idol from a previous era, especially when your own career was temporarily in the doldrums. The tour ended in controversy with Morrissey abandoning ship in Scotland due to alleged illness. By this stage even his former record company could no longer muster much interest in old product. The rare 'Sunny' was rushed out in December 1995, but even Morrissey's loyal fan base failed to push the single beyond a chart low of number 42.

1996 was dominated by the High Court action in which Joyce secured his claim for 25 per cent of the Smiths earnings, bar songwriting, and Morrissey was famously described by Judge Weeks in his summing up as "devious, truculent and unreliable". No concerts or recordings were undertaken that year and Morrissey was further burdened by the pressure of mounting an Appeal which would also prove unsuccessful.

It was in this climate that Morrissey commenced work on his next album during the first week of 1997. "There was almost a sense of relief that we were actually there doing something," Bridgwood recalls. "Obviously he'd been somewhat embroiled in things the previous year and just really wanted to get on. So suddenly we were back doing an album and it was business as usual. We actually did a lot of work that year. We did what we thought we were going to do the year before but with another album. This session was probably the easiest going of any of them. It was really relaxed and Morrissey was more sociable than at any other time."

Three months before the album's release Morrissey issued a press statement under the pseudonym Stoney Hands, in which he told the world: "Morrissey has no interest in world politics and prefers the company of animals to humans. His ambition is to play Fremantle in Western Australia, otherwise he has no interest whatsoever in modern life. He lives in Spain." This was gallows humour at its best, for Morrissey was still seething over the recent court case, increasingly disillusioned about the state of his career and seemingly ready to abandon his birthplace. "I'm in exile . . . I'm box-office poison as far as I can gather. I'm simply a roadside curiosity, no more, no less. I don't know whether a real hit single would change things." Another switch of record label, far from suggesting a new start, merely underlined Morrissey's caprice and disenchantment.

There was a time when Morrissey's albums were seemingly regarded as sacrosanct by the artiste and if anyone dared to tamper with the contents, the entire project would have been placed in jeopardy. Yet here, probably for the first time, Morrissey found himself under the record company hammer. First there was the cover artwork which is generally regarded as the most prosaic and unflattering of his career. As Morrissey told Keith Cameron: "I made such a holy mess of *Southpaw Grammar* that I left *Maladjusted* to be pieced together by the record company – and it was even worse than *Southpaw Grammar*. I've got Tony Blair's hairline and I look as if I'm sat on the lavatory crying my eyes out. Nothing new there then . . ." Delegating decisions about artwork was worrying enough, but there was another bow to company pressure that was far more uncharacteristic. A key track, 'Sorrow Will Come In The End', was suddenly excised from the UK edition of the album. No public complaint was heard from Morrissey and no other track substituted in its place. Could it be that he was past caring?

Maladjusted remains the most mysterious, problematical and underrated album of Morrissey's career. Despite his good spirits in the studio, a sense of world-weariness permeates the work. It still sounds like a tired, distant record, impenetrable and unfocused in places, a bitter testament to his artistic uncertainty and lack of direction. While the relative strengths and weaknesses of *Southpaw Grammar* had been fairly transparent, *Maladjusted* was genuinely perplexing.

There were some spine-chilling moments on the album, but it was worryingly inconsistent. At its centre lay an emotional distance that made it difficult to love. It remains Morrissey's most neglected and misunderstood work – complex, awkward, resistant to categorization and strangely lost, just like the artiste himself at the time. As such it is well worthy of re-evaluation.

Critical reaction was salutary. Apathy appeared the dominant response. It was as if it didn't matter any more whether Morrissey made a good album or not. Suddenly he was a living anachronism. As ever, the *NME* picked away at the supposedly decaying corpse. "During *Maladjusted* Moz seems to be so detached from the stuff of pop-life that the only image of him you can conjure up is at a pool-side somewhere, sipping Pimm's and listening to the playback in between the cricket scores on the World Service . . . What effect such a curiously anodyne collection will have on the world at large remains to be seen . . . To wit, Johnny Rogan will have to wait for his autographed copy, hapless Smiths' bassist Andy Rourke will have to tape it off a friend and Mike Joyce will no doubt become familiar with it drifting over the airwaves whilst reclining on a yacht in the Bahamas."

In *The Times*, Alan Jackson could not resist the old Smiths comparisons. "Nine albums into his increasingly quixotic solo career, is it profitable still to lament the breakup of a once glorious creative partnership with Johnny Marr? Of course, the answer is no. But *Maladjusted*, for all its moments of near satisfaction, provokes nostalgia all the same: where are the soaring melodies, the chiming guitars, the deftness and grace with which a complementary band leavened the bequiffed one's famous tendency towards mordancy and introspection? Such virtues are in short supply here, as is another old-fashioned commodity, the tune that can be whistled . . ."

Uncut's Bob Stanley reckoned Morrissey should consider a new career. "There's nothing wrong with making consistently quite good records but, Christ, Morrissey is such a wasted talent. He needs a new challenge – maybe as a columnist or a TV pundit. At the very least he needs a new songwriting foil. Wrapped up tight in the old-Ted, old-time world of Morrissey, he probably doesn't care."

Others were more succinct in their barbs. Q proffered an all-time low two-star review, concluding, "It's just not good enough". The *Independent*'s James Delingpole reckoned "the tunes sound like the work of a Morrissey tribute band; the lyrics are a parade of tired clichés and cringeworthy puns." In *Gay Times*, Richard Smith borrowed the words of Oscar Wilde to add a sting to his review: "*Maladjusted* largely is the sound of a man who has no interest in modern life. And to paraphrase some old queen or other, to make one boring album may be regarded as misfortune, to make two in a row looks like he couldn't care less. Maybe Morrissey shouldn't be surprised if these days people care less and less about him."

It was left to *Melody Maker*'s Taylor Parkes to provide the executioner's axe. "Morrissey . . . is still capable of producing good work but he will never again produce great work, and there's some awful acknowledgement of that fact in everything about him these dull days, in his stunted ambition and his inability to do anything but rot in public . . . If Morrissey's masochistic refusal to just get on with his life – even to think about what the hell that might mean – once put him in the perfectly precarious position that invariably inspires great pop, then nowadays, its steady, wasting effect has taken its toll. He refuses to change as a person; he's left it so long that he can no longer change as an artiste. He hates surprises. He will never surprise us again . . ."

The doom sayers probably felt vindicated when the album entered at number 8, then dropped out of the chart the following week. In America, it peaked at number 61. Common wisdom suggests that Morrissey was at a creative all-time low during this period, but the truth is more complicated. If *Maladjusted* had been released at a different time it would probably have received an easier ride. Even some of the critics who sneered at its contents admitted that there were some fascinating moments. More importantly, Morrissey was anything but the washed-up character incapable of surprise. That summer he entered the studio to work on some B-sides and emerged with a small catalogue of songs, many of which were superior to those included on *Maladjusted*. Forgotten B-side releases during this period like 'I Can Have Both', 'Lost', 'The Edges Are No Longer Parallel', 'This Is Not Your Country' and 'Now I Am A Was' indicated that Morrissey was still keen to push forward creatively. There were also a few numbers that ended up on the cutting-room floor or were never completed, including Boz Boorer's sprightly 'I Know Who I Love' and 'Kit', an elaborate production that Bridgwood described as "fairly bold" with "a *Scott Walker Sings Brel* approach in three musical sections". In addition there was 'Hanratty', Morrissey's comment on the fate of James Hanratty, who was convicted of the 'A6 murder' at Dead Man's Hill in 1961 and subsequently hanged. But most amazing of all was the evidence of several compositions that would not be premièred until Morrissey's next studio album seven years later. 'The Leeches Go On Removing' was transformed into the brilliant 'You Know I Couldn't Last', and 'It's Hard To Walk Tall When You're Small' was revived with a new melody. "We could have done more albums than we did," Bridgwood notes, "and the last two could have been better. Certainly *Maladjusted* could have been a much better album if those B-sides had been there earlier when we recorded the album."

Finally, it's worth noting that Morrissey, far from taking a break, still felt committed enough to embark on an extensive tour of America from September through to mid-December. But even he had to acknowledge that the times were now against him.

Maladjusted

Like *Southpaw Grammar*, the album opens on a strong note with a snatch of feedback followed by Anthony Newley's speech "on this glorious occasion of the splendid defeat" from the film *Cockleshell Heroes*, which also starred Patric Doonan, later a bit part player in 'Now My Heart Is Full'. Morrissey's urban mini-drama is a fascinating, oblique composition whose insistent musical refrain adds a claustro-phobic ambience that becomes more intense as this bleak tale unfolds. As Jonny Bridgwood reveals: " 'Maladjusted' is just one piece of music that repeats over and over. The original demo was quite a long track but Morrissey only liked a certain section of it. So he discarded the rest of the music. We tried doing it a couple of different ways. When I was recording the bass, Steve Lillywhite wanted me to track up different things. I did a melodic bass line and then a pumping one which Steve preferred. 'I like the low-end guy better,' he used to say. After I did that we built up the rest of the track."

The enticing melody is enhanced by Morrissey's densely packed lyrics. With its images of a forbidden capital, it recalls the Smiths' 'London', only this time the journey is not from the north to the south, but from dowdy Stevenage to affluent Fulham. The narrator's impatience is evident in Morrissey's wonderfully sarcastic aside: 'Anyway, do you want to hear our story or not?' It proves more than enough to recapture the listener's interest. The story itself is one of desperate thrill seekers taking in the late night sights of SW6 – Chelsea and Fulham – seemingly with a mixture of resentment and envy. In their great song of Chelsea 'You Can't Always Get What You Want', the Rolling Stones had noted that 'you might be able to get what you need'. Such redemption is evidently beyond the leading character in Morrissey's morality tale who we're told can never get the 'things I need'. Midway through the song, in one of his great gender switches, Morrissey adopts the voice of a 'working girl' – a lost 15-year-old attempting to find some salvation in prostitution. The mantra 'maladjusted' is repeated like a Greek chorus followed by the desperate, defensive cries of the young teenager insisting that nothing is mentally wrong with her. As an opening track, it's a stunning scene setter and probably one of the most underrated compositions in Morrissey's extensive canon.

Alma Matters
A pleasant melody accompanies this slight lyric which, like 'Maladjusted', seems partly a plea from an individual to act out a life that many might consider self-destructive. The line 'it's my life to ruin in my own way' sees Morrissey returning to one of his former set texts, *A Taste Of Honey* (in which Jo's mother retorts: "Anyway it's your life, ruin it your own way"). Coincidentally or otherwise, the title brings to mind the actress Amanda Barrie, the former *Carry On* star who played the role of Alma Baldwin in the Granada television series *Coronation Street*. There's also the possibility that Morrissey might be name-checking the late UK singer Alma Cogan, who died from a cancer-related illness in 1966. Her name was later used as a title for a novel by Gordon Burn whose subplot dealt with the horror of the Moors Murderers which, of course, takes us back to 'Suffer Little Children'. In 1983, the *Sun* had misinterpreted Morrissey's lyrics,

causing a minor furore, but this time around it was the *Independent*'s
concert reviewer who made a hilarious gaffe by suggesting that
Morrissey was singing about double-entry sex: 'Alma matters in
mind, body and soul, *in bottom and hole*'.

Pressed for a quick critique, Morrissey reverted to the old stand-by
of ambisexuality. "It really means something specific. I think it means
that we should be pleased and proud of the female side of our character, of our nature. Or if we're female we should be proud of the male
side of our character and give it just as much importance as the other
side. So everybody's fine, it doesn't matter how you behave."

Ambitious Outsiders

With its quaint baroque backing, this featured Morrissey's band-
mates playing a role never heard before. Midway through there's a
riveting yet disconcerting section that sounds like it's emerged from
Keith West's teenage opera. "I don't think the song was originally
conceived as being part of the album," Bridgwood notes. "Much of
it is Alain Whyte's demo with strings on it. That's to say it's a keyboard linked to a computer with all the processed sounds. Morrissey
decided not to use real strings. They could easily have scored it on
the computer and got people in to play. I think Steve Lillywhite
would have preferred real strings. Anyway no string players came in
and the only strings you'll hear are me on my double bass here and
there."

Lyrically, this was one of Morrissey's most menacing songs and the
stalking subplot resembles a perverted reworking of 'The More You
Ignore Me, The Closer I Get'. As the story progresses the mystery
assailants, whose identities are never made clear, move 'closer' to
their prey. The sinister outsiders, who remain undetected, are evidently on a mission to annihilate children, an act which they justify
by blaming parents for the sin of reproduction. Ultimately, the song
provokes more questions than answers. Is it some oblique comment
on the paedophile hysteria that dominated the news pages in the
Nineties? Or is Morrissey simply trying to take us back to the terrain
of 'Suffer Little Children'? The results are inconclusive, but never less
than intriguing. Morrissey was wise enough not to be drawn into a
debate about the meaning of the composition, merely stating: "I like

music to be slightly dangerous. I like to be pushed. There's not really much point making safe music."

Trouble Loves Me

Before presenting this tune to Morrissey, Alain Whyte wrote a completely different set of lyrics under the title 'It's Really Over'. When the singer heard the bare-bones melody, he felt it would fit his own ruminations on troubles past and present. Beneath the maudlin musings, there are some humorous asides including a fictional trip to Soho, the home of clandestine sex. Morrissey also jokes about musically scraping the barrel, as if inviting more trouble from catty reviewers.

Musically, the backing features Whyte's stark piano followed by a concordance of changes from the school of mainstream rock, tinged with flashes of jazz balladry and some fine vocal phrasing. If the lyrics had been written a few years later, then over-eager source hunters would have sworn blind that Morrissey was referencing Kylie Minogue with the line 'I can't get you out of my head'. "We recorded the song towards the end of the album," Bridgwood recalls. "It starts with a blues turnaround which is a refrain that comes in here and there. It's good use of a blues turnaround in a pop song because it's used as an intro. From a compositional point of view that's quite interesting. I thought it was a bit Beatley in the middle."

Morrissey regarded the song as a good example of his minimalist aesthetic and use of a singular voice. "The process used on this record was very, very spartan. What's always been most important to me are the vocal melodies, even more than the lyrical content. That's really the key to the songs surviving. For better or worse what I do is distinctive. And that's a very unusual thing to be able to say in Nineties pop because most people sound exactly the same, and you can be with somebody and they can be speaking in a perfectly normal English accent and as soon as they stand behind a microphone they develop this swirling West Coast twang. They can't just sing as they speak. And I completely sing as I speak."

Papa Jack

A surprise feature of this album was the extent to which Morrissey's rockabilly-styled band had transformed themselves into a competent recording unit. Here they sound uncommonly like seasoned session musicians. The track reaches a thrilling climax, ending up like a tribute to the Who's *Quadrophenia*, laced with some late period Beatles. "I also thought the outro was like the Who," Bridgwood agrees. "Alain liked them. It was Alain's trademark to have a totally different outro. Quite often he would modulate up a tone like he does at the end of 'Dagenham Dave' where the same section is repeated in a different key."

Lyrically, the song can be read as a rumination on lost time and squandered chances by a lonely father or a superannuated pop star. Some lines no doubt encourage a quasi-autobiographical interpretation focusing, unfairly perhaps, on Morrissey's father as the likely protagonist. Alternatively, it can be read as a wistful contemplation on a once messianic rock star. The image of the kids reaching up for approval is reminiscent of David Bowie's crowd-pleasing 'Rock 'n' Roll Suicide' ('give me your hands!') and, of course, Morrissey's own devoted audience.

Ammunition

Given the singer's penchant for Sixties' female vocalists, it is a beautiful coincidence that the first 20 seconds of this song should include a guitar riff recalling the chorus of Clodagh Rodgers' 1969 hit 'Come Back And Shake Me'. Rarely for Morrissey, this is a fatalistic song in which the desire for wrath is quelled by the realization that something of value has been found. Nevertheless, there is a worrying ambiguity in the allusion to 'veering cliffwards' which sounds like a reference to suicide. The closing lines, in which he states that there is no longer any room in his life for revenge, will soon be contradicted by the sentiments of 'Sorrow Will Come In The End'. "Morrissey did remark on that contradiction," says Bridgwood. "He saw the humour in it."

Wide To Receive

The first song in which Morrissey has ever used computers as a metaphor ends with one of his more mournful meditations on loneliness. Is it a love song? "Yes," Morrissey says, "it's supposed to be, but I'd never dash out on a limb. It's supposed to be an Internet song. You know, lying by your computer waiting for someone to tap into you and finding that nobody is, and hence being wide to receive. How awful, of course, to be wide to receive and finding there's no reason to be."

Boz Boorer closes the track with an attractive clarinet solo but even that cannot disguise the lack of musical adventure. The sole Morrissey/Cobrin collaboration on the album, this appears to have been included almost as an afterthought. "It was originally a B-side," Bridgwood confirms. "It was then promoted to the album in favour of Boz's 'I Know Who I Love' which was itself demoted to a B-side, then dropped completely. The end of 'Wide To Receive' features the same chord progression as the Beatles' 'Dear Prudence'. I remember when we were doing it, it was so tempting just to duplicate that bass part but obviously we didn't want to make it sound like that. It's an iconic chord progression and once you hear it you know exactly what it is. I wasn't too keen on the track really. I thought it was probably the weakest song on the album, along with the throwaway 'Roy's Keen'."

Roy's Keen

A painful pun on the name of the famous former Manchester United captain Roy Keene, this was another of Morrissey's whimsical pieces. Its positioning on the album amid a series of aridly downbeat songs actually proved rather welcoming. The otherwise banal lyrics satirize football clichés, using those terms to describe the noble art of window cleaning which, in turn, takes Morrissey into George Formby territory. Not content with bad puns, Morrissey even includes one of the most painfully strained metaphors in pop, imagining the window cleaner's ladder as a planet, Roy as a star and himself as a burning satellite. The lyrics were a far cry from what Whyte envisaged when he submitted the song under the title 'You'll Leave Me Behind'. Released as the second single from the album, 'Roy's Keen' performed appallingly in the market-place, peaking at number 42 in the UK charts.

He Cried

One of the more emotive songs on the album, this featured Morrissey's familiar reticence in describing feelings that can 'never be heard' alongside warnings about lines that cannot be crossed. Catholic guilt is revealed in the allusions to martyrdom with a 'soul' being stoned to death while the body remains frozen, shock-still, like Christ on the cross staring at the ground. The chilling immobility is only relieved by the shedding of tears, seemingly in deference rather than pain. The track concludes with an overwrought mock orchestral accompaniment and chorus. "That was Alain and his backing vocals," says Bridgwood. "I tend to favour real strings because no matter how good a sound sample is you can't beat the real thing. It would have been better with actual strings but that's down to taste as much as anything."

Oddly, nobody asked Morrissey about religion or repression when discussing the song. Instead there was a polite enquiry about when he had last cried. "Not for a long time," he admitted. "I used to cry very regularly. And it's a fantastic cleansing process – I felt three stone lighter afterward. But I haven't recently. I've had cause to – we all know that. But I truly haven't cried in a long time."

Sorrow Will Come In The End

Conspicuously absent from the UK edition of the album, this sometimes shocking and reckless outburst never looked likely to be sanctioned for release in Morrissey's home country given his recent adventures in the High Court. Judged as a song, it has a camp melodrama which Morrissey surely did not intend given his genuine bitterness about the legal system. The backing sounds almost filmic, like the soundtrack from a Seventies horror B-movie, complete with Morrissey intoning the words with the ham stateliness of a Vincent Price. At times it sounds like a cross between the Shangri-Las and Jacques Brel. It also has the feel of a circus, complete with the crack of a lion tamer's whip, which probably sums up Morrissey's subjective feelings about his treatment by the judiciary. After some explosive lyrics in the early verses it closes with the aggrieved narrator stalking his adversary while fantasizing about cutting his throat. "I just found it funny," quipped Mike Joyce, when asked for his reaction. "If Lemmy had written it I might be concerned."

Morrissey's musicians were mildly amused by the composition, which proved the most elaborate recording on the album. "He wasn't scared, was he!" says Bridgwood. "We knew the title while we were recording the backing track. We didn't do any live routine for it – the drums went down, I did some double bass, things were added and it evolved as a track. Morrissey definitely had an idea of how he wanted it to sound. He said, 'I want something quite dramatic and filmic.' When he'd give you a musical instruction it was never that specific. He never ever said, 'Can you play it like *this*?' either to anyone individually or collectively."

Satan Rejected My Soul

Despite its portentous and despairing title, this finale was an upbeat romp, opening with a musical flourish reminiscent of the Tornados' 1962 number 1 hit 'Telstar'. In common with much of the album, the music sounds like a cornucopia of familiar rock riffs that zoom by leaving vague traces of recognition but never staying around long enough to provoke accusations of plagiarism. Indeed, identifying the likely musical influences, unconscious or otherwise, is part of the fun. Towards the end, Morrissey's persistent plea 'come on come on' recalls the chorus of the Beatles' 'Please Please Me'. There's a second or two of glam rock circa the Sweet's 'Blockbuster', a delightful riff redolent of 'This Charming Man' and an oompah ending straight out of 'Sheila Take A Bow'. Students of Morrissey's cosmology and peculiar theology will find much to amuse them here, especially when comparing the lyrics with 'There's A Place In Hell For Me And My Friends'.

The third and best single to be released from the album, its late showing hampered its chances, resulting in a disappointing peak of number 39. Despite its attractive rockabilly feel, critical reaction was surprisingly tepid. *NME*'s reviewer seemed particularly harsh: "'Satan Rejected My Soul' sounds about as cutting edge in these burnt-out distorted times as something you'd hear emanating from a wax cylinder. And Moz, who's always had something of a Narcissus in his demeanour, seems too fascinated with the trials and tribulations of his own life to really care either way."

For the band, however, the song was always an enjoyable romp. "It's straight ahead rock 'n' roll isn't it?" says Bridgwood. "As the albums took shape there was always a running order before we left the studio. Morrissey always knew. Obviously 'Maladjusted' was conceived as the first track and this was the last. Musically it was a Boz track and on his demo the drum pattern is sampled from 'Come And Play With Me In The Garden' by John's Children. So that became the drum part. Obviously with the descending part, we put loads of basses on to make it feel big. Some had effects on and some were just straight. It was fun to do. Morrissey was in the control room while I was recording, listening to it take shape. He must have really enjoyed it. It was always a good one to play. Perhaps it wasn't his greatest song lyrically but it was a great live rocker. It was the last song that both Spencer and myself ever played live with him – you can hear it on *TFI Friday*. That was the end of the band."

SUEDEHEAD – THE BEST OF MORRISSEY

Released: September 1997

EMI EMC 3771, 7243-8-59665-2-1 CD, September 1997, February 2000

This compilation was another attempt by EMI to make sense of Morrissey's back catalogue with a formidable 'best of' concentrating largely on his single releases. Although not following any chronological order, all his A-sides from 'Suedehead' to 'Sunny' are featured with the odd exceptions of 'Sing Your Life' and 'Certain People I Know', both missing in action. Given its limited brief, the work serves as a reasonable introduction for mid-price purchasers in search of some additional tracks to the more prized albums. Critical reaction was probably better than expected and even *NME* awarded an 8 out of 10 rating. Reviewer Mark Beaumont may have missed the point about the compilation's *raison d'être* as a singles emporium, but was otherwise positive: "It's hard to fathom who this all-but-complete singles collection is for . . . Nevertheless, despite the majority of Moz's singles output being of the inconsequential, jangling lah-de-dah-give-us-a-twirl-Kirsty-m-darlin' variety, there are enough treasures here to make it worth a rummage . . . To get ever so slightly anal for a second, any Mozzer's 'Best Of . . . ' that ignores the likes of 'Now My Heart Is Full', 'Disappointed' and 'I Know It's Gonna Happen Someday' while venturing within a million miles of 'You're The One For Me, Fatty' deserves to be shot for Trades Description violations. But listen without prejudice, and somehow you know there will always be a place reserved in the low 20s for Mr Morrissey and friends." That final sentence sounded condescending and dismissive but accurately reflected Morrissey's chart standing at the time. Following recent trends this UK album reached number 26 and when it was reissued in February 2000 climbed to number 25.

The work included four tracks previously unavailable on album in the UK, as follows:

Sunny

Following Morrissey's defection to RCA, Parlophone EMI belatedly released this as a single in December 1995, one week after their rivals had just charted with 'The Boy Racer' at number 35. Nobody won in this Christmas chart war as the understated 'Sunny' peaked at number 42. With its graphic allusion to shooting-up, 'Sunny' was never likely to pick up much radio airplay and sounded a fairly light, if affective, composition. Morrissey had originally intended to issue the track the previous year but perhaps found the subject matter – a declaration of unrequited affection – too personal for public display. His band seemed firmly convinced that the composition was auto-biographical and privately named the person in question. Predictably, Morrissey said nothing to confirm such speculation.

Interlude (Extended)

Originally recorded towards the end of the *Vauxhall And I* sessions, this was a unique opportunity to hear Morrissey singing with punk icon Siouxsie Sioux. The song, a romantic classic, featured in the 1968 film *Interlude* and was sung by Timi Yuro, with original screen-play credits by Lee Langley and Hugh Leonard, and music composed and conducted by Georges Delerue with lyrics by Hal Schaper. The Morrissey/Siouxsie rendition was beautifully performed, complete with a string section, which enhanced their sensitive handling of the song. Surprisingly, Boz Boorer produced the track in favour of the more experienced Steve Lillywhite, and did a fine job. The take included here was the extended vocal version which was a full two minutes longer with a lengthy string coda.

"Although it was part of the *Vauxhall And I* sessions, it was a project completely aside from the album," Jonny Bridgwood stresses. "It was never a contender and was always considered as a single. 'Interlude' was the only song Morrissey and Siouxsie did together. It all went down in those couple of days when I wasn't there. I came back and did the double bass. The timpani on it is a tom-tom. It was a trick that Steve came up with. He recorded it with the track played faster so that when it's played at the right speed the tom-tom is slowed down and it sounds like a timpani. So it saved hiring one."

What seemed like a palpable hit, bringing together two iconic figures, soon went sour. Morrissey and Siouxsie had a falling-out and neither promoted the record which eventually stumbled into the charts in August 1994, peaking at a disappointing number 25.

That's Entertainment

Formerly the B-side of 'Sing Your Life', this was another of Morrissey's rare cover versions. Oddly, he had never spoken of the Jam while listing his teenage icons, but evidently felt favourably disposed towards Paul Weller's songwriting. Recorded during the *Kill Uncle* sessions, this was always likely for B-side status. "I remember hearing a bit of it when I turned up to do 'Born To Hang'," Bridgwood remembers. "It was on the desk, but I don't know what plans they had for it then."

Mark Nevin was also in attendance for what turned out to be his final session with Morrissey. "We recorded it after *Kill Uncle* at West Side Studios in Hammersmith. We did 'Skin Storm' at the same session. 'That's Entertainment' was a one-off for a single. The comedians were on that one. Vic Reeves came down, Chas Smith was there, and Suggs too. Reeves was definitely there and I think he sung backing vocals. Shortly afterwards he did an impersonation on television: the Morrissey Monkey! Kate St John was brought in to play cor anglais, which was a nice touch. But it was a weird recording. There's some strange noise on it, but I can't remember what it was. Obviously we'd sampled something and shoved it on the record."

The 'noise' Nevin refers to sounds like the shuttling of a train carriage, and neatly bookends the song. As a reading of the Jam classic, it works surprisingly well. Morrissey tackles the vocal in a higher register and transforms Weller's proletariat saga into a poignant ballad. Even the violent imagery, notably the kick in the balls, is denuded of aggressive intent and made to sound vaguely romantic.

Pregnant For The Last Time

This single was a remnant from the short-lived 'rockabilly experiment' in the immediate aftermath of *Kill Uncle*. Gradually, the idea devolved from an LP to an EP and finally this single. The line-up on the track was unique, bringing together Jonny Bridgwood, Alain Whyte, Boz Boorer and Andrew Paresi. "I had no idea it was going to be a single," says Bridgwood. "As far as I knew we were going to go down to do a few tracks. We did a couple of them and then it was all aborted – and then it was a single. By then he'd got the band together. It all seemed to happen so quickly. It was strange because obviously I had people from EMI wanting me to give permission for Gary Day to mime to it."

"That was my last attempt, really," Andrew Paresi recalls of his final session. "We just turned a rubbish bin upside down, miked it up and I was whacking it. So I was trying. And it had a great spirit to it." Indeed, it was a brave departure for Morrissey and the attempt to produce a rockabilly feel was largely successful. Regrettably, it was not rewarded with significant sales and a mediocre chart peak of number 25 concluded this fascinating rockabilly excursion.

Full track listing: *Suedehead; Sunny; Boxers; Tomorrow; Interlude (Extended); Everyday Is Like Sunday; That's Entertainment; Hold On To Your Friends; My Love Life; Interesting Drug; Our Frank; Piccadilly Palare; Ouija Board, Ouija Board; You're The One For Me, Fatty; We Hate It When Our Friends Become Successful; The Last Of The Famous International Playboys; Pregnant For The Last Time; November Spawned A Monster; The More You Ignore Me, The Closer I Get.*

RARE TRACKS

Released: April 1998 (Japan)

Japan issue: Mercury PHCR 4080, April 1998

Although foreign releases are not featured in this analysis of Morrissey's oeuvre, an exception has to be made for this six-track mini-album, exclusively issued in Japan. It provides something of a missing link in the Morrissey story, bringing together the B-sides that he unveiled after the release of the unfairly maligned *Maladjusted*. It has become something of a critical cliché to suggest that the singer was all but washed-up during 1997 and went into a creative slump and career retreat that continued until the 2004 'comeback' with *You Are The Quarry*. The truth, of course, was more complicated. At the time he cut these B-sides, Morrissey was still writing some of his best songs. Arguably all the tracks herein deserved a place on *Maladjusted* and had they been recorded a few months earlier they would certainly have been in contention. It is regrettable that Mercury (US) or Island (UK) never considered releasing an expanded version of *Maladjusted* featuring these largely forgotten B-sides. Such a release would undoubtedly have prompted a reappraisal of this period and given the lie to the view that Morrissey was in a parlous state. It is also worth noting that the singer spent more time touring in late 1997 than in virtually any other period of his career. Indeed, it is now clear that he could have produced an album of new material with ease at any stage during 1998–2003 had anyone offered a satisfactory deal. Given his changes of record company, it seems unlikely that *Rare Tracks* will be issued in the UK or US anytime soon, but a 'best of the Mercury years' featuring these songs in the context of *Maladjusted* would be most welcome for old and new listeners alike.

Lost

The B-side of 'Roy's Keen', the second single to be released from *Maladjusted*, this lush orchestrated track was ostensibly Morrissey's comment on the 'all humanity is spiritually lost' motif. Musically and especially thematically, it recalls R.E.M.'s 'Everybody Hurts', albeit with Morrissey's familiar self-effacement thrown in for additional poignant effect. A closer inspection, however, suggests that the pat philosophizing is a clever device which the narrator uses as a legitimate excuse for his predatory romantic interest. According to Jonny Bridgwood, the sessions that produced these series of B-sides were the most enjoyable and positive that he ever experienced during his time working with Morrissey.

Heir Apparent

This breezy pop arrangement, complete with a strong rhythmic coda, is set against some intriguing lyrics that reveal much about Morrissey's current state of mind. What begins as an apparent reflection on a troubled homecoming to Manchester soon emerges as a salutary comment on the vagaries of pop fame. At a time when Oasis were in the ascendant, Morrissey adopts the role of elder statesman, offering spiritual and career advice from the standpoint of the recently abandoned. While acknowledging the possibility that his successors may win the public over with a winning smile and an intense hunger for fame, the greater likelihood is that they too will be discarded. 'They'll seduce your heart and then slap your arse', he warns in a voice of resignation rather than bitterness.

The Edges Are No Longer Parallel

The third track on the 12-inch and CD single of 'Roy's Keen' showed Morrissey successfully introducing geometry into the lexicon of songwriting. There's even a touch of chaos theory in a universe where the meaningful suddenly becomes meaningless. Warming to his metaphysical, mathematical theme, Morrissey creates a new cosmos in which the law of averages ceases to exist and negativity rules. Alain Whyte once nominated this tune as one of his favourites, largely because he was allowed free rein to combine acoustic and electric guitar to strong effect along with one of his Who-inspired solos which took the song over the five-minute mark.

This Is Not Your Country

In January 1967, the Northern Ireland Civil Rights Association

(NICRA) was founded. Inspired by the civil rights campaigns in America, it brought together university students, liberals, trade unionists and enlightened republicans as a united front to protest against the British government's discriminatory policies in Northern Ireland. After hearing news about the 30th anniversary of the movement, Morrissey wrote this piercing and poignant broadside. Some time before he had expressed his feelings about the Troubles to Irish journalist George Byrne. "You can turn on the news and hear that six innocent people have been shot dead in Belfast, and it doesn't warrant comment, which I say with massive regret because death and murder are part of a situation which is obviously unbridgeable. I certainly don't think that in England there's any desire, politically, to make life any easier in Belfast. Distance gives great comfort to the politicians who have to deal with it."

'This Is Not Your Country' was Morrissey's best political song by some considerable distance. The cello backing adds a chilling ambience to his vivid descriptions of armoured cars, barbed wire and menacing, trigger-ready British soldiers. Images of locals being harassed by soldiers, the suddenness with which a walk home has to become a desperate run, and the media's indifference to the shooting and death of a child are evoked with a poignant but dispassionate vocal. Morrissey throws in the sarcastic 'home sweet fortress' and his favourite catch-phrase 'born and braised', already familiar from interviews during the *Vauxhall And I* period. Often Morrissey's political songs have fallen into the agitprop category but 'This Is Not Your Country' is soundly based on fact and minus the usual overstatement favoured by the singer. Even the reference to 'BBC scum' is not vicious hyperbole but a telling reference to the policies of the IBA which was responsible for censoring and cancelling countless television programmes during the Troubles. Even in the years before the Troubles, the British media had ignored Northern Ireland, partly through apathy, but mainly as a reflection of government policy which discouraged such reporting. Morrissey articulates such shame with understated vituperation. 'This Is Your Country' should have been the centrepiece of Morrissey's live shows during visits to Ireland but regrettably it was ignored by the singer despite its topicality.

Now I Am A Was

The B-side of 'Satan Rejected My Soul', this deceptively catchy melody and upbeat vocal featured some of Morrissey's most revealing and negative statements on his recent life. Thematically, it reiterated the sentiments of 'Heir Apparent', this time using the fragmentation of a personal relationship as a parallel commentary on the decline of the singer's standing in the music world. When I first heard this track, having failed to peruse the title, I assumed Morrissey was singing 'Now I Am A *Wus*', a sentiment that would no doubt have been seized upon by media detractors. Morrissey's familiar tendency to contrast light melodies with dark lyrics was well applied here while the guitar riff was reminiscent of the recent 'Ammunition' from *Maladjusted*.

I Can Have Both

With its Smiths-style arrangement and pleasing melody this addition to the 12-inch and CD versions of 'Alma Matters' was another of Morrissey's forgotten songs, although its quality was self-evident. Innocently presented as a shopper's dilemma, the song obviously contained 'bisexual' connotations in its arch title. Morrissey subtly plays with the innuendo, telling us the tale of a boy who is brainwashed into believing that he can never 'have both'. Other lines such as the coy *double entendre* 'I've not been feeling myself' bring a *Carry On* humour to the proceedings.

Although this compilation was a fascinating artefact, it was regrettable that the tracks were not presented in chronological order of release. Had this occurred then the final track would have been 'This Is Not Your Country', the third song on 'Satan Rejected My Soul'. Given that Morrissey's commentary on the Troubles was both an epic and one of his best songs of the period, it seemed a perverse decision to change the running order and make 'I Can Have Both' the concluding song. As the last composition to be released by Morrissey for seven years, 'This Is Not Your Country' would have been a perfect closer here and, had he never recorded again, a fitting finale to the singer's career.

MY EARLY BURGLARY YEARS

Released: September 1998

US issue: Reprise 9-46874-2, September 1998.

Over the years there had been numerous limited edition and promotional releases coming to and emanating from the US market, but this was their first attempt at a fully fledged official compilation. It is included in this essentially UK based discography on the grounds of exclusivity. As Reprise's Howie Klein explained: "It's not a greatest hits, because he already did that. It wouldn't have been much different from *Bona Drag*, which was a straight singles collection, so I asked Morrissey for his ideas on what other kinds of things could be included . . . These are basically tracks that Morrissey thought were overlooked or were his favourite tracks, some were imports." For American purchasers, this was a rewarding release which allowed them to hear a number of tracks previously only available in the European market-place. There was also the added bonus of an enhanced CD of 'Sunny'. At the time of writing, there are firm plans to release this compilation in the UK in late 2006. Discussed below are the six tracks previously unavailable on album in the UK.

Cosmic Dancer

Morrissey's interest in Marc Bolan stemmed from his school-days when, according to fellow pupils, he would spend entire lessons sketching the pop star's photograph. Morrissey's appreciation of Bolan reached its apogee in 1972 when he saw T. Rex perform at the Belle Vue, Kings Hall, Manchester. Later, during the Smiths era, Morrissey's fascination with Bolan was evident when he and Marr took the template of 'Metal Guru' as a key influence on their hit single 'Panic'. It was therefore unsurprising that, unlike Morrissey's cover of the Jam's 'That's Entertainment', this live version of T. Rex's 'Cosmic Dancer' was entirely faithful to the original.

255

Nobody Loves Us

The B-side of 'Dagenham Dave', this was arguably the equal or superior to some of the tracks on *Southpaw Grammar*. It certainly would have improved the latter which offered only eight songs in total. Of course, Morrissey was always strict about providing fresh B-sides for singles even when the parent album was urgently in need of enhancement. This was another song about lost, troublesome boys whose four-day stubble and insistence upon pleasing themselves cannot disguise a strange maternal dependency. The references to being called home, the need to be held by the hand and the desire to stuff themselves with cake and home-made jam all testify to a child-like affection. Indeed, if it wasn't for the 'stubble' allusion, this could easily have been a song about a bunch of 10-year-old tearaways. Morrissey evidently felt a fondness for the composition. "I think he once said it was his best B-side," Bridgwood recalls. "I'm not entirely sure but I believe he felt, in retrospect, that it should have been on the album."

Swallow On My Neck

Coincidentally or otherwise, this catchy track, first released on the 12-inch version of 'Sunny', brought together several of Morrissey's themes in one place. Part of the song is set in a funeral parlour, bringing to mind Billy Fisher's employers Shadrack And Duxbury in the frequently referenced *Billy Liar*. The tattoo motif of the swallow, visually present on the cover of *Vauxhall And I* and on the rear sleeve of 'The More You Ignore Me, The Closer I Get', can be traced back to the Birkenhead boy described in 'What She Said'. Finally, there is gang camaraderie and that familiar furtive evasion ('more I will not say') when discussing male bonding. Once the man has drawn a tattoo on the narrator's neck 'everyone knew' – although, as ever with Morrissey, precisely what they knew is not spelt out.

Sister I'm A Poet

Amazingly, the original studio version of this song escaped inclusion on both *Bona Drag* and the 1997 reissue of *Viva Hate*. With its Smiths-like melody and arch lyrics, it was one of Morrissey's much loved songs of the period, particularly in concert where its stop/start rhythm worked to dramatic effect. Originally recorded in February 1988 on the flip-side of Morrissey's second single, it displayed the full potential of the Street, Reilly, Paresi line-up. The performance is noticeably tight, with Paresi urgently attempting to make a good impression with metronome precision drumming and an uneasy Reilly trying to flesh out the track and add some colour via keyboards. For Street, whose relationship with Reilly was at its sourest, the session was 'frustrating' and 'unbearable' but Paresi felt it was a peak, made more moving by lost opportunities. "Nothing matches 'Everyday Is Like Sunday' in terms of quality B-sides. And 'Sister I'm A Poet' was an important part of that. It was another of those stompy swing-type tracks where I just hit the drums hard to get that big bouncy sound off . . . If we'd gone out and toured after those B-sides we'd have nailed it."

Black-Eyed Susan

An oddity in the Morrissey canon, this was recorded early in the *Vauxhall And I* sessions and eventually found a home on the B-side of 'Sunny'. It's tempting to think that the tart lyrics and gothic allusions might be an unsubtle dig at Siouxsie Sioux who recorded 'Interlude' with Morrissey during the same period. If some of the words are arresting then the musical execution is plain puzzling. After a reverberating cymbal introduction, the song moves along at a sprightly pace, only to be dramatically interrupted one minute in by an elongated ambient interlude of strange instrumental effects, after which Morrissey returns to complete the track in more orthodox fashion. Jonny Bridgwood recalls the strange evolution of this unheralded composition: "We did that before Steve Lillywhite arrived for the session and the cymbals were one of the only things that were kept. We tried the track a few different ways. It's still fairly rocky anyway, but at one point it was even more so. We really liked the cymbal intro that Woodie came up with so that was just spliced and put on to the track. Originally the song was going to be on the album, but it just went somewhere else really. It was one of the few tracks where we actually sat down and had a chat. I remember me and Boz talking to Morrissey about it and he wanted something different in the middle. He was trying to explain. Eventually I said, 'Do you mean like a sound collage?' and he said, 'Yeah! For two minutes!' That was almost avant-garde by his standards. Steve Lillywhite had us in the studio and said, 'I'm just setting up the sound. Do something!' So everybody did and he just recorded it. I used a lot of double bass, just messing about, but I had a feeling he would use it, which he did. Steve then had some guitar bits put over the top to ensure that it wouldn't sound like something from a weird sci-fi movie spliced in the middle. We kept coming back to it because it wasn't that good really. In the end, obviously we tried it lots of different ways, just trying to improve and make it more rocky and in keeping with the evolution of the album. But it didn't fit really, so it wasn't on there and instead ended up on 'Sunny'."

Jack The Ripper

One night Boz Boorer was at home watching television with the sound down and a tune appeared in his head. He swiftly wrote it down, placed it in his back pocket and, soon after, presented the results to Morrissey. During the run-through, some startling cascading and descending guitar lines were added and Morrissey's vocals were compressed for maximum atmospheric effect. Lyrically, it was a fascinating song, seductive and predatory at the same time. Thematically, it recalled 'The More You Ignore Me, The Closer I Get' but with greater sophistication. The Ripper's menacing line 'I'm gonna get you' was later revived and incorporated, most appropriately, into the menacing 'Sorrow Will Come In The End'.

Full track listing: *Sunny; At Amber; Cosmic Dancer; Nobody Loves Us; Swallow On My Neck; Sister I'm A Poet; Black-Eyed Susan; Michael's Bones; I'd Love To; Reader Meet Author; Pashernate Love; Girl Least Likely To; Jack The Ripper; I've Changed My Plea To Guilty; The Boy Racer; Boxers.*

THE CD SINGLES '88–91'

Released: June 2000

EMI 7243 8 87293 2 1, June 2000

This box set featured the first 10 Morrissey CD singles on individual discs, complete with the original cover artwork. Presumably aimed at album collectors who had neglected to invest in the singles at the time of their release, it was the perfect opportunity to witness the progression of an artiste who had always believed in the potency of the '45 rpm record' as an important statement. While the A-sides were familiar to everyman, the B-sides must have seemed like hidden treasures to the uninitiated. Ranging from the quirky to the brilliant, this was the best way to understand Morrissey's continuing appeal and mystique as a songwriter. Regrettably, not everyone was convinced. The *NME*'s headline 'Viva – Second Rate' betrayed a weary disdain and one of their leading critics, John Mulvey, could only offer a sarcastic attack on Morrissey's supposedly anachronistic world-view. "Back in the days when we had an empire, the manor was run by gangsters who looked after their own and there was always lard for tea, it might have meant something. A deluxe set of Morrissey's first 10 solo singles, something to listen to between a hard day fighting on the beaches and the night's bouts of boxing and self-loathing . . . Now, in the wake of Tony Blair's brave and shiny New Britain . . . and the widespread availability of electricity, the lone Morrissey sounds sillier than ever. It's a traumatic time covered here, as he drifts from widespread acclaim to the zealously guarded property of fanatics counting the days until the Internet is invented . . . There's an air of tragedy about this box set, of a rare talent pissed away and a limited, increasingly embittered range of expression. It's a long decline that has now reached the point where labels keep recycling his back catalogue rather than release new songs. An antique curio, a relic from an England that's slowly, mercifully dying – and that, ironically, he now chooses to keep far away from. Let's hope Hollywood's roustabouts are more inspiring." A disappointing 4 out of 10 grading was even harsher given the quality of the songs under discussion.

Below are the tracks from the set that had not previously been released in album form in the UK/US market-place.

I Know Very Well How I Got My Name

The B-side of 'Suedehead' this delicate ballad was animated by Vini Reilly's subtle guitar work, enhanced by a six-piece string section. Effectively Morrissey's autobiography in miniature, it tells the story of a child going through a 'curious phase' who grows into a man with 'southern ways'. The anecdote about the hair-dyeing disaster was actually true, as Morrissey revealed to Len Brown. "When I was 13 I did experiment with bottles of bleach and so forth. I tried to dye it yellow and it came out gold, then I tried to get rid of it and it came out purple. I was sent home from school." Several of Morrissey's former classmates recall the incident vividly, although they insist that all he did was add a blond streak to his hair and none were aware of any multi-colour experiments in righting the condition. It was probably no coincidence that Morrissey placed this song alongside 'Hairdresser On Fire' on the 'Suedehead' single.

Oh Well, I'll Never Learn

This composition was so slight as to appear almost fragmentary. The last track on the 'Suedehead' single, it contained the memorable image of Morrissey falling into a fountain of youth. Musically, it was alarmingly sparse and sounded in urgent need of some intricate, expressive guitar work from Reilly. His complaints about Stephen Street's basic chord sequences appear to have hit home here. According to Andrew Paresi: "There were frequently wobblers where Vini would just explode. 'I'm not playing these bloody stupid chords, they're boring!' And he'd storm out of the control room and that would be the end of that."

Sweet And Tender Hooligan (Live)

This was the breathless finale of Morrissey's first live solo outing, which took place at Wolverhampton's Civic Hall on 22 December 1988. It also served as a farewell to the Smiths, with litigious colleagues Rourke, Joyce and Gannon joining the singer for the last time onstage. 'Sweet And Tender Hooligan' had never been played live by the Smiths, but this was far from a welcome début. Musically, the performance sounds wayward and Morrissey is noticeably off key throughout. Constant stage invasions threw everyone's timing, creating chaos in the process. An unedifying reminder of better days, this track was tolerable as a video memento, but sounds like a travesty on CD.

East West

It was typical of Morrissey to dredge up this minor hit by fellow Mancunians Herman's Hermits as his latest exercise in kitsch, following similar covers of Twinkle and Cilla Black. Relatively obscure, even to Sixties' pop aficionados, this was the song that broke a two-year run of UK hits for the group when it failed to reach the Top 30 in late 1966. Recorded just before 'Ouija Board, Ouija Board', to which it was appended as an extra B-side, it heralded the return of drummer Andrew Paresi after a year's absence. Unfortunately, he had just sold his drum kit and was forced to borrow a new set, much to his embarrassment. "The thing is, I'd bought this flat and the mortgage got a bit out of hand and I had to sell the kit. I was sad to see it go and I thought, 'I've got to get another kit from somewhere.' Of course, no sooner had I sold the drums than I received a phone call from Clive Langer saying, 'We need you.' I turned up with this kit I'd borrowed from a friend . . . It seemed like it was made out of 'papier mâché'. It didn't even sound like a drum kit and was more like a dustbin which, in some later Morrissey music, might have been effective, but it wasn't right at the time for highly respected producers like Clive and Alan. Here was me arriving at this session with this laughable drum kit. I remember Alan Winstanley saying, 'Bloody drum kit, we can't possibly get a sound out of that.' It was hilarious. But we used it on 'East West'. After that we hired a Gretsch drum kit, a brand which I've remained attached to ever since." Oddly enough, the 'papier mâché' drums were not out of place on this dated pop pastiche and brought a not entirely unwelcome Sixties audio-vérité to an otherwise unremarkable song.

Get Off The Stage

"The Rolling Stones are an after-death experience, the ultimate freak-show," Morrissey once said. It was their longevity and continued popularity that irked him sufficiently to compose this playful but spiteful attack on geriatric rock. Sounding like a piece of music hall whimsy, complete with concertina, it lampooned the Peter Pan pretensions of the ageing rock star in a series of nasty put-downs, ably abetted by guest vocalist Suggs who ends the song with the warning 'For whom the bell tolls'. Rather like Pete Townshend with the immortal 'I hope I die before I get old', the lyrics were always likely to catch up with Morrissey in middle age. Despite hints at retirement during the mid-Nineties, he continues to tread the boards and will probably do so well into his senior years. At the time of the record's release, of course, he was in full flow about the inequities of dinosaur rock stars. Speaking to Nick Kent in 1989 about 'Get Off The Stage', he observed: "If you look at the Top 10 albums of the moment you'll find the Rolling Stones, Bob Dylan, Neil Young, Eric Clapton and the Grateful Dead. I find that horrifying. There's a song that has the Rolling Stones in mind because I've been so disgusted by their recent comeback that I no longer find it sad or pitiful. I just feel immense anger that they don't just get out of the way. You open papers in this country, and every day there's the obligatory picture of Mick with bags at the airport, or Keith saying he's completely normal now. They just won't move away."

Journalists Who Lie

Artless polemic was never Morrissey's strong point and this bitter swipe against journalists who apparently write 'sickening lies' had the same one-dimensional lyric quality as 'Get Off The Stage'. Interestingly, it was written long before the *NME* backlash of 1992 which Morrissey no doubt felt justified his complaints here. The arrangement was unexpected and the minimal instrumentation worked well. "'Journalists Who Lie' was a track we spent a lot of time on," Andrew Paresi remembers, 'and it just didn't work. I don't know why. I put this big drum fill at the beginning of it and half-way through. It was always a big epic event from a drumming point of view. I don't know . . . There were lots of things in there that didn't work." Actually, the drumming is anything but overwhelmingly loud and at times Paresi sounds as though he's still playing the aforementioned 'papier mâché' kit, creating a chugging rockabilly beat in the process. Along the way, other effects are thrown in, including what sounds like sampled shots from a rifle range.

Skin Storm

Morrissey championed many new groups over the years, but it was rare for him to record their material. Along with James' 'What's The World?' and later Raymonde's 'No One Can Hold A Candle To You', this song from the indie band Bradford was given the honour of an official release, appearing on the B-side of 'Pregnant For The Last Time'. It was unusual to hear Morrissey sing such passionate lyrics without a smidgen of his customary irony or ambiguity. Although no lost classic, the composition is treated with deference and performed with careful enunciation.

Disappointed (Live)

This was the same live version of the track from Holland that appeared on the 1997 reissue of *Viva Hate* although this original boasted an extra 19 seconds of applause and audience audio-vérité at the end of the track. Once again, it proves an amusing way to end a Morrissey record, a trick used most notably with the studio recording at the close of *Bona Drag*.

Full track listing: CD 1 *Suedehead; I Know Very Well How I Got My Name; Hairdresser On Fire; Oh Well, I'll Never Learn;* CD 2 *Everyday Is Like Sunday; Sister I'm A Poet; Disappointed; Will Never Marry;* CD 3 *The Last Of The Famous International Playboys; Lucky Lisp; Michael's Bones;* CD 4 *Interesting Drug; Such A Little Thing Makes Such A Big Difference; Sweet And Tender Hooligan (Live);* CD 5 *Ouija Board, Ouija Board; Yes, I Am Blind; East West;* CD 6 *November Spawned A Monster; He Knows I'd Love To See Him; Girl Least Likely To;* CD 7 *Piccadilly Palare; Get Off The Stage; At Amber;* CD 8 *Our Frank; Journalists Who Lie; Tony The Pony;* CD 9 *Sing Your Life; That's Entertainment; The Loop;* CD 10 *Pregnant For The Last Time; Skin Storm; Cosmic Dancer (Live); Disappointed (Live).*

THE CD SINGLES '91–95'

Released: September 2000

EMI 7243 879745 2 4, September 2000

Three months after *The CD Singles '88–91'*, this companion set was issued in September 2000. Although not as arresting as its predecessor, and with one less CD in the package, it served the purpose of rounding up the EMI years. For collectors wishing to obtain all Morrissey's singles in one place these two boxed sets were a welcome addition to his discography.

Below are the tracks not previously issued on album in the UK/US market-place.

Suedehead (Live)

A strumming guitar tentatively opens this unsteady live version of Morrissey's first solo hit. At times it sounds tuneless and Morrissey's vocal also strays off-key. Midway through he attempts to rescue the song by substituting energy and excitement for craft, and playing around with the pronunciation of a word or two as a distracting device. But it hardly makes riveting listening. Stephen Street at his mildest would probably have called this 'appalling'.

I've Changed My Plea To Guilty (Live)

One of the first Morrissey songs to employ judicial imagery, this composition was originally unveiled as the B-side of 'My Love Life'. This live reading is not the most spectacular of Morrissey's career but he takes the song towards a powerful climax. It's hardly surprising that these in-concert B-sides never previously found their way on to any of the various compilations.

Pregnant For The Last Time (Live)

Probably the best of the four tracks featured on the CD single of 'We Hate It When Our Friends Become Successful', this found the band more at home playing rockabilly. It's an exuberant outing that recalls the time when Morrissey first discovered his compatriots at the Camden Workers' Social Club. Regrettably, the definitive rockabilly album or EP that would have cemented this era was never completed.

Alsatian Cousin (Live)
The final live cut on the 'We Hate It When Our Friends Become Successful' single returned to the opening chords of Morrissey's first solo album. The major difference was the lack of Vini Reilly's distinctive whiny guitar which Whyte and Boorer do not attempt to duplicate. Instead, there's a shift towards an early Sixties' instrumental style. The audience evidently appreciate the band's work and the track ends with loud applause.

There Speaks A True Friend
In the tradition of 'We Hate It When Our Friends Become Successful', this was another of Morrissey's sarcastic tirades against false friends. Unfortunately, the simple melody is largely tuneless despite an attempt to liven up matters with a brief guitar solo. The abrupt ending was the only interesting feature. "It was Morrissey's idea I think," Alain Whyte told Rob Nebeker. "I think he thought the tune was too long. It actually had a long outro that was really melodic. The tune was really sweet, maybe too sweet. It had to be chopped to make it unusual."

You've Had Her
Backed by a desolate, howling wind, Morrissey adopts his most mournful tone for this reflection on the emotional vacuity of the stereotypical womanizer. Essentially it's Bacharach/David's 'Alfie' without the *joie de vivre* or the incessant questioning. The 'it's all over now' refrain is a familiar song theme from the Rolling Stones to Bob Dylan. Although the effects are atmospheric in the tradition of the Smiths' 'Asleep', the emotional quality at the heart of that song is sadly missing.

Moonriver
Surprisingly, this was the first time that the short, three-minute

version of 'Moonriver' appeared on album. The superior extended version was previously issued in the UK on *World Of Morrissey*. For reasons unspecified, Morrissey changed the title from 'Moon River' to 'Moonriver' and omitted the lyrics 'my Huckleberry friend'. Perhaps they reminded him of the cartoon series *Huckleberry Hound*, or it may have been that he felt uncomfortable with the phrase or phrasing.

Interlude

The CD of 'Interlude' featured three different mixes of the title track, one of which, 'Interlude (Extended)' was issued on the aforementioned compilation *Suedehead – The Best Of Morrissey*. The shorter version had not previously appeared on any album. Evidently the single's delayed release came to the attention of bootleggers. "Well I know you could get it before it came out," says Bridgwood. "It was on a bootleg. Effectively it was a track that Boz was going to produce. Whether it was originally conceived that we would do it at the end of the sessions after Steve Lillywhite had gone and we'd mixed the album, I don't know. But we did it during the sessions. We'd just record bits."

Interlude (Instrumental)

The instrumental 'Interlude' at 7 minutes 37 seconds even outlasted the 'extended' version by nearly two minutes. It's fascinating to hear the structure of the composition, the intricacy of the string arrangement and the added involvement of Boorer as producer and instrumentalist. "It's just Boz playing guitar and harmonium on that," Bridgwood concludes.

Full track listing: *CD 1 My Love Life; I've Changed My Plea To Guilty; There's A Place In Hell For Me And My Friends; CD 2 We Hate It When Our Friends Become Successful; Suedehead (Live); I've Changed My Plea To Guilty (Live); Pregnant For The Last Time (Live); Alsatian Cousin (Live); CD 3 You're The One For Me, Fatty; Pashernate Love; There Speaks A True Friend; CD 4 Certain People I Know; You've Had Her; Jack The Ripper; CD 5 The More You Ignore Me, The Closer I Get; Used To Be A Sweet Boy; I'd Love To; CD 6 Hold On To Your Friends;*

Moonriver; Moonriver (Extended); CD 7 Interlude; Interlude (Extended); Interlude (Instrumental); CD 8 Boxers; Have-A-Go Merchant; Whatever Happens, I Love You; CD 9 Sunny; Black-Eyed Susan; Swallow On My Neck.

THE BEST OF!

Released: November 2001 (US)

US issue: Rhino/Reprise R2-78375, November 2001

This American issue added little to the story, unless you count an edit of 'Now My Heart Is Full' but it is specifically mentioned here as a result of the final track, 'Lost', which had escaped all the UK compilations to date. The song was previously included on the aforementioned Japan-only mini-album *Rare Tracks*, issued in April 1998, and is discussed therein. Within the context of this compilation, it serves as a filmic closing theme, like the strings at the end of a concert. Looking at the track listing of this 'Best Of' it seems clear that the compilers have sacrificed chronology and coherence in favour of placing Morrissey's more commercial and well-known songs at the start of the disc. This would probably have been castigated in the UK music press had anybody bothered to offer a review. Rhino/Reprise probably felt it served its purpose in the US market.

Full track listing: *The More You Ignore Me, The Closer I Get; Suedehead; Everyday Is Like Sunday; Glamorous Glue; Do Your Best And Don't Worry; November Spawned A Monster; The Last Of The Famous International Playboys; Sing Your Life; Hairdresser On Fire; Interesting Drug; We Hate It When Our Friends Become Successful; Certain People I Know; Now My Heart Is Full; I Know It's Gonna Happen Someday; Sunny; Alma Matters; Hold On To Your Friends; Sister I'm A Poet; Disappointed; Tomorrow; Lost.*

YOU ARE THE QUARRY

Released: May 2004

Attack ATKLP 001, ATKCD 001, ATKDX 001 [CD/DVD], May 2004
Reissued as 'Deluxe Edition': Attack ATKDD 013, November 2004.
US issue: Attack 86001-1, 86001-2 [CD jewelcase], 86002-2 [CD cardboard],
86003-2 [CD/DVD], May 2004

Morrissey's fall from commercial grace was punctuated by a gap of seven years without a record release. Wealthy from the sale of his publishing, the singer had relocated to LA, emerging occasionally for some highly successful live performances which testified to his enduring appeal. Remarkably, he was unable to reach mutually agreeable terms with any record company throughout this long period. Finally, in May 2003, Sanctuary signed Morrissey, allowing him exclusive use of the Attack imprint – a label previously associated mainly with reggae acts. Originally, this album was scheduled for release under the superior title *Irish Blood, English Heart* and among the short list of tracks mentioned was the live 'Women Don't Seem To Like Me' (which actually turned out to be the already released song 'Lost') and 'Home Is A Question Mark'. The latter failed to appear and, along the way, Morrissey decided to change the album's title to the less impressive sounding *You Are The Quarry*. "I have been the quarry for so many years," he said, "and people have taken so many repeated pot-shots at me . . . I've been through so many managers and so many record companies and so many musicians – and they never let go, even though they may walk away of their own accord . . . And they will do all in their power to stop you from fulfilling your dreams. I have a lot of enemies. But let it be. So be it."

For the new album, Morrissey re-enlisted several members of his former backing band, including guitarists Boz Boorer, Alain Whyte and Gary Day, plus drummer Deano Butterworth and keyboardist Mikey V. Farrell. Producer Jerry Finn, best known for his work with Blink-182 and Green Day, was recruited to add a contemporary gloss. "I was introduced to Jerry Finn by a mutual friend," Morrissey explained. "He made me feel very confident. He's not easily pleased

269

and he's not prepared to be overwrought. He knows exactly what he
wants to do. He was able to help me create the sound for this album
that I had already been hearing in my head. This is a much brighter
sounding album than much of my previous work. We've turned the
page with '*Quarry*'. It's a dynamic album and I couldn't be any
happier."

You Are The Quarry was certainly a formidable comeback album
that served to reintroduce Morrissey to a new generation of listeners.
During his absence, younger musicians had continued to pick up on
the Smiths' legacy and acknowledged his importance as one of the
great pop icons. Anticipation for this release was considerable and
Morrissey did not disappoint, appearing in concert and on television
and radio. He boasted that the album was the finest of his career, an
exaggeration no doubt, but it was clear that he was pleased with the
results. Reviews in the music press were consistently excellent. Most
agreed that Morrissey had defied the passage of time and returned
more powerful than ever.

Mojo's Victoria Segal awarded the work four stars out of five,
arguing: "It seems that there's been a slow, sheepish realization that
one of our national treasures has been treated shabbily. *You Are The
Quarry* has generated a genuine sense of anticipation as those who
have denied him are beginning to realize that they've missed his
voice, his charisma, his world-view . . . After all this time, this album
is still a charisma masterclass, a mature work from a teenage icon. The
knives might have been out, but for Morrissey the Ides of March are
long gone. The king is dead. Long live the king."

In the rehabilitated *NME*, Mark Beaumont wrote a meandering
appreciation, before concluding that the album was worth an impressive 8 out of 10. Beaumont admitted his hope that the work might
prove a career-topping masterpiece, but was forced to disallow that
ultimate accolade. "Sadly, as with so much of his post-Smiths output,
it's not quite. It's undoubtedly the best thing he's done since *Vauxhall
And I* but that's hardly the most hysterical of plaudits . . . While certainly something of a return to form, *You Are The Quarry* scares no
stylistic horses: musically we're not a million miles from 1997's
much-maligned *Maladjusted*, but with a bit of the rock swagger of
Your Arsenal, the languid croonery of *Vauxhall And I* . . . and much

better tunes . . . Yet there's no deflating the true triumph of this album. It's a solid, occasionally spectacular comeback record . . ."

In *Q*'s Special Edition, Stuart Maconie provided another balanced commentary, concluding: "When Chairman Mao was asked about the legacy of the French Revolution, he famously said that it was too early to say yet. Well, it's too early to say whether *You Are The Quarry* is the glorious prodigal's return that some are trumpeting, or just another episode in one of the rummest and most entertaining soap operas in modern pop."

It was only the broadsheet papers that seriously questioned Morrissey's artistic worth. The most damning comments came from the *Independent*'s well-respected music critic Andy Gill, who awarded the album a paltry two stars out of five and dared question the prevailing notion of Morrissey godhead. "This is Morrissey's first new work since 1997's *Maladjusted*, an album whose feeble puns, self-parodic misery and mechanical riffing suggested a talent in apparently terminal decline. *You Are The Quarry* simply confirms it: in almost every respect – subject matter, musical settings, language and particularly the seemingly oceanic self-pity in which the singer wallows – it could have been made the week after *Maladjusted*, so infinitesimal is his progress . . . Alas not only is he fighting battles that everyone else has long ago forgotten, he's fighting them in almost identical terms, lyrically and musically, as he did a decade ago."

In one sense, Gill was correct. Outside of a glossy production, there was little evidence of any significant lyrical or musical development on Morrissey's part. But those points could have been argued at virtually every stage of his career. His work had never been about musical radicalism and the lyrics, apart from occasional forays into political polemic or social commentary, were largely concerned with the dialogue between self and soul. It was that ongoing drama along with the self-creation of Morrissey as a pop entity that enshrined his appeal. The importance of *You Are The Quarry* was to be found not only in the enjoyment of many excellent songs but in its re-establishment of Morrissey as a key modern icon whose history now took on an even greater significance. It was amazing to consider that the gap between *Maladjusted* and *You Are The Quarry* was two years longer than the entire career of the Smiths. In short, Morrissey had been missed and there was a growing awareness that a national treasure, seemingly lost, was more than ready to recapture former glories. The drama implicit in his return to recording was part of the same myth. Comeback albums by long-missed artistes often fare well, but hubris usually awaits with the follow-up and therein lay the real test for Morrissey. *You Are The Quarry* proved an enormous success on both sides of the Atlantic, reaching number 2 in the UK and number 11 in the US. It also provided Morrissey with the biggest single of his career when 'Irish Blood, English Heart' climbed to number 3 in the UK, at last outperforming, although not outselling, his 1988 début 'Suedehead'. By the time the chart statistics had been logged, the tantalizing question 'What next?' was in the air. Could Morrissey sustain this impressive comeback and build on this strong work to create something even greater?

America Is Not The World

Morrissey's ambivalence towards America had been evident since his teenage years and here it spilt forth in a combination of invective and confused love. Set against an almost funky backing, Morrissey derides the land of the free for its failure to elect a black, female or gay president and the apparently unpardonable sin of enslaving the western world with hamburgers. As he explained: "I imagined the sexy and sharp people of Estonia – which is not considered to be a world leader in anything – as far as I know – looking at the Burger King fast-food hell of the modern American food industry and actually feeling sorry for Americans." The lyrics are notable for their amusing bathos, particularly the childish chant, 'you fat pig', which brilliantly conveys the politics of the school playground. There is also a charac-teristically messianic arrogance in the complaint, 'For haven't you me with you now', as if Morrissey's presence alone ought to rehabilitate the country. As a twisted love song to a nation this was Morrissey at his supremely endearing.

In 2005, Christy Moore, a connoisseur of great songwriters, included a moving version of the song on his acclaimed album *Burning Times*. "When we played Glastonbury last year we heard the man and then in Dublin went to hear him again," he wrote. "Superb. Heard this song and it just summed up what I felt about this great land. Wondered if *I* could sing it and slowly found a way in." Un-intentionally retitling the composition 'America, I Love You', Moore appreciated Morrissey's sentiments more subtly than some critics. It was fascinating to hear his work in the context of such august protest songs as Bob Dylan's 'The Lonesome Death Of Hattie Carroll', Phil Ochs' 'Changes' and Joni Mitchell's 'The Magdalene Laundries'. Moore, a courageous campaigner during the hunger strikes in the Maze Prison in 1981, was never a stranger to controversy but must have been surprised to experience the vicarious whiplash so often administered to Morrissey. "We played in the TF Theatre in Castlebar and after the gig I was waylaid by this tank of a female Texan. She tore into me like nobody's business. 'You called me a pig, Mr Moore. I want my money back.' The promoter refunded her despite my cries that it was the only song she did not like." Moore's tale underlines the power of Morrissey's work when unleashed upon the mainstream, a rare enough occurrence.

Irish Blood, English Heart
This, the first acknowledgement in song of Morrissey's Irish roots (discounting the political commentary 'This Is Not Your Country'), displayed the power of his band with Boz Boorer providing some reverberating guitar offset by Deano Butterworth's powerful drum-ming. Belatedly addressing the racist debate, Morrissey dreams of reclaiming the English flag, bemoans the state of the British political system, denounces the monarchy and rekindles his republican dreams. Oliver Cromwell, the scourge of the Irish, is predictably castigated for his crimes against humanity, although the suggestion that the royal line still 'salute him' makes no historical sense whatsoever. Explaining this anomaly, Morrissey countered: "It's a comment on the whole British monarchy. Oliver Cromwell was no more than a general, but he behaved like some of them by slaughtering thousands of Irishmen just to get them out of the way." Although Morrissey's 'Englishness' has been extensively analysed, few, apart from myself, have spent much time on the crucial Irish connection. One excep-tion was the celebrated *Irish Times* critic John Waters who noted with characteristic precision: "The Smiths needed no translation in Ireland. Their dark introspection, tragic narcissism, ironic world-view and

swirling tunefulness fashioned a profound, existential connection with those of us born into the era of the First Programme for Economic Expansion, a connection which it is impossible to explain in other than mystical terms. The Smiths, more than most of the native-grown rock bands, can claim citizenship of that elusive territory so beloved of the President Mrs Robinson and Richard Kearney – The Fifth Province."

Later, Waters' colleague Brian Boyd questioned Morrissey about the Irish dimension in light of this composition's release. "My Irishness was never something I hid or camouflaged. I grew up in a strong Irish community. I was very aware of being Irish and we were told that we were quite separate from the scruffy kids around us – we were different to them. In many ways, though, I think I had the best of both places and the best of both countries. I'm 'one of us' on both sides. It was always odd later on with the Smiths when I was described as being 'extremely English' because other people would tell me I looked Irish, I sounded Irish and had other tell-tale signs."

I Have Forgiven Jesus

Setting the scene with a thoughtful piano opening, this remarkable reproach against the Almighty sees Morrissey taking his case to the celestial court. His list of grievances centres largely around the Deity's bestowing him with physical desires that evidently cannot be sated. There's also an amusing diary of the week which brings humiliation, suffocation and condescension. By the time he reaches the fourth day, Morrissey is so exasperated he cannot even muster a suitable adjective: 'Thursday is . . . pathetic'. By Friday, life has killed him off and there's just time for the familiar complaint about the state of his body. What other LA-based rock star multimillionaire could pull off a lyric like this and make it sound plausible enough to warrant sympathy? And who else but Morrissey would dare try? Years before, Morrissey had addressed the song's underlying theme when discussing his religious upbringing with the *Guardian*'s Suzie Mackenzie. "It is probably the worst thing you can do to a child, to make it feel guilty, and guilt is astonishingly embedded in Catholic children without [them] knowing why. It is a ferocious burden to carry. How evil can children be?" While promoting his latest work, Morrissey appeared in priest's clothes but even in Ireland this caused only passing comment rather than any national controversy. As a final act of subversion, 'I Have Forgiven Jesus' was issued as a single in a quixotic attempt to secure a Christmas number 1 hit.

Come Back To Camden

Given its declarations of being alone forever with only despair for company, this lament occasionally sounded even more self-pitying than 'I Have Forgiven Jesus'. Of course, as so often with Morrissey, there is self-disparaging wit and wry comments, this time on the state of London tea and garrulous taxi drivers. There is also a touch of droll eroticism in the suggestion 'every last inch of me's yours' which is sung in a hyena falsetto. The same effect can be heard in the closing plea 'come back to Camden and *I'll be good*', the vocabulary of which suggests a dependency similar to that of a young child who has misbehaved. At times, the effect is almost mock romantic as Morrissey's voice soars against swirling strings in overwrought adolescent yearning. Although there are hints of sexual longing, the song's focus is the heart rather than the loins. Significantly, it is the loss of somebody who enjoys laughing at the narrator's jokes which prompts the opening reminiscence. Private speculation that this part of the lyric might be a reference back to Morrissey's 'best friend on the payroll' evidently proved plausible. "That song is about a particular person," Morrissey confirmed. "I have a history, yes. And that whole time in my life is a very emotive period for me."

I'm Not Sorry

Apart from the philosophic aphorism about existence being a game, this song sounded like a private journey into Morrissey's inner world. The reference to slipping below the waterline recalled the suffocating image of the soil falling over his head in the Smiths' 'I Know It's Over'. There was also the coy, disparaging reference to a dream woman in the anti-climactic admission that there never was one. In interviews when asked about this fantasy he alluded to "the woman of my nightmares". But what comes across most forcibly is Morrissey's self-justification as alluded to in the title. Musically, Rhys Williams' unexpected flute interjection adds a pastoral note, playing out the song in poignant fashion.

The World Is Full Of Crashing Bores

This world-weary attack on a variety of matters that offend Morrissey's sensibilities employs diction redolent of Noël Coward, while the words echo Oscar Wilde. In the first two verses, Morrissey places himself among the catalogue of crashing bores but by the final stanza he insists that he is 'not one'. Among his targets are the legal system ('educated criminals') and pusillanimous pop stars whose careerist motives anger him sufficiently to provoke an uncharacteristic vulgarity: 'pigshit'. His complaint about uniformed whores was clearly an allusion both to the US police and the immigration officials who detained him for three hours following confusion over an alleged passport irregularity. "The police in America are terribly heavy and are themselves beyond the law, so they can do anything. They can shoot you and it doesn't matter to anybody. They don't have to account for themselves. But they're very very aggressive. And that's quite shocking, when you're surrounded, dragged into a room and cross-examined." But after all the barbs, it's the Gladys Knight & The Pips refrain 'Take Me In Your Arms And Love Me' that lingers most, a plea that is at once desperate and narcissistic.

Musically, Morrissey added his customary advice prior to recording. "'The World Is Full Of Crashing Bores' had a little piano bit before each verse," Boz Boorer recalls. "Morrissey said, 'Just cut those bits out, they're not necessary.' We try not to stress any strong melodies in the demo so there's a freedom. By the time a song gets to Morrissey it can be completely turned around."

How Can Anybody Possibly Know How I Feel?

With a fiercer musical attack reminiscent of mid-period Smiths, this was an even more splenetic assault than its predecessor. Morrissey again uses the word 'shit' in song for only the second time in his career. The subjects of his outburst are those uniformed whores mentioned in 'The World Is Full Of Crashing Bores' only this time Morrissey intensifies his attack, selecting one poor individual for the crime of being rude to him and wearing a smelly uniform. A female who claims to love him is declared insane and a man who respects him is deemed to have faulty judgement. This froth of self-loathing overflows in the final few lines in which the narrator lists all his deficiencies, sickness and depravity in order to throw them back into the face of his detractors with the punch-line that he would never exchange places with them. Morrissey's wonderfully arrogant solipsism is expressed through the repeated self-reference: 'the only one around here who is me is me'.

First Of The Gang To Die

A concert favourite prior to the album's release, this continued Morrissey's fascination with life's criminal underbelly, albeit with a shift of geographical location. Latino street gangs are the subject of his reverence here, but while admiring the pretty petty thieves, he treats the gang leader Hector with condescending sympathy describing him as a 'silly boy'. Any illusions about Hector's role as a quasi-Robin Hood are also dispelled at the end by the revelation that he stole from the rich and the 'very poor'. Evidently, his one saving grace is the charm that allows him to steal 'all hearts away'. Morrissey's shift from Moors Murderers and London East End gangsters to LA street gangs coincided with the discovery that he had become a minor icon in the Hispanic community. Guitarist Alain Whyte recalls: "We first noticed it at the Coachella's Festival in Palm Springs in 1999. All these Hispanic kids were coming to see us, with quiffs and leather jackets, shouting for Morrissey. The Latinos embraced him because they relate to all that isolation in his lyrics. They feel like outsiders in their own country. Plus, they have a very romantic sensibility and love the whole rocker image."

Let Me Kiss You

Opening with the pop cliché 'There's a place in the sun . . .', familiar from Stevie Wonder onwards, this romantic opus sounds like a repository of well-versed reference points. The guitar style and arrangement are redolent of Johnny Marr, at times recalling 'Girl Afraid', while the lyrics 'my heart is open' are straight out of *Vauxhall And I*. In reprising old ideas and referencing himself as a source Morrissey nevertheless plays to his strengths. A form of vicarious seduction is attempted by encouraging the recipient to fantasize about somebody else, a typical example of Morrissey's theatrical self-loathing in song. Sensing the sensuality beneath the lyrics, Nancy Sinatra, who had befriended the singer during this period, recorded her own version soon after.

All The Lazy Dykes

According to Morrissey, he wrote this song after witnessing a scene outside the Palms nightclub on Hollywood's Santa Monica Boulevard. "The clientele were all spilling out on to the pavement and they looked absolutely fascinating. Really very, very strong women; women who know who they are and what they want and where they're coming from and where they're going. Fascinating." Although the song title sounds pejorative, this is anything but a criticism of lesbians. Morrissey always admired laziness as a virtue and had championed lesbianism since discovering feminist literature during his teenage years. This song is very much a recruiting poster for lesbianism – 'Come and join the girls' – and a call to reject the servility of marriage in favour of a more fulfilling life. The musical arrangement is suitably sumptuous and those seeking some minor lyrical reference points would do well to listen to P.J. Proby's 'Hold Me'.

I Like You

A sprightly arrangement, this beautifully self-deprecating lyric again recalls Morrissey's early work with the Smiths in its adolescent sense of love as an uncertain discovery. There's a palpable feeling of joy and wonderment in the realization that one of his severest critics must be the object of his desire. Why else does he let the person get away with speaking to him in such an irreverent fashion? And what they evidently share is that neither is right in the head. Along the way Morrissey, in search of similes, cannot resist another gratuitous attack on the legal establishment, denouncing envious magistrates and complaining about their 'fat faces'. It is typical of Morrissey to throw such jarring asides into an otherwise joyful love song. According to Morrissey, Robbie Williams offered to perform this song with him at the Brit Awards, but the invitation was either ignored or declined.

You Know I Couldn't Last

Perhaps in an attempt to sum things up, Morrissey's final song on the album attacked just about everyone – journalists, critics, record companies, voracious teenagers, evil legal eagles, northern leeches, racist accusers and rampant accountants. All seemingly conspire to transform the fruits of Morrissey's labours into a form of mental squalor. The beguiling image of a cash register weighing heavily on his back becomes a powerful metaphor for the compound interest owed to Mike Joyce. There is even a Wildean allusion to death by the printed word which simultaneously conjures the libel trial that Oscar brought against the Marquess of Queensbury and Morrissey's own hounding by the music press. As Morrissey told the *NME*: "It's addressing people who have been critical of me through the years and never quite given credit for my having sustained a barrage of unrelenting criticism, which is quite difficult for most people to take. Most people can't take criticism. And I think I've been accused of everything except murder – which is bound to come at some stage, I don't doubt." Musically, the sumptuous waltz-time arrangement provided a dramatic and stunning conclusion to the album recalling the great Smiths' song 'That Joke Isn't Funny Anymore'.

A 'Deluxe Edition' of this album was subsequently issued in November 2004 as a 2-CD set. The bonus disc included an enhanced CD featuring video performances of 'Irish Blood, English Heart', 'First Of The Gang To Die', 'I Have Forgiven Jesus' and 'Let Me Kiss You' taken from *The Late Late Show With Craig Kilborn*. There was also an audio collection of B-sides, featuring the following nine songs:

Don't Make Fun Of Daddy's Voice

With its thrashy musical backdrop and slight lyrics, this was typical good quality B-side material, complete with a smidgen of sexual innuendo concerning how the father may have ended up with a funny voice. Those in search of coincidental autobiographical footnotes might wish to consult *The Severed Alliance* which reveals that as a young teenager Morrissey's voice was also the subject of some schoolboy ridicule.

279

It's Hard To Walk Tall When You're Small

Having just made fun of daddy's voice, Morrissey's sardonic humour now descends upon the vertically challenged. They represent another easy target for his cruel wit and the treatment recalls Randy Newman's lyrically and satirically superior 'Short People'. Although it was assumed that the songs on *You Are The Quarry* and its B-sides were relatively recent, Jonny Bridgwood reveals that this composition was around during the recordings for *Maladjusted*. "Originally, it had a different tune written by Spencer Cobrin. We did it in 1997. It's the same title and I believe the lyrics are the same but the tune is different."

Teenage Dad On His Estate

One of the better B-sides, this acerbic put-down satirized judgemental middle-class types who self-righteously condemn the lifestyles of teenage parents living on council estates. It contains one of Morrissey's more baffling but funny insults in the line, 'you're a dipper, a slider, cart-house provider'. The satire extends to the teenage dad who is portrayed as a methadone-assisted plebeian, living off basic but hedonistic pleasures who nevertheless is deemed happier than his materialistically minded middle-class critics. Musically, the anthemic chorus brings a mock-heroic quality to the teenage dad's lifestyle, allowing Morrissey to empathize with and patronize his subject in the same breath. The same technique was later used on 'The Slum Mums', whose theme provided a companion piece to this composition.

Munich Air Disaster 1958

Although its title recalled the 1967 Bee Gees' hit 'New York Mining Disaster 1948', this featured Morrissey returning to his Manchester heritage for one of the most famous footballing tragedies of all time. On 6 February 1958, following a match against Red Star Belgrade, a triumphant Manchester United team set off home. Their plane stopped for refuelling at Munich, where the passengers disembarked for refreshments, before reboarding. After a couple of false starts, the plane sped to the end of the runway, then plunged through a perimeter fence, collided with a house, lost a wing and sliced itself in two. There were 24 fatalities, including eight young players. The tragedy became a part of Manchester's history and although the event happened before Morrissey's birth, he was all too aware of its significance. Both he and his father Peter were supporters of the club. If this song had been written at the start of the Smiths' career, it might have brought them the same kind of disapprobation that followed the Moors' Murders saga 'Suffer Little Children'. But 1958 now seemed an age away. Morrissey's treatment of the tragic event is sympathetic but the attempted empathy in wishing to join them merely serves to transmute the tragedy into a metaphor for his own morbidity.

Friday Mourning
In keeping with its bleak punning title, the tempo of this tune was suitably funereal in the style of Mark Nevin's mournful melody on *Kill Uncle*'s 'Asian Rut'. The lyrics also recalled the mordant humour of *Viva Hate*'s 'Late Night Maudlin Street'. Midway through, there is even an echo of the comic revulsion of a nation turning its back and gagging at Morrissey's nakedness in the wry 'I will never stand naked in front of you'. There's also a probable allusion to his retirement from the pop pantheon in the demand to douse the houselights because 'I'm not coming back'. That threat was last heard in more comic mode at the close of 'Disappointed'. Of course the words could equally refer to suicide, especially in view of the funeral imagery that closes the song. Amid this maudlin meditation the singer roll calls the views of teachers, parents and bosses all of whom offer the denigrating litany, 'You are a loser'.

The Never-Played Symphonies
Dramatized as a death-bed confession, with piano dominant, this near elegy looks back on a life of lost opportunities with particular punning emphasis on 'the never laid'. In effect, it was a musical reiteration of Poet Laureate Sir John Betjeman's famous quip that his greatest regret was not having had more sexual intercourse. The synth string background was a pleasing touch considering the metaphorical title, but it was regrettable that Morrissey or his producer declined to invest in a full-scale orchestra whose contribution would have transformed this track into a true epic.

My Life Is A Succession Of People Saying Goodbye

This high-quality arrangement was made even more striking by the luscious harp playing of Camilla Pay. Passing time and the prospect of old age now dominate the singer's thoughts. The image of the future stretching ahead, then behind, recalls a near identical allusion in 'How Can Anybody Possibly Know How I Feel?' Here, perhaps, lies a clue to a theme that may come to dominate Morrissey's lyrical observations hereafter. An exceptionally strong B-side, this was the final track on the CD single of 'First Of The Gang To Die' which also featured 'Teenage Dad On His Estate' and 'Mexico', any of which would have been worthy of a place on the original *You Are The Quarry*.

I Am Two People

First issued as the B-side to 'Let Me Kiss You', the third single from *You Are The Quarry*, this was musically weaker than most of the other tracks, but by no means unpleasing. The slight lyric relates the story of two faces, one that can never be shown – just like the portrait of Dorian Gray. There's an enticing ad-lib at the end recalling Morrissey's vocal tricks of yore reinforced by a strong piano accompaniment by Michael Farrell.

Less than two months after this song's release, a fourth single from the album was issued: 'I Have Forgiven Jesus'. Unfortunately, the latter's B-sides arrived too late for inclusion on this 'Deluxe Edition'. As a result, we still await the album débuts of the Raymonde cover 'No One Can Hold A Candle To You', the social commentary 'The Slum Mums' and the sardonic 'The Public Image'.

Mexico

A touching conclusion to the B-side collection, this was Morrissey's love song to Mexico, complete with the same anti-American senti-ments that framed this album's opening track. The incomplete lyric sheet mistakenly prints 'you'll be alright' instead of the superior 'you think you're so right'. Coincidentally or not, the refrain 'In Mexico I lay on the grass and I cried my heart out' was reminiscent of the title of Elizabeth Smart's novel *By Grand Central Station I Sat Down And Wept*. The connection is less tenuous than it sounds, given that

Smart's work was a lyrical touchstone for Morrissey in the past and even inspired the title of the Smiths' compilation, *Louder Than Bombs*. Morrissey's affection for Mexico and Hispanic culture was mentioned in several promotional interviews, including his audience with the *Word* where he stressed the country's musical heritage. "When you go to Mexico, you constantly hear people singing and music playing, and it's very soft, loving music, not harsh, brittle hip-hop or very nasty urban social messages . . . It might be the emotional outpouring, which Mexicans also do very well: the high pitch and the stretching-out of songs. The songs are reaching out towards people and asking for some form of communication, they're not mumbled or sung into the chest."

LIVE AT EARLS COURT

Released: March 2005

Attack ATKCD 014 [CD jewelcase], ATKDP 014 [CD cardboard], April 2005.
US issue: Attack 86012-2, March 2005

After such a long absence from the recording studio and the acclaim achieved by *You Are The Quarry*, it was not entirely surprising that Morrissey took advantage of his renewed profile to rush out a live album. Even during his wilderness years as an unsigned exile, he had always been a fantastic draw in concert. In September 2002, for instance, he sold out two nights at London's Royal Albert Hall without any pre-publicity, let alone a new album. All his shows were well-attended events seemingly proving the theory that he could exist in a vacuum outside the usual machinations of the music industry. The live set captured herein not only featured recordings from Earls Court but also selections from shows in Glasgow, Birmingham, Brighton and Dublin, all recorded in December 2004. Although far from indispensable, the album offered an eclectic selection of songs including four compositions from the Smiths era.

The recording's provenance was reflected in its contrasting chart fortunes on either side of the Atlantic: number 18 (UK) and number 118 (US).

How Soon Is Now?

It took real audacity for Morrissey to start a live album with arguably the Smiths' most famous recording. This serves partly as an exorcism, indicating that there is little, if anything, in the Smiths' canon that he is afraid to tackle. The reverberating guitar was a clever signifier, offering a facsimile of Marr's original without fully knowing how the guitarist achieved every effect. As Marr once told *Total Guitar*: "The lead is just slide guitar put through a couple of AMSs. The way we did the vibrato bit was to put the track down straight, then we fed the guitar track out to four Fender Twins. The producer, John Porter, was changing the timing on one side, I was changing it on the other, to keep it in time with the track. So that's what the sound is. Most people pick up on the vibrato part, but the slide's also great, really tense."

The approximation from Boz Boorer and Jesse Tobias was apparently enough to keep the audience happy. Morrissey's vocal sounds more mature and thankfully the occasional whistle is still in evidence. He even attempts an amusing yodel while singing 'what do you really mean?' The song rumbles towards its conclusion amid a barrage of applause. Although this particular performance is pleasant enough, the feeling remains that the audience's appreciation is directed more towards the memory of a great song, unexpectedly resurrected.

First Of The Gang To Die

Inevitably the solo show is heavily focused on the recent album, *You Are The Quarry*. Morrissey enjoys his vocal here, stretching syllables and stressing particular words for no apparent reason. The elongated lines are so convoluted that he can play with them in various ways. Even the name of his protagonist has a slightly comic edge. Although it is possible that 'Hector' is a common name in the gangland community of LA, the suspicion remains that Morrissey has employed a deliberately unfashionable monicker for his bumbling anti-hero, recalling the cartoon character Hector Heathcote, a popular tea-time television attraction during the singer's school-days. It might also be worth considering that Hector is the name of the school teacher in Alan Bennett's play *The History Boys*. As the song fades, Morrissey offers the humble, "Thank you for being here – thank you for being you."

November Spawned A Monster

A burst of feedback prefaces one of the more recognizable riffs among Morrissey's solo work. This was the song's second live outing on CD and it has the edge over the previous reading on *Beethoven Was Deaf*. The most notable difference is the interrogative use of the word 'Why?' at key moments, with Morrissey sounding like a teacher expressing a maths formula. Lyrically, but not musically, it is even more biting than the original studio version with subtle changes like '*idiots* discussing me' and the forthright admission, 'yes I am a freak'. Following the reference to 'sex mad lovers' Morrissey offers an amazing growl which adds to the drama. Although Mary Margaret O'Hara's unearthly expostulations cannot be replicated, the group throw in a raga-like instrumental break which reaches a suitably cacophonous crescendo. Given the appearance of 'Subway Train' later on the album, it's worth remembering that 'November Spawned A Monster' was partly inspired by the New York Dolls' 'Frankenstein'.

Don't Make Fun Of Daddy's Voice

Morrissey's capacity to transform a minor B-side into a strong live track is demonstrated here with some aplomb. Although the arrangement and execution are completely faithful to the original recording, the song finds new life in a concert setting where its understated merriment provides light relief. At one point Morrissey soars into a few seconds of his famous falsetto, in mock tribute to the song's title.

Bigmouth Strikes Again

A roar of approval can be heard within seconds of this song's opening which again testifies to the audience's love of Morrissey revisiting his past. Here he alters the second line to 'sweetness, I *wasn't* joking . . .' while imagining his adversary being bludgeoned in bed. In deference to technology, the hearing aid which melts in the fire of martyrdom is replaced by an iPod. The group play the tune at a faster pace than the Smiths' original and Morrissey's vocal sounds grittier, with little attempt to sing in a higher register. As the song ends, Morrissey reflects on the evident incongruity of hearing a Smiths' classic re-invented for a new century: "The past is a strange place."

I Like You

Even more impressive than 'Don't Make Fun Of Daddy's Voice', 'I Like You' emerges as a live highlight. Indeed, it is one of the best examples of Morrissey rehabilitating a seemingly minor song and transforming it into a concert classic, a trick seldom shown since the excellent 'Disappointed'. This version sounds slightly more earnest than its studio counterpart, so much so that Morrissey makes it seem eminently reasonable that mutual mental problems should provide the perfect basis for an enduring friendship. Whatever else, it's a wonderfully amusing dissection of a singular psyche.

Redondo Beach

The importance of Patti Smith to Morrissey should never be under-estimated. Her acclaimed 1975 album *Horses* enthralled the 16-year-old and helped spearhead an interest in feminist literature and sexual politics that would dominate his late teenage life and reach fruition in the lyrics of his earliest recordings. It was surely no coincidence that he named his group the Smiths or that his first brief encounter with Johnny Marr took place at a Patti Smith concert. Morrissey was so enamoured of the New York singer/writer/poet that a harsh word about her could bring a crashing end to a budding friendship. Wythenshawe contemporary Phil Fletcher, whose circle included Billy Duffy and Johnny Marr, once wrote a letter to *Sounds* support-ing a scathing review of Patti Smith's Rainbow concert by journalist Jane Suck. Two days after its publication he received a stinging missive from Morrissey defending the singer and dismissing his "pedestrian prose".

'Redondo Beach' proved an eminently suitable song to cover and can now be seen as a lyrical blueprint for Morrissey's style of mordant humour. The setting offers a neat contrast to the dismal seaside imagery of 'Everyday Is Like Sunday', while the childish vocabulary ('have you gone gone?') and delicate tone are a clever distraction from the real drama in which a friend or lover abruptly leaves, then drowns herself. The pointlessness of the death is expressed in cruel word-play (the girl is 'washed up') and a bathetic finale in which the narrator's surprise is equalled only by an insouciant carelessness which is comically callous: 'The girl who died, it was *you*. Because you've gone, gone – oh, goodbye.'

Let Me Kiss You

"If you don't mind and you've got the time . . ." Morrissey intones, before launching into another selection from the recent *You Are The Quarry*. It's a faithful reproduction, complete with the Smiths-influenced guitar refrain and a snatch of brass courtesy of Michael Farrell. Of the six selections from the first edition of his last album, this is arguably the least desirable, although it is performed reasonably well. It's interesting that Morrissey chose this rather than a bigger statement such as 'America Is Not The World'.

Subway Train/Munich Air Disaster 1958

Morrissey's enduring love for the New York Dolls has been documented in countless interview quotes since the beginning of the Smiths. He even wrote a short and undistinguished booklet on the group, published by John Muir's Babylon Books. Clearly there were moments during the early stages of his solo career when they fell out of favour on his turntable. Speaking in 1984, he said: "I was so fanatical about the Dolls to an almost unhealthy obsession and then, one day, I suddenly woke up and it didn't mean a thing to me, which was quite frightening. For me now to look back on records from a particular period which were the sole reason why I existed and to listen to those records today and I hear *nothing* is really quite strange." During that same year, he told another magazine, "That was a horrible period and I *hate* the Dolls now." After leaving the Smiths he rekindled his teenage passion and regularly performed the Dolls' 'Trash', which was featured on his 1991 video *Live In Dallas*. 'Subway Train', another track from 1973's *New York Dolls* was his second tribute to his adolescent heroes, this time featuring a single verse as a 50-second lead-in to his morbid tribute to the dead players of Manchester United. 'Subway Train' previously served as a preamble to 'Everyday Is Like Sunday', most notably on television's *Jonathan Ross Show* and the DVD *Who Put The 'M' In Manchester?* In June 2004, 20 years after dismissing the Dolls, Morrissey reunited the surviving members for an appearance as part of the Meltdown series of concerts on London's South Bank.

There Is A Light That Never Goes Out

The third Smiths song on the album, this was the sole rival to 'How Soon Is Now?' as the group's most famous offering. Unlike 'Bigmouth Strikes Again', Morrissey makes no playful attempt to alter the lyrics and sings with the expected earnestness. The only small addition is a truculent 'so what?' after the '10-ton truck' line. As expected, the audience reaction is celebratory from the outset. The placing of the song on the live album is subtle, following other compositions with a death theme including 'Munich Air Disaster 1958', 'Redondo Beach', 'Bigmouth Strikes Again' and 'First Of The Gang To Die'.

The More You Ignore Me, The Closer I Get

"Time will prove everything," Morrissey observes ominously before reprising one of the more spry moments from *Vauxhall And I*. The song's age is acknowledged in a slight change of lyric with Morrissey now suggesting his prey 'take the *difficult* way and give in to me'. What was once a typical Morrissey song of obsessive attachment, akin to a stalker's romantic quest, takes on a new subtext in view of his long-standing legal feud with Mike Joyce. The reference to high court judges proves more prescient than Morrissey ever intended. Indeed, given Joyce's dogged pursuit of Morrissey's assets and the singer's convoluted attempts to ignore his adversary, the lyrics would now sound more appropriate if they were sung by the drummer who once told me, "I'll get there in the end."

Friday Mourning

"I really can't help it – it's either this or prison," Morrissey announces, sounding as if judicial matters are still on his mind, subconsciously or otherwise. A catalogue of self-revulsion and vicious diatribes follow amid contemplations of retirement or suicide, the latter hinted at in the reference to being dressed in black. Unlike the suicide in 'Redondo Beach', this demise seems like blessed relief. It says much for Morrissey that he can still write mournful, self-pitying lyrics that ooze with conviction rather than self-parody. His audience, ever aware of this, greet the song with loud appreciation.

I Have Forgiven Jesus

"I know it isn't mutual, but I have forgiven Jesus," Morrissey proclaims. One of the most unlikely festive hits of all time was promoted by Morrissey complete with a priest's vestments. In the new Ireland, his antics were greeted with mild amusement rather than outrage or tabloid controversy. Whether he received any letters from aggrieved proselytizing Christians attempting to teach him the finer points of theology remains uncertain. The song fits well into Morrissey's repertoire amid the allusions to death elsewhere on the album. Similarly, the reference to life killing him 'by Friday' echoes the theme of 'Friday Mourning'. Unusually for a Morrissey lyric there is a lapse into Americanism with the phrase 'mooning', which sounds deliberately jarring in a song about Jesus. Then again, fantasies about dropping trousers can be traced back to the lyrics of both 'Nowhere Fast' and 'The World Is Full Of Crashing Bores'. As Morrissey's lament reaches a dramatic climax his voice grows more anguished as he envisages taking on the Deity himself in true Miltonic fashion.

The World Is Full Of Crashing Bores

Although the arrangement is faithful to the recent version on *You Are The Quarry*, this performance sounds less arresting minus its professional studio gloss. Morrissey takes gleeful revenge on contemporary plastic pop stars, audibly sneering the line about them smearing their 'lovely careers'. Nor was there any shortage of other boorish targets. "I could name 505," he told *NME*'s Alex Needham, "but that's not the point. Let's just say the world is full of crashing bores. They know who they are, particularly within music. It's the entire culture of so-called pop music and the assumption that all you have to do is stand and smile and you're a pop idol. They are the aspects of modern society that scare me to death. They're worse than terrorists."

Shoplifters Of The World Unite

For the fourth time on the album, Morrissey performs a Smiths song, significantly one of their less successful singles. Speaking of its inclusion in his solo repertoire, Morrissey insisted: "It's one of my all-time favourite songs, a great song that means so much to me. Contrary to popular belief, I am proud to the point of absolute conceitedness of the Smiths. Being in the Smiths for five years wasn't the worst way to spend a life. I'd like to do much more Smiths songs in the future live. They are shockingly good songs really." Unfortunately, this live version fails to match the power of the original and Morrissey's croaky vocal is less appealing.

Irish Blood, English Heart

"So, you see, I can't be wrong about everything. I can't be. It's impossible." Morrissey's preamble takes the form of a defensive soliloquy, more appropriate for a High Court setting. This song was introduced live long before the release of *You Are The Quarry* and emerges as one of the highlights of this collection with an impressive performance by the band. Morrissey's republican anthem endeared him to Irish audiences, particularly as this was the first time he had celebrated his Dublin roots in song. Speaking to *Mojo*'s Keith Cameron, Morrissey acknowledged the ambivalence felt by many second-generation Irish children, separated from their ancestry by a new and challenging culture. "Obviously the Irish feel resentment towards England because England has historically been appalling to Ireland. So it was somewhat confusing for me growing up . . . But of course the English laugh at everybody and ridicule everybody, which is often quite funny."

You Know I Couldn't Last

With its Beatlesque opening and waltz-time melody this wonderful summation of Morrissey's trials and tribulations is like a medieval pageant of allegories slowly wandering past to receive condemnation. In common with 'Friday Mourning', Morrissey is reduced to listing offences, as if a single song can no longer contain merely one subject of complaint. Even his royalties are tainted by misery, but at least he takes stoic satisfaction in pointing out that the critics who attempted to break him have failed. Appropriately, this realization is accompanied by a Rottweiller growl closing with a cacophony of colliding instrumentation.

Last Night I Dreamt That Somebody Loved Me

A slow, stately piano opening from Michael Farrell ushers in Morrissey's favourite song from *Strangeways, Here We Come*. That he chooses to bookend the album with Smiths' songs underlines the extent to which he now feels comfortable with his own history and legacy. In singing 'the story is old . . . but it goes on' Morrissey evidently acknowledges that the old themes are ever present and so are memories of the Smiths. Boz Boorer adds a clarinet to proceedings but this is clearly a paean to past glories. The need to remember is emphasized by Morrissey in some final words that coincidentally paraphrase his admonition in 'Rubber Ring': "Don't forget me. I love you. Goodnight."

RINGLEADER OF THE TORMENTORS

Released: April 2006

Attack ATKCD 016, ATKDX 016 [CD/DVD], April 2006.
US issue: Attack 86014, 86015 [CD/DVD], April 2006

The follow-up to *You Are The Quarry* was a crucial album for Morrissey who could no longer rely on a returning warrior's champagne reception from the music press or media. Its recording signalled another important change in his life, ending his lengthy stay in Los Angeles. After relocating to Rome, he elected to write and record a new work using the nucleus of Boz Boorer, Alain Whyte and Gary Day, along with recent recruit Michael Farrell and experienced session musicians Jesse Tobias (guitar) and Matt Chamberlain (drums). The sessions took place during the summer of 2005 at the Forum Music Village. Unfortunately, the intended producer Jeff Saltzman, best known for his work with the Killers, was unavailable. It was at this point that Morrissey arrived at the novel idea of inviting a figure renowned for working on the early Seventies recordings of T. Rex and David Bowie. In September 2005, Tony Visconti was surprised to receive a call demanding immediate attention. This was actually his second chance to collaborate with Morrissey having previously been approached as a likely candidate for *Your Arsenal*, which was subsequently passed on to Mick Ronson. Within 72 hours of receiving Morrissey's offer, Visconti was on a plane to Rome. "They'd started on their own and it wasn't going very well. There was no one in charge. There were a lot of problems, so I just had to go in and sort things out. But they had already recorded their drum tracks and some guitars, which we ended up using. It wasn't in bad shape but it just wasn't organized."

Thereafter, the sessions proceeded exceptionally smoothly and a release date was scheduled for spring 2006. The album's title was scrutinized for possible hidden meanings, but none were forthcoming. In a pre-release press statement Morrissey explained: "By *Ringleader Of The Tormentors* I mostly mean disturber of the peace. It would be easy to call the album something nicey wishy-washy, but it doesn't come naturally to me to endear myself to the public. In fact, if it was 1773, I probably would've been hanged and burned by now, which gives even more credence to the album title."

The first major review was printed in the *Observer Music Monthly* and could hardly have been more encouraging. Morrissey's Mancunian contemporary Paul Morley preferred five stars and declared the work "the Morrissey masterpiece", a soundbite that was eagerly seized upon and plastered across the front of the CD upon its release, along with an 8 out of 10 recommendation by *NME* which concluded that it was "his boldest, most adventurous and intensely personal collection to date". The *Guardian*'s Alexis Petridis was equally ecstatic, although he could not resist a hilarious analysis of "Morrissey's combustible crown jewels" under a review pointedly headed 'Never mind the bollocks'. In uncannily similar fashion to the reviews of *You Are The Quarry* there was a tailing off of appreciation after this point and it was telling that three of the major music monthlies, *Q*, *Uncut* and the *Word* each concluded that the work was worth no more than three stars out of five. Although the *Word* had Morrissey on the cover and interviewed him at length, their reviewer Andrew Harrison retained a professional detachment. In an overview of the singer's career it was revealing to observe that the new album was ranked alongside the three-starred *You Are The Quarry* and *Southpaw Grammar*, with *Viva Hate* and *Your Arsenal* receiving four stars and *Vauxhall And I* an unassailable five.

In *Q*, Tom Doyle felt similar reservations, arguing: "Ultimately what we are left with is a sense of something not quite finished, a recurring problem in Morrissey's solo catalogue. It makes *Ringleader Of The Tormentors* feel like a transitional album, which is frustrating when much of it is as focused as he's ever been."

Arguably the most perceptive, best written and provocative analysis came from *Uncut*'s Stephen Troussé who provided a piercing overview of Morrissey's career before concluding, less harshly than it appears in this short extract: "*Ringleader Of The Tormentors* isn't a bad record, it's just no better or worse than *You Are The Quarry* or *Maladjusted* and demonstrates, if nothing else, that Morrissey is quite consistent. But more and more it seems that, like Wilde, he has put all his genius into the creation of the persona, and only his talent into his songs."

Whatever else, the reviews confirmed that Morrissey was still taken seriously, even by his detractors. It must have been especially gratifying when the album entered the UK charts at number 1, reigning in the same glory as *Vauxhall And I* and *Viva Hate*. An accompanying tour proved a delight, with Morrissey appearing at some unexpected venues and performing with a confidence and charisma that showed no sign of diminishment in middle age.

The success of *Ringleaders Of The Tormentors* promised much for the future and there were clearly more risks for Morrissey to take should he possess the nerve. Looking back at his career, and particularly his latest album, made you wonder where he might travel next. Revealingly, he had described *Ringleaders . . .* as unlike "any previous Morrissey album" and "a completely new sensation". This made some sense in view of Visconti's Technicolor production, the sensuous use of strings and the involvement of a couple of seasoned session musicians. However, for all those plusses, the album was no great radical departure from the main body of his work. Far from an overwhelming testament to his artistic ambition, it gave the impression of being all things to all men, a well-calculated combination of Morrissey songs that structurally echoed the light and shade of *You Are The Quarry*. It was almost as if Morrissey had a preconceived notion of how his work should be constructed, complete with the customary epic centrepiece and two or three commercial songs to be plundered as potential A-sides, this time from the pen of former Alanis Morissette guitarist Jesse Tobias. There were some thrilling moments along the way from the staggering 'I Will See You In Far-Off Places' to the flamboyant exuberance of 'At Last I Am Born' but for every artistic leap forward there were safety steps in reverse. Perhaps this tells us much about Morrissey's philosophy of pop. It may be that he has no wish to produce anything as 'out there' as *Low* or *Tilt* or sees no point in taking the experimental route into areas that might cause us to question what exactly Morrissey is about musically. Over the years he has stuck closely to a small core of musicians and collaborators even during periods when critics and fans were willing him out of that orbit of comfort. Within the perimeters of his enclosed universe, he continues to surprise us with works brimming with passion, irony and all those familiar Morrissey traits. Maybe one day he will provide us with something even greater or more disconcerting, a work of epic ambition or a grand failure – his own *Metal Machine Music* meets *The Drift*, or simply a bleak, undiluted album that resolutely shows no concession to the singles market. Whatever else, there remains plenty of scope and fresh tactics available to Morrissey during his autumnal years.

I Will See You In Far-Off Places

With an opening that recalls Led Zeppelin's Eastern-flavoured 'Kashmir', this grand production proved the most dramatic and astounding track on the album. As early as the first line Morrissey speculates philosophically about the nature of human life before the sonic assault takes us into questions about death, immortality and the consequences, in human terms, of the war in Iraq. Here the sarcastic quip 'if the USA doesn't bomb you' recalls the flippancy of the bomb references in 'Ask' and 'Everyday Is Like Sunday', only this time Morrissey sounds deadly serious. Questioned about the line by *NME*'s Mark Beaumont, he admitted: "Yes, I do feel very sad for the people of Iraq having been invaded by Bush and Blair – so many people have unnecessarily lost their lives and Bush and Blair don't care. But within the song I feel there's a spiritual sensation whereby, although we know that life will end, we all have a feeling that we will meet again. Now why should we all have that feeling? If we realize that everything is temporary, why do we all have this innate feeling that we will be together in some place?"

As the song reaches a dramatic close, Morrissey provides a brilliant wordless mantra that echoes the apocalyptic sound effects. In the great tradition of 'The Queen Is Dead', 'I Will See You In Far-Off Places' ranks alongside the greatest of Morrissey's album-opening tracks.

Dear God Please Help Me

This was the most discussed track on the album, largely due to its sexual lyrical content. In complete contrast to the preceding track, it begins as a reflective acoustic piece built upon a string arrangement written by the great Ennio Morricone. Speaking to journalist Ian Harrison, producer Tony Visconti explained how he edited Morricone's work into the mix. "He did a lovely arrangement, but it was a little baroque and flowery, and we had to take the saddest, most beautiful part and make it more elegiac. The song's part prayer, but it has this dark, sexual nature. Ennio doesn't speak English, and he made it more of a prayer. He didn't understand the naughty bits."

In the song the narrator pleas directly to God about the temptations of the flesh before comparing his testicles to exploding kegs. The effect is typically jarring, with Morrissey continuing his tradition of mixing humour, longing and tragedy in a single song. The enduring image of detonating testicles simultaneously conjures visions of Guy Fawkes mixed with a *Tom And Jerry* cartoon. A stately, swelling organ accompaniment adds another contrasting effect, complicating the listener's response once more. It says much for the power of Morrissey's heartfelt vocal that not an ounce of poignancy is lost along the way. Ultimately, the lyrical interpretation hinges upon a fascinatingly ambiguous third verse in which the narrator addresses either God or alternatively a mortal suitor to track him down and win his heart. Thereafter, we are presented with the most explicit sexual imagery ever featured in a Morrissey song. In 'Come Back To Camden' there was a reference to raised knees in recline, but here a 'he' places his hand on the narrator's knee who then takes the sexual lead in what sounds like attempted buggery. The homosexual act, if that's what it is, ultimately serves to free the stifled heart. Although the sexual allusions provided countless comments in the press, the theological aspects of the song were no less interesting. When discussing the composition, Morrissey was predictably evasive about the subject matter. Speaking to *Mojo*'s Andrew Male, he appeared to suggest that the line about leg-spreading was autobiographical, but on closer inspection he was only saying it was 'true' without confirming the identity of the speaker or subject. "Well I didn't think there was ever something I couldn't write about, but unless it was a strip of me then I didn't really want to venture into anything. The song has to be true, otherwise it's pointless. And it is, very true." He was far more ambiguous in conversation with *NME*'s Mark Beaumont, obtusely observing, "I don't think homosexuality is mentioned in the song . . .

Well there are 'he's' all over the place. It's a matter of having interest from someone who is a 'he', which one can't help and one can't orchestrate, and so turning to God and saying, 'Did this happen to you?' We don't really know about His personal relationships but He must have had a few. Somebody must have put their hand on His knee . . ." Of course, contrary to Morrissey's suggestion, the 'he' mentioned in the song is clearly distinct from the God who is pleaded to in the same verse. Pushed for further explication, Morrissey concluded: "It's best I say nothing . . . It's all down to the ear of the beholder." Finally, in a penetrating interview with *The Times*' Andrew Billen in May 2006, he denied some of the sexual allusions mentioned in *Mojo* and *Q* and furthermore insisted that he was not in love with anybody. "It isn't true. Everything remains the same. I am an island."

You Have Killed Me

The first single released from the album reached number 3 in the UK charts, repeating the achievement of 'Irish Blood, English Heart' but still failing to reward Morrissey with his first ever number 1. Commentators were quick to remind readers that Morrissey was name-checking the gay Italian film directors Pasolini and Visconti in the song. The singer was equally quick to quash an over-literal interpretation of the opening words 'Pasolini is me'. "I understand him and I appreciate his art, but we weren't scrubbed off together in the same bathtub." Elsewhere he was content to pay tribute to the film director's work. "I've seen all the films . . . There's nothing flash about them. You're seeing real people without any distractions, just the naked person, with everything taking place on the streets . . . He didn't have to be anybody else, he was being himself in his own world and even though he was obsessed with the low-life, that was all he wanted." Within the song, the memorable line 'I entered nothing . . .' vividly describes the way in which celibacy is replaced by sexual union, leading to a sense of bewilderment ('who am I that I came to be here?'). In keeping with the religious motifs scattered throughout the album, Morrissey closes the song with an utterance of papal forgiveness.

The Youngest Was The Most Loved

Commencing with the street sounds of Rome, drowned out by an ambulance siren, this saga of a spoilt child turned killer resembled the plot of a predictable mini-Mafia television script, minus any dramatic relief. That said, it was a rocking single whose thin lyrics were saved by some decent one-liners. As Tony Visconti noted: "The lyrics will provoke you to think, but that's not high on his agenda, and at the same time he'll make big jokes about the songs – 'Who the hell would use the term "retroussé nose"?'" What transfoms the song, however, is the inspired idea of employing a children's choir to sing about the redundancy of the word 'normal', a subversive act that recalled the 'Hang the DJ' chorus on 'Panic'. Morrissey described the Italian kiddie chorus as a "perverse joy" and he deserved some praise of his own for the scat singing at the end.

In The Future When All's Well

Undistinguished in comparison to the stronger songs on the album, this was another contender for single status with a catchy but rather basic melody line. While it serves partly as light relief, you cannot help thinking that the album might have been even better if Morrissey had chosen to tackle something more adventurous rather than ensuring that sufficient singles were ready and waiting. The lyrics here are directed towards a character named Lee whose role, personality traits and significance are completely undeveloped. Similarly, the pat philosophy on the dangers of postponing the problems of today by focusing on the fantasies of tomorrow are relieved only by a familiar Morrissey punch-line in which the future is revealed as a lengthy sleep in the grave, punctuated by an admittedly impressive Fifties-style falsetto.

The Father Who Must Be Killed

Morrissey's take on this intriguing song was that it was written from the standpoint of "the stepchild who feels like the unwanted over-spill from a failed previous marriage, feels in the way and is determined to get rid of the father, as one does quite naturally." As narrator, of course, Morrissey is anything but objective and takes the side of the stepchild whose point of view sounds perverse at best. In the opening lines, the child is described as a waste of space, made worse by being ground down by his overbearing legal guardian. However, it soon emerges that the 'evil' stepfather's major crime appears to be chewing his food in an unattractive manner. Morrissey gleefully encourages the grisly stabbing, but the mood of the song changes with the stepfather's noble apology as he lies dying. The introduction of the children's chorus works even more effectively than on 'The Youngest Was The Most Loved', adding a macabre ambience made additionally effective by the suspicion that the innocent kids have no idea what they are singing about. The composition has several fine touches, notably the delayed revelation that the stepchild is a girl, a fact we are not told until the fourth verse. This, in itself, prompts memories of a similarly troubled father/daughter relationship in 'Have-A-Go Merchant'. The song ends on a dramatic and ambiguous note involving either suicide or matricide. Morrissey evidently intended the listener to accept the notion of the girl's suicide, explaining: "The second the stepfather is slipping away he apologizes, too late of course, because every artery is spilling over the carpet. So the stepchild also makes the journey and exits." That said, the reference to 'motherless birds flying high' inevitably recalls a fantasy release from maternal apron strings that can be traced back to 'The Queen Is Dead'.

Life Is A Pigsty

At 7 minutes 22 seconds, this was the longest track on the album and was clearly intended as its centrepiece. Bleak as its title suggests, it sets Morrissey's mournful mood against a backdrop of suitably stormy weather. Lyrically, the composition seems more likely to be a direct address to his audience rather than to a specific person. Several critics noticed that the effects were comparable to the work of Massive Attack which conjured the unlikely vision of Morrissey and trip-hop being mentioned in the same sentence. In concert, the song became a *tour de force* highlighted by the pounding, spectral beat of Matt Chamberlain's massive, illuminated drum kit. For Morrissey the composition articulated an ever increasing sense of mortality as he grew slowly closer to his 50th birthday. "People don't last and it's the thinnest of lines that you step over and make that final journey," he told Mark Beaumont. "When you're younger you feel that it's a great leap to take but it isn't, it's the batting of an eyelid and you're no longer. And all this brain matter that you've been working on for the past 50 years, perfecting, and all these elongated words that you now know and use, it comes to nothing and you're rubble."

I'll Never Be Anybody's Hero Now

For an album supposedly concerned with erotic release and new-found happiness, it was reassuring to hear Morrissey reiterating his negative world-view on consecutive tracks. Here we learn that his one true love is already buried and there is no hope offered of ever finding a replacement. As desperation increases, his falsetto soars towards notes that he can barely command. Although the song attempts to offer some passing comments on class differences this lyrical idea remains undeveloped while the melody and arrangement aren't especially memorable.

On The Streets I Ran

Opening with a strong riff and engaging rhythm, this intriguing lyric reflected on Morrissey's past and present as the undisputed purveyor of sickness into popular or unpopular song. The streets of his youth can now offer only a 'kill or be killed' philosophy which causes him to throw in a wonderfully expressive verbal footnote – 'which isn't very nice'. Towards the end there is another plea to 'Dear God', the third song on the album to mention the Deity. Like Graham Greene, Morrissey's Catholicism casts a long shadow over his work, now more than ever before. "I don't think you have any choice," he told *Mojo*'s Andrew Male. "It's sandblasted into you. And it will take one hell of a blowtorch to get rid of it. That will never happen, regardless of what your feelings are, regardless of what your intentions are." In response to a palmist's prediction, the narrator ends the song on a sublimely egotistical note of Faustian cowardice, imploring God to save him at the expense of the new-born, infirm and the entire population of Pittsburgh, Pennsylvania. There is great humour here, both in the peculiarity of choice and the dramatic irony implicit in the listener's knowledge that Morrissey had previously been singing for years about being half in love with easeful death.

To Me You Are A Work Of Art
Probably Alain Whyte's least ambitious melody on the album, this troubled meditation on the plight of the artist attempts to find salvation in romantic love for a special one, but even that is tainted by the admission that the narrator is bereft of a heart or an ability to love. An anthemic arrangement plays up the melodramatic sentiments, complete with the usual Morrissey similes of sickness. The composition is partly saved by the introduction of strings midway through, although they remain uncredited in the notes at the end of the CD booklet.

I Just Want To See The Boy Happy
The religious motif continues here as early as the first line in which Morrissey on his death-bed beseeches the Lord in a final act of atonement. In contrast to the egotistical self-interest displayed in 'On The Streets I Ran' and the pathological viciousness of 'The Father Who Must Be Killed' the narrator here emerges as a serene altruist whose dying wish is solely to bring happiness to an idealized boy. A predictable attempt at an easy-going rocking single, this betrayed the commercial influence of guitarist/co-writer Jesse Tobias whose other contributions, 'You Have Killed Me', 'In The Future When All's Well' and 'On The Streets I Ran', emphasized the lighter side of Morrissey. This song's saving grace was the final combination of Chamberlain's fierce drumming and Farrell's trombone blast.

At Last I Am Born
With its spectacular orchestral opening, this track brilliantly bookended the album. Morrissey always displayed care and calculation in ordering his work so that the first and last track served a dramatic purpose. Evidently freed from sexual repression and the guilt of the flesh, the narrator informs historians to take note of this epochal event. Chamberlain's military drumming serves as a call to arms for Morrissey whose passionate vocal displays sheer wonderment at the prospect of discovering a new life, evidently free of the old neuroses. Being Morrissey, of course, there is always a sting in the tale. What is the nature of this great rebirth that he celebrates and what does he hope to achieve? Seemingly precious little. For all its lyrical exuberance, the pay-off appears to be a pleasing apathy which allows the

narrator to sit back, yawn at the world and no longer care about any-thing. It says much for Morrissey's strength as a performer that he can transform all this into a heart-stopping event. Amid the celebrations are some odd moments, notably a semi-chorus mysteriously placed in inverted commas in which he chronicles a baffling progression from a difficult childhood 'to Claude Brasseur', referring, for reasons unknown, to the French actor and occasional rally-driver. There is also the return of the children's choir, this time in the role of a Greek chorus whose chants have a taunting ring, presumably directed at the world rather than Morrissey. Never less than absorbing 'At Last I Am Born' ends the album on a vigorous and resounding note.

SINGLES/VIDEOS/DVDS

SMITHS SINGLES

The Smiths always placed great pride in their singles work, carefully ordering releases that featured a healthy selection of material unavailable on album. Over the years, most of these tracks have been issued on CD compilations, most notably *Hatful Of Hollow*, *The World Won't Listen* and *Louder Than Bombs*. However, as the singles discography below indicates, several live tracks, remixes and a handful of songs have yet to appear on any official album. These include 'Jeane', 'Wonderful Woman' and 'The Draize Train' (studio version). 'Jeane' and 'Wonderful Woman' were later issued on CD singles in August 1992 (see Smiths CD Singles). 'Work Is A Four Letter Word', 'I Keep Mine Hidden' and the cover of James' 'What's The World?' (cassette issue) are not available on CD in the UK but all three were featured on a US CD in May 1995 (see Smiths CD Singles section for details). At present there are no plans for the missing tracks to be issued on CD in the UK but they may become available on a compilation or box set some time in the future. Barring some instrumental backing tracks and the occasional cover such as 'A Fool Such As I', unreleased songs from the Smiths' sessions are amazingly sparse. Indeed, there is no known Morrissey song to be found on the official recording sessions unless you count the early take of 'Bengali In Platforms' which was recorded after Marr's departure. Cassette rehearsal tapes exist featuring 'Don't Blow Your Own Horn' and 'A Matter Of Opinion', but neither appears to have been recorded professionally. For anything else, you would have to travel back further to Morrissey's pre-Smiths history as documented in this book's Introduction.

SMITHS 7-INCH SINGLES

Hand In Glove/Handsome Devil (Live)
Rough Trade RT 131, May 1983 *(The B-side was recorded live at the Haçienda, Manchester on 4 February 1983)*

This Charming Man/Jeane
Rough Trade, RT 136, November 1983 *(A limited number of test pressings of the cancelled 'Reel Around The Fountain'/'Jeane' are in existence. 'Jeane' is unavailable on CD but the track has been discussed previously in the Troy Tate demos section at the start of this book)*

What Difference Does It Make?/Back To The Old House
Rough Trade RT 146, January 1984 *(The A-side is an edited version. During February 1984 a limited number of DJ-only promotional copies of 'Still Ill'/ 'You've Got Everything Now' [R61 DJ] were circulated in order to plug the group's début album)*

Heaven Knows I'm Miserable Now/Suffer Little Children
Rough Trade RT 156, May 1984

William, It Was Really Nothing/Please Please Please Let Me Get What I Want
Rough Trade RT 166, August 1984 *(In several European territories the A-side was replaced by 'How Soon Is Now?')*

How Soon Is Now?/Well I Wonder
Rough Trade RT 176, February 1985

Shakespeare's Sister/What She Said
Rough Trade RT 181, March 1985

That Joke Isn't Funny Anymore (Edited)/Meat Is Murder (Live)
Rough Trade RT 186, July 1985

The Boy With The Thorn In His Side [Single mix]/Asleep
Rough Trade RT 191, September 1985

Bigmouth Strikes Again/Money Changes Everything
Rough Trade RT 192, May 1986

Panic/Vicar In A Tutu
Rough Trade RT 193, July 1986

Ask [Single take]/Cemetry Gates
Rough Trade RT 194, October 1986

Shoplifters Of The World Unite/Half A Person
Rough Trade RT 195, January 1987

Sheila Take A Bow/Is It Really So Strange?
Rough Trade RT 196, April 1987

Girlfriend In A Coma/Work Is A Four Letter Word
Rough Trade RT 197, July 1987

I Started Something I Couldn't Finish/Pretty Girls Make Graves
Rough Trade RT 198, October 1987

Stop Me If You Think You've Heard This One Before/I Keep Mine
Hidden
Sire 9-28136-7 (US only) *(This was released in various territories, but not in the
UK. It is mentioned here because of the relatively rare B-side)*

Last Night I Dreamt That Somebody Loved Me/Rusholme Ruffians [John
Peel session version]
Rough Trade RT 200, December 1987

This Charming Man/Jeane
WEA YZ 0001, August 1992

How Soon Is Now?/Hand In Glove
WEA YZ 0002, September 1992

There Is A Light That Never Goes Out/Hand In Glove [David Jensen
radio session]
WEA YZ 0003, October 1992

Ask [album version]/Cemetry Gates
WEA YZ 0004, February 1995

SMITHS 12-INCH SINGLES

This Charming Man (Manchester)/This Charming Man (London)/
Accept Yourself/Wonderful Woman
Rough Trade RTT 136, November 1983 *(This formidable rarity features the
Matrix mix of 'This Charming Man' subtitled London, the original studio version
of 'Accept Yourself' and the Troy Tate produced 'Wonderful Woman'. For further
details see the songs as discussed in the Albums section)*

This Charming Man (New York Mix – Vocal)/This Charming Man (New
York Mix – Instrumental)
Rough Trade RTT 136 NY, December 1983

What Difference Does It Make?/Back To The Old House/These Things
Take Time
Rough Trade RTT 146, February 1984

Heaven Knows I'm Miserable Now/Girl Afraid/Suffer Little Children
Rough Trade RTT 156, May 1984

William, It Was Really Nothing/Please Please Please Let Me Get What I
Want/How Soon Is Now?
Rough Trade RTT 166, August 1984 (*The Italian version of 'How Soon Is
Now?' on the flip-side of the 12-inch 'William, It Was Really Nothing' [Italy:
Virgin VINX 71] is supposedly an alternate take*)

Barbarism Begins At Home/Barbarism Begins At Home
Rough Trade RTT 171, January 1985 (*A promotion only edited release in a
limited edition of 500 copies*)

How Soon Is Now?/Well I Wonder/Oscillate Wildly
Rough Trade RTT 176, February 1985

Shakespeare's Sister/What She Said/Stretch Out And Wait
Rough Trade RTT 181, March 1985

That Joke Isn't Funny Anymore/Nowhere Fast (Live)/Stretch Out And
Wait (Live)/Shakespeare's Sister (Live)/Meat Is Murder (Live)
Rough Trade RTT 186, July 1985

The Boy With The Thorn In His Side/Rubber Ring/Asleep
Rough Trade RTT 191, September 1985

Bigmouth Strikes Again/Money Changes Everything/Unloveable
Rough Trade RTT 192, May 1986

Panic/Vicar In A Tutu/The Draize Train [studio version]
Rough Trade RTT 193, July 1986

Ask/Cemetry Gates/Golden Lights
Rough Trade RTT 194, October 1986

Shoplifters Of The World Unite/Half A Person/London
Rough Trade RTT 195, January 1987 (*Initial versions of 'Shoplifters Of The
World Unite' were despatched with 'You Just Haven't Earned It Yet, Baby' on the
A-side*)

Sheila Take A Bow/Is It Really So Strange? [John Peel session version]/
Sweet And Tender Hooligan [John Peel session version]
Rough Trade RTT 196, April 1987

Girlfriend In A Coma/Work Is A Four Letter Word/I Keep Mine Hidden
Rough Trade RTT 197, July 1987

I Started Something I Couldn't Finish/Pretty Girls Make Graves/Some Girls Are Bigger Than Others (Live)
Rough Trade RTT 198, October 1987 *(Cassette versions of the single included a cover version of James' 'What's The World?', recorded live at Glasgow's Barrowlands on 25 September 1985. 'Some Girls Are Bigger Than Others', which includes some additional lyrics, was recorded at London's Brixton Academy on 12 December 1986)*

Last Night I Dreamt That Somebody Loved Me/Rusholme Ruffians [John Peel session version]/Nowhere Fast [John Peel session version]
Rough Trade RTT 200, December 1987 *(The CD version of this single featured an extra track: the John Peel session version of 'William, It Was Really Nothing')*

SMITHS CD SINGLES

Rough Trade retrospectively issued the Smiths' 12-inch singles on CD in November 1988. Strangely, the transference from vinyl to CD single was apparently never completed and the ordering of releases was neither logical nor chronological. I have been unable to locate any UK CD versions of the 12-inch singles of 'That Joke Isn't Funny Anymore', 'Bigmouth Strikes Again', 'Shoplifters Of The World Unite', 'Sheila Take A Bow', 'Girlfriend In A Coma' or 'I Started Something I Couldn't Finish'. Items whose release is uncertain have the words 'Unconfirmed release, presumed unissued' added to the track listing.

What Difference Does It Make?/Back To The Old House/These Things Take Time
Rough Trade RTT 146 CD, November 1988

Heaven Knows I'm Miserable Now/Girl Afraid/Suffer Little Children
Rough Trade RTT 156 CD, November 1988

William, It Was Really Nothing/Please Please Please Let Me Get What I Want/How Soon Is Now?
Rough Trade RTT 166 CD, November 1988

Barbarism Begins At Home/Shakespeare's Sister/Stretch Out And Wait
Rough Trade RTT 171 CD, November 1988 *(This was a belated first UK issue of a single previously released as a 12-inch in Germany back in April 1985. Rough Trade used the serial number previously allocated to the 'Barbarism Begins At Home' promotional release. See '7-inch Singles' entry for January 1985)*

That Joke Isn't Funny Anymore/Nowhere Fast (Live)/Stretch Out And
Wait (Live)/Shakespeare's Sister (Live)/Meat Is Murder (Live)
Rough Trade RTT 186 CD [*Unconfirmed release, presumed unissued*]

The Boy With The Thorn In His Side/Rubber Ring/Asleep
Rough Trade RTT 191 CD, November 1988

Bigmouth Strikes Again/Money Changes Everything/Unloveable
Rough Trade RTT 192 CD [*Unconfirmed release, presumed unissued*]

Panic/Vicar In A Tutu/The Draize Train [studio version]
Rough Trade RTT 193 CD, November 1988

Ask/Cemetry Gates/Golden Lights
Rough Trade RTT 194 CD, November 1988

Shoplifters Of The World Unite/Half A Person/London
Rough Trade RTT 195 CD [*Unconfirmed release, presumed unissued*]

Sheila Take A Bow/Is It Really So Strange? [John Peel session version]/
Sweet And Tender Hooligan [John Peel session version]
Rough Trade RTT 196 CD [*Unconfirmed release, presumed unissued*]

Girlfriend In A Coma/Work Is A Four Letter Word/I Keep Mine Hidden
Rough Trade RTT 197 CD [*Unconfirmed release, presumed unissued*]

I Started Something I Couldn't Finish/Pretty Girls Make Graves/Some
Girls Are Bigger Than Others (Live)/What's The World? (Live)
Rough Trade RTT 198 CD [*Unconfirmed release, presumed unissued*]

Last Night I Dreamt That Somebody Loved Me/Rusholme Ruffians [John
Peel session version]/Nowhere Fast [John Peel session version]/William, It
Was Really Nothing [John Peel session version]
Rough Trade RTT 200 CD, November 1988

The Headmaster Ritual/Nowhere Fast (Live)/ Stretch Out And Wait
(Live)/Meat Is Murder (Live)
Rough Trade RTT 215 CD, November 1988 *(This was originally issued in
Holland back in June 1985)*

This Charming Man (Manchester Mix)/Jeane/Wonderful Woman/Accept
Yourself
WEA YZ 0001 CD1, August 1992

This Charming Man (Manchester Mix)/This Charming Man (London Mix)/This Charming Man (New York Mix)/This Charming Man (New York Instrumental)/This Charming Man (Peel Session)/This Charming Man (Single Remix)/This Charming Man (Original Single Version)
WEA YZ 0001 CD2, August 1992

How Soon Is Now? (Edited)/The Queen Is Dead/Handsome Devil [John Peel session version]/I Started Something I Couldn't Finish
WEA YZ 0002 CD1, September 1992

I Know It's Over/Suffer Little Children/Back To The Old House/How Soon Is Now? [Album version]
WEA YZ 0002 CD2, September 1992

There Is A Light That Never Goes Out/Hand In Glove (Live)/Some Girls Are Bigger Than Others (Live)/Money Changes Everything
WEA YZ 0003 CD1, October 1992

There Is A Light That Never Goes Out/Hand In Glove (featuring Sandie Shaw)/I Don't Owe You Anything (featuring Sandie Shaw)/Jeane (featuring Sandie Shaw)
WEA YZ 0003 CD2, October 1992

Ask [Album version]/Cemetry Gates/Golden Lights
WEA YZ 0004 CDX1, February 1995

Sweet And Tender Hooligan [John Peel session version]/I Keep Mine Hidden/Work Is A Four Letter Word/What's The World? (Live)
Reprise 9-43525-2 (US only), May 1995

EP

The Peel Sessions
What Difference Does It Make?/Miserable Lie/Reel Around The Fountain/Handsome Devil
Strange Fruit SF PS 055, October 1988

In addition to the above, the Smiths have appeared on various samplers, imports and rare special promotion discs and test pressings. Among these are the supposedly alternate version of 'How Soon Is Now?' on the flip-side of the 12-inch 'William, It Was Really Nothing' (Italy: Virgin VINX 71). At one point, a live EP was rumoured for release featuring 'Meat Is Murder', 'Nowhere Fast', 'What She Said', 'Stretch Out And Wait', 'William, It Was

Really Nothing' and 'Miserable Lie'. The tracks later appeared on various 7-inch and 12-inch B-sides. These included the free 7-inch EP *Poll Winners* (GIV 1) available with *NME* on 25 May 1985, which included 'What She Said'. A live version of 'Girl Afraid' was also available, by mail order only, on the *NME* Various Artistes compilation *Department Of Enjoyment* (CS NME 011). No doubt there are many more such one-offs and anomalies scattered throughout the group's lengthy discography.

SMITHS VIDEO/DVD

The Complete Picture
This Charming Man/What Difference Does It Make?/Panic/Heaven Knows I'm Miserable Now/Ask/The Boy With The Thorn In His Side/How Soon Is Now?/Shoplifters Of The World Unite/Girlfriend In A Coma/Sheila Take A Bow/Stop Me If You Think You've Heard This One Before/The Queen Is Dead/There Is A Light That Never Goes Out/Panic
WEA 91155-3 [Video], November 1992
WEA 91155-3 [DVD], April 2000
(Includes promotional videos and mimed appearances on BBC Television's Top Of The Pops*)*

MORRISSEY SINGLES

In common with the Smiths, Morrissey's solo releases include several tracks that have never appeared on CD album releases in the UK. Apart from the contents of the Japanese CD *Rare Tracks*, which rounded up the immediate post-*Maladjusted* B-sides, there were a number of live tracks from the RCA Victor era like 'London', 'Billy Budd', 'Spring-Heeled Jim' and 'Why Don't You Find Out For Yourself', as well as several tracks on the US only *My Early Burglary Years*. 'You Must Please Remember', the final track on the CD single of 'Dagenham Dave', has still not appeared on album. Given Morrissey's changes of record company it seems unlikely that we will hear any as yet unissued RCA Victor period material in the near future. The expanded edition of *You Are The Quarry* did not include the cover of Raymonde's 'No One Can Hold A Candle To You', 'The Slum Mums' or 'The Public Image'. Similarly, the Janice Long session for the retro pastiche 'Noise Is The Best Revenge' remains on CD single only. Presumably, the B-sides from *Ringleader Of The Tormentors* (including 'Good Looking Man About Town', 'I Knew I Was Next', 'If You Don't Like Me, Don't Look At Me', 'Ganglord' and the cover of Magazine's 'A Song From Under The Floorboards') will appear on some expanded edition later down the line or, if not, a compilation of the Attack years. As discussed in the main text, there are also a number of unreleased songs and fragments from the solo years that may turn up eventually on some future box set or similar enterprise. These include, among others, 'Lifeguard On Duty', 'Safe, Warm Lancashire Home', 'Treat Me Like A Human Being', 'Please Help The Cause Against Loneliness', 'Oh Phoney', 'Jodie's Still Alive', 'Striptease With A Difference', 'Kill Uncle', 'Born To Hang', 'Stay As You Are', 'Honey You Know Where To Find Me', 'Laughing Anne' (the last three definitely minus vocals), 'Sharp Bend, Fast Car, Goodbye', 'Kit', 'I Know Who I Love', 'The Leeches Go On Removing', 'Hanratty', 'I'm Playing Easy Tonight' and 'Home Is A Question Mark'.

MORRISSEY 7-INCH SINGLES

Suedehead/I Know Very Well How I Got My Name
HMV POP 1618, February 1988

Everyday Is Like Sunday/Disappointed
HMV POP 1619, June 1988

The Last Of The Famous International Playboys/Lucky Lisp
HMV POP 1620, February 1989

Interesting Drug/Such A Little Thing Makes Such A Big Difference
HMV POP 1621, April 1989

Ouija Board, Ouija Board/Yes, I Am Blind
HMV POP 1622, November 1989

November Spawned A Monster/He Knows I'd Love To See Him
HMV POP 1623, April 1990

Piccadilly Palare/Get Off The Stage
HMV POP 1624, October 1990

Our Frank/Journalists Who Lie
HMV POP 1625, February 1991

Sing Your Life/That's Entertainment
HMV POP 1626, April 1991

Pregnant For The Last Time/Skin Storm
HMV POP 1627, July 1991

My Love Life/I've Changed My Plea To Guilty
HMV POP 1628, September 1991

We Hate It When Our Friends Become Successful/Suedehead (Live)
HMV POP 1629, April 1992

You're The One For Me, Fatty/Pashernate Love
HMV POP 1630, July 1992

Certain People I Know/Jack The Ripper
HMV POP 1631, November 1992

The More You Ignore Me, The Closer I Get/Used To Be A Sweet Boy
Parlophone R 6372, February 1994

Hold On To Your Friends/Moonriver
Parlophone R 6383, May 1994

Interlude/Interlude (Extended)
Parlophone R 6365 (with Siouxsie), July 1994

Boxers/Have-A-Go Merchant
Parlophone R 6400, January 1995

Dagenham Dave/Nobody Loves Us
RCA Victor 29980 2, August 1995

The Boy Racer/London (Live)
RCA Victor 33294 7, November 1995

Sunny/Black-Eyed Susan
Parlophone R 6243, December 1995

Alma Matters/Heir Apparent
Island IS 667, July 1997

Roy's Keen/Lost
Island IS 671, October 1997

Satan Rejected My Soul/Now I Am A Was
Island IS 686, December 1997

Irish Blood, English Heart/It's Hard To Walk Tall When You're Small
Attack/Sanctuary ATKS 1002, May 2004

First Of The Gang To Die/My Life Is A Succession Of People Saying
Goodbye
Attack/Sanctuary ATKS 1003, July 2004

Let Me Kiss You/Don't Make Fun Of Daddy's Voice
Attack/Sanctuary ATKSE 008, October 2004

I Have Forgiven Jesus/No One Can Hold A Candle To You
Attack/Sanctuary ATKSE 011, December 2004

Redondo Beach (Live)/There Is A Light That Never Goes Out (Live)
Attack/Sanctuary ATKSE 015, March 2005

You Have Killed Me/Good Looking Man About Town
Attack/Sanctuary ATKSE 017, March 2006

The Youngest Was The Most Loved/If You Don't Like Me, Don't Look
At Me
Attack/Sanctuary ATKSE 018, June 2006

MORRISSEY 12-INCH SINGLES

Although this discography does not include foreign releases, I have used my discretion in featuring certain American issues which differ significantly or are of especial interest.

Suedehead/I Know Very Well How I Got My Name/Hairdresser On Fire
HMV 12 POP 1618, February 1988

Everyday Is Like Sunday/Sister I'm A Poet/Disappointed/Will Never Marry
HMV 12 POP 1619, June 1988

The Last Of The Famous International Playboys/Lucky Lisp/Michael's Bones
HMV 12 POP 1620, February 1989

Interesting Drug/Such A Little Thing Makes Such A Big
Difference/Sweet And Tender Hooligan (Live)
HMV 12 POP 1621, April 1989

Ouija Board, Ouija Board/Yes, I Am Blind/East West
HMV 12 POP 1622, November 1989

November Spawned A Monster/He Knows I'd Love To See Him/Girl
Least Likely To
HMV 12 POP 1623, April 1990

Piccadilly Palare/At Amber/Get Off The Stage
HMV 12 POP 1624, October 1990

Our Frank/Journalists Who Lie/Tony The Pony
HMV 12 POP 1625, February 1991

Sing Your Life/That's Entertainment/The Loop
HMV 12 POP 1626, March 1991

Pregnant For The Last Time/Skin Storm/Cosmic Dancer (Live)/
Disappointed (Live)
HMV 12 POP 1627, July 1991

My Love Life/I've Changed My Plea To Guilty/There's A Place In Hell
For Me And My Friends (KROQ radio version)
HMV 12 POP 1628, October 1991

We Hate It When Our Friends Become Successful/Suedehead (Live)/I've
Changed My Plea To Guilty (Live)/Pregnant For The Last Time (Live)
HMV CD POP 1629, April 1992

You're The One For Me, Fatty/Pashernate Love/There Speaks A True Friend
HMV 12 POP 1630, July 1992

Tomorrow/Let The Right One Slip In/There Speaks A True Friend
Sire/Reprise 940580-0 (US only), September 1992

Certain People I Know/You've Had Her/Jack The Ripper
HMV 12 POP 1631, November 1992

The More You Ignore Me, The Closer I Get/Used To Be A Sweet Boy/
I'd Love To
Parlophone 12R 6372, February 1994

Hold On To Your Friends/Moonriver/Moonriver (Extended Version)
Parlophone 12R 6383, May 1994

Interlude/(Extended)/(Instrumental)
Parlophone 12R 6365 (with Siouxsie), July 1994

Boxers/Have-A-Go Merchant/Whatever Happens I Love You
Parlophone 12R 6400, January 1995

*The singles 'Dagenham Dave', 'The Boy Racer' and 'Sunny' do not appear to
have been available officially on 12-inch in the UK. See 7-inch and CD Singles
sections for related releases.*

Alma Matters/Heir Apparent/I Can Have Both
Island 12 667, July 1997

Roy's Keen/Lost/The Edges Are No Longer Parallel
Island 12 671, October 1997

Satan Rejected My Soul/Now I Am A Was/This Is Not Your Country
Island 12 686, December 1997

*Morrissey's singles on Attack/Sanctuary were not available on 12-inch. However,
at the time of writing, two vinyl discs have been made available "for a limited period
only".*

Irish Blood, English Heart/It's Hard To Walk Tall When You're
Small/Munich Air Disaster 1958/The Never-Played Symphonies
Attack/Sanctuary ATKTW 019, June 2006

First Of The Gang To Die/Teenage Dad On His Estate/Mexico/My Life
Is A Succession Of People Saying Goodbye
Attack/Sanctuary ATKTW 020, June 2006

MORRISSEY CD SINGLES

This list of CD singles excludes foreign releases, except in the case of certain US issues that I have featured at my discretion. Please note that promotional items, DJ-only releases and other special issues outside the artiste's main discography are not featured here.

Suedehead/I Know Very Well How I Got My Name/Hairdresser On Fire/
Oh Well, I'll Never Learn
HMV CD POP 1618, February 1988

Everyday Is Like Sunday/Sister I'm A Poet/Disappointed/Will Never Marry
HMV CD POP 1619, June 1988

The Last Of The Famous International Playboys/Lucky Lisp/Michael's
Bones
HMV CD POP 1620, February 1989

Interesting Drug/Such A Little Thing Makes Such A Big Difference/
Sweet And Tender Hooligan (Live)
HMV CD POP 1621, April 1989

Ouija Board, Ouija Board/Yes, I Am Blind/East West
HMV CD POP 1622, November 1989

November Spawned A Monster/He Knows I'd Love To See Him/
Girl Least Likely To
HMV CD POP 1623, April 1990

Piccadilly Palare/At Amber/Get Off The Stage
HMV CD POP 1624, October 1990

Our Frank/Journalists Who Lie/Tony The Pony
HMV CD POP 1625, February 1991

Sing Your Life/That's Entertainment/The Loop
HMV CD POP 1626, March 1991

Pregnant For The Last Time/Skin Storm/Cosmic Dancer (Live)/
Disappointed (Live)
HMV CD POP 1627, July 1991

My Love Life/I've Changed My Plea To Guilty/There's A Place In Hell
For Me And My Friends (KROQ radio version)
HMV CD POP 1628, October 1991

We Hate It When Our Friends Become Successful/Suedehead (Live)/
I've Changed My Plea To Guilty (Live)/Alsatian Cousin (Live)
HMV CD POP 1629, April 1992

You're The One For Me, Fatty/Pashernate Love/There Speaks A True
Friend
HMV CD POP 1630, July 1992

Tomorrow/Let The Right One Slip In/Pashernate Love
Sire/Reprise 940580-2 (US only), September 1992

Certain People I Know/You've Had Her/Jack The Ripper
HMV CD POP 1631, November 1992

The More You Ignore Me, The Closer I Get/Used To Be A Sweet Boy/
I'd Love To
Parlophone CDR 6372, February 1994

Hold On To Your Friends/Moonriver/Moonriver (Extended Version)
Parlophone CDR 6383, May 1994

Interlude/(Extended)/(Instrumental)
Parlophone CDR 6365 (with Siouxsie), July 1994

Now My Heart Is Full/Moonriver (Extended Version)/
Jack The Ripper (Live)
Sire/Reprise 41700-2 (US only), August 1994

Boxers/Have-A-Go Merchant/Whatever Happens I Love You
Parlophone CDR 6400, January 1995

Dagenham Dave/Nobody Loves Us/You Must Please Remember
RCA Victor 74321 29980 2, August 1995

The Boy Racer/London (Live)/Billy Budd (Live)
RCA Victor 33294 2, November 1995

The Boy Racer/Spring-Heeled Jim (Live)/Why Don't You Find Out For
Yourself (Live)
RCA Victor 33295 2, November 1995

Sunny/Black-Eyed Susan/Swallow On My Neck
Parlophone CDR 6243, December 1995

Alma Matters/Heir Apparent/I Can Have Both
Island CID 667, July 1997

Roy's Keen/Lost/The Edges Are No Longer Parallel
Island CID 671, October 1997

Satan Rejected My Soul/Now I Am A Was/This Is Not Your Country
Island CID 686, December 1997

Irish Blood, English Heart/It's Hard To Walk Tall When You're Small
Attack/Sanctuary ATKS 1002, May 2004

Irish Blood, English Heart/Munich Air Disaster 1958/The Never-Played
Symphonies
Attack/Sanctuary ATKXD 002, May 2004

First Of The Gang To Die/My Life Is A Succession Of People Saying
Goodbye
Attack/Sanctuary ATKXS 003, July 2004

First Of The Gang To Die/Teenage Dad On His Estate/Mexico/My Life
Is A Succession Of People Saying Goodbye
Attack/Sanctuary ATKXD 003, July 2004

Let Me Kiss You/Don't Make Fun Of Daddy's Voice
Attack/Sanctuary ATKXS 008, October 2004

Let Me Kiss You/Friday Mourning/I Am Two People
Attack/Sanctuary ATKXD 008, October 2004

I Have Forgiven Jesus/No One Can Hold A Candle To You
Attack/Sanctuary ATKXS 011, December 2004

I Have Forgiven Jesus/The Slum Mums/The Public Image
Attack/Sanctuary ATKXD 011, December 2004

Redondo Beach (Live)/There Is A Light That Never Goes Out
(Live)/Noise Is The Best Revenge [Janice Long Session 2004]
Attack/Sanctuary ATKXD 015, March 2005

You Have Killed Me/Good Looking Man About Town
Attack/Sanctuary ATKXS 017, March 2006

You Have Killed Me/Human Being/I Knew I Was Next
Attack/Sanctuary ATKXD 017, March 2006

The Youngest Was The Most Loved/Ganglord/A Song From Under The
Floorboards
Attack/Sanctuary ATKXD 018, June 2006

Several of the Attack singles also contain enhanced music videos of their
title tracks.

EPs

Morrissey At KROQ
There's A Place In Hell For Me And My Friends/My Love Life/Sing Your Life
Sire 9-40184-2, October 1991. This EP was issued in the US only. The session was recorded at Capitol Studios, Hollywood, 3 June 1991 and concludes with a series of recorded messages from fans.

Sessions@aol
First Of The Gang To Die/The World Is Full Of Crashing Bores/I Like You
September 2004. (US only) This iTunes download was recorded on 27 September 2004 at the Reading Festival on the day before Morrissey's performance.

MORRISSEY VIDEOS/DVDS

Hulmerist
The Last Of The Famous International Playboys/Sister I'm A Poet (Live)/
Everyday Is Like Sunday/Interesting Drug/Suedehead/Ouija Board, Ouija
Board/November Spawned A Monster
PMI MVP 9912183 [Video] June 1990
*(Includes videos, plus footage from Morrissey's performance at the Wolverhampton
Civic Hall, 22 December 1988)*

Live In Dallas
The Last Of The Famous International Playboys/Interesting Drug/
Piccadilly Palare/Trash/Sing Your Life/King Leer/Asian Rut/
Mute Witness/November Spawned A Monster/Will Never Marry/
Angel, Angel Down We Go Together/There's A Place In Hell For Me
And My Friends/That's Entertainment/Our Frank/Suedehead/
Everyday Is Like Sunday
PMI MYP 4911193 [Video] May 1992
EMI 7243 4 81234 9 7 [DVD] November 2000
*(Recorded live at the Dallas Starplex Amphitheatre, 17 June 1991, supposedly
"before an audience of 11,000 people")*

The Malady Lingers On
Glamorous Glue/Certain People I Know/Tomorrow/We Hate It When
Our Friends Become Successful/My Love Life/You're The One For Me,
Fatty/Sing Your Life/Pregnant For The Last Time
PMI MVR 4900063 [Video] November 1992
EMI 7243 5 99636 9 3 [DVD] November 2004
(Collection of promotional videos)

Introducing Morrissey
Billy Budd/Have-A-Go Merchant/Spring-Heeled Jim/You're The One
For Me, Fatty/The More You Ignore Me, The Closer I Get/Whatever
Happens I Love You/We'll Let You Know/Jack The Ripper/Why Don't
You Find Out For Yourself/The National Front Disco/Moonriver/Hold
On To Your Friends/Boxers/Now My Heart Is Full/Speedway
Warner Reprise 3-36418 [Video] August 1996 (US)
Warner Reprise 3-38418 [Video] October 1996 (UK)
*(Recorded live, Sheffield City Hall, 7 February 1995, and Blackpool Winter
Gardens, 8 February 1995)*

¡Oye Esteban!
Everyday Is Like Sunday/Suedehead/Will Never Marry/November
Spawned A Monster/Interesting Drug/The Last Of The Famous
International Playboys/My Love Life/Sing Your Life/Seasick, Yet Still
Docked/We Hate It When Our Friends Become Successful/Glamorous
Glue/Tomorrow/You're The One For Me, Fatty/The More You Ignore
Me, The Closer I Get/Pregnant For The Last Time/Boxers/Dagenham
Dave/The Boy Racer/Sunny
Warner Reprise 38515-2 [DVD] (US only), October 2000
(Collection of promotional videos, including material from Hulmerist *and* The
Malady Lingers On*)*

Who Put The 'M' In Manchester?
First Of The Gang To Die/Hairdresser On Fire/Irish Blood, English
Heart/The Headmaster Ritual/Subway Train/Everyday Is Like Sunday/
I Have Forgiven Jesus/I Know It's Gonna Happen Someday/How Can
Anybody Possibly Know How I Feel?/Rubber Ring/Such A Little Thing
Makes Such A Big Difference/Don't Make Fun Of Daddy's Voice/
The World Is Full Of Crashing Bores/Let Me Kiss You/No One Can
Hold A Candle To You/Jack The Ripper/A Rush And A Push And The
Land Is Ours/I'm Not Sorry/Shoplifters Of The World Unite/There Is A
Light That Never Goes Out.
DVD Extras include five live performances from the Move Festival,
Manchester, 11 July 2004: First Of The Gang To Die/ I Have Forgiven
Jesus/Everyday Is Like Sunday/There Is A Light That Never Goes
Out/Irish Blood, English Heart. Music Videos: Irish Blood, English
Heart/First Of The Gang To Die (UK version)/First Of The Gang To Die
(US version)/I Have Forgiven Jesus
Attack Films SVE 4010 [DVD] March 2005
*(Recorded live, Manchester MEN Arena, 22 May 2004, plus selections from the
Move Festival, Manchester, 11 July 2004, plus music videos)*

Recently, promotional video and television appearances by Morrissey have
started to appear as extras on his CD releases. As previously mentioned, the
expanded 'bonus disc enhanced' edition of *You Are The Quarry* featured
'Irish Blood, English Heart', 'First Of The Gang To Die' (live), 'I Have
Forgiven Jesus' (live) and 'Let Me Kiss You' (live). The video of 'You Have
Killed Me' has already appeared on the single of the same name, and further
material including 'The Youngest Was The First Loved' and 'In The Future
When All's Well' are included on the CD/DVD edition of *Ringleader Of
The Tormentors* which, like *You Are The Quarry*, may well be reissued at a
later date with additional B-sides and enhancements.

INDEX

Singles releases are in roman type and albums in italics

A Certain Ratio, 56
'Accept Yourself' (Smiths), 17, 19, 28, 43,
    65
Adonais (poem) (Shelley), 84
Aizlewood, John, 179–181
Ali, Lorraine, 181
Alice Adams (film), 52–53
'All The Lazy Dykes' (Morrissey), 278
Allen, Richard, 128, 139
Allman, Robin, 3–7, 25, 29
Alma Cogan (novel) (Gordon Burn), 239
'Alma Matters' (Morrissey), 239–240, 254,
    268
'Alsatian Cousin' (Morrissey), 129–131,
    191, 265–266
'Ambitious Outsiders' (Morrissey), 240
'Amelia' (Joni Mitchell), 101
'America, I Love You' (Christy Moore),
    273
'America Is Not The World' (Morrissey),
    272–273, 288
'Ammunition' (Morrissey), 242, 254
Among The Thugs (book) (Bill Buford),
    183
Anderson, Brett, 153, 180
Andrews, Chris, 65
'Andy Warhol' (David Bowie), 131
'Angel, Angel Down We Go Together'
    (Morrissey), 128, 135–136
Angels Are Genderless, 5
Angstee, Bill, 10
Armstrong, Kevin, 165, 197
'Asian Rut' (Morrissey), 169–170, 184, 281
'Ask' (Smiths), 74–75, 89, 110, 117,
    119–120, 296
'Asleep' (Smiths), 80, 84, 89, 187, 189, 265
Associates, The, 36
'At Amber' (Morrissey), 161, 230, 258, 263
'At Last I Am Born' (Morrissey), 1, 295,
    302–303
Attenborough, Richard, 202
Austen, Jane, 5
Aztec Camera, 40

Babylon Books, 288
Bacharach, Burt, 265
Bachelors, The, 84
'Back To The Old House' (Smiths), 44, 55,
    85, 88–89
Bailie, Stuart, 201
Baker, Anita, 61
Banger, Ed, 4
'Barbarism Begins At Home' (Smiths),
    56–57
Barrie, Amanda, 70, 239
Bartlett, Neil, 148
Bassey, Shirley, 114
'Batman Theme, The' (Marketts), 180, 198
Beach Boys, The, 93
Beatles, The, 34, 40, 48–49, 53, 60, 98, 118,
    120, 143, 187, 202, 210, 241, 243, 245,
    291
Beatles, The (Beatles), 98
Beaujolais, Roger, 170
Beaumont, Mark, 247, 270, 296–297, 301
Bedford, Mark 'Bedders', 168, 218
Bee Gees, The, 280
Beethoven Was Deaf (Morrissey), 190–198,
    216, 218, 285
Bellis, Pat, 68
'Bells' (Buffy Saint-Marie), 40
'Bells' (Leonard Cohen), 40
Bend Sinister (Fall), 61
'Bengali In Platforms' (Morrissey), 129,
    133–135, 152, 169, 184, 209
'Bengali In Platforms' ('Smiths'), 94,
    133–134
Bennett, Alan, 285
Best . . . (Smiths), 115–116, 120
Best . . . II (Smiths), 117, 120
Best Of!, The (Morrissey), 268
'Best Friend On The Payroll' (Morrissey),
    221, 227
Betjeman, John, Sir, 132, 281
Beyond Belief (book) (Emlyn Williams), 31
'Bigmouth Strikes Again' (Morrissey), 286,
    288–289

'Bigmouth Strikes Again' (Smiths), 67–68, 76–77, 80, 113–114, 117, 119–120
Billen, Andrew, 298
'Billy Budd' (Morrissey), 204–205, 208, 220
Billy Budd (film), 205
Billy Budd (short story) (Herman Melville), 205
Billy Liar (novel) (Keith Waterhouse), 35, 64–65, 67, 75–76, 256
Black, Cilla, 84–85, 261
Black Tie, White Noise (David Bowie), 188
'Black-Eyed Susan' (Morrissey), 201, 257–258, 267
Blair, Tony, Prime Minister, 235, 259, 296
Blink-182, 269
'Blockbuster' (Sweet), 181, 245
Blondie, 41
Blue Lamp, The (film), 202
Blue Rondo A La Turk, 11
Blur, 222
Bolan, Marc, 74, 155, 160, 184–185, 192, 255
Bona Drag (Morrissey), 145–163, 166, 195, 216, 229, 255–256, 263
Bonham, John, 214
Boon, Richard, 10n., 11n., 12, 28
Boorer, Boz, 166, 178, 184, 192, 194–196, 202–203, 209, 211, 217, 219, 223–224, 227, 232, 238, 243, 246, 248, 249, 257–258, 265–266, 269, 273, 276, 285, 291, 293
Born In The USA (Bruce Springsteen), 46
'Born To Hang' (Morrissey), 166, 218, 249
Bowie, David, 86–87, 131, 155, 178, 181, 188, 222, 224, 234, 242, 293
Bowie, Zowie, 87
'Boxers' (Morrissey), 217–221, 250, 258, 267
'Boy Racer, The' (Morrissey), 221, 225–226, 248, 258
'Boy With The Thorn In His Side, The' (Smiths), 68–70, 78–79, 83, 111, 117–120
Boyd, Brian, 274
Bradford, 263
Brady, Ian, 32
Bragg, Billy, 19, 180
Brasseur, Claude, 303
'Break Up The Family' (Morrissey), 128, 139–140, 142
Breakfast At Tiffany's (film), 219
Breakthrough: An Amazing Experiment In Electronic Communication With The Dead (book) (Dr Konstantin Raudive), 83–84

Brel, Jacques, 238, 244
Bresslaw, Bernard, 230
Bridgwood, Jonny, 166, 200–201, 203–214, 217–219, 221, 223–225, 227–228, 234, 238, 240–246, 248–250, 252, 256–258, 266, 280
Brighton Rock (film), 202
Brighton Rock (novel) (Graham Greene), 202
Broad, Tim, 199
Brolan, Dave, 210
Bronski Beat, 47
Bros, 145
Brown, Angie (see Angie Marr)
Brown, James (journalist), 108
Brown, Len, 82, 95, 148, 152, 156, 230, 260
Browne, David, 117
Bucks Fizz, 125–126
Buffalo Springfield, 11n.
Buford, Bill, 183
Burke, Clem, 41
Burn, Gordon, 239
Burning Times (Christy Moore), 272
Burns, Pete, 56, 142
Bush, George W., President, 296
Bush, Kate, 136
Butterworth, Deano, 269, 273
Buzzcocks, 27, 83, 100
By Grand Central Station I Sat Down And Wept (novel) (Elizabeth Smart), 52, 282–283
Byrne, George, 253

Cameo, 61
Cameron, Keith, 216, 235, 291
'Candy Everybody Wants' (10,000 Maniacs), 217
Carr, John 'Cornelius', 218
Carrack, Paul, 23
Carry On Cleo (film), 70
CD Singles '88–91', The (Morrissey), 259–263
CD Singles '91–95', The (Morrissey), 264–267
Celebrity Big Brother (television programme), 142
'Cemetry Gates' (Smiths), 66–67, 111–112
'Certain People I Know' (Morrissey), 184–185, 191–193, 195, 220, 247, 266, 268
Chamberlain, Matt, 293, 300, 302
'Changes' (Christy Moore), 273
'Changes' (Phil Ochs), 273

Charles, Prince, 62
Chevalier Brothers, The, 170
Chic, 56
'Chirpy Chirpy Cheep Cheep' (Middle Of The Road), 156
Clapton, Eric, 262
Clarke, Stanley, 56
Clash, The, 94, 210
Clearmountain, Bob, 191
'Cloudbusting' (Kate Bush), 136
Cluskey, Declan, 84
Cobrin, Spencer, 178, 200, 219, 221, 225, 243, 246, 280
Cochran, Eddie, 180
Cockleshell Heroes (film), 202, 238
Cogan, Alma, 239
Cohen, Leonard, 40
Collector, The (film), 23, 30
Collins, Andrew, 179, 185, 200
'Come And Play With Me In The Garden' (John's Children), 246
'Come Back And Shake Me' (Clodagh Rodgers), 242
'Come Back To Camden' (Morrissey), 275, 297
Control (Janet Jackson), 61
Cookies, The, 8
Coronation Street (television programme), 7
Corr, Alan, 224
'Cosmic Dancer' (Morrissey), 178, 255, 258, 263
'Cosmic Dancer' (T. Rex), 255
Coupland, Douglas, 99
Courtneidge, Cicely, 62
Coward, Noël, 173, 276
Cradle Snatchers, The (bootleg) (Smiths), 17
Crak Therapy (Freak Party), 7
Cromwell, Oliver, 273
'Cry Baby Cry' (Beatles), 98
Culture Club, 47
Cunliffe, Grant (see Grant Showbiz)

'Dagenham Dave' (Morrissey), 221, 226, 242, 256
Daly, Johnny, 158
David, Hal, 265
Davies, Ray, 67
Day, Gary, 178, 200, 219, 230, 250, 269, 293
Day In The Death Of Joe Egg, A (play) (Joe Orton), 151
'Day Tripper' (Beatles), 49
'Deacon Blues' (Steely Dan), 132
Dead Or Alive, 56

Deaf School, 171
Dean, James, 6, 81, 108
'Dear God Please Help Me' (Morrissey), 296–298
'Dear Prudence' (Beatles), 243
'Death At One's Elbow' (Morrissey), 103
'Death At One's Elbow' (Smiths), 103
'Death Of A Disco Dancer' (Smiths), 98–99
Delaney, Shelagh, 19, 40, 42, 112, 203
Delerue, Georges, 248
Delingpole, James, 237
Devoto, Howard, 4, 67, 155
Dexys Midnight Runners, 188
'Dial A Cliché' (Morrissey), 143
Diana, Princess, 55
Dickens, Charles, 49, 205
Dickie, Chris, 205
Diddley, Bo, 38
'Disappointed' (Morrissey), 143, 153–154, 161–162, 231, 247, 263, 268, 281, 286
'Do Your Best And Don't Worry' (Morrissey), 227–228, 268
Donelly, Tanya, 180
'Don't Blow Your Own Horn' (Smiths), 8, 11n.
'Don't Make Fun Of Daddy's Voice' (Morrissey), 279, 286
Doonan, Patric, 202, 238
Dors, Diana, 118
Douglas, Alfred, Lord, 97
Downey, Lesley Ann, 32, 232
Doyle, Tom, 170–171, 174, 176, 294
Draize, John, 113
'Draize Train, The' (Smiths), 113
Drift, The (Scott Walker), 296
'Driving Your Girlfriend Home' (Morrissey), 174–176
Duffy, Billy, 3–7, 287
Durham, Geoffrey, 186
Durkin, Bobby, 7
Durutti Column, 125–127
Dwyer, Elizabeth (Morrissey's mother), 156, 211
Dylan, Bob, 262, 265, 273

'East West' (Herman's Hermits), 261
'East West' (Morrissey), 161, 261, 263
Easterhouse, 10, 94, 107, 133
Echo & The Bunnymen, 132
'Edges Are No Longer Parallel, The' (Morrissey), 237, 252
Eliot, George, 38
Ellen, Barbara, 186

Elmhirst, Tom, 225
Eminem, 213
Eno, Brian, 156
'Everybody Hurts' (R.E.M.), 252
'Everybody's Happy Nowadays'
    (Buzzcocks), 83
'Everyday Is Like Sunday' (Morrissey), 129,
    132–133, 153, 158, 161, 195, 202, 212,
    229–230, 250, 257, 263, 268, 287–288,
    296
'Everyday Is Like Sunday' (10,000 Maniacs),
    217
Evol (Sonic Youth), 61
'Excerpt From A Teenage Opera' (Keith
    West), 240

Fagin, Michael, 62
Fairground Attraction, 164, 220
Faith, Adam, 171
Fall, The, 61, 68
Fallada, Hans, 131
Farrell, Gary, 10, 107
Farrell, Michael, 269, 282, 287, 291, 293,
    302
'Father Who Must Be Killed, The'
    (Morrissey), 299–300, 302
Fawkes, Guy, 297
Ferry, Bryan, 79
Finn, Jerry, 269–270
Finn, Neil, 78
'First Of The Gang To Die' (Morrissey),
    277, 279, 282, 285, 289
Flash, Grandmaster, 56
Fletcher, Phil, 3–4, 6, 287
Formby, George, 85, 243
Forty Years On (play) (Alan Bennett), 131
'Found Found Found' (Morrissey),
    173–174
'Fourteen Again' (Victoria Wood), 36, 50
Fowler, Nadia, 83–84
Frame, Pete, 176
Frame, Roddy, 133
'Frankenstein' (New York Dolls), 286
Frankie Goes To Hollywood, 47, 118
'Frankly Mr Shankly' (Smiths), 64–65, 71,
    107, 169
Freak Party, The, 7–8, 12, 56
'Friday Mourning' (Morrissey), 281,
    289–291
Friedman, Ken, 91
From Reverence To Rape (book) (Molly
    Haskell), 23
'Funny How Things Turn Out' (Victoria
    Wood), 50

Fury, Billy, 102

Gannon, Craig, 60, 74–75, 88, 90, 105,
    107–113, 133, 145–146, 155, 261
Garbo, Greta, 163
Geldof, Bob, 68
'Get Off The Stage' (Morrissey), 161,
    262–263
Get Yer Ya-Yas Out (Rolling Stones), 192
Gill, Andy (journalist), 271
Gill, Andy (musician), 39
'Girl Afraid' (Smiths), 43–44, 52, 88, 117,
    277
'Girl Least Likely To' (Morrissey), 161,
    186, 231–232, 258, 263
Girlfriend In A Coma (novel) (Douglas
    Coupland), 99
'Girlfriend In A Coma' (Smiths), 98–99,
    116, 119, 120
'Give Him A Great Big Kiss' (Shangri-Las),
    10
'Glamorous Glue' (Morrissey), 181–182,
    191, 198, 268
Glitter, Gary, 86, 181
Glitter Band, The, 113
Goddard, Simon, 11n.
'Golden Lights' (Smiths), 84, 86, 89
'Golden Lights' (Twinkle), 84
'Good Looking Man About Town'
    (Morrissey), 315
'Goodbye My Love' (Searchers), 103
Graceland (Paul Simon), 61
Grandmaster Flash, 56
Grateful Dead, The, 262
Green Day, 269
Greene, Graham, 202, 301
Griffin, Dale, 37
Guerin, John, 138
Gutteridge, Reg, 218

'Hairdresser On Fire' (Morrissey), 140–141,
    157–158, 229, 260, 263, 268
'Half A Person' (Smiths), 1, 80–81, 88, 116,
    155, 187
Halliwell, Kenneth, 103
'Hand In Glove' (Sandie Shaw), 31
'Hand In Glove' (Smiths), 12, 19, 28–29,
    39–41, 89, 103, 105, 116, 118–120, 232
'Hand That Rocks The Cradle, The'
    (Smiths), 8–11, 19, 25–26, 99
Hand That Rocks The Cradle, The (Smiths
    bootleg) (Smiths), 16–17
Hand That Rocks The Cradle, The [Troy
    Tates Demos] (Smiths), 15–19

'Handsome Devil' (Smiths), 17, 19, 39–40, 44, 152, 224
'Handy Man' (Jimmy Jones), 23
Hanratty (Morrissey), 238
Hanratty, James, 238
Happy Mondays, The, 150
Harris, John, 91, 191–192
Harrison, Andrew, 183, 294
Harrison, George, 49
Harrison, Ian, 297
'Harsh Truth Of The Camera Eye, The' (Morrissey), 175
Haskell, Molly, 23
Haslam, Dave, 73, 92
Hatful Of Hollow (Smiths), 34–46, 72, 88, 147, 216
'Have-A-Go Merchant' (Morrissey), 217, 220, 267, 300
Hawtrey, Charles, 18, 120
'He Cried' (Morrissey), 244
'He Knows I'd Love To See Him' (Morrissey), 153, 158–159, 191, 197, 263
'He's Got The Whole World In His Hands' (Laurie London), 225
'Headmaster Ritual, The' (Smiths), 1, 48–50, 52, 117, 223
Heart, Steve, 170–171, 175
Heartbreakers, The, 3
'Heaven Knows I'm Miserable Now' (Smiths), 31, 41–43, 89, 117, 119–120
'Heaven Knows I'm Missing Him Now' (Sandie Shaw), 41–42
'Heir Apparent' (Morrissey), 252, 254
Hendrix, Jimi, 193
Herman's Hermits, 92, 261
Hibbert, Dale, 8–12
Hibbert, Tom, 59
Hindley, Myra, 9, 31–33, 41, 58, 81, 152
'Hippiechick' (Soho), 39
'His Latest Flame' (Elvis Presley) [see (Marie's The Name) His Latest Flame]
Hissing Of Summer Lawns, The (Joni Mitchell), 137–138
History Boys, The (play) (Alan Bennett), 285
Hitler, Adolph, 165
Hoax, The, 11
'Hold Me' (P.J. Proby), 278
'Hold On To Your Friends' (Morrissey), 205–207, 219, 250, 266, 268
'Hole In My Shoe' (Neil), 136
Holliday, Michael, 81
Holly, Buddy, 186

'Home Is A Question Mark' (Morrissey), 269
'Honey, You Know Where To Find Me' (Morrissey), 201
Hood, Fred, 113
Horses (Patti Smith), 25, 287
Hounds Of Love (Kate Bush), 136
'How Can Anybody Possibly Know How I Feel?' (Morrissey), 276–277, 282
'How Soon Is Now?' (Morrissey), 284–285, 288
'How Soon Is Now?' (Smiths), 38–39, 45, 53–55, 82, 107, 113, 116, 118–120
Howerd, Frankie, 181
Huckleberry Hound (television cartoon), 266
Hulmerist (video) (Morrissey), 195
Hunky Dory (David Bowie), 131
Hynde, Chrissie, 32, 219

'I Am Hated For Loving' (Morrissey), 1, 209–210
'I Am Two People' (Morrissey), 282
'I Can Have Both' (Morrissey), 237, 254
'I Don't Mind If You Forget Me' (Morrissey), 142–143
'I Don't Owe You Anything' (Sandie Shaw), 32
'I Don't Owe You Anything' (Smiths), 19, 30–31
'I Get Nervous' (Nosebleeds), 5
'I Have Forgiven Jesus' (Morrissey), 159, 274–275, 279, 282, 289–290
'I Just Want To See The Boy Happy' (Morrissey), 302
'I Keep Mine Hidden' (Smiths), 85, 93
'I Knew I Was Next' (Morrissey), 315
'I Know It's Gonna Happen Someday' (David Bowie), 188
'I Know It's Gonna Happen Someday' (Morrissey), 181, 187–188, 196, 247, 268
'I Know It's Over' (Smiths), 65–66, 112, 121, 214, 275
'I Know Very Well How I Got My Name' (Morrissey), 161, 260, 263
'I Know Very Well How I Got My Note Wrong' (Vincent Gerard & Steven Patrick), 127
'I Like You' (Morrissey), 278, 286–287
'I Started Something I Couldn't Finish' (Smiths), 18, 97–98, 119, 121
'(I Think) I'm Ready For The Electric Chair' (Nosebleeds), 5

'I Want A Boy For My Birthday'
(Cookies), 8
'I Want A Boy For My Birthday' (Smiths),
8, 10
'I Want The One I Can't Have'
(Morrissey), 52
'I Want The One I Can't Have' (Smiths),
51–52, 107, 185
'I Will See You In Far-Off Places'
(Morrissey), 295–296
'I Won't Share You' (Smiths), 103
'I'd Love To' (Morrissey), 232, 258, 266
'I'll Never Be Anybody's Hero Now'
(Morrissey), 301
'I'm Not Sorry' (Morrissey), 275–276
'I'm So Tired' (Beatles), 98
'(I'm) The End Of The Family Line'
(Morrissey), 176
'I'm Your Man' (Wham!), 73
'I've Been A Bad, Bad Boy' (Paul Jones),
25
'I've Changed My Plea To Guilty'
(Morrissey), 233, 258, 264, 266
'If Love Were All' (Noël Coward), 173
Impossible Dreamers, The, 113
'In The Future When All's Well'
(Morrissey), 299, 302
Inglot, Bill, 120
'Interesting Drug' (Morrissey), 146,
150–151, 154, 156, 207, 250, 253, 268
'Interlude (Extended)' (Morrissey &
Siouxsie), 201, 211, 214, 248–250, 257,
266–267
Interlude (film), 248
'Interlude (Instrumental)' (Morrissey &
Siouxsie), 201, 211, 214, 266–267
'Interlude' (Morrissey & Siouxsie), 201,
211, 214, 257, 266–267
'Interlude' (Timi Yuro), 248
'Irish Blood, English Heart' (Morrissey),
272–274, 279, 291, 298
'Is It Really So Strange?' (Smiths), 86, 88,
101, 111
'It's Hard To Walk Tall When You're
Small' (Morrissey), 238, 280

Jablonska, Annalisa, 31, 152
'Jack The Ripper' (Morrissey), 195–196,
220, 258, 266
'Jack The Ripper' (Screaming Lord Sutch),
196
Jackson, Alan, 236
Jackson, Janet, 61
Jackson, Michael, 145

Jacques, Hattie, 18
Jagger, Mick, 84, 106, 262
Jake, 227
Jam, The, 46, 186, 190, 249, 255
James, 180, 263
Jarman, Derek, 74
'Jeane' (Billy Bragg), 19
'Jeane' (Sandie Shaw), 19
'Jeane' (Smiths), 17, 19
Jensen, David, 12, 18, 20, 37, 43, 45, 88
Jo Jo Gunne, 29
Jobriath, 2
'Jodie's Still Alive' (Morrissey), 164
Johansen, David, 4
John Marr And Other Sailors: With Some Sea
Pieces (poem) (Herman Melville), 205
John's Children, 246
Johnson, Matt, 7
Jolson, Al, 26
Jones, Allan, 21
Jones, Brian, 84
Jones, Jimmy, 23
Jones, Paul, 25
'Journalists Who Lie' (Morrissey), 262–263
Joy Division, 23
Joyce, Mike, 11–12, 16, 20, 22, 27–31, 37,
41–42, 47–48, 51–52, 56, 58, 62–63,
66–67, 69, 84, 88, 91, 93–96, 101–102,
106, 108, 112, 115, 145–146, 155, 199,
207, 232, 234, 236, 244, 261, 279, 289
Joyce, Tina, 108
'Jumpin' Jack Flash' (Rolling Stones), 68
Justice, Jimmy, 52

'Kashmir' (Led Zeppelin), 296
Kearney, Richard, 274
Keats, John, 67
Keene, Roy, 243
Kelly, Danny, 145, 169, 232–233
Kennedy, Kevin, 7
Kent, Nick, 10n., 19, 61, 129, 147–148, 262
Kevorkian, Francois, 28
Khan, Nawazish Ali, 169
Kilborn, Craig, 279
Kill Uncle (Morrissey), 159, 163–178,
180–181, 187, 191, 195, 200, 218, 222,
233, 249, 281
'Kill Uncle' (Morrissey), 165
Killers, The, 293
Kilminster, Lemmy, 245
'Kimberly' (Patti Smith), 25, 99
King Lear (William Shakespeare), 159
'King Leer' (Morrissey), 159, 172–175
Kinks, The, 67, 190

'Kit' (Morrissey), 238
Kite (Kirsty MacColl), 83
Klein, Howie, 255
Kleiner Mann, Was Nun? (book) (Hans Fallada), 131
Knight, Gladys, & The Pips, 276
'Kooks' (David Bowie), 86–87
Kopf, Biba, 51
Kray, Reggie, 154–155, 233
Kray, Ronnie, 154–155, 233

Langer, Clive, 146–148, 156, 164–166, 168–175, 177, 181, 220, 233, 261
Langley, Lee, 248
Langtry, Lillie, 19
Last Exit To Brooklyn (Hubert Selby Jnr), 63
'Last Night I Dreamt That Somebody Loved Me' (Morrissey), 291–292
'Last Night I Dreamt That Somebody Loved Me' (Smiths), 55, 100–101, 117, 119, 121
'Last Of The Famous International Playboys, The' (Morrissey), 154–155, 191, 196, 216, 220, 232, 250, 263, 268
Late Late Show With Craig Kilborn (television programme), 279
'Late Night, Maudlin Street' (Morrissey), 136–139, 281
'Layla' (Derek & The Dominos), 54
'Lazy Sunbathers, The' (Morrissey), 212–213
Lean, David, 205
Led Zeppelin, 105, 296
'Leeches Go On Removing, The' (Morrissey), 238
Lemmy (see Lemmy Kilminster)
Leonard, Hugh, 248
'Let Me Kiss You' (Morrissey), 277–279, 282, 287–288
'Let Me Kiss You' (Nancy Sinatra), 278
'Let The Right One Slip In' (Morrissey), 229
Let's Kill Uncle (film), 165
'Life Is A Pigsty' (Morrissey), 300–301
'Lifeguard On Duty' (Morrissey), 127, 211
'Lifeguard Sleeping, Girl Drowning' (Morrissey), 210–211, 232
Lillywhite, Steve, 75, 200, 203–207, 209–212, 214, 221–222, 224–225, 227, 238, 240, 248, 257–258, 266
Linder (see Linda Mulvey)
'Little Man, What Now?' (Morrissey), 128, 131

Live At Earls Court (Morrissey), 284–292
Live In Dallas (video) (Morrissey), 288
'Living Juke-Box, The' (Nosebleeds), 5
Lolita (novel) (Vladimir Nabokov), 39
'London' (Smiths), 75–76, 86, 88, 112, 141, 239
London, Laurie, 225
'Lonesome Death Of Hattie Carroll, The' (Bob Dylan), 273
'Lonesome Death Of Hattie Carroll, The' (Christy Moore), 273
Looks Familiar (television programme), 131
'Loop, The' (Morrissey), 166, 194–195, 218, 220, 263
'Lost' (Morrissey), 237, 251–252, 268–269
Louder Than Bombs (Smiths), 82, 85–89, 102, 283
'Love Me Do' (Beatles), 40
Love Thy Neighbour (television programme), 135
Low (David Bowie), 295
Lowe, Nick, 7
'Lucky Lips' (Cliff Richard), 160
'Lucky Lisp' (Morrissey), 160, 263

MacColl, Kirsty, 83–84, 150, 186, 247
Machiavelli, 83
MacKenzie, Billy, 36
Mackenzie, Suzie, 274–275
Maconie, Stuart, 135, 219, 224, 271
'Mad Passionate Love' (Bernard Bresslaw), 230
Madness, 168, 171, 190
Magazine, 4–5
'Magdalene Laundries, The' (Christy Moore), 273
'Magdalene Laundries, The' (Joni Mitchell), 273
Maher, Johnny (see Johnny Marr)
Maker, James, 11–12
Maladjusted (Morrissey), 234–246, 251, 254, 270–271, 280, 294
'Maladjusted' (Morrissey), 238–239, 246
Male, Andrew, 297, 301
Man Who Came To Dinner, The (film), 67
Mancini, Henry, 219
Manzanera, Phil, 49
Mao Tse-tung, Chairman, 271
'March Of The Capulets' (Philharmonic Orchestra), 109
'Margaret On A Guillotine' (Morrissey), 142–144, 159
Marie Celeste (boat), 227

'(Marie's The Name) His Latest Flame'
    (Elvis Presley), 50, 110
Marlowe, Christopher, 159
Marr, Angie, 29
Marr, Johnny, 3, 6–12, 15–16, 20, 22–23,
    25–31, 36, 37–41, 44–45, 47–50, 52–60,
    62–80, 84, 85, 87, 90–106, 108–113,
    117–118, 120, 125–126, 128, 133, 136,
    145, 158, 160, 165, 169, 186–187, 199,
    205, 214, 218, 236, 255, 277, 284, 287
Marvin, Hank, 79
Massive Attack, 300
Matlock, Glen, 3
'Matter Of Opinion, A' (Smiths), 11n.
MC5, The, 49, 63–64
McCartney, Linda, 59, 65
McCartney, Paul, 173, 210
McCullough, Dave, 17
McGuinn, Roger (formerly Jim), 49
'Meat Is Murder' (Johnny Marr), 59
'Meat Is Murder' (Smiths), 1, 57–59, 82,
    107, 144
Meat Is Murder (Smiths), 46–60, 82, 96, 111,
    129
Melville, Herman, 205
Mensi, 179
Mercer, Johnny, 219
Merchant, Natalie, 217
'Metal Guru' (T. Rex), 74, 255
Metal Machine Music (Lou Reed), 296
'Mexico' (Morrissey), 282–283
'Michael's Bones' (Morrissey), 161,
    232–233, 258, 263
Middle Of The Road, 156
Middlemarch (novel) (George Eliot), 38
Milton, John, 159, 290
Minogue, Kylie, 241
'Miserable Lie' (Smiths), 19, 24–25, 44,
    112, 136
Miss America (Mary Margaret O'Hara), 153
Mitchell, Joni, 48–49, 101, 137, 273
'Money Changes Everything' (Smiths), 79
Montsho, Quibilah, 4
'Moon River' (Danny Williams), 219
'Moonriver (Extended)' (Morrissey),
    219–220, 266–267
'Moonriver' (Morrissey), 265–267
Moore, Christy, 272–273
Moore, Scotty, 69
'More You Ignore Me, The Closer I Get,
    The' (Morrissey), 207–208, 232, 240,
    250, 256, 258, 266, 268, 289
Morgan, Vincent 'Jet', 49
Morissette, Alanis, 295

Morley, Paul, 294
Morricone, Ennio, 297
Morrissey, 1–12, 15, 17–59, 61–88, 91–104,
    106–107, 109–115, 117–118, 120, 123,
    125–161, 163–214, 216–266, 268–303
Morrissey, Elizabeth (see Elizabeth Dwyer)
Morrissey, Jackie (see Jackie Rayner)
Morrissey, Kevin (Morrissey's cousin), 176
Morrissey, Lee (Morrissey's cousin), 176
Morrissey, Perry (Morrissey's cousin), 176
Morrissey, Peter (Morrissey's cousin), 176
Morrissey, Peter (Morrissey's father), 211,
    242, 281
Morrissey, Rheece (Morrissey's cousin),
    176
Morrissey, Rhett (Morrissey's cousin), 176
Morrissey, Thomas (Morrissey's cousin),
    176
Morrissey, Thomas (Morrissey's uncle), 176
Morrissey & Marr: The Severed Alliance
    (book) (Johnny Rogan), 1, 9, 11n., 16,
    24, 33, 41, 64, 87, 99, 179, 185, 199,
    279
Moss, Joe, 12, 15–16, 40
Mott The Hoople, 171
'Mr Soul' (Buffalo Springfield), 11n.
Muir, John, 6, 288
Mulvey, John, 259
Mulvey, Linda, 19, 25, 67, 174, 180
'Munich Air Disaster 1958' (Morrissey),
    280–281, 288–289
Murderers' Who's Who, The (book), 66
'Mute Witness' (Morrissey), 171–172
My Early Burglary Years (Morrissey),
    255–258
'My Generation' (Who), 262
'My Insatiable One' (Morrissey), 191
'My Insatiable One' (Suede), 191
'My Life Is A Succession Of People Saying
    Goodbye' (Morrissey), 282
'My Love Life' (Morrissey), 178, 219–220,
    233, 250, 264, 266

'National Front Disco, The' (Morrissey),
    183–184, 191, 193
Nebeker, Rob, 187, 265
Needham, Alex, 290
Neil, 136
'Never Had No One Ever' (Smiths), 66,
    107
'Never-Played Symphonies, The'
    (Morrissey), 281–282
Nevin, Mark, 164–178, 181, 187–188, 196,
    198, 219–220, 249, 281

New Order, 132, 150
New York Dolls, The, 2–6, 286, 288
New York Dolls, The (book) (Morrissey), 6, 288
New York Dolls (New York Dolls), 2
'New York Mining Disaster 1948' (Bee Gees), 280
Newley, Anthony, 238
Newman, Randy, 280
Nice Bit Of Meat 3 (bootleg) (Smiths), 17
Nicholson, Viv, 28, 32–33
NICRA (see Northern Ireland Civil Rights Association)
Nieve, Steve (see Steve Heart)
'No One Can Hold A Candle To You' (Morrissey), 263, 282
'No One Can Hold A Candle To You' (Raymonde), 263, 282
'Nobody Loves Us' (Morrissey), 226, 256, 258
Northern Ireland Civil Rights Association, 252–253
Nosebleeds, The, 4–6, 10
Not Waving But Drowning (poem) (Stevie Smith), 211
'November Spawned A Monster' (Morrissey), 151–153, 164–165, 168, 172, 193–194, 230–231, 250, 263, 268, 285–286
'Now I Am A Was' (Morrissey), 237, 254
'Now My Heart Is Full' (Morrissey), 202–203, 208, 238, 247, 268
'Nowhere Fast' (Smiths), 54–55, 63, 82, 117, 290

O'Hara, Mary Margaret, 151–153, 158–159, 164, 194, 197, 286
Oasis, 222, 252
Ochs, Phil, 273
'Oh Phoney' (Morrissey), 165
'Oh Pretty Woman' (Roy Orbison), 140
'Oh Well, I'll Never Learn' (Morrissey), 161, 260, 263
Old Grey Whistle Test, The (television programme), 2
Oliver Twist (film), 205
Oliver Twist (novel) (Charles Dickens), 205
'On The Streets I Ran' (Morrissey), 301–302
'Operation, The' (Morrissey), 225–226, 228
Orbison, Roy, 140
Ordinary Boys, The, 142
'Ordinary Boys, The' (Morrissey), 141–143

Orton, Joe, 103, 151
'Oscillate Wildly' (Smiths), 82, 89, 117
Other Side Of Midnight, The (television programme), 107
'Ouija Board, Ouija Board' (Morrissey), 146, 151, 155–157, 164–165, 179, 185, 194, 250, 261, 263
'Our Frank' (Morrissey), 168–169, 177, 179, 250, 263

'Paint A Vulgar Picture' (Morrissey), 102
'Paint A Vulgar Picture' (Smiths), 102–103, 208
'Panic' (Smiths), 72–74, 87–88, 109, 113, 116, 119–120, 255, 299
'Papa Jack' (Morrissey), 241–242
Paresi, Andrew, 125–127, 130–133, 137–143, 153–154, 157–158, 161–164, 173–174, 176–177, 220, 231–232, 249–250, 257, 260–263
Paris Valentinos, The, 7
Parker, Dorothy, 112
Parkes, Taylor, 237
Parsons, Tony, 192
'Pashernate Love' (Morrissey), 230, 258, 266
Pasolini, Pablo, 298
Pattison, Ian, 88
Pay, Camilla, 282
Pearson, Hesketh, 97
Peel, John, 12, 17, 35, 36–39, 41, 44–45, 55, 76, 81, 86, 88, 161
Peeping Tom (film), 175
'Peppermint Heaven' (Nosebleeds), 5
'Perfect' (Fairground Attraction), 164, 220
Perry, Ivor, 10, 94, 107, 133–134
Petridis, Alexis, 294
Philadelphia Orchestra, The, 109
Phillips, Shaun, 134
'Piccadilly Palare' (Morrissey), 148–149, 151, 164, 230, 250, 263
Piering, Scott, 32–33, 42, 44–45, 77
Pink Floyd, 98
'Please Help The Cause Against Loneliness' (Morrissey), 127
'Please Help The Cause Against Loneliness' (Sandie Shaw), 127
'Please Please Me' (Beatles), 245
'Please Please Please Let Me Get What I Want' (Smiths), 1, 45, 89, 116, 120
Polecats, The, 181
Polsky, Ruth, 78
Pomfret, Stephen 'Pommy', 3–4, 6–8, 11*n*., 25

Pomus, Doc, 50, 110
Pop, Iggy, 29
Porter, John, 16, 18, 20–21, 23–24, 26–30,
    37–38, 43, 45, 47, 55, 65, 75–76, 83–84,
    87–88, 132, 172, 284
'Pregnant For The Last Time' (Morrissey),
    166, 178, 200, 218, 231, 249–250,
    263–266
Presley, Elvis, 38, 55, 110, 168, 176, 222
Preston, Samuel, 142
'Pretty Girls Make Graves' (Smiths), 17–19,
    25
Price, Vincent, 244
Pride And Prejudice (novel) (Jane Austen),
    5
Prince, 137
Proby, P.J., 278
Prokofiev, Sergei Sergeyevich, 114
'Public Image, The' (Morrissey), 282
'Purple Haze' (Jimi Hendrix Experience),
    193
Pusey, Roger, 36, 42, 44
Pye, Ian, 48, 69, 80

Quadrophenia (Who), 242
Quantick, David, 166, 168, 222
'Queen Is Dead, The' (Smiths), 62–64, 66,
    107, 109, 181, 205, 296, 300
Queen Is Dead, The (Smiths), 60–71, 79, 85,
    90, 95–96, 103, 110, 144, 201
Quinlan, Karen, 99

Raging Bull (film), 218
Raisin' Hell (Run DMC), 61
Ramones, The, 2, 64, 112
Rank (Smiths), 105–114
Rapture (Anita Baker), 61
Rare Tracks (Morrissey), 251–254, 268
Raudive, Konstantin, Dr, 83
Ray, Johnnie, 188
Raymonde, 180, 263, 282
Rayner, Jackie (Morrissey's sister), 8
'Read It In Books' (Richard Thompson),
    181
'Reader Meet Author' (Morrissey), 221,
    224, 258
Rebel Without A Cause (film), 81
'Redondo Beach' (Morrissey), 287, 289
'Redondo Beach' (Patti Smith), 211, 287
Reed, Lou, 170, 222, 295–296
'Reel Around The Fountain' (Smiths),
    17–19, 23, 33, 37, 44–45, 117, 152
Reel Around The Fountain (bootleg)
    (Smiths), 16–17

Reeves, Vic, 249
Reilly, Vini, 1, 125–127, 130–133, 135,
    137–138, 140, 142–144, 155, 158,
    161–162, 229, 257, 260, 265
Reisz, Karel, 204
R.E.M., 174, 252
Résumé (poem) (Dorothy Parker), 112
Reynolds, Simon, 144
Rich Kids, The, 3
Richard, Cliff, 160
Richards, Keith, 106, 262
'Ride A White Swan' (T. Rex), 184
'Right Stuff, The' (Bryan Ferry), 79
Riley, Audrey, 18
Ringleader Of The Tormentors (Morrissey),
    293–303
Riviera, Jake, 7
Robinson, Mary, President, 274
'Rock And Roll (Parts 1 And 2)' (Gary
    Glitter), 181
'Rock 'n' Roll Suicide' (David Bowie),
    188, 242
Rodgers, Clodagh, 242
Rodgers, Nile, 56
Rogan, Johnny, 1, 9, 11n., 16, 24, 33, 41–42,
    64, 99, 163, 179, 185, 201, 224, 236
Rolling Stones, The, 7, 60, 68, 84,
    105–106, 118, 192, 239, 261, 265
Romeo And Juliet (Philharmonic Orchestra),
    109
Ronson, Mick, 178–179, 181, 188, 199,
    230, 293
Room Of One's Own, A (essay) (Virginia
    Woolf), 76
Ross, Jonathan, 288
Rostock, Gary, 107
Round The Home (radio programme),
    149
Rourke, Andy, 7, 9, 11–12, 15–16, 18, 22,
    24, 27, 29–30, 37, 40, 47–48, 51, 56–58,
    60, 63, 69, 82–84, 88, 90, 93–94, 97,
    103, 109, 145–146, 155, 159–160, 165,
    199, 230–231, 236, 261
Roxy Music, 49, 168–169, 171
'Roy's Keen' (Morrissey), 243, 251–252
'Rubber Ring' (Smiths), 66, 83–84, 89,
    111, 116, 292
Run DMC, 61
'Run Run Run' (Jo Jo Gunne), 29
'Rush And A Push And The Land Is Ours,
    A' (Smiths), 97, 140
'Rusholme Ruffians' (Smiths), 50–51,
    110–111, 214
Ryan, Michael, 100

'Safe, Warm Lancashire Home' (Morrissey), 127

Saint-Marie, Buffy, 40

Saltzman, Jeff, 293

Samson Agonistes (poem) (John Milton), 159

'Satan Rejected My Soul' (Morrissey), 245–246, 254

Saturday Night And Sunday Morning (film), 142

Schaper, Hal, 248

Scritti Politti, 40

Searchers, The, 103

Searching For The Young Soul Rebels (Dexys Midnight Runners), 188

'Seasick, Yet Still Docked' (Morrissey), 186–187, 194

Segal, Victoria, 270

Selby Jnr, Hubert, 63

'Send Me The Pillow You Dream On' (Johnny Tillotson), 71

Seven Worlds Collide (Neil Finn), 78

Severed Alliance, The (book) (see *Morrissey & Marr: The Severed Alliance*)

Sex Pistols, The, 2–3

Sexton, Dave, 106

Shakespeare, William, 70

'Shakespeare's Sister' (Smiths), 76–77, 82, 88, 107, 117, 119, 121

Shanakies, The, 210

Shangri-Las, The, 10, 70, 244

'Sharp Bend, Fast Car, Goodbye' (Morrissey), 202

Shaw, Sandie, 19, 29, 31, 42, 64, 127, 189, 226

Shaw, William, 206

'Sheila Take A Bow' (Smiths), 86–88, 116, 119, 121, 245

Shelley, Percy Bysshe, 84

Sheppard, David, 29

Sheppard, Jeane, 19

'Shoplifters Of The World Unite' (Morrissey), 290

'Shoplifters Of The World Unite' (Smiths), 78, 82–83, 88, 116, 119, 121

'Short People' (Randy Newman), 280

Shostakovich, Dmitri, Dmitrievich, 223

Showbiz, Grant, 106–107

Shuman, Mort, 50, 110

Simon, Paul, 61

Sims, Joan, 156

Sinatra, Nancy, 278

'Sing Your Life' (Morrissey), 170–171, 185, 195, 218, 247, 249, 263, 268

Singles (Smiths), 118–120

Sioux, Siouxsie, 201, 248–249, 257

'Sister I'm A Poet' (Morrissey), 143, 153, 161, 195, 220, 256–258, 263, 268

Sister Ray, 7, 10

'Skin Storm' (Bradford), 263

'Skin Storm' (Morrissey), 249, 263

Slade, 230

Slaughter And The Dogs, 5

Sleuth (film), 37

Slough (poem) (John Betjeman), 132

'Slum Mums, The' (Morrissey), 280, 282

Smart, Elizabeth, 52, 56, 112, 203, 282–283

Smith, Bessie, 11*n*.

Smith, Chas, 249

Smith, David, 33

Smith, Mark E., 68, 180

Smith, Patti, 2, 6–7, 25, 99, 211, 287

Smith, Richard, 149, 237

Smith, Stevie, 211

Smiths Indeed (fanzine), 97

Smiths, The, 1, 4, 9–13, 15–18, 20–32, 34–48, 52–63, 67–69, 72–74, 76–80, 82, 84–88, 90–97, 99–115, 117–118, 120, 125–130, 133–134, 136, 144–147, 149–150, 152, 158–159, 165, 168–169, 174, 179–180, 185, 187, 189–191, 199, 201, 203, 205, 208, 222–223, 229, 231, 234, 236, 239, 254, 256, 260–261, 265, 270, 272–276, 278, 281, 283–284, 286–288, 290–291

Smiths, The (Smiths), 10, 15, 17, 19–33, 41, 43–44, 46, 48, 96

Smiths, The: The Visual Documentary (book) (Johnny Rogan), 9, 11*n*.

Snow, Mat, 155

Soho, 39

Soil, 107

'Some Girls Are Bigger Than Others' (Smiths), 70–71, 98, 116, 120

'Something Else' (Eddie Cochran), 180

Sonic Youth, 61

'Sonny Boy' (Al Jolson), 26

'Sorrow Will Come In The End' (Morrissey), 1, 235, 242, 244–245, 258

Sound Of Music, The (soundtrack album), 37

South Bank Show, The (television programme), 95

'Southpaw' (Morrissey), 227–228

Southpaw Grammar (Morrissey), 221–228, 235, 238, 256, 294

Sparks, 2, 154, 171

Spector, Phil, 28

'Speedway' (Morrissey), 213–215, 217
Spend Spend Spend (autobiography) (Viv
    Nicholson), 28
'Spring-Heeled Jim' (Morrissey), 203–204,
    220
Springsteen, Bruce, 46
St John, Kate, 249
'Stairway To Heaven' (Led Zeppelin), 38
Stamp, Terence, 30, 205
Stanley, Bob, 236
Staunton, Terry, 145
'Stay As You Are' (Morrissey), 201
Steely Dan, 132
Stein, Seymour, 38
'Steven, You Were Really Something'
    (Associates), 36
'Still Ill' (Smiths), 28, 41, 51, 103, 113, 117
Stipe, Michael, 174
Stone, Sly, 92
Stone Roses, The, 150
'Stop Me If You Think You've Heard This
    One Before' (Smiths), 100–101,
    115–116, 121
'Story Of My Life, The' (Michael
    Holliday), 81
Strangeways, Here We Come (Smiths),
    90–104, 129, 291
Stranglers, The, 226
Street, Stephen, 47, 51, 56–57, 62, 64–66,
    68, 70, 76–77, 80, 83, 87, 90–91, 94,
    97–98, 100–101, 103, 125–127,
    130–133, 135–140, 142–144, 146–148,
    153–156, 158, 160–162, 164–165, 167,
    172, 196–197, 257, 260, 264
'Stretch Out And Wait' (Smiths), 81–82, 89
'Striptease With A Difference' (Morrissey),
    147, 165
Stubbs, David, 128
'Subway Train' (New York Dolls), 286
'Subway Train/Munich Air Disaster 1958'
    (Morrissey), 286, 288
'Such A Little Thing Makes Such A Big
    Difference' (Morrissey), 153, 196, 263
Suck, Jane, 287
Suede, 191
'Suedehead' (Morrissey), 128, 138–140,
    160–161, 185, 191, 197, 229, 247, 250,
    260, 263–264, 266, 268, 272
Suedehead (novel) (Richard Allen), 128, 139
Suedehead – The Best Of Morrissey
    (Morrissey), 247–250, 266
'Suffer Little Children' (Smiths), 1, 8–11,
    19, 31–33, 41, 58, 79, 152, 196, 232,
    239–240, 281

Suggs, 148, 164, 171, 249, 262
Sulky Youth, 3
'Sunny' (Morrissey), 218, 234, 247–248,
    250, 255–258, 267–268
Supple, Danton, 205, 213, 228
'Suspicious Minds' (Elvis Presley), 176
Sutch, Screaming Lord, 196
Sutherland, Steve, 73, 167
'Swallow On My Neck' (Morrissey), 256,
    258, 267
'Sweet And Tender Hooligan' (Morrissey),
    260–261
Sweet And Tender Hooligan (novel) (Ian
    Pattison), 88
'Sweet And Tender Hooligan' (Smiths),
    87–88, 260–261, 263
Sweet, The, 181, 245
Sylvain, Sylvain, 4
Symphony No. 5 (Shostakovich), 223
Sztumph, Matthew, 58

T. Rex, 74, 97, 178, 185, 255, 293
'Take Me Back To Dear Old Blighty'
    (Cicely Courtneidge), 63
'Take Me In Your Arms And Love Me'
    (Gladys Knight & The Pips), 276
Tamburlaine The Great (play) (Christopher
    Marlowe), 159
Taste Of Honey, A (play) (Shelagh
    Delaney), 19, 42, 239
Tate, Troy, 15–18, 20, 43, 45, 48
Taylor, Woodie, 166, 200, 203, 210, 212,
    214, 217, 221, 257
'Teachers Are Afraid Of The Pupils, The'
    (Morrissey), 221, 223–224
Teardrop Explodes, The, 15
Tebbitt, Norman, 107
Tee Shirts, The, 4
'Teenage Dad On His Estate' (Morrissey),
    280, 282
'Teenage News' (Sylvain Sylvain), 4
'Telstar' (Tornados), 245
10,000 Maniacs, 217
TFI Friday (television programme), 246
'That Joke Isn't Funny Anymore' (Smiths),
    52–53, 55, 70, 82, 117, 119–120, 176,
    187, 279
'That's Entertainment' (Jam), 249, 255
'That's Entertainment' (Morrissey),
    249–250, 255, 263
'That's The Story Of My Life' (Velvet
    Underground), 81
Thatcher, Margaret, Prime Minister, 47,
    144, 159, 182

'There Is A Light That Never Goes Out' (Morrissey), 288–289

'There Is A Light That Never Goes Out' (Smiths), 65, 69–70, 77–78, 107, 117, 119–120, 175, 187

'There Speaks A True Friend' (Morrissey), 265–266

'There's A Place In Hell For Me And My Friends' (Morrissey), 176–177, 202, 245, 266

'These Things Take Time' (Smiths), 17, 19, 37, 51, 85, 88–89

'This Charming Man' (Smiths), 18–19, 26–28, 37, 40, 43, 53, 70, 115, 119–120, 187, 245

'This Is Not Your Country' (Morrissey), 237, 252–254, 273

'This Night Has Opened My Eyes' (Smiths), 42, 89

Thomas, Nigel, 199

Thompson, Richard, 181

Thunders, Johnny, 3

Tillotson, Johnny, 71

Tilt (Scott Walker), 295

Tiny Tim, 24

'To Me You Are A Work Of Art' (Morrissey), 302

Tobias, Jesse, 285, 293, 295, 302

Tom And Jerry (television cartoon), 297

'Tomorrow' (Morrissey), 189, 191, 229, 250, 268

'Tomorrow' (Sandie Shaw), 189

'Tony The Pony' (Morrissey), 177, 263

Top Of The Pops (television programme), 27, 79, 118, 129

Tornados, The, 245

Townshend, Pete, 262

Transformer (Lou Reed), 170

'Trash' (Morrissey), 288

'Trash' (New York Dolls), 288

Travis, Geoff, 16, 20, 26–28, 37–38, 40, 54, 64, 77, 102, 107, 113

'Treat Me Like A Human Being' (Morrissey), 127

'Trouble Loves Me' (Morrissey), 241

Troussé, Stephen, 294

Troy Hand Rocks The Cradle (bootleg) (Smiths), 17

Troy Tate Demos, The (bootleg) (Smiths), 17

Tseng, David, 97

Tube, The (television programme), 27

Twinkle, 70, 84, 261

Udo, Tommy, 226

'Unhappy Birthday' (Smiths), 101–102

'Unloveable' (Smiths), 80, 89, 187

Up The Junction (novel) (Nell Dunn), 51

'Used To Be A Sweet Boy' (Morrissey), 211–212, 215, 266

Van Der Graaf Generator, 228

Vauxhall And I (Morrissey), 199–217, 219, 221–222, 224, 248, 253, 256–257, 270, 277, 289, 294–295

Velvet Underground, The, 81

Very Best Of The Smiths, The (Smiths), 120–121

'Vicar In A Tutu' (Smiths), 69, 71, 103, 110

Victim, 11

Victim (film), 25

Village People, The, 81

Vini Reilly (Durutti Column), 127

'Virginia Plain' (Roxy Music), 171

Visconti, Luchino, 298

Visconti, Tony, 293, 295, 297–299

Viva Hate (Morrissey), 125–144, 161, 185, 191, 200, 211, 229, 256, 263, 281, 294–295

Viva Hate (Extended Edition) (Morrissey), 229–233

Voidoids, The, 3

Walker, Scott, 238, 295–296

Walsh, Teresa, 201

Waterhouse, Keith, 35, 76

Walters, John, 45

Waters, John, 273–274

Watson, Don, 21

We Are The Lambeth Boys (television documentary), 204

'We Hate It When Our Friends Become Successful' (Morrissey), 185–186, 192, 198, 250, 264–266, 268

'We'll Let You Know' (Morrissey), 182–183, 187, 191, 196–197, 220

Weeks, Judge, 234

'Well I Wonder' (Smiths), 55–56

Weller, Paul, 249

West, Ann, 32

West, Keith, 240

Wham!, 73

'What Difference Does It Make?' (Smiths), 19, 29–30, 36–37, 44, 88, 115, 119–120

'What Do You See In Him?' (Smiths), 18

'What She Said' (Smiths), 52, 111, 256

'What's The World?' (James), 263

'What's The World?' (Smiths), 263

'Whatever Happens, I Love You'
(Morrissey), 217, 220, 267
'When My Little Girl Is Smiling' (Jimmy
Justice), 52
White Dice, 7, 10, 25
Whittall, Paul, 7
Who, The, 60, 190, 242, 252
Who Put The 'M' In Manchester (DVD), 288
*Who Was That Man? A Present For Oscar
Wilde?* (book) (Neil Bartlett), 148
'Why Don't You Find Out For Yourself'
(Morrissey), 208, 210
Whyte, Alain, 178, 183, 187, 192, 194, 196,
198, 201, 206–207, 210, 212–213,
217–218, 230, 240–244, 249, 252, 265,
269, 277, 293, 302
'Wide To Receive' (Morrissey), 242–243
Wilde, Jack, 131
Wilde, Oscar, 19, 47, 67, 82–83, 97, 101,
148, 175, 181, 185–186, 237, 276, 279,
294
'Will Never Marry' (Morrissey), 143,
153–154, 263
'William, It Was Really Nothing' (Smiths),
35–36, 38, 44–45, 76, 88–89, 115,
119–120, 141
Williams, Danny, 219
Williams, Emlyn, 31
Williams, Kevin (see Kevin Kennedy)
Williams, Rhys, 275
Williams, Robbie, 278
Williams, Steve, 162
Wilson, Tony, 12, 27, 107
Winstanley, Alan, 146–148, 156, 164, 166,
170–171, 173, 175, 177, 195, 220, 233,
261
Wolstencroft, Simon, 7–10, 12, 56
Wonder, Stevie, 277
'Wonderful Woman' (Smiths), 17–19, 28
Wonderful Woman (Smiths bootleg)
(Smiths), 17
Wood, Victoria, 35, 50, 112, 186, 203
Woolf, Virginia, 76
Word Up (Cameo), 61
'Work Is A Four Letter Word' (Cilla
Black), 84–85
'Work Is A Four Letter Word' (Smiths),
84–85, 93

'World In Motion' (England New Order),
150
'World Is Full Of Crashing Bores, The'
(Morrissey), 276, 290
World Of Morrissey (Morrissey), 72–84,
216–221, 266
World Won't Listen, The (Smiths), 85–86,
102, 220
Wright, Steve, 109

'Y.M.C.A.' (Village People), 81
Yardbirds, The, 217
'Year In Song' (Mary Margaret O'Hara),
153
Yeats, W.B., 67
'Yes, I Am Blind' (Morrissey), 159–160,
263
'Yesterday Man' (Chris Andrews), 65
Yield To The Night (film), 119
You Are The Quarry (Morrissey), 251,
269–285, 287, 290–291, 293–295
'You Can't Always Get What You Want'
(Rolling Stones), 239
'You Have Killed Me' (Morrissey), 298,
302
'You Just Haven't Earned It Yet, Baby'
(Smiths), 82–83, 89, 102
'You Know I Couldn't Last' (Morrissey),
186, 238, 279, 291
'You Must Please Remember' (Morrissey),
226
'You'll Never Walk Alone' (Shirley
Bassey), 114
'You're Gonna Need Someone On Your
Side' (Morrissey), 180–181, 191, 198
'You're The One For Me, Fatty'
(Morrissey), 179, 186, 191–192, 220,
229, 247, 250, 266
'You've Got Everything Now' (Smiths),
19, 23–24, 43
'You've Had Her' (Morrissey), 265–266
Young, Neil, 7, 11n., 262
'Youngest Was The Most Loved, The'
(Morrissey), 299–300
Your Arsenal (Morrissey), 164, 178–191,
196–201, 208, 222, 230, 233, 270,
293–294
Yuro, Timi, 248